A NEW PSYCHOLOGY OF MEN

EDITED BY

Ronald F. Levant
and
William S. Pollack

BasicBooks
A Division of HarperCollins*Publishers*

To the memory of Harry G. Levant (1913–1994),

to Marsha and Sarah,

and to the next generation of "new" men and women.

Grateful acknowledgment is made for permission to reprint a portion of Robert Bly's "For My Son Noah, Ten Years Old." Reprinted with permission of the author. Copyright © 1981 by Robert Bly.

Designed by Ellen Levine

Library of Congress Cataloging-in-Publication Data
A new psychology of men / edited by Ronald F. Levant, William S. Pollack.
    p. cm.
  Includes bibliographical references and index.
  ISBN 0–465–08656–X
  1. Masculinity (Psychology)—United States. 2. Men—United States—Psychology. 3. Sex role—United States. I. Levant, Ronald F. II. Pollack, William S.
  BF692.5.N48 1995
  155.6'32—dc20   94–41028
                                       CIP

---

95 96 97 98 ❖/HC 9 8 7 6 5 4 3 2 1

Contents

PART III—APPLICATIONS

PART IV—THE VARIETIES OF MASCULINITY

Co-Editors and
Contributing Authors

Ronald F. Levant, Ed.D.

Ronald F. Levant earned his doctorate in clinical psychology and public practice from Harvard in 1973 and for 13 years was on the faculty of the Counseling Psychology Program at Boston University, where he served as the founder and director of the nationally prominent Fatherhood Project. He is now on the faculty at Cambridge Hospital/Harvard Medical School. He has also established Counseling for Men, a psychological practice in Brookline, Massachusetts, that provides individual, group, and family counseling for men and their families. He is the co-founder and co-chair of the Society for the Psychological Study of Men and Masculinity (PsyMen), which is in line to become an APA division on the psychology of men.

Dr. Levant's research interests are in the fields of family and gender psychology. He has authored, co-authored, or edited 7 books and over 65 articles and book chapters in the areas of family psychology and the psychology of men. His publications include *Between Father and Child* (Viking/Penguin, 1989, 1991), co-authored with John Kelly, and *Masculinity, Reconstructed* (Dutton, 1995), co-authored with Gini Kopecky. In addition, he serves as editor for the *Journal of Family Psychology*, published by the American Psychological Association.

William S. Pollack, Ph.D.

William S. Pollack is the director of continuing education (psychology) and the co-director of the Center for Men at McLean Hospital in Belmont, Massachusetts, and is assistant clinical professor of psychology in the

Department of Psychiatry at Harvard Medical School. Dr. Pollack earned his Ph.D. from Boston University in clinical psychology in 1981. He is a past president of the Massachusetts Psychological Association, for which he presently serves as chair of the Advocacy (Legislative) Steering Committee. He is a candidate at the Boston Psychoanalytic Institute and a diplomate in clinical psychology (ABPP, board-certified).

Dr. Pollack is the co-author (with Dr. William Betcher) of *In a Time of Fallen Heroes: The Re-creation of Masculinity* (Atheneum, 1993). His research interests are in the areas of parenting (fathering), gender studies (men and male-female relationships), psychoanalytic psychotherapy, and professional issues in the practice of psychology. He is the author of and/or contributor to numerous scholarly journal articles and book chapters, serves on several editorial boards, and is a member of the Steering Committee of the Society for the Psychological Study of Men and Masculinity (PsyMen). Dr. Pollack maintains a private practice in Newton, Massachusetts, in psychotherapy and in organizational consultation (as a principal in the psychological consulting firm Spectrum, O.E.D., Inc.).

Stephen J. Bergman, M.D., Ph.D.

Stephen J. Bergman is a lecturer in psychiatry at Harvard Medical School and chairman of the Committee on Clinical Projects at the Harvard Medical School Division on Addictions. He is also an affiliated scholar at the Stone Center, Wellesley College. With his wife, Dr. Janet Surrey, he is co-director of the Center for Gender Relations in Boston and co-author of the forthcoming *Something Might Happen: When Women and Men Get Together*. He was a Rhodes Scholar at Oxford, where he received his Ph.D in physiology, and he graduated from Harvard Medical School Alpha Omega Alpha. Under the pen name of Samuel Shem, he has published *The House of God* (1978), *Fine* (Dell, 1985), and the sequel to *House of God, Mount Misery* (in preparation). He has been selected as one of the Boston Public Library's "Literary Lights" and as one of "Boston's Best Authors." With Janet Surrey, he is the author of the play *Bill W. and Dr. Bob* (Samuel French, 1990), about the founding of Alcoholics Anonymous. Two other plays have been published in *The Best Short Plays* anthologies.

Gary R. Brooks, Ph.D.

Gary R. Brooks received his Ph.D. from the University of Texas at Austin in 1976. He currently is the assistant chief of psychology service at the O. E.

Teague Veterans Center, Temple, Texas. He is an associate professor in psychiatry and behavioral sciences with the Texas A&M University Health Sciences Center, an adjunct faculty member at Baylor University, and an instructor in men's studies with Texas Women's University. He has been an executive board member of the National Organization of Men Against Sexism (NOMAS), co-chair of gender concerns committees of two APA divisions, and co-chair of the Society for the Psychological Study of Men and Masculinity (PsyMen). His primary clinical and scholarly activities are focused on understanding and treating traditional men.

Richard M. Eisler, Ph.D.

Richard M. Eisler received his doctorate in clinical psychology at the State University of New York at Buffalo in 1967. He received a diplomate in clinical psychology from the American Board of Professional Psychology in 1975. At present Dr. Eisler is professor and director of psychological services in the Department of Psychology at Virginia Polytechnic Institute and State University. He is currently a consulting editor for the *Journal of Men's Studies*, an associate editor of the book series *Behavior Modification*, and editor-in-chief of the *Journal of Gender, Culture, and Health*. He is the author of the Masculine Gender Role Stress Scale. He has an active research program in the areas of gender role behavior, psychological stress, and health issues for men and women and has published over 75 theoretical and research articles and chapters.

Lucia Albino Gilbert, Ph.D.

Lucia Albino Gilbert, professor of educational psychology at the University of Texas at Austin, studies the career development of women and various aspects of dual-career family life. She has published widely in the areas of work and family and career development. Her books include *Men in Dual-Career Families* (Lawrence Erlbaum, 1985), *Sharing It All* (Plenum, 1988), and *Two Careers, One Family: Prospects for Gender Equality* (Sage, 1993). Her recent work also concerns the effects of gender processes on professional development, family functioning, and mental health. Dr. Gilbert is a fellow of the American Psychological Association and the American Psychological Society, an associate editor of *Psychology of Women Quarterly*, an editorial board member of *Journal of Family Psychology* and *Contemporary Psychology*, and a consulting reviewer for many other journals. She has received two teaching excellence awards during her 15 years at the University of Texas at Austin and is also the recipient of the John Holland Award for Excellence in Research.

Glenn E. Good, Ph.D.

Glenn E. Good is a lecturer, writer, and researcher known for his expertise in psychotherapy with men. He has made more than 50 presentations at national conventions. Among his recent papers are "Masculinity Research: A Review and Critique" and "Gender Aware Therapy: A Synthesis of Feminist Therapy and Knowledge About Gender." He was also a co-editor of Scher et al., *The Handbook of Counseling and Psychotherapy with Men* (Sage, 1987). He earned his doctorate in counseling psychology from Ohio State University in 1987. Dr. Good is currently an assistant professor in the Department of Psychology at the University of Missouri–Columbia. He is also a licensed psychologist and maintains a private practice in Columbia, Missouri.

James Harrison, Ph.D.

James Harrison, a psychologist, is a graduate of the University of North Carolina (1956) in sociology, Yale University Divinity School (1959, M. Div.), and New York University (1975, Ph.D.). For 10 years, he worked for the Presbyterian Church, but only so long as he could do organizing for the civil rights and peace movements. From 1975 to 1993, he worked for New York State and was in private practice in New York City. In 1993, he returned to North Carolina to write, garden, and train dogs. He is establishing a private practice in counseling and doing community organizing and consulting. His identity is antiauthoritarian; his role is muckraker.

Sarah Holmes, M.A.

Sarah Holmes is a Ph.D. student in the Marriage and Family Therapy Program in the School of Family Studies at the University of Connecticut–Storrs. She received her master's degree from the same university. Her interests include gender as a social construction, family-of-origin influences on adult functioning, and family caregiving of the elderly.

Steven Krugman, Ph.D.

Steven Krugman is a clinical psychologist in private practice in Boston. He is a senior supervisor at the Trauma Clinic at the Massachusetts General Hospital and an instructor in the Department of Psychiatry, Harvard Medical School. Dr. Krugman's interests include male development, the impact of psychological trauma, integrative psychotherapy, and group treatment. He has written on men, shame, and psychotherapy; the intergenerational transmission of traumatic violence; and men in group treatment. He has been leading a seminar on the treatment and management of psychological trauma for the past five years. He is currently working on the relationship between male development and psychological trauma. He earned his Ph.D in clinical psychology from New York University in 1978.

Richard F. Lazur, Psy.D.

Richard F. Lazur is a licensed psychologist in the practice of Lazur & Lazur, Ltd., and clinical supervisor of the Addictive Behavior Center of the Alaska Regional Hospital in Anchorage. He earned a doctor of psychology degree from the Massachusetts School of Professional Psychology in 1983. He is a member of the core faculty of the University of La Verne, Elmendorf residence campus, and an adjunct faculty member at Alaska Pacific University and the University of Alaska–Anchorage. He is the author of "Identity Integration: Counseling the Adolescent Male," in *The Handbook of Counseling and Psychotherapy with Men* (Sage, 1987), edited by Scher et al. Dr. Lazur is active in exploring the impact of male gender roles in both his personal and professional activities and has lectured in the United States and Canada.

Richard Majors, Ph.D.

Richard Majors is a senior research associate at the Urban Institute in Washington, DC. He earned a doctorate in counseling psychology at the University of Illinois–Urbana-Champaign. He was an assistant professor at the University of Wisconsin–Eau Claire and a clinical fellow in psychiatry at Harvard Medical School. He is co-founder of the National Council of African-American Men and co-founder and deputy editor of the *Journal of African-American Male Studies*. He is co-author of *Cool Pose: The Dilemma of Black Manhood in American* (Lexington, 1992) and *The American Black Male:*

His Present Status and His Future (Nelson Hall, 1994). Dr. Majors has lectured extensively around the country on the issues facing the African-American male.

James O'Neil, Ph.D.

James M. O'Neil received his Ph.D. in counseling psychology from the University of Maryland. He is currently professor of family studies and educational psychology at the University of Connecticut–Storrs. He has served on the editorial boards of *Psychology of Women Quarterly, Journal of Counseling Psychology,* and *Journal of Men's Studies.* He is co-chair of the Special Interest Group on Men, Masculinity, and Men's Studies (Division 17, Counseling Psychology, APA), co-chair of the Gender Concerns Committee (Division 43, Family Psychology, APA), administrative director of the Society for the Psychological Study of Men and Masculinity (PsyMen), and a member of the Committee on Women (Division 17, Counseling Psychology). In 1991, he was awarded a Fulbright Teaching Scholarship by the Council for International Exchange of Scholars to Russia, where he lectured on the psychology of gender and researched Russian men's gender role conflict. He has been involved in the new psychology of men since the late 1970s, when he created the Gender Role Conflict Scale, the first scale to assess men's gender role conflict.

Joseph H. Pleck, Ph.D.

Joseph H. Pleck is on the faculty in human development and family studies at the University of Illinois–Urbana-Champaign. He is the author of *Men and Masculinity* (Prentice Hall, 1974), *The American Man* (Prentice Hall, 1980), *The Myth of Masculinity* (MIT Press, 1981), and *Working Wives, Working Husbands* (Sage, 1985) and has edited or co-edited several collections of articles on male roles and men's roles in the family. Dr. Pleck's research interests include adolescent health, particularly male sexual and contraceptive behavior, and relationships between family and work roles. Since 1986, he has been co-principal investigator of the National Survey of Adolescent Males, a national longitudinal survey of young men funded by the National Institute of Child Health and Human Development (NICHD). He is also directing the evaluation of the Classroom, Clinic, and Community Project and is chair of the Measurement Committee of NICHD's Minority Youth Health Initiative. Dr. Pleck was a founder of the National Organization of Men Against Sexism (NOMAS) and editor of the organization's publication, *Brother.* He is currently a contributing editor to *Masculinities* and a member of the advisory board of the *Journal of Men's Studies.* He holds a Ph.D. in clinical psychology from Harvard University and is a fellow of the American Psychological Association.

Louise B. Silverstein, Ph.D.

Louise B. Silverstein received her Ph.D. in school psychology from New York University in 1981. She is currently an assistant professor and director of the master's degree program in general psychology at the Ferkauf Graduate School of Psychology at Yeshiva University. Dr. Silverstein is secretary of the Division of Family Psychology, and chair of the Task Force on Feminist Family Therapy, of the Division of the Psychology of Women in the American Psychological Association. She has written extensively about child care and maternal employment, fathering, and the social construction of gender.

Edward H. Thompson, Jr., Ph.D.

Edward H. Thompson, Jr., is associate professor of sociology at Holy Cross College in Worcester, Massachusetts. He earned his Ph.D. in sociology from Case Western Reserve University. He has published numerous articles in the fields of family life, gerontology, and gender studies in such journals as *American Behavioral Scientist* and *Sex Roles.* He is currently editing a volume titled *Older Men's Lives,* which will be published by Sage Publications. His research interests currently are the effects of constructed masculinities on men, particularly on the well-being of middle-aged and elderly men.

Acknowledgments

First, we would like to acknowledge the involvement and support of our senior editor at Basic Books, Jo Ann Miller, whose vision made this book possible; and to thank Stephen Francoeur, our assistant editor, whose hard work and dedication helped bring this project to fruition.

We would like to express our gratitude to our many colleagues and friends who had a hand in the development of this book. In addition to the distinguished authors of each of the chapters, we would like to recognize Drs.: Jim Barron, William Betcher, Robert Brannon, Michael Diamond, Joel Eichler, Marion Gindes, Alan Gurwitt, Judith Jordan, James Levine, Sam Osherson, Robert Pasick, E. Anthony Rotundo, Jon Reusser, Jerry Shapiro, Lenore Walker, Kathy Weingarten, and Marty Wong in particular for their encouragement and wise counsel.

Dr. Levant would like to express his gratitude to the men who participated in his fatherhood courses and workshops, and his clients, from whom he has learned an incalculable amount about the new psychology of men. Thanks are also due to colleagues Jeff Fischer, University of Florida, Gainesville, and Wu Ronxian, Suzhou University, The People's Republic of China, with whom he has collaborated recently on research in masculinity ideology. He would also like to acknowledge his wife, Carol L. Slatter, for her support, patience, and wise counsel about many aspects of this project.

Dr. Pollack would like to acknowledge the gracious support of his colleagues at McLean Hospital—its chief, Dr. Steven Mirin, and the members of the Department of Continuing Education: Drs. Robert Aranow and Shervert Frazier, Carol Brown, and Cathy Toon. Thanks are also due to the excellent secretarial support of Patti Brown. He would also like to acknowledge his family—his wife, Dr. Marsha Padwa, and daughter, Sarah Faye Pollack—for their understanding, patience, and wisdom during the course of this project. Dr. Shervert Frazier, Psychiatrist in Chief Emeritus at McLean Hospital, has been a special mentor in the development of his intellectual "voice"; and Dr. Joseph Coyle, Harvard Medical School, a believer in the scientific merit of the new psychology of men. Dr. Pollack expresses his special thanks to them both.

Last, but not least, we extend our gracious thanks to the many men and women—colleagues, friends, and patients alike—who have lent us their trust, opened their hearts to us, told us their stories, and urged us to create a *new psychology of men.*

Introduction

RONALD F. LEVANT AND WILLIAM S. POLLACK

Why Study the Psychology of Men?

This volume attempts to lay the foundation for a new psychology of men. Those not familiar with this new work sometimes ask, "Why do we need a psychology of men? Isn't all psychology the psychology of men?" The answer is, yes, males have been the focal point of most psychological research, but in studies that viewed the male gender as representative of humanity as a whole. Feminist scholars challenged this traditional viewpoint by arguing for a gender-specific approach and, in the past quarter-century, have rewritten the canon on women's development. In the same spirit, men's studies scholars over the past 15 years have begun to examine masculinity not as a normative referent but as a complex and problematic construct. In so doing, they have provided a framework for a psychological approach to men and masculinity that questions traditional norms for the male role, such as the emphases on competition, status, toughness, and emotional stoicism, and that views certain male problems (such as aggression and violence, homophobia, misogyny, detached fathering, and neglect of health) as unfortunate but predictable results of the male role socialization process.

This gender-aware examination of the psychology of men is both overdue and urgently needed. For one thing, a new psychology of men might contribute to the solution of some of the male problems alluded to above, problems that have long had a negative impact on women, men, children, and society. For another thing, owing to long delays in dealing with these problems, the pressures on men to behave in ways that conflict with various aspects of traditional masculinity ideology have never been greater. These new pressures—to commit to relationships, to communicate one's innermost feelings, to nurture children, to share in housework, to integrate sexuality with love, and to curb aggression and violence—have shaken traditional masculinity ideology to such an extent that the resulting masculinity crisis has left many men feeling bewildered and confused, and the pride associated with being a man is lower than at any time in the recent past. A new psychology of men is required to provide men with a sense of direction as they attempt to reconstruct the male code.

The Gender Role Strain Paradigm

The new psychology of men views gender roles not as biological or even social "givens" but rather as psychologically and socially constructed entities that bring certain advantages and disadvantages and, most important, can change. This perspective acknowledges the biological differences between men and women but argues that it is not the biological differences of sex that make for "masculinity" and "femininity." These notions are socially constructed from bits and pieces of biological, psychological, and social experience to serve particular purposes. Traditional constructions of gender serve patriarchal purposes; nontraditional constructions, such as those that Gilmore (1990) described as operating among the Tahitians and the Semai, appear to serve equalitarian purposes.

The gender role strain paradigm, originally formulated by Joseph Pleck in *The Myth of Masculinity* (1981), is the forerunner in the new psychology of men of social constructionism and of modern critical thinking about masculinity, having been formulated before social constructionism emerged as a new perspective on masculinity. Pleck's contribution spawned a number of major research programs, which in turn have produced important data that deepen our understanding of the strain men experience when they attempt to live up to the impossible standards of the traditional male role.

Pleck demonstrated that the paradigm that had dominated the research on masculinity for 50 years (1930–80)—the gender role identity paradigm—not only poorly accounts for the observed data but also promotes the patriarchal bifurcation of society on the basis of stereotyped gender roles. The gender role identity paradigm assumes that people have an inner psychological need to have a gender role identity and that their personality development hinges on its formation. The extent to which this "inherent" need is met is determined by how completely men and women embrace their traditional gender role. From such a perspective, the development of appropriate gender role identity is viewed as a failure-prone process; failure for men to achieve a masculine gender role identity is thought to result in homosexuality, negative attitudes toward women, or hypermasculinity. This paradigm springs from the same philosophical roots as the "essentialist" or "nativist" view of sex roles—the notion that, for men, there is a clear, historically invariant masculine "essence."

In contrast, the replacement paradigm offered by Pleck, the gender role strain paradigm, proposes that contemporary gender roles are contradictory and inconsistent; that the proportion of persons who violate gender roles is high; that violation of gender roles leads to condemnation and negative psychological consequences; that actual or imagined violation of gender roles leads people to overconform to them; that violating gender roles has more severe consequences for males than for females; and that certain prescribed gender role traits (such as male aggression) are too often dysfunctional. In this paradigm, gender roles are defined by gender role stereotypes and norms and are imposed on the developing child by parents, teachers, and peers—the cultural transmitters who subscribe to the prevailing masculinity ideology. As noted above, this paradigm springs from the same philosophical roots as social constructionism—the view that notions of masculinity and femininity are relational, socially constructed, and subject to change.

Overview of the Book

Recently a large number of books on men have been published, responding to the crisis of masculinity described above. These books either arise out of one of the factions of the "men's movement" (Clatterbaugh, 1990) or attempt to summarize the new gender-specific insights into the meanings of masculinity for the general public. There also exists a scholarly, interdisciplinary literature on men's studies (e.g., Brod, 1987; Kimmel, 1987). In the field of psychology, the new gender-aware work on men has come in two forms: an earlier literature on fatherhood, which sought to underscore the importance of fathers in children's lives (e.g., Lamb, 1981; Cath, Gurwitt, & Ross, 1982), and more recent work on psychotherapy for men (e.g., Scher, Stevens, Good, & Eichenfeld, 1987; Meth & Pasick, 1990). The present volume is the first book that provides broad coverage of the new psychology of men by bringing together four major facets—theory, research, applications, and considerations of diversity.

As an overarching theme, the contributing authors share an open view of what has heretofore been constructed as masculinity and a perspective on male-female relations and dynamics that blames neither gender for the quagmire the sexes presently find themselves in but does acknowledge the corrosive effects of sexism and patriarchy. Even though this is a book about men, we think it is central to a 21st-century view of women's roles, and therefore to any substantial rethinking of gender.

There are four parts to the book. Part I of the book, "Theory," first provides an update on the gender role strain paradigm and then presents two evocative theoretical approaches to the psychological study of men: a critical psychoanalytic approach, and the "relational" approach inspired by the groundbreaking work of Jean Baker Miller on the psychology of women. This section concludes with a discussion, from the perspective of psychoanalytic theory, of the role of shame in male development. In this section, we have chosen to emphasize psychoanalytic perspectives, a choice that deserves a bit of explanation. Social learning and cognitive perspectives have been strongly associated with the gender role strain paradigm from the beginning and are represented in a number of chapters in this volume. Traditional psychoanalytic perspectives, on the other hand, have long been at the heart of the gender role identity paradigm. However, the most recent theoretical work on the psychology of men has attempted to develop a gender-aware psychoanalytic perspective on male development. Representative of this perspective, the chapters by Krugman and Pollack revise modern psychoanalytic theory to take into account the social construction of gender—integrating this critical perspective into a depth psychology.

Part II, "Research," first provides a review of the research on men and masculinity conducted over the past 15 years and then focuses on two research programs that have been inspired by the gender role strain paradigm. Part III, "Applications," presents a program designed to reconstruct masculinity, considers the issues relating to men's family roles, and casts a long hard look at the "dark side" of masculinity. Finally, in keeping with the idea that rigid gender role socialization according to a monolithic set of norms is not only unnecessary (contrary to the gender role identity paradigm) but also dysfunctional, Part IV, "The Varieties of Masculinity," promotes the notion that there are many valid forms of manhood in our society by discussing variations according to ethnocultural status and sexual orientation.

PART I: "THEORY"

The first part of this volume focuses on psychological theories of men and masculinity. In Chapter 1, Joseph Pleck updates the gender role strain paradigm. His original formulation of the paradigm stimulated research on three varieties of male gender role strain, which he terms "discrepancy-strain," "trauma-strain," and "dysfunction strain." Pleck then addresses the critique of the concept of the "male role" made by social constructionist writers, pointing out the confusion in some of these writings between the gender role strain paradigm and the gender role identity paradigm. Finally, Pleck considers the ongoing contention for cultural dominance between the strain and "identity-ist" perspectives on masculinity. Although the insights of the male gender role strain perspective are now widely accepted, the popularity of the mythopoetic perspective on masculinity and the emerging neoconservative critique of recent changes in family roles suggest that the identity-ist model of masculinity continues to exert strong influence.

William Pollack, in Chapter 2, provides a redefinition of boys' early developmental struggles for gendered selfhood from a critical, psychoanalytic perspective. He specifically proposes that historically salient cultural and interpersonal models of parenting have made it likely that, as boys, men suffer a traumatic abrogation of their early holding environment. This is a gender-linked, normative, developmental trauma or loss that may leave boys at risk later, as adult men, for specific psychological sequelae that often manifest as deficits in the arenas of intimacy, empathy, and struggles with commitment in relationships. Such a premature push toward disidentification yields a prototypic character style of defensive autonomy or pseudo-self-sufficiency. Early biological gender proclivities and later gender-bifurcated patterns of role socialization often exacerbate these unconscious traumas, shaming boys and men into suppressing the expression of a whole range of deeply felt emotions and needs. Pollack utilizes modern psychoanalytic theories of development, empirical research, biological gender differences, reinterpretations of Greek myths, and findings of cross-cultural anthropology to support new interpretive pathways of masculine development that are empathic to men while remaining respectful of women.

In Chapter 3, Stephen Bergman presents the "relational" approach to the study of men. He notes that current theories of male psychological development emphasize the primary importance of the self and fail to describe the whole of men's experiences in relationship. Men as well as women are motivated by a primary desire for connection, and it is less accurate and useful to think of "self" than to think of "self-in-relation" as a process. As with women, the sources of men's misery are in disconnections, violations, and dominance and in participating in relationships that are not mutually empowering.

Steven Krugman, in Chapter 4, presents a contemporary perspective on the interrelationship between dilemmas of male development and integration of the shame response. The author argues that strains within normative male development mitigate against effective shame integration, and that this lack of integration, in turn, accounts for a particularly male emotional vulnerability and male proclivities for social withdrawal and recourse to violence.

PART II: "RESEARCH"

In Part II, we consider the empirical research on men and masculinity that has been conducted over the past 15 years. Chapter 5, written by Edward

Thompson and Joseph Pleck, provides a review and classification of 18 instruments that have been developed since the late 1970s to study the male gender role, including masculinity ideology measures as well as measures of other masculinity-related constructs. The authors derive four conclusions from this review. First, there is evidence that gender orientation and gender ideologies are independent and have differential correlates. Second, there is also evidence that gender ideologies about men are distinct from and have different correlates than gender ideologies about women and gender relations in general. Third, measures that directly tap how men personally experience their gender are more likely to predict male behavior. Finally, a number of the existing instruments direct attention too narrowly toward a single definition of masculinity.

In Chapter 6, James O'Neil, along with his collaborators, Glenn Good and Sarah Holmes, summarize the results of 15 years of work on gender role conflict, discussing the large number of correlates of gender role conflict and strain. The centerpiece of this research program is an empirically derived measure of four patterns of gender role conflict, the Gender Role Conflict Scale (GRCS). The authors review 34 studies that have used the GRCS in relationship to demographic, personality, psychological health, relational-interpersonal, and therapy process variables. They conclude that gender role conflict is a documented area of difficulty for men and potentially hazardous to their well-being.

In Chapter 7, Richard Eisler, originator of the Masculine Gender Role Stress Scale (MGRSS) based on cognitive psychology, reviews his program of research focused on men's health. He presents data that describe associations between the MGRSS, its component factors, emotional expressiveness, stress, Type A behavior, and health habits. He also reviews a series of studies, employing cardiovascular measures of stress-response, that explore the relationships between men's vulnerability to masculine gender role stress and the gender relevance of the challenge. The author concludes that there are important relationships between masculine gender role stress and cardiovascular reactivity. This area of men's health is very important because of men's higher mortality rates and the association of the resulting shorter life spans with gender role strain. Research in this area could have an important impact on men's health.

PART III: "APPLICATIONS"

The third part of the book focuses on applications. In Chapter 8, Ronald Levant provides a framework for this part by proposing a "reconstruction of masculinity" based on several principles. First, it recognizes that there is a problem: The concerns expressed by women about men have basis in fact, and the feminists are essentially correct in their analyses of the relationship between gender and power. Second, it breaks with the essentialist tradition of viewing gender roles as "inherent" and adopts a social constructionist perspective on masculinity. In keeping with this perspective, the reconstruction allows for many versions of masculinity (or "masculinities"). Third, it strives to be empathic to men. To reconstruct masculinity, the author examines the strain of growing up male through three lenses. He considers: (1) gender role socialization and the ordeal of male emotional socialization, using the lens of social learning theory; (2) normative developmental traumas, using the lens of modern psychoanalytic developmental psychology; and (3) cultural requirements, using the lens of cultural anthropology. Along the way, he distinguishes those aspects of traditional masculinity that remain valuable, honors them, and discusses in some depth how the dysfunctional aspects of traditional masculinity might be changed.

Gary Brooks and Lucia Albino Gilbert, in Chapter 9, take up the issue of men in families as husbands and fathers. Traditionally, men have entered marriage and fatherhood with severe role limitations rooted in male gender role socialization and in the prevailing ideological perspectives on the institution of marriage and the role of fathers. Brooks and Gilbert analyze these restrictive forces before discussing the changing nature of being a husband and father in contemporary society. Finally, the authors consider prospects for changing masculinity ideology to allow men the option of more complete participation in family life.

In Chapter 10, Gary Brooks and Louise Silverstein take on the "dark side" of masculinity and consider a set of special problems that are most often the province of men but are also significant social and public health problems in their own right: violence, sexual excess, socially irresponsible behaviors (e.g., chemical dependence and risk-taking behavior), and relationship dysfunctions. Contemporary etiological explanations for dark side behavior are reviewed in order to lay the foundation for the authors' "interactive systems model of gender role strain." This model integrates cultural, social, psychological, and political variables to provide an explanatory framework for understanding the dark side of masculinity. The chapter concludes with a set of recommendations for changing traditional masculinity ideology.

PART IV: "THE VARIETIES OF MASCULINITY"

In this part of the book, we make good on one of the promises of the gender role strain paradigm—namely, the promise that this paradigm does not have to make its predecessor's mistake of setting up a monolithic, hence restrictive, notion of what it means to be a man. Instead, we view masculinity as capable of taking a variety of forms in response to the demands of different contexts. In Chapter 11, Richard Lazur and Richard Majors examine masculinity in ethnocultural and social-class perspective, looking specifically at how men of four cultures of color in the United States—African-American, Latino, American-Indian, and Asian-American—experience and express gender role strain. They address, from a social constructionist perspective, the dilemmas faced by men of color when they try to remain faithful to ethnocultural values while adapting to the requirements of the dominant culture. James Harrison, in Chapter 12, examines the relevance of the gender role strain paradigm for understanding the experience of homosexual and bisexual men. In a wide-ranging discussion that considers the development of Western culture as a context in which to understand the historical evolution of thought regarding sexual orientation, the author attempts to address four basic questions: Is homosexual status intrinsically good or bad? Is homosexual activity intrinsically right or wrong? Is homosexuality a preference or a way of being? And is homosexuality unique to contemporary Western culture, or is it a human universal?

To conclude this volume, the editors will pose the summary question: On the psychology of men, where are we now, and where are we going as we move forward into the 21st century?

References

Brod, H. (1987). *The making of the masculinities: The new men's studies.* Boston: Unwin Hyman.

Cath, S. H., Gurwitt, A. R., & Ross, J. M. (1982). *Father and child: Developmental and clinical considerations.* Boston: Little, Brown.

Clatterbaugh, K. (1990). *Contemporary perspectives on masculinity.* Boulder, CO: Westview Press.

Gilmore, D. D. (1990). *Manhood in the making: Cultural concepts of masculinity.* New Haven, CT: Yale University Press.

Kimmel, M. S. (1987). *Changing men: New directions in research on men and masculinity.* Newbury Park, CA: Sage.

Lamb, M. E. (1981). *The role of the father in child development.* New York: Wiley.

Meth, R. L., & Pasick, R. S. (1990). *Men in therapy: The challenge of change.* New York: Guilford Press.

Pleck, J. H. (1981). *The myth of masculinity.* Cambridge, MA: MIT Press.

Scher, M., Stevens, M., Good, G., & Eichenfeld, G. A. (1987). *The handbook of counseling and psychotherapy for men.* Newbury Park, CA: Sage.

PART I

THEORY

CHAPTER 1

The Gender Role Strain Paradigm: An Update

JOSEPH H. PLECK

I FIRST PROPOSED the "gender[1] role strain" model for masculinity in the early 1980s (Pleck, 1981). In presenting this model, my goal was to integrate the new ideas about masculinity then starting to appear in the professional literature into a systematic theoretical framework. I hoped that this new approach would replace the "gender role *identity*" model of masculinity, the theoretical perspective that had dominated American social science since the 1930s. Research since then has developed the concept of male gender role strain in varying ways. At the same time, new ideas about masculinity have emerged and some of the old ideas have been revived.

In this chapter, I present an overview of the often lively debate about male gender role strain in the research and theoretical literatures of the last dozen years. First, I distinguish the three major arguments inherent in the gender role strain model and describe how they have fared in recent research. Second, I develop the construct of masculinity ideology as a central "co-factor" in male gender role strain. Third, I analyze and respond to the criticisms of the gender role strain model made by a more recent theoretical perspective on masculinity, social constructionism. Finally, I consider the recent revival of "male identityism" (the older dominant theory of masculinity) and reflect on the broader cultural contention between the strain and identity models of masculinity.

Male Gender Role Strain: Three Concepts

My formulation of male gender role strain in Chapter 9 of *The Myth of Masculinity* (1981) drew particularly on Turner's (1970) and Komarovsky's

[1]In my 1981 book and earlier literature, the term was "sex role identity." To be consistent with contemporary usage, "sex role" has been updated to "gender role" here and elsewhere.

(1976) presentations of role strain as a more general sociological and social-psychological concept and on Hartley's (1959) and Hacker's (1957) analyses of the dynamics of masculinity. This formulation involved ten different propositions, each corresponding to a specific line of research.[2]

1. Gender roles are operationally defined by gender role stereotypes and norms.
2. Gender role norms are contradictory and inconsistent.
3. The proportion of individuals who violate gender role norms is high.
4. Violating gender role norms leads to social condemnation.
5. Violating gender role norms leads to negative psychological consequences.
6. Actual or imagined violation of gender role norms leads individuals to overconform to them.
7. Violating gender role norms has more severe consequences for males than females.
8. Certain characteristics prescribed by gender role norms are psychologically dysfunctional.
9. Each gender experiences gender role strain in its paid work and family roles.
10. Historical change causes gender role strain. (Pleck, 1981, p. 9)

Implicit in these propositions are three broader ideas about how cultural standards for masculinity, as implemented in gender socialization, have potentially negative effects on individual males. The first idea is that a significant proportion of males exhibit long-term failure to fulfill male role expectations. The resulting disjuncture between these expectations and these males' characteristics leads to low self-esteem and other negative psychological consequences. This dynamic is "gender role *discrepancy*" or "incongruity."

Second, even if male role expectations are successfully fulfilled, the socialization process leading to this fulfillment is traumatic, or the fulfillment itself is traumatic, with long-term negative side effects. This is the "gender role *trauma*" argument.

And the third theoretical notion is that the successful fulfillment of male role expectations can have negative consequences because many of the characteristics viewed as desirable or acceptable in men (e.g., low level of family participation) have inherent negative side effects, either for males themselves or for others. This is the "gender role *dysfunction*" argument.

These three ideas correspond to three theoretical subtypes of male gender role strain: discrepancy-strain, trauma-strain, and dysfunction-strain. Let us

[2]In propositions 2–8, I have updated "roles" to "role norms."

consider these concepts in more detail and review how they have been developed in research in the last decade.

MALE GENDER ROLE "DISCREPANCY"

Gender roles entail standards, expectations, or norms that individual males fit or do not fit to varying degrees. Not conforming to these standards has negative consequences for self-esteem and other outcomes reflecting psychological well-being because of negative social feedback as well as internalized negative self-judgments. The idea underlying discrepancy-strain seems particularly relevant to males. Erving Goffman (1963) gives a concrete description:

> In an important sense there is only one complete unblushing male in America: a young, married, white, urban, northern, heterosexual Protestant father of college education, fully employed, of good complexion, weight, and height, and a recent record in sports. Every American male tends to look out upon the world from this perspective, this constituting one sense in which one can speak of a common value system in America. Any male who fails to qualify in any one of these ways is likely to view himself—during moments at least—as unworthy, incomplete, and inferior. (p. 128)

The process Goffman describes has wide application in male experience: boys inadequate in sports, gay male adolescents and adults taught their sexuality is perverse, men unable to support families.

Discrepancy-strain is the argument in the first social science book in the early 20th century to pose a fundamental challenge to traditional concepts of gender: Margaret Mead's *Sex and Temperament in Three Primitive Societies* (1935). Mead's work is occasionally cited in textbooks today, but generally only as a source of somewhat exotic cross-cultural examples that disconfirm Western patterns of gender behavior (Arapesh men are gentle and artistic, Mundugumor women are aggressive, etc.). Mead's real point, however, was not that different societies vary in the sexes' actual characteristics. Rather, her central insight was that societies differ in their definitions of the sexes' *ideal* characteristics. As a result, a man or woman perfectly adapted to the gender norms of one culture would be a "misfit" (a term Mead used repeatedly) in another.

Empirical Research: Assessing Discrepancy Between Real Self and Same-Gender Ideal

Discrepancy-strain has been explored in two different ways. One line of research attempts to directly assess the two theoretical ingredients of this form of role strain—gender role standards and individuals' own characteristics—and then relates discrepancies between the two to various outcomes. Using adjectival rating scales, respondents describe the "ideal woman" (for women) or "ideal man" (for men) and then describe themselves. Gender role strain is operationalized as the discrepancy score between the two ratings and then analyzed as an influence on self-esteem. An early study by Deutsch and Gilbert (1976) produced some confirming results, but other research of this type has been limited and has not produced strong confirmation.

There are several possible reasons this line of research has not provided better validation. One important theoretical issue is that the research ought to take into account the degree to which gender role norms are actually psychologically salient or important to the individual. If the individual is deeply psychologically enmeshed in traditional gender concepts, gender role discrepancy should have strong correlates, but if the individual is not, discrepancy should not. In other words, the effect of gender discrepancy is, in the statistical sense, moderated by the salience of gender roles to the individual. However, prior studies testing this moderator hypothesis have not produced validation (Garnets, 1978; Suslowitz, 1979).

A second theoretical issue is that discrepancy-strain may be not a static outcome but a process. When individuals experience gender role discrepancy, they probably do not remain frozen in this state for extended periods of time. Rather, they cope with or adapt to it by changing their behavior, by changing their perception of gender role norms or disengaging from them, or by changing their reference group. Thus, gender discrepancy's impact on psychological well-being may not persist in a way that will be evident in cross-sectional correlational studies.

Third, research needs to take into account the possibility that not fitting masculinity standards can have positive as well as negative consequences and to seek to determine when these differential outcomes occur. One possible basis for positive consequences is that the normatively prescribed characteristics may be inherently dysfunctional, as I discuss in a later section. In addition, the process of confronting and disengaging from traditional gender role standards may actually confer psychological benefits. Some therapists have argued, for example, that among many gay men and lesbians, confronting external oppression and internalized homophobia seems to promote psychological maturity and integration (Harrison, 1987). If this process occurs more generally around gender role standards, then it may not be surprising that discrepancy measures between same-sex ideal and the self-concept are not correlated with low self-esteem.

Finally, this research design correlates ideal-self discrepancies assessed on a set of extremely global masculine personality characteristics (e.g., "aggressive") with an equally global outcome, self-esteem. Self-esteem may be too stable a component of personality to be a good outcome measure for gender role strain research. There may be too many intervening processes and too many other influences on global self-esteem for a strong overall relationship to be evident. A strength of the adjective checklists used in this research is that they can be used to assess ideal and real self in the same format. But are these adjectives really meaningful to respondents as dimensions through which they categorize themselves or perceive gender role expectations? Knowing what level of "aggressiveness" a respondent checks off for the "ideal man" does not tell us how strongly—or even whether—he links this characteristic to masculinity in a deeper sense.

Some summary recommendations for future research and theory in this area include: Pay attention, both theoretically and in terms of assessment, to the degree to which a perceived same-sex standard is psychologically salient to the individual. Assess potential discrepancies in more specific areas, such as making a lot of money, having many sexual partners, or excelling at one or more sports. Likewise, use outcomes that are theoretically narrower and more proximal to the hypothesized strain, for example, being uncomfortable in situations in which others know your level of performance.

Experiencing Gender Role Discrepancy as Stressful

A second line of research on discrepancy-strain, represented by O'Neil et al.'s (1986) Gender Role Conflict Scale-II, and by Eisler and Skidmore's (1987) Masculine Gender Role Stress instrument, takes a somewhat different approach. (See also Chapters 6 and 7.) In this research, rooted in the cognitive appraisal approach to stress, individuals self-report not *whether* gender role discrepancy exists for them, but the extent to which, *if* a gender discrepancy did exist, they would experience it as stressful. Eisler's Masculine Gender Role Stress measure, for example, asks respondents to judge how stressful it would be for them to experience various circumstances that raters have judged to be more stressful for men than women (e.g., feeling that you are not in good physical condition, having your lover say that she/he is not satisfied). Work using these scales has found that this disposition is related to measures of self-reported stress such as anger and anxiety, to homophobia, and even to psychophysiological outcomes such as responses to the "cold pressor" test. Thus, O'Neil's and Eisler's approach to discrepancy-strain provides empirical validation. This research has the strength of focusing on the disposition to experience gender role discrepancies as stressful and of investigating narrower and more specific outcomes as concomitants of gender role strain.

MALE GENDER ROLE TRAUMA

The second form of male gender role strain in my theoretical framework is trauma-strain. In recent years, the concept of "trauma" has become

increasingly important in clinical fields (Herman, 1992; Herman, Perry, &
Van der Kolk, 1989). The concept has been implicit in several qualitative
studies of male socialization in different contexts, such as professional ath-
letics (Messner, 1992) and Little League baseball (Fine, 1987). Particularly
vivid examples come from Best's (1983) ethnography of an elementary
school, Pine Hill, focusing on the "hidden curriculum" of gender roles. She
describes how the proscription of any behavior remotely "feminine" in boys
becomes consolidated during the second grade. She notes, for example, that
"if this 'be a nonfemale' lesson was cruel, so was the teaching of it. It was not
unusual for Pine Hill mothers to report that their sons had arrived home in
tears because peers had called them 'fags,' 'queers,' or 'gay'" (p. 82). The
concept of trauma has also been implicit in analyses of the "coming-out"
process (Harrison, 1987).

The concept of trauma is beginning to be applied to masculinity in a more
explicit way. Levant (1992; Chapter 8) integrates social learning and psychoanalytic developmental perspectives in his examination of the traumas
inherent in the male gender role socialization process and of their effects on
adult male emotional experience. He has hypothesized that such male ills as
overreliance on aggression and difficulties with emotional tenderness and
intimacy stem from a nearly universal socialization of males to be "alex-
ithymic" (unable to put emotions into words). Pollack (1992) has argued that
boys' need to become independent of their mothers at an early age leads to a
"traumatic abrogation of the holding environment."[3] Brooks (1990) extends
the trauma paradigm in another direction in his reformulation of post-
traumatic stress syndrome in Vietnam-era veterans as "post-Vietnam gender
role strain." Brooks argues that the notion of post-Vietnam gender role strain
is an extension of earlier efforts to differentiate post-traumatic stress syndrome from its imitators. To Brooks, it is a "sociocultural condition that
results from the failure of Vietnam veterans to move beyond their military
socialization and adopt gender roles more in harmony with contemporary
culture" (p. 18). Recent literature on shame in males is giving more attention
to its dynamic connection to trauma (Chapter 4; Osherson & Krugman,
1990). The trauma perspective clearly offers a promising new direction in the
understanding of masculinity.

MALE GENDER ROLE DYSFUNCTION

The third major subtype of male gender role strain is male gender role
dysfunction. The core idea here is that the fulfillment of gender role stan-

---

[3]However, Pollack interprets boys' need to be independent as deriving from their recognition of being of a different gender than their mothers (consistent with the male identity
argument), rather than from cultural prescriptions.

dards can have negative consequences because the behaviors and character-istics these standards prescribe can be inherently dysfunctional, in the sense of being associated with negative outcomes either for the male himself or for others. Several bodies of recent work exemplify this approach.

Correlates of Gender-Related Personality Characteristics

First, research has investigated the association between various outcomes and masculine gender-related personality characteristics, as assessed by the M (masculinity) scales of the Bem (1974) Sex Role Inventory and by Spence and Helmreich's (1978) Personal Attributes Questionnaire. The construct assessed by these measures is often referred to as "gender role orientation" (Lenney, 1991). A few studies suggest that being high in M (masculinity) is correlated with negative outcomes such as delinquency (Horwitz & White, 1987) and psychological violence toward dating partners (Thompson, 1990). However, such negative correlates are not found in other comparisons within these studies, or in a variety of other studies. (For a fuller review, see Pleck, Sonenstein, & Ku, 1993b.) The lack of more consistent negative corre-lates is perhaps not surprising when one realizes that the scale developers explicitly designed their M scales to assess the *socially desirable* component of traits associated with masculinity.

At a later stage in this line of research, researchers theoretically differenti-ated between the socially positive and the socially negative components of masculinity. In particular, Spence, Helmreich, and Holahan (1979) did this in a later form of the PAQ, the *Extended* PAQ, which distinguished between the components of masculinity they called M+ (achieving, responsible, etc.) and M– (aggressive, exploitative, etc.). M– has been found to be correlated with measures of fighting (Spence, Helmreich, & Holahan, 1979) and alcohol and drug use (Snell, Belk, & Hawkins, 1987).

Other research provides further documentation that socially negative male personality styles have correlates that are problematic for males themselves and/or for others, thus providing empirical support for the notion of male dysfunction-strain. One group of studies uses O'Neil et al.'s (1986) Gender Role Conflict Scale-I, which includes a strong component of self-reported negative masculine characteristics. In studies by Davis (1987) and Sharpe and Heppner (1991), this measure has been found to predict low self-esteem, anxiety, and depression. Another line of supporting studies uses Mosher and Sirkin's (1984) Hypermasculinity Inventory, which has been found to be correlated with self-reported drug use, aggressiveness, driving after drinking, and delinquent behavior. Yet another is Majors and Billson's (1992) work on "cool pose" in black males. In Majors's analysis, cool pose is a particular form of masculine behavior that functions as an adaptation to racial oppression but at the same time exacts considerable costs on black males themselves.

Research on the negative sequelae of traditional masculinity is becoming more common in the health area. For example, Helgeson (1990) has documented that among males with coronary heart disease, Bem's M scale predicted Type A behavior, poor health practices, impaired social networks, and an overall prognostic indicator of heart attack severity. Another recent study reports that during doctor visits, men are more passive than women and may suffer poorer health as a result. In an analysis of 296 taped visits by patients with serious illnesses, men gave less information and asked fewer questions; in a 15-minute office visit, women asked an average of six questions, while men typically asked none! However, men seeing female doctors gave twice as much information as those seeing male doctors and reported fewer functional limitations. The press report of the study concludes that "real men are lousy patients, particularly when their doctors are also men" (cited in Winslow, 1993).

Correlates of Functioning in Social Roles

Another line of research providing documentation for male gender role dysfunction concerns men's involvement in social roles, particularly family roles. To cite one example from my own research, in a long-term longitudinal study, fathers who reported less involvement with their children's development, especially social-emotional development, were judged by clinicians as showing lower levels of marital success and "psychosocial generativity" (a measure operationalizing Erikson's [1950] concept) when interviewed decades later, in their fifties and sixties (Snarey & Pleck, 1993). Interestingly, contrary to the possible argument that these low-involved fathers traded off involvement with their children for career success, they also showed somewhat lower occupational mobility. In addition, in analyses of effects on children, also assessed later in life, low father involvement also predicted lower educational and occupational mobility for both sexes (Snarey, 1993). Thus, this study showed that the low paternal involvement prescribed by traditional masculinity has negative consequences for both fathers and their offspring.

In another study, using data from two national samples, fathers who spend less time in housework and child care report lower levels of well-being (Pleck, 1985). In a third study, with men in two-earner couples from a mixed middle-class/working-class community, men reporting lower "quality" in their marital and parental roles register significantly higher levels of psychological distress (Barnett, Marshall, & Pleck, 1992). The larger dynamic underlying these studies' results is that traditional male role expectations foster commitment to paid work and breadwinning at the expense of marriage and family. When men conform to these expectations by showing less involvement or getting less from the latter roles, they and those around them pay a price.

Masculinity Ideology: Co-Factor in Male Gender Role Strain

In my current thinking, the concept of "masculinity ideology" is central to male gender role strain. Masculinity ideology refers to beliefs about the importance of men adhering to culturally defined standards for male behavior. My recent research focuses on this concept (Pleck, Sonenstein, & Ku, 1991, 1993a, 1993b, 1994a, 1994b; Thompson, Grisanti, & Pleck, 1985; Thompson & Pleck, 1986; Chapter 5; Thompson, Pleck, & Ferrera, 1992). Masculinity ideology is implicated in all three forms of male role strain. At a broader level, it is a vital co-factor in male role strain.

As argued in detail elsewhere (Pleck, Sonenstein, & Ku, 1993a, 1993b, 1994a, 1994b; Chapter 5; Thompson, Pleck, & Ferrera, 1992), this concept differs from masculine gender orientation and is also distinct from other gender-related beliefs. The construct of masculinity ideology derives most directly from research on what is generally termed "attitudes toward masculinity." Although the latter term is often the generic label for these measures, masculinity ideology is conceptually preferable. Better than the more neutral term "attitudes," masculinity ideology conveys the full significance of what these scales really assess: the individual's endorsement and internalization of cultural belief systems about masculinity and male gender, rooted in the structural relationship between the two sexes. Masculinity ideology also connotes better the superordinate, organizing nature of these beliefs, at both the individual level and the social-structural level. They are not just beliefs about a particular social object but constitute a belief system about masculinity connected to a broad network of more specific attitudes and dispositions. Some previous research also conceptualizes gender-related beliefs as ideologies (e.g., Levinson & Huffman, 1955; Lipman-Blumen, 1972; Mason & Bumpass, 1975).

There is clearly not a single masculinity ideology, but many. The concept refers to a variety of component beliefs that may be endorsed to different degrees and related to each other in varying ways, both in different individuals and in different social subgroups. For example, the masculinity ideology held on the average by men in the profeminist men's movement is probably different from the average ideology held by men in the career military. Complementing this average difference is the undoubtedly great variance within both groups. The coexistence of between-group differences and within-group diversity is also documented by quantitative data from late adolescent males showing associations between masculinity ideology and sociodemographic background characteristics such as age, family income, and race-ethnicity (Pleck, Sonenstein, & Ku, 1994a).

Thus, the concept of masculinity ideology does not assume that there is a single, unvarying, universal standard for masculinity. Rather, the theoretical notion is that within the diversity of actual and possible standards about men

and masculinity in contemporary U.S. culture, there is a *particular* constellation of standards and expectations that individually and jointly have various
kinds of negative concomitants. These standards and expectations have been
formulated in various ways in theoretical analyses of masculinity (Brannon,
1976; Doyle, 1989; Franklin, 1984; Pleck, 1981). These formulations emphasize different distinctions but nonetheless focus on common dimensions, including achievement, emotional control, antifemininity, and homophobia.
Though they have many pitfalls, terms such as "traditional," "conventional,"
and "conservative" are the best available labels for this configuration of standards. Anyone using these terms must, of course, recognize that they have to
be placed in the context of particular cultures: There is no one "traditional"
masculinity across culture and time. A particular masculinity ideology scale
may *assess* a single masculinity ideology, but this does not mean that the
scale, or the broader concept of masculinity ideology, assumes that only one
universal standard or dimension of masculinity ideology exists. Using such
scales, research can determine empirically whether "traditional" masculinity
ideology is associated with negative correlates and whether it has the same
correlates in different groups.

What are the dynamic links between masculinity ideology and male gender role strain? Masculinity ideology plays an essential part in all its forms.
For the discrepancy form of male strain, the individual male's level of
endorsement of traditional masculinity ideology translates into the gender
expectations he personally applies to himself. In addition, it influences the
subjective consequences of any existing discrepancies between his self-concept
and male role standards. At the social level, the masculinity ideology held in
the broader culture and in the immediate reference group structures the social
expectations experienced by males.

Masculinity ideology directly creates trauma in male socialization, as documented by the examples discussed earlier. It influences, if not regulates,
how trauma from other sources is psychologically resolved. The phrase
"men can't cry" is sometimes dismissed as a trite truism. Nevertheles, within
it is the deeper insight that in many segments of contemporary culture, men
are denied the right to grieve—recognized in all theories as the essential first
stage in the resolution of trauma, however they differ in other respects. Masculinity ideology also affects men's willingness to risk, even seek, trauma.
For example, many males enter situations such as the military, gangs, and
college fraternities fully knowing that they will include dangerous "hazing"
ordeals (trauma) and in many cases actually seeking these ordeals out.

Masculinity ideology also plays a part in the tendency of many men to
persist in behaviors whose consequences are dysfunctional for themselves
and for others. It influences the extent to which males attempt to fulfill traditional role expectations in spite of their inherent negative side effects or dys-
functionality. My research has focused particularly on this third process,

reflected in the association between traditional masculinity ideology and negative consequences such as inconsistent condom use. The negative concomitants found for traditional masculinity ideology in my own research and that of others are recounted in detail in Chapter 5. Taken together, these studies provide considerable support for the hypothesis that traditional masculinity ideology has dysfunctional correlates.

In my own work, I have taken particular pains to test empirically whether masculinity ideology has similar correlates within white, black, and Hispanic males—a critical test to conduct in light of the possible criticism that the particular masculinity ideology assessed in my own and others' scales is relevant only to whites, or only to middle-class whites. Empirically, levels of both traditional masculinity ideology and the outcome variables differed somewhat in the three groups. At the same time, the relationships between masculinity ideology and outcomes were highly similar (Pleck, Sonenstein, & Ku, 1993a, 1993b, 1994b). This suggests that adolescent males endorse traditional masculinity ideology to different degrees in different racial-ethnic groups, but that it has generally similar concomitants in these three groups.

In summary, by shaping the gender expectations that men apply to themselves (and others apply to men) and by influencing how discrepancies from these expectations are experienced, masculinity ideology is an essential cofactor in male role strain. It also promotes trauma, inhibits the working-through of trauma, and leads men to persist in dysfunctional behavior.

Social Constructionism and Its Critique of Gender Role

Alongside gender role strain, "social constructionism" has emerged in the last decade as a new perspective on masculinity (Brod, 1987; Kimmel, 1987; Kimmel & Messner, 1989). First introduced by Gagnon and Simon (1973) and Rubin (1975), social constructionism has become a dominant theoretical framework in gender studies (e.g., Hunter College Women's Studies Collective, 1983), although recently the concept of the social construction of homosexuality has come under attack (see Stein, 1992). As Kimmel and Messner (1989) apply the constructionist perspective to men, "the important fact of men's lives is not that they are biological males, but that they become men. Our sex may be male, but our identity as men is developed through a complex process of interaction with the culture in which we both learn the gender scripts appropriate to our culture, and attempt to modify those scripts to make them more palatable" (p. 10).

The central arguments in social constructionism and gender role strain are theoretically compatible. Social constructionism's model of the learning of gender "scripts" is analogous to the gender role strain paradigm's equally central concept of gender role socialization. Social constructionism implies that masculinity can have negative consequences for men. The gender role strain model for masculinity is, in the broad sense, a social constructionist perspective that simply predated the term. The concept of role strain was applied to gender (Mead, 1935; Turner, 1970) before the notion of social construction was (Gagnon & Simon, 1973; Rubin, 1975). The role strain interpretation of masculinity (Hacker, 1957; Hartley, 1959; Pleck, 1981) appeared prior to the social constructionist interpretation (Brod, 1987; Kimmel, 1987; Kimmel & Messner, 1989).

However, social constructionists make several arguments that fundamentally challenge the concept of gender role and, by extension, male gender role strain. In my view, their critiques are ill founded. Kimmel and Messner (1989) claim that the gender role perspective casts these roles "as static containers of behaviors and attitudes, and biological males and females are required to fit themselves into these containers, regardless of how ill-fitting these clusters of behaviors and attitudes felt. Such a model was ahistorical and suggested a false cultural universalism, and was therefore ill-equipped to understand the ways in which sex roles change, and the ways that individuals modify these roles through the enactments of gender expectations" (p. 8). These authors also assert that this model makes the "unexamined assumption that . . . one version of masculinity—white, middle age, middle class, heterosexual—was the sex role into which all men were struggling to fit in our society" (p. 9; see also Kimmel, 1987, p. 12). Kimmel and others cite my work (particularly *The Myth of Masculinity,* 1981) as the formulation of the gender role model they critique. Let us compare my formulation of this model—specifically, the 10 propositions from *The Myth of Masculinity* summarized at the outset of this chapter—with these assertions.

For example, contrary to the charge that my model views gender roles as "static," the discussion of Proposition 2 ("Gender role norms are contradictory and inconsistent") includes an explicit analysis of how gender role expectations vary over the life cycle. Whereas they claim that the gender role model is ahistorical, falsely assuming that gender role norms do not change, Proposition 10 states, "Historical change causes gender role strain." This argument is linked to my presentation of Proposition 2, which explicitly analyzes how historical changes in gender norms contribute to the contradictions and inconsistencies in expectations experienced by men. The view of historical change in social constructionism may be more elaborate than in the role strain model, but the claim that the role model is "ahistorical" is a misrepresentation.

Contrary to the claim that the gender role model assumes a single, universal male gender role norm, Proposition 2 examines how the existence of different male gender norms in different cultural groups creates a potential for inconsistent expectations. I argue there and elsewhere (Pleck, 1976) that there are multiple, competing conceptions of masculinity. In fact, the existence of multiple standards is central to the gender role perspective. In arguing against biological interpretations of gender, I and other role theorists in fact give central attention to cross-cultural variations in each sex's actual and expected behavior, using them as one of the most obvious pieces of evidence that gender behavior should be understood as role behavior. In addition, I have analyzed how the assumption of a single standard was a central failing of the earlier, male role *identity* model. In a particularly important example, I deconstructed the fallacious interpretation of black males as having "inadequate" male identity because their scores on masculinity-femininity tests were "feminine" relative to whites' (Pleck, 1981, pp. 126–128).

In my view, Kimmel and other social constructionist theorists have never grasped the fundamental difference between the gender *role* model and the older, male gender role *identity* theory—the distinction at the heart of *The Myth of Masculinity* (see also Pleck, Sonenstein, & Ku, 1993a). Constructionists use the term "role" to refer to both (e.g., Kimmel, 1987, p. 12; Kimmel & Messner, 1989, p. 8).[4] They apparently see the identity and role perspectives as only two slight variants within the role model and dismiss both in a single stroke. But the differences between the two models are profound, particularly with respect to their criticisms. The identity model does indeed have the failings they misattribute to the role perspective: assuming that psychological masculinity and "male identity" had a single, static, unvarying form, holding true across all cultures and all time, assessable with "masculinity-femininity" tests in any population with equal validity.

Finally, social constructionists claim that the gender role strain model is fundamentally reactionary because it ignores issues of power in gender relations and assumes a false equivalence in the experiences of women and men (Kimmel, 1993). This criticism is faulty on several grounds. Like any theory, the theory of gender role strain cannot explain everything, but it was never intended to do so. Unlike the male identity theory it was intended to replace, the role strain model provides an interpretation of the psychological and social-psychological dynamics associated with masculinity that locates the "problem" of masculinity in the cultural definition of manhood itself, not in men's inability to live up to it.

Focusing on these dynamics does not assume an absence of power dynamics between the genders or an equivalence in their experience. The concept of "role" does not intrinsically assume that incumbents in all roles have equal power. Bosses and workers can be analyzed as having different roles without ignoring the fact that bosses can fire workers but the reverse is

---

[4]Kimmel's phrasing in his earlier writing allows room for the interpretation that he is criticizing only the identity model and simply mislabeling it as the role perspective (Kimmel, 1987; Kimmel & Messner, 1989). I interpreted his criticisms this way in a previous publication (Pleck, Sonenstein, & Ku, 1993b).

not true. Just as psychoanalytic theory and other theories can be used in ways that either contribute to the understanding of power dynamics or ignore or mystify them (Chodorow, 1978), the same is true for role theory. Both I and most others who have developed the role perspective on masculinity (e.g., Brannon, 1976; Levant, 1992) have clearly grounded this analysis in the recognition that, as social groups, men have power over women. The constructionist analysis may develop power dynamics more than does the role analysis, but the claim that the concept of gender role strain inherently ignores or mystifies power dynamics cannot be sustained.

SOCIAL CONSTRUCTIONISM: STRENGTHS AND WEAKNESSES

At a broader level, what are the strengths and weaknesses of the social constructionist approach as an alternative approach to masculinity? First, it does have the strength of making power dynamics between men and women central to the understanding of gender, which they should be. However, in my view, constructionism distorts this point by holding that power is the *only* important dynamic in gender and that focusing on any other dynamic is intellectually and politically reactionary.

Second, social constructionists exaggerate the extent to which the role perspective views gender socialization as acting on passive individuals and focuses on early childhood. As evidence, a simple comparison of the proportion of the studies involving children cited in *The Myth of Masculinity*'s discussion of the identity model with the proportion for the role model would reveal that the identity perspective, not the role perspective, focuses on early childhood. Nonetheless, social constructionism has the virtue of reinforcing an emphasis on individuals' adaptation to gender expectations as a lifelong process, as well as one in which individuals are not only acted upon but act.

Third, in their criticism that the role perspective is universalistic, constructionists have a double standard, applying these criteria to one theory but not another. Constructionist theorists criticize the role perspective for assuming universalism in the psychological dynamics surrounding gender. However, constructionist writing often incorporates Chodorow's (1978) psychoanalytic arguments about the mother-son relationship shaping male personality (Messner, 1992). These arguments, of course, assume the same dynamics in personality development across all cultures (Segura & Pierce, 1993). Further, the concept of "identity" is a central one in the constructionist perspective (e.g., "Our sex may be male, but our identity as men is developed," Kimmel & Messner, 1989, p. 10; see also Messner, 1992). But the concept of identity is unanalyzed and taken for granted.

Finally, social constructionism vastly underestimates the amount of attention that research rooted in the role perspective gives to differences in the conceptions and dynamics of masculinity in varying cultural groups. In many important areas, such as sexual behavior and family behavior, racial and other group differences are arguably the central focus of current research (e.g., Sonenstein, Pleck, & Ku, 1989). Constructionism has a valid point, nonetheless, in stating that these differences should receive even more attention.

However, constructionist theorists make this statement the end point of their discussion, rather than a starting point from which to examine what research has actually found about the extent of these differences and commonalities. As a result, besides stating that across all cultures and all time men have power in relation to women, constructionist descriptions of the *substance* of masculinity (e.g., Carrigan, Connell, & Lee, 1985; Kimmel, 1987; Kimmel & Messner, 1989) seem oddly content-free and empty, even sterile. In their effort to not mischaracterize any particular issue as affecting *all* men, these writings give little acknowledgment of specific issues that affect *any* men.

Male Gender Role Strain in Broader Cultural Perspective

Up to this point, I have reviewed several lines of research within the male gender role strain paradigm and responded to social constructionism's critique of it. In concluding, I turn to a deeper question: What contribution does the gender role strain perspective make at a broader cultural level, and how is it faring? As I have recounted, gender role strain is being pursued in research, and being pursued by social constructionist theorists. But outside this debate between adherents of the role and constructionist views within the rather narrow field of gender studies, does the concept of gender role strain have any bearing on intellectual currents in other academic fields, or any connection to broader gender dynamics in contemporary society? In concluding, I can offer only some preliminary reflections.

At one level, it seems that the core insights underlying the concept of male gender role strain have been broadly accepted. This is certainly so in the mental health field, and this acceptance seems just as widespread in the media and popular culture. Television comedies, newspaper advice columns, and media analyses of events (from why we bombed Iraq to the impact of unemployment) seem to take almost as a given that cultural expectations about masculinity shape male behavior, often negatively. Gender role strain has become assimilated into the consensus cultural perspective on men and masculinity—quite a different perspective from the early 1970s when I wrote my first article on the topic, let alone two decades before that, when I was a young boy. A particularly important example is John Bradshaw's public education work in the "adult children of alcoholics" and "recovery" movements. Bradshaw's message is probably reaching as many people today as any popular trend in mental health in recent years. In his presentations and tapes,

Bradshaw routinely connects dysfunctional male behavior patterns to mistaken cultural beliefs about what men should do and feel. In terms of breadth of impact, Bradshaw, for all his idiosyncrasies, may be today's single most important exponent and disseminator of the core insights of male gender strain.

But at the same time, it seems that the other leading candidate for the dominant cultural view of masculinity is as strong as ever. This alternative contender is not, of course, social constructionism but the male gender role *identity* model, which predated constructionism by several generations. The core argument of this model is that males have an intrinsic psychological nature that is deformed by modern culture and its key institutions (especially families). As a result, it is a constant struggle for men to assert and maintain their masculinity. In philosophical terms, the male identity model holds a particular kind of "essentialist" view of male nature. To help mark this view of masculinity as only a theory, I suggest the term "male identity-ism" for it.

There is an ongoing contention for cultural dominance between the strain and identity-ist perspectives on masculinity. Although male identity-ism has been almost completely abandoned in academic research in psychology and sociology, it has been amazingly persistent in other intellectual fields. It, of course, continues to have considerable hold in academic psychoanalysis (e.g., Fast, 1984). But more surprisingly, it also appears in recent feminist clinical writing. For example, an analysis of male sexual violence recently appearing in the prestigious journal *Signs* in essence restates the classic male identity view (Lisak, 1991). Miedzian's (1991) otherwise excellent feminist analysis of male violence likewise appropriates, with no critical comment, many features of the identity interpretation of male violence. Male identity-ism has made a resurgence in anthropology through Gilmore's *Manhood in the Making* (1990). This influential book's core argument is that male aggression is ultimately a response to males' needs to psychologically separate from their mothers. The identity model also persists in social history. For example, Carnes's (1989) elaborate analysis of male fraternal and secret societies in U.S. history resurrects the identity-based arguments of the 1950s about male initiation rites.

Male identity-ism is also on the upswing in popular culture, as evidenced by two broader social trends. First, the "mythopoetic" men's movement (Harding, 1992) has arisen. While the true extent of its impact on men is exaggerated by the media, this movement does seem to have involved more men in a direct, personal way than the fathers' rights movement, and certainly more than the profeminist men's movement. The mythopoetic men's movement has become one of the major current cultural repositories of male identity-ism. While this movement has many different intellectual themes, if there is a dominant one it is that too many males today have never truly become men because they never really separated from their mothers, and therefore that men need more contact with their fathers and other older men to become mature (Bly, 1990). This is, of course, the central argument in the male gender identity paradigm. What men actually get from involvement in the mythopoetic men's movement may bear little relation to this idea, but the idea's intellectual centrality is nonetheless noteworthy.

Second, but as yet not as well known, a new neoconservative perspective on fatherhood is emerging (Blankenhorn, 1991; see also Gibbs, 1993). As the sociologist David Popenoe (cited in Gibbs, 1993, p. 61) puts it: "Parenting of young infants is not a natural activity for males." By making men do the "unnatural," feminism violates men's essential gendered nature, leading to manifold negative consequences. Feminist expectations that fathers be more involved with young children, especially that fathers be "androgynous," have undermined fathers' distinctive parental role. This has led men in increasingly higher numbers to abandon the family through divorce and other irresponsible behavior. In turn, the resulting increase in father absence is the direct source of negative behavior in children and youth, especially males. In this neoconservative analysis of contemporary fatherhood, we see simply an updated recapitulation of most of the central arguments of the theory of male gender role identity, as I systematized it in 1981. "Feminine" behaviors in men, promoted by women, desex men's essential psychological nature. This desexing—not dysfunctional definitions of masculinity—accounts for men's problems. Father absence is once again invoked as a specific mechanism linking the presumed deformations of identity of male adults and male children.

Concluding Reflections

The idea that a man behaves in a certain way because he "needs to prove his masculinity" has a powerful emotional resonance for many people. That this notion is so widely accepted is one of the core truths about masculinity in American culture. By contrast, the analogous idea that women act to "prove their femininity" would sound odd and alien.

But this observation by itself begs the question, *Why* do men seem to need to prove their masculinity? This fundamental question has two possible answers, and it is vital to recognize how they are different. Men need to prove their manhood (a) because men are socialized to believe that their masculinity is something they have to prove, or (b) because it is men's essential nature that their masculinity can never be fully established, as women's femininity is. Position A is the strain answer, and Position B is the identity-ist answer. In the identity-ist view, men's psychological frailty derives from allegedly universal psychological dynamics in the mother-father-son triangle or, in other accounts, from men's lack of any experience that validates their gender comparable to childbirth for women.

A recent *Newsweek* article on gays in the military illustrates the unexamined intellectual leap from the *observation* that men seem especially motivated to prove their masculinity to the identity-ist *interpretation* of why. "Sigmund Freud observed half a century ago that men seldom live comfortably with their manhood: they are stuck with constantly having to prove it. . . . Freud said men are engaged in a constant struggle against what he called their 'feminine' or 'passive' side" (Gelman, 1993, pp. 28–29).[5] The linguistic difference between the first sentence and the second may seem small, but the conceptual leap is great. Yes, many men feel uncomfortable with manhood, and seem to have to prove it. But why is struggling against internal femininity the explanation, and what consequences does this explanation have?

At a broad cultural level, male identity-ism capitalizes on the apparent truth of the observation that men "need to prove it" to promulgate an essentialist gender insecurity as its taken-for-granted and only interpretation. But the gender role strain perspective challenges the taken-for-granted-ness of the identity model. Because the identity interpretation has social implications that are so fundamentally conservative, it is ever more important that adherents of the gender role strain perspective continue their work with renewed dedication.

References

Barnett, R. C., Marshall, N. L., & Pleck, J. H. (1992). Men's multiple roles and their relationship to men's psychological distress. *Journal of Marriage and the Family, 54*(2), 358–367.

Bem, S. L. (1974). The measurement of psychological androgyny. *Journal of Personality and Social Psychology, 42,* 155–162.

Best, R. (1983). *We've all got scars: What boys and girls learn in elementary school.* Bloomington: Indiana University Press.

Blankenhorn, D. (1991). *The good family man: Fatherhood and the pursuit of happiness in America* (Publication No. W.P. 12). New York: Institute for American Values.

Bly, R. (1990). *Iron John.* Reading, MA: Addison-Wesley.

Brannon, R. (1976). The male sex role: Our culture's blueprint for manhood and what it's done for us lately. In D. David & R. Brannon (Eds.), *The forty-nine percent majority: The male sex role* (pp. 1–48). Reading, MA: Addison-Wesley.

[5]These two quotations also show how our culture pays the identity-ist interpretation one of its highest compliments: the idea is attributed to Freud. In reality, this is a projection of later views onto Freud. Freud did theorize that individuals of each sex had what he called the "character traits of masculinity and femininity" as part of a constitutional bisexuality. But Freud did not describe them as in constant struggle; neither did he conclude that men had a special contest against their femininity. The idea of male struggle against internal femininity was in fact introduced to psychoanalytic theory much later by Felix Boehm and Karen Horney in the 1930s (Pleck, 1981, p. 157).

Brod, H. (Ed.). (1987). *The making of masculinities: The new men's studies.* Winchester, MA: Allen & Unwin.

Brooks, G. R. (1990). Post-Vietnam gender role strain: A needed concept? *Professional Psychology: Research and Practice, 21*(1), 18–25.

Carnes, M. C. (1989). *Secret ritual and manhood in Victorian America.* New Haven, CT: Yale University Press.

Carrigan, T., Connell, B., & Lee, J. (1985). Toward a new sociology of masculinity. *Theory and Society, 14,* 551–604.

Chodorow, N. (1978). *The reproduction of mothering: Psychoanalysis and the sociology of gender.* Berkeley: University of California Press.

Davis, F. (1987). *Antecedents and consequents of gender role conflict: An empirical validation of sex role strain analysis.* Unpublished doctoral dissertation, Ohio State University.

Deutsch, C., & Gilbert, L. (1976). Sex role stereotypes: Effects on perceptions of self and others and on personal adjustment. *Journal of Counseling Psychology, 23,* 373–379.

Doyle, J. A. (1989). *The male experience* (2nd ed.). Dubuque, IA: William C. Brown.

Eisler, R., & Skidmore, J. (1987). Masculine gender role stress: Scale development and components factors in the appraisal of stressful situations. *Behavior Modification, 11,* 123–136.

Erikson, E. (1950). *Childhood and society.* New York: Norton.

Fast, I. (1984). *Gender identity: A differentiation model.* Hillsdale, NJ: Lawrence Erlbaum.

Fine, G. A. (1987). *With the boys: Little League baseball and preadolescent culture.* Chicago: University of Chicago Press.

Franklin, C. W. (1984). *The changing definition of masculinity.* New York: Plenum.

Gagnon, J. H., & Simon, W. (1973). *Sexual conduct: The social sources of human sexuality.* Chicago: Aldine.

Garnets, L. (1978). Sex role strain analysis: Effects of sex role discrepancy and sex role salience on adjustment (Ph.D. dissertation, University of Michigan, 1978). *Dissertation Abstracts International, 39* (1979), 5064B. (University Microfilms No. 7907078).

Gelman, D. (1993, July 26). Homoeroticism in the ranks. *Newsweek,* pp. 28–29.

Gibbs, N. R. (1993, June 28). Bringing up father. *Time,* pp. 52–56, 58, 61.

Gilmore, D. (1990). *Manhood in the making: Cultural concepts of masculinity.* New Haven, CT: Yale University Press.

Goffman, E. (1963). *Stigma: Notes on the management of spoiled identity.* Englewood Cliffs, NJ: Prentice-Hall.

Hacker, H. (1957). The new burdens of masculinity. *Marriage and Family Living, 3,* 227–233.

Harding, C. (1992). *Wingspan: Inside the men's movement.* New York: St. Martins Press.

Harrison, J. (1987). Counseling gay men. In M. Scher, M. Stevens, G. Good, & G. A. Eichenfield (Eds.), *Handbook of counseling and psychotherapy with men* (pp. 220–231). Newbury Park, CA: Sage.

Hartley, R. L. (1959). American core culture: Continuity and change. In G. Seward & R. Williamson (Eds.), *Sex roles in a changing society* (pp. 160–180). New York: Random House.

Helgeson, V. S. (1990). The role of masculinity in a prognostic predictor of heart attack severity. *Sex Roles, 22*(11/12), 755–776.

Herman, J. L. (1992). *Trauma and recovery*. New York: Basic Books.

Herman, J. L., Perry, J. C., & Van der Kolk, B. A. (1989). Childhood trauma in border-line personality disorder. *American Journal of Psychiatry, 146,* 490–495.

Horwitz, A. V., & White, H. R. (1987). Gender role orientation and styles of pathology among adolescents. *Journal of Health and Social Behavior, 28,* 158–170.

Hunter College Women's Studies Collective. (1983). *Women's realities, women's choices.* New York: Oxford University Press.

Kimmel, M. S. (1987). Rethinking "masculinity": New directions in research. In M. S. Kimmel (Ed.), *Changing men: New directions in research on men and masculinity* (pp. 9–24). Newbury Park, CA: Sage.

Kimmel, M. S., & Messner, M. (1989). Introduction. In M. S. Kimmel & M. Messner (Eds.), *Men's lives* (pp. 1–14). New York: Macmillan.

Komarovsky, M. (1976). *Dilemmas of masculinity.* New York: Norton.

Levant, R. F. (1992). Toward the reconstruction of masculinity. *Journal of Family Psychology, 5*(3/4), 379–402.

Lenney, E. (1991). Sex roles: The measurement of masculinity, femininity, and androgyny. In J. P. Robinson, P. R. Shaver, & L. S. Wrightsman (Eds.), *Measures of personality and social psychological attitudes* (pp. 573–660). New York: Academic Press.

Levinson, D. J., & Huffman, P. E. (1955). Traditional family ideology and its relations to personality. *Journal of Personality, 23,* 251–273.

Lipman-Blumen, J. (1972). How ideology shapes women's lives. *Scientific American, 226*(1), 34–62.

Lisak, D. (1991). Sexual aggression, masculinity, and fathers. *Signs: Journal of Women in Culture and Society, 16*(2), 238–262.

Majors, R., & Billson, J. M. (1992). *Cool pose: The dilemmas of black manhood in America.* New York: Lexington Books.

Mason, K. O., & Bumpass, L. L. (1975). U.S. women's sex-role ideology, 1970. *American Sociological Review, 40,* 1212–1219.

Mead, M. (1935). *Sex and temperament in three primitive societies.* New York: Morrow.

Messner, M. A. (1992). *Power at play: Sports and the problem of masculinity.* Boston: Beacon Press.

Miedzian, M. (1991). *Boys will be boys: Breaking the link between masculinity and violence.* New York: Doubleday.

Mosher, D., & Sirkin, M. (1984). Measuring a macho personality constellation. *Journal of Research in Personality, 18,* 150–162.

O'Neil, J. M., Helms, B., Gable, R. K., David, L., & Wrightsman, L. S. (1986). Gender-role conflict scale: College men's fear of femininity. *Sex Roles, 14,* 335–350.

Osherson, S., & Krugman, S. (1990). Men, shame, and psychotherapy. *Psychotherapy, 27*(3), 327–339.

Pleck, J. H. (1976). The male sex role: Problems, definitions, and sources of change. *Journal of Social Issues, 32,* 155–164.

Pleck, J. H. (1981). *The myth of masculinity.* Cambridge, MA: MIT Press.

Pleck, J. H. (1985). *Working wives, working husbands.* Beverly Hills, CA: Sage.

Pleck, J. H., Sonenstein, F. L., & Ku, L. C. (1991). Adolescent males' condom use: Relationships between perceived cost-benefits and consistency. *Journal of Marriage and the Family, 53*, 733–746.

Pleck, J. H., Sonenstein, F. L., & Ku, L. C. (1993a). Masculinity ideology: Its impact on adolescent males' heterosexual relationships. *Journal of Social Issues, 49*(3), 11–29.

Pleck, J. H., Sonenstein, F. L., & Ku, L. C. (1993b). Masculinity ideology and its correlates. In S. Oskamp & M. Costanzo (Eds.), *Gender issues in social psychology* (pp. 85–110). Newbury Park, CA: Sage.

Pleck, J. H., Sonenstein, F. L., & Ku, L. C. (1994a). Attitudes toward male roles: A discriminant validity analysis. *Sex Roles, 30*, 481–501.

Pleck, J. H., Sonenstein, F. L., & Ku, L. C. (1994b). Problem behaviors and masculinity ideology in adolescent males. In R. Ketterlinus & M. E. Lamb (Eds.), *Adolescent problem behaviors* (pp. 165–186). Hillsdale, NJ: Lawrence Erlbaum.

Pollack, W. S. (1992). Should men treat women? Dilemmas for the male psychotherapist: Psychoanalytic and developmental perspectives. *Ethics and Behavior, 2*(1), 39–49.

Rubin, G. (1975). The traffic in women. In R. R. Reiter (Ed.), *Toward an anthropology of women* (pp. 157–210). New York: Monthly Review Press.

Segura, D. A., & Pierce, J. L. (1993). Chicana/o family structure and gender personality: Chodorow, familism, and psychoanalytic sociology revisited. *Signs: Journal of Women in Culture and Society, 19*, 62–78.

Sharpe, M. J., & Heppner, P. P (1991). Gender role, gender role conflict, and psychological well-being in men. *Journal of Counseling Psychology, 38*, 323–330.

Snarey, J. (Ed.). (1993). *How fathers care for the next generation*. Cambridge, MA: Harvard University Press.

Snarey, J., & Pleck, J. H. (1993). Midlife consequences of paternal generativity for fathers themselves. In J. Snarey (Ed.), *How fathers care for the next generation* (pp. 84–118). Cambridge, MA: Harvard University Press.

Snell, W. E., Belk, S. S., & Hawkins, R. C. (1987). Alcohol and drug use in stressful times: The influence of the masculine role and sex-related personality attributes. *Sex Roles, 16*, 359–373.

Sonenstein, F. L., Pleck, J. H., & Ku, L. C. (1989). Sexual activity, condom use and AIDS awareness among adolescent males. *Family Planning Perspectives, 21*, 152–158.

Spence, J. T., & Helmreich, R. L. (1978). *Masculinity and femininity: Their psychological dimensions, correlates, and antecedents*. Austin: University of Texas Press.

Spence, J. T., Helmreich, R. L., & Holahan, C. T. (1979). Negative and positive components of psychological masculinity and femininity and their relationships to self-reports of neurotic and acting out behaviors. *Journal of Personality and Social Psychology, 37*, 1673–1682.

Stein, E. (Ed.). (1992). *Forms of desire: Sexual orientation and the sexual constructionist controversy*. New York: Routledge.

Suslowitz, P.D. (1979). *Sex role self-concept, ego development, and self-esteem*. Unpublished doctoral dissertation, University of Massachusetts at Amherst.

Thompson, E. H. (1990). Courtship violence and the male role. *Men's Studies Review, 7*(3), 1, 4–13.

Thompson, E. H., Grisanti, C., & Pleck, J. H. (1985). Attitudes toward the male role and their correlates. *Sex Roles, 13,* 413–427.

Thompson, E. H., & Pleck, J. H. (1986). The structure of male role norms. *American Behavioral Scientist, 29,* 531–543.

Thompson, E. H., Pleck, J. H., & Ferrera, D. (1992). Men and masculinities: Scales for masculinity ideology and masculinity-related constructs. *Sex Roles, 27*(11/12), 573–607.

Turner, R. (1970). *Family interaction.* New York: Wiley.

Winslow, R. (1993, July 9). Male patients suffer for being taciturn. *Wall Street Journal,* p. B1.

CHAPTER 2

No Man Is an Island: Toward a New Psychoanalytic Psychology of Men

WILLIAM S. POLLACK

If I am not for myself, who will be for me?
And if I am for myself alone, then what am I?
If not now, then when?

HILLEL

Introduction

SUBLIME ISOLATION OR DEFENSIVE SELF-SUFFICIENCY?

Centuries ago this Jewish sage's existential plea for a balance between an investment in the self and a connection with or a commitment to others—a balance between the sense of an I and a We—foreshadowed our modern-day, gender-based struggles concerning autonomy, affiliation, and intimacy. Although many men, like women, have come to intellectually accept the necessity for a type of emotional interdependence in life, the deepest personal meanings of their dependent needs are often experienced as a frightening anathema to men. John Donne, the poet, advised in the 17th century, "No man is an island, entire of itself; every man is a piece of the continent, a part of the main; . . . any man's death diminishes me, because I am involved in mankind; and therefore never send to know for whom the bell tolls; it tolls for thee."

Yet most modern men continue to function emotionally much more like Robert Frost's neighbor in the poem "Mending Wall," who felt, "Good fences make good neighbors." Men are often found walling themselves off from their own feeling states, fending off sadness and depression as well as empathic intimate relationships—especially with women—in ways that cause their significant others to feel a great deal of pain and consternation and, I will argue, in ways that often tend to hurt and confuse the men themselves. Frost goes on to state, "Before I built a wall I'd ask to know / What I was walling in or walling out." Indeed, that is the poignant and important question we must consider to understand why men so often find themselves in search of a type of sublime isolation, worshiping an idol of emotional stoicism—while continuing to yearn for connection and intimate fulfillment.

THE DECONSTRUCTION OF TRADITIONAL THEORY

Over 10 years ago in his groundbreaking work *The Myth of Masculinity* (1981), Joseph Pleck critically deconstructed so-called male sex role identity theories, creating in their stead the paradigm of gender role strain. In so doing, he highlighted the sometimes devastating conflicts and stressors that gender stereotyping and ("macho") cultural expectations have created for men. Since that time, a decade of feminist scholarship (Chodorow, 1978, 1989; Gilligan, 1982; Jordan, Kaplan, Miller, Stiver, & Surrey, 1991; Miller, 1976) has taken to task our phallocentric theories of human development, deftly recasting women's growth from a relational, bonded perspective. Where does that leave men? Boys and men have been left out in the cold, in the midst of the discredited, discarded shards of biased, outmoded theory.

Research and clinical experience alike have shown that many men do indeed manifest difficulties with commitment to relationships, including dysfunction in the expression of affiliative openness and the proclivity for a style of emotional suppression and *defensive autonomy* or self-sufficiency (Pollack, 1990), which at times frustrates the capacity for any mutual intimacy. How then do we help men to "understand"? Equally significant, how do we as psychologists in turn expand our empathic capacity to genuinely understand men? How do we explore—from a gender-sensitive perspective—the normative, developmental pathways, that is, the childhood precursors that lead eventually to adult males' dilemmas with affect, dependency, closeness, connection, and love?

I will argue that many men are desperately searching for love, indeed yearning for genuine intimate union, for connection, for a sense of making what now seems only "half" eventually "whole." Yet, powerful unconscious forces in the form of gender-specific dilemmas in the resolution of identity-connectedness (autonomy-affiliation) conflicts—dating back as far as the pre-Oedipal childhood period of separation-individuation—often leave men defending against the very intimate merger that they seek! Such defenses often take the form of behavior and personality characteristics that, to frustrated partners or critical therapists alike, may look cold, narcissistic, unfeeling, and nonrelational. Yet when one delves deeper into classic male struggles with tender feelings and intimacy, from an experience-near/empathic mode of listening, new insight may emerge. Men often form what to them subjectively appear to be open, intimate relationships, yet to their significant others these men continue to appear to have difficulty accepting mutuality. This dilemma ensues, I believe, because many men cannot tolerate recognizing their interdependence or their dependence—especially dependence on a woman.

Indeed, if we truly want men to become more empathic, *we need to become more empathic to men.*

This chapter is a beginning effort in that direction of empathic understanding: toward redefining a new, postfeminist masculinity. It is an attempt at creating a masculinity that distills what is historically, proactively, and positively male-gendered yet remains respectful of women's specialness as well. This chapter moves in the direction of creating an empathic and solid theoretical foundation for a new psychology of men by focusing on a redefinition, from a critical, psychoanalytic perspective, of boys' early developmental struggles for gendered selfhood. Specifically addressed will be the author's theory that historically salient cultural and interpersonal models of parenting (motherhood and fatherhood) have made it likely that, as boys, men suffer a traumatic abrogation of their early holding environment, that is, a premature psychic separation from both their maternal and paternal caregivers. This is a gender-linked, normative, *developmental trauma* or loss that may leave boys at risk later, as adult men, for specific psychological sequelae often manifest as deficits in the arenas of intimacy, empathy, and struggles with commitment in relationships (Betcher & Pollack, 1993; Pollack, 1992).

In addition, gender-bifurcated patterns of role socialization often exacerbate these unconscious traumas, shaming boys and men into suppressing the expression of a whole range of deeply felt needs—warm or sad feelings—so as to eschew being called a "sissy" and being viewed as shamefully unmanly. Yet there is every reason to believe that male qualities of succor, care, sacrifice, giving, and, indeed, empathy exist that could form the nexus of a positive, substantial, and proactive sense of masculinity.

Modern psychoanalytic theories of development, empirically derived concepts of autonomy-affiliation balance (replacing our emphasis on a "separation morality"), gender role socialization research, reinterpretations of Greek myth (including a critique of the fate of Oedipus), the findings of cross-cultural anthropology, and evidence of "male" models of empathy will be utilized to support new interpretive pathways of masculine development. These in turn will be woven into a fabric for a new psychoanalytic developmental psychology of men—a reframed and re-created psychology—

respectful of women's needs precisely because it is empathic to men's own unique sense of developmental conflict. As we reframe masculinity from this new perspective, we may be able to re-create a sense of manhood that frees men and women alike from the shackles of gender bias and the straitjackets of self-defeating gender stereotypes—creating in turn bridges for respectful understanding.

A Mythical Sojourn

Early psychoanalysts often turned to the classics of Greek literature—mythos and tragedy—to elucidate universal psychological, unconscious undercurrents in human behavior. Freud (1900/1953), of course, came to view the journey and fate of Oedipus as representing the quintessential male struggle for identity. In recent years, commentators on the fate of men's psychology—most notably Robert Bly (1990)—have unearthed a new mythos of cthonic Iron Men to mentor forgotten males back into a network of healthy, vibrant masculinity. As a cultural schema for men's psychological development—that is, heuristic explanatories within the arenas of love and intimacy—I will take exception to both approaches: with Freud because I believe we must go to even earlier layers of self-development, to the so-called pre-Oedipal period, to understand men's dilemmas with intimacy and dependency; and with Bly because, although his poetic approach brings men back to deep affective, often primitive developmental levels, some of his concepts have been used to obscure the postmodern complexity of gender issues in a way that could easily lead, in the wrong hands, to a misogynist antifeminist sentiment. Instead, I will revisit classic Greek myths, which, analyzed in depth, yield further insight into modern men's struggles with connection and emotion.

THE MISSING HALF

In Plato's *Symposium*, the Socratic emphasis is on the idealization of abstract beauty and self-sufficiency, predating many of our Western cultural concerns about autonomy. Yet there is one notable exception—Aristophanes' speech about a mythos of love. Each symposiast is required to give a talk on the definition, and in praise, of love. Aristophanes' tale is usually presented as a humorous after-dinner speech. However, on closer reflection, it goes to the heart of men's dilemma over love and loss.

Aristophanes presents a prehistory of creation in which we were all large, round, roly-poly double creatures. Each had two faces, four hands, and four feet. Each was outfitted with two sets of genitals (male and female) that fit together perfectly. Men and women were merged together, bouncing around and enjoying the greatest pleasure. We could engage in all types of athletic feats successfully, and we considered ourselves perfect because we matched the Greek ideal of perfection—the shape of a sphere. Eventually, our tragic flaw of hubris brought down upon us the wrath of the gods. To humble us, Zeus split us in two. Our sense of oneness and wholeness was lost, leaving each of us as "but the indenture of a man . . . always looking for our *other half*" (Jowett 1956; p. 355, my emphasis).

In Aristophanes' myth, each man is engaged in a search for lost "oneness" and yearns to find a mirror self, a complete self, within the connection to another—in order to be whole again. In finding our special other, we are truly finding ourselves. And even more significant, it is not mere sexuality that drives us:

> When one of them finds his other half . . . the pair are lost in amazement of love and friendship and intimacy. . . . The intense yearning which each of them has toward the other does not appear to be in the desire of intercourse but of something else which the *soul desires and cannot tell, and of which she only has a dark and doubtful presentiment.* (Jowett, 1956, pp. 356–357; my emphasis)

This discovery is seen to be at the very heart of man's struggle, "so ancient is the desire of one another that is implanted in us, reuniting our original nature, making one of two and *healing the state of man.*"

> There is not a man among them when he heard this who would deny or would not acknowledge that this meeting and melting in one another's arms . . . this becoming one instead of two, was the very expression of his ancient need. *And the reason is that human nature was originally one and we were whole, and the desire and pursuit of that whole is called love.* (Jowett, 1956, p. 357; my emphasis)

This myth of intimacy, *ab origino*, is indicative of man's search for a partner, his attempt to replace and/or repair his earlier lost love and to regain a state of connection abruptly disrupted in his earlier developmental history. Unknowingly, men wish to merge with women precisely because of their "feminine" caring qualities, while they deny having any such yearnings. Men seek special women to love them with an exceptional blend of understanding, caring, and giving—qualities that men see as feminine and therefore unacceptable within their *own* selves.

THE MYTH OF NARCISSUS: A TALE OF MEN'S LOVE FOR OUR AGE

Perhaps even more than the classical myth of Oedipus, the story of Narcissus may be a central, guiding mythological tale for our present age. In particular, men are often seen as engaged in the type of self-involvement and self-love that makes them appear "narcissistic" to their female partners.

But can there be discerned in the tale of Narcissus insight for a deeper understanding of men and their needs for intimacy, just as Oedipus was once interpreted by Freud?

A woman's attraction to a man who cannot love was well known in antiquity. In the classic tale of Ovid, Narcissus is the son of the river god Cephisus and the nymph Liriope and is most distinctive for his beauty. Upon his birth, his mother seeks out the advice of the wise seer Teiresias, who prophesies that Narcissus will live a long life, but only if he never comes to know himself.

As a young man, Narcissus's striking beauty causes all the girls who see him to long to be his. But he is indifferent even to the loveliest of them, and their broken hearts mean nothing to him. Even the sad plight of the nymph Echo does not touch him.

Echo has been falsely accused by the goddess Hera of seducing her husband, Zeus. Her punishment is to be able only to repeat what is said to her, to have no power to speak first. Echo falls in love with Narcissus, but he flees at her approach, saying, "You must not touch—go, take your hands away, may I be dead before you throw your fearful chains around me." Echo's wish for bonding is experienced by Narcissus as bondage. Echo, since she can only repeat his words, cannot allay his fears about intimacy. She is left to hide her shame in a cave.

One day a suitor who has been scorned by Narcissus issues a vengeful prayer that someday he will feel what it is to love and receive no return of affection. The goddess Nemesis (meaning "righteous anger") hears this prayer and grants it. As Narcissus bends over a clear spring to drink, he sees his own reflection and immediately falls in love with it. He cannot tear himself away, but, of course, neither can he bring this mirror lover to him. There he kneels, calling upon his reflected beauty, "Why, beautiful being, do you shun me?" but never able to achieve union.

Accompanying him to the end is his unrequited lover, Echo, who, as Narcissus dies, can only repeat his last words, "Farewell . . . farewell."

As this is the myth of the pain of reflection, we may see mirrored in the myth itself the modern-day dilemma of many men and women and their often unrequited quest to understand each other. Each is condemned to a painful isolation in which they can be with each other but are unable to communicate. Ovid's tale suggests that the root of most of the trouble lies in a man's self-absorption and lack of empathy, which can be remedied only by painful experience. Women, too, are implicated by Ovid. While not to blame for their predicament, they are limited by the opposite incapacity of men—they appear to have *no* self, existing only as the echo of a man's hopes and dreams. Ovid clearly then foretells the modern dilemma: Men are overly "autonomous," women are too reliant on "connection," and the casualty is mutuality. Lost, too, is the potential for new syntheses of masculinity and femininity.

Rethinking Development: Men and Women

Research has begun to show that a man's need to cling to independence at the cost of intimacy seems driven by emotional imperatives that begin in boyhood. As feminist scholars (e.g., Chodorow, Gilligan, and Miller) have pointed out, girls and boys develop quite differently. Girls are generally encouraged to maintain their closeness to their mother, while boys are usually pushed to make a more clear-cut separation. Boys are expected to "*disidentify*" (Greenson, 1968) from their mothers, that is, become different in order to become masculine. As a result, men try to create a strong sense of independent identity, no matter what the cost to their relationships. Only with greater maturity do they sometimes reestablish connections. But to openly acknowledge such a need, especially to notice a dependency upon a woman, feels quite shameful to men.

EARLY DEVELOPMENT

Chodorow (1978, 1989) asserted that because women are still largely responsible for caretaking in the early years of a child's life, the consequent issues of gender identity formation differ in critical ways for boys and girls. For females, identity formation occurs through the integration of, or identification with, an ongoing relational attachment to their mother. However, for boys to define themselves as masculine, they must be different. They must clearly separate from the mother, both intrapsychically and interpersonally. Achieving and maintaining this separation may require more of a defensive hardening of the self and ego boundaries of little boys, and later of adult males, on both a conscious and an unconscious level.

This process has a socially constructed basis and may change as child-rearing patterns shift. Yet until that occurs, differential developmental processes of nurture, according to Chodorow, will generally propel men and women in different directions. If one accepts Chodorow's argument, one must basically agree with her that, "because women mother, the sense of maleness in men differs from the sense of femaleness in women," and that masculinity (or maleness) becomes more conflictual and more problematic than femaleness:

> Underlying, or built into, core male gender identity is an early, non-verbal, unconscious and almost *somatic sense of primary oneness with the mother, an underlying sense of femaleness that continually, usually unnoticeably but sometimes consistently challenges and undermines the sense of maleness.* Thus, because of the primary oneness and identification with his mother, a primary femaleness, a boy's and man's core gender identity . . . is an issue. (1989, p. 109; my emphasis)

What becomes clear, from this perspective, is that little boys, and grown men, unconsciously need to fend off an earlier sense of oneness with their mother, which tends to threaten their gender identity and/or independent sense of self. So, while girls "grow up with a sense of continuity and similarity to their mother, a relational connection to the world" (p. 110), boys, by contrast, do not have this opportunity. Because of both current child-rearing practices, which create the significance of the mother, and the consequent "absence of concrete, real, available male figures of identification and love who are [equally] salient" for the boy, "learning what it is to be masculine comes to mean learning to be . . . not womanly" (p. 109). As a result, separateness becomes more salient for boys. Boys, and later men, tend to eschew "feminine" identifications and experiences such as dependency, strong feelings, and relational bonding.

BEYOND FREUD: BENEATH THE OEDIPUS

Although Freud and his early followers linked core sexual and gender identity to the crucible of the Oedipus complex and its resolution, it has become clear that core identity issues and the sense of masculinity emerge much earlier than this in children's psychic development. Deep in the adult man's psyche lies the formative experience of a little boy struggling to maintain a sense of a masculine self vis-à-vis his attachment to his mother. Yet he is also struggling with the very real loss of an earlier affiliative oneness— which can never be regained, within this model, without a threat to masculine identity.

While Chodorow's discussion of gender identity development is insightful, it does not adequately capture what this experience of development must feel like for a little boy. The emphasis remains on the bond between mothers and daughters. Nowhere do we get a sense of the loss associated with the boy's definition of his own identity and core gender self, an experiential process that requires separation from the most cherished, admired, and loved object in his life—at what would be a phase-inappropriate time from the point of view of girls' development. Equally significant, this broken maternal connection or *disidentification*[1] occurs within a social context of child rearing in which (1) girl siblings are allowed to remain connected, and (2) the father often remains absent or emotionally unavailable to his young son as an alternative nurturing figure for the "lost" mother.

---

[1]Although disidentification in its traditional use (Greenson, 1968) is not meant to represent "a broken maternal connection," it is precisely my argument that the term and process have functioned as a normative psychoanalytic "cover-up" for what I have suggested is, in fact, closer to a traumatic disruption of the holding environment.

A NORMATIVE (GENDER-LINKED) DEVELOPMENTAL TRAUMA

Chodorow (1978) makes the suggestion that the intrapsychic developmental events so significant to the young boy may actually be played out reciprocally and interpersonally between mother and son: "Though children of both sexes are originally part of her self, a mother unconsciously and often consciously experiences her son as more of an 'other' than her daughter. Reciprocally, a son's male core gender identity develops away from his mother" (p. 166). This difference in the mother is more than just a subtle emotional shift. Indeed, it is akin to a behavioral push:

> Mothers tend to experience their daughters as more like, and continuous with themselves. . . . By contrast, mothers experience their sons as a male *opposite*. Boys are more likely to have been *pushed out of the pre-oedipal relationship* and to have had to curtail their primary love and sense of empathic tie with their mother. A boy has been engaged *and been required to engage* in a more emphatic individuation and a more defensive firming of experienced ego boundaries. (1978, p. 166; my emphasis)

As a consequence, males may be more vulnerable to traumatic and premature actual separations—disruptions that may later be experienced by the child as a loss or abandonment—than females are.

I have argued (Pollack, 1992) that we may be seeing a developmental basis for a gender-specific vulnerability to *traumatic abrogation* of the early holding environment (Winnicott, 1974), an *impingement* in boys' development—a normative life-cycle loss—that may, later in life, leave many adult men at risk for fears of intimate connection. This traumatic experience of abandonment occurs so early in the life course that the shameful memory of the loss is likely to be deeply repressed.

Boys, then, have not only a more problematic course toward identity but a continuing need to defend against urges toward affiliation and intimacy because of the repressed trauma of shameful and premature separation. This is a loss that ensued with their mothers and was probably unassuaged when their fathers proved unable to assume an alternative nurturant role. Having experienced a sense of hurt in the real connection to their mothers (as a result of her societally constructed role to make gender differentiation clear) and the subsequent loss of finding no equally salient alternative in their fathers, many boys, and later men, are left at risk for empathic disruptions in their affiliative connections, doomed to search endlessly, as in Aristophanes' myth, and yet fend women off because of their fear of retraumatization (as in the tale of Narcissus).

Later relationships may revive the deeply repressed yearnings toward the early mother. The result may be the creation of *transitional* or *self-object* relationships with mother substitutes that are meant to repair and assuage the unspeakable hurt of premature traumatic separation and

simultaneously to deny the loss of the relational bond. In their unconscious yearning for closeness, men may seek out women who meet their
needs—only to deny them any mutually empathic response in order to
protect themselves from the fears or dangers of reexperiencing the
repressed pain, sadness, or depression that affiliation now conjures forth.
Such men maintain that they are self-sufficient while they are in the
midst of an interdependent connection! This paradox, combined with
women's reasonable expectation that the significance of their relational
capacities will be recognized, may lead to much of the misunderstanding
seen in the traditional intimate relationships that men and women form.
It accounts for much of the pain experienced by men and women as they
attempt to listen to and interpret each other's "voices" (Gilligan, 1982). It
may also account for the preponderance of males diagnosed with narcissistic personality disorder and the requirement that what Modell (1976)
calls the symbolic actualization of the holding environment be brought
into our understanding of psychoanalytic treatment. Kohut (1971, 1977)
also addresses this issue by concentrating on stabilizing selfobject trans-
ferences in the treatment of patients with narcissistic issues—patients
who quite often are *men*.

OEDIPUS REVISITED

For Freud and generations of psychoanalysts and child researchers who
followed, the myth of Oedipus was the central paradigm for illustrating
unconscious forces at work in self and gender identity formation in childhood, especially for little boys. The story came to represent, in particular, a
boy's unconscious sexual wishes for his mother, fears of retributive castration
by his father, and finally, the renunciation of this wish—leading to a more
stable sense of self through the boy's identification with his father's masculine role. Indeed, Freud believed that the great power this myth has continued to hold for us in our present generations lay in our fearful recognition
that all men harbor the same wishes that Oedipus lived out, and that such
unconscious conflicts are the stuff that men's neuroses are made of. Freud felt
that "the poet, as he unravels the past, brings to light the guilt of Oedipus, . . .
compelling us to recognize our own inner minds, in which those same
impulses, though suppressed, are still to be found. . . . Like Oedipus, we live
in ignorance of these wishes, . . . [and] seek to close our eyes to the scenes of
our childhood" (Freud, 1900/1953, p. 263). Yet it appears to be Freud himself
who failed to recognize two central components in the myth he analyzed.

First, the tragedy is set in motion not by a child's fantasies but by an
adult's hurtful actions. Upon hearing of the birth of a son, Laius, Oedipus's
father, is so frightened that his power on the throne will be usurped by this
heir that he hires a herdsman to murder him. In fact, Oedipus's name,

roughly translated as "swollen foot," represents the herdsman's ambivalence about carrying out the murderous intentions of the father: he leaves the child, bound by the feet, hanging from a branch to die.[2] One rendering of the myth goes even further, suggesting that it is not Laius alone but also Oedipus's mother, Jocasta, who attempts to sacrifice the infant to appease the gods.

Oedipus survives, is adopted into another family, and on his return to Thebes, inadvertently murders his father. He is soon to marry the queen, whom he does not consciously know is his mother. Oedipus is worried, however, by dark prophesies and, reflecting upon his planned marriage, contemplates withdrawal. Again he is betrayed by one of his parents, this time Jocasta, who mocks the dire predictions and urges Oedipus to marry her without further delay.

Significantly for us all, Freud chose to ignore Oedipus's earliest trauma and to blame the fantasies of the unconscious. But, in fact, the story of Oedipus is about a young boy betrayed and abandoned to die by his own mother and father. It is not Oedipus's unconscious lust for his mother or jealousy of his father that sets the stage for downfall, but his parents' hurtful rejection of him. I have no argument with Freud's pivotal belief in unconscious fantasy as the nidus of neurosis. But just as women have come to acknowledge much of the hurt that occurs to little girls during their childhood and the consequent effects on adult women's functioning, I believe that boys also deserve an empathic understanding of what may be a gender-specific trauma for males. The point is not to vilify Jocasta or cast aspersions on Laius—to condemn mothers or fathers—but rather to highlight that men may either feel or unconsciously experience a sense of having been abandoned, betrayed, or hurtfully separated. Like Oedipus, most men may have no conscious memory of this earlier trauma, though their vulnerabilities (especially to shame) in adult life may be the evidence of the unhealed wound.

Nature *and* Nurture

Side by side with my argument for powerful unconscious sequelae in the functioning of adult men, due to gender differentiation processes in the parenting of young boys, are two additional influences on the developmental psychology of men: first, the historically insidious, psychoeducationally oriented, skill-based, gender-tracked role socialization models in schools and

[2]John Munder Ross (1982) coined the term "Laius complex" to refer to the father's aggressive, rivalrous fantasies and actions toward the son and to highlight the intergenerational transmission of these often submerged, too often enacted forms of hatred or sadism. Here, I am more specifically reanalyzing the myth as a "bearer," if you will, of normative, yet painfully traumatic, premature separations—for boys—which translate into later abandonment fears.

homes (see Chapter 8); and second, the biological predispositions to male fragility from infancy onward.

GENDER-BIFURCATED ROLE SOCIALIZATION

The very systems of gender-bifurcated role socialization that have been strongly criticized by feminist scholars for tracking girls into doll play and sibling care and away from assertion and mathematics skills have been equally devastating and limiting for boys in their developmental pathways. David and Brannon (1976) have delineated four stereotyped male ideals or admonitions through which we have historically socialized boys into manhood. The injunction to become a Sturdy Oak refers to men's stoicism: We teach little boys not to share pain or openly grieve. The Give 'em Hell stance of our sports coaches creates the false self of daring, bravado, and love for violence, while the ideal of being a Big Wheel stresses the need to achieve status and power at any cost. But perhaps the most traumatizing, straitjacketing social role training is that of No Sissy Stuff—the condemnation of the expression in boys of any strong, dependent, or warm feelings or urges that are seen as feminine and therefore as totally unacceptable or even taboo. The "mommy track" for women and its equally destructive counterpart, the "daddy with no feelings, work til you drop" track for men, begin long before the work-career ladder is in view. It is the fruition of our early, rigid, gender-bifurcated socialization systems.

Pleck (1981; Chapter 1) has argued that men are ground down trying to live up to such inhuman standards of masculinity or what he calls "gender role strain." Levant (see Chapter 8) has pointed cogently to the skill deficits in adult men due to these gender-based training experiences in boyhood. Especially, he notes a severe inability of men to identify, express, and describe their own feeling-states, particularly those of warmth, caring, sadness, and pain. He links this deficit to the psychological disorder of alexithymia—the inability to connect words with feelings; men often experience a vague "buzz" of undifferentiated affect rather than a clear or articulate emotional message of caring and love to convey to their loved ones.

THE BIOLOGICAL IMPERATIVES

Although it is difficult to parse out the distinct contributions of nature versus nurture in gender socialization, some infancy research data are telling. A critical review of the developmental and biological data concerning the differences between female and male babies reveals evidence significant enough to support the claim that girl infants are generally more calm, less irritable, and more alert than boy infants (Malatesta & Haviland, 1982). As a result, there may be reason to suspect that little girls can engage in an earlier socialization, and in a more comfortable connection with their mothers, than little boys (Silverman, 1987). Of particular note are the findings that girl infants are more able to engage the gaze of their mothers, and to feel enhanced attunement in such gaze, than little boys. Indeed, there are gender-linked gazing patterns in both humans and nonhuman primates that tend to make it more difficult for males to remain focused on their mother's gaze and, in turn, for mothers to remain connected in this attuned way with their male children. If one adds to this the corpus of research support for enhanced and early vocalization in girl babies, what appears to be emerging is a potential biological base for easier bonding between mother and daughter than between mother and son—a biogenetic predisposition to the psychodynamic issues raised earlier. Silverman (1987) summarizes:

> The less stable state system of the male infant leads to decreased social interaction. Not only is it difficult to establish social interchange during fussy irritable states, but the parents' task during these states becomes one of soothing and calming rather than socializing. The animated face of the mother is highly arousing . . . and may overstimulate the male infant, given his less stable state system. Extended eye contact with mother also increases arousal and leads to gaze aversion when it is overstimulating. . . . The male infant's greater vulnerability and instability may lead to easier overarousal, with irritability, crying and gaze aversion. This then produces diminished social interchange between mother and infant, and, as does not happen with female infants, provides increasing separation with mothers and sons. (p. 328)

Brody (1993, in press) takes a different route to a strikingly similar conclusion: Gender-bifurcated, biologically based temperamental predispositions in infants, in combination with specific caretaker interactions, lead to radically different affective socialization experiences for boy and girl babies. Following from Cunningham and Shapiro (1984) and Weinberg (1992), Brody (in press) opines that "infant boys are more emotionally expressive than are infant girls, and hence their expressions are easier for . . . parents to read."[3]

Supported by her interpretation of the findings by Tronick and his research laboratory (Tronick, 1989; Tronick & Cohn, 1989)—that mothers and their infant sons have an easier time matching their emotional interactive states—Brody suggests that "both mothers and daughters may have to work harder to read each others' emotional signals than do mothers and sons." The result may be the beginning of a long journey toward affective bonding for mothers and their daughters, and an increasing emotional inexpressiveness and disconnection for parents and their young sons:

> Working harder may translate into talking more to daughters about feelings, as well as in displaying a wider range of feelings to daughters. . . . For females,

---

[3]The author gratefully acknowledges the assistance of Dr. Leslie Brody in sharing her ideas about the gendered nature of affective socialization of infants and young children, which is central to this section of my argument (see Brody, in press).

this may eventually result in both amplified facial expressiveness in order to communicate more clearly, as well as in better emotional recognition abilities. In contrast, in adapting to their sons' higher emotional intensity, parents may respond with more constraint and a de-emphasis on emotional expressiveness. These types of socialization patterns also represent the conformity to the cultured gender role stereotype that girls should be more emotionally expressive and that boys should be more emotionally constrained. (Brody, in press)

The empirical findings on differential socialization of emotion language for young boys and girls do not disappoint us in this regard. It has been shown that mothers appear to use more words about emotions when they speak to their young daughters than to their sons (Dunn, Bretherton, & Munn, 1987; Fivush, 1989) and tend to speak more about sadness with girls, and about anger with boys (Fivush, 1989). By the time they are school age, little girls expect more positive reaction from mothers for expressing sadness than for showing anger, and their male counterparts expect negative reactions from both parents if they express sadness (Fuchs & Thelen, 1988). In an unpublished paper by Greif, Alvarez, and Ulman (cited in Brody, in press), it was found that, in creating a storybook for their daughters, mothers *never* used the word *angry*, while they used it frequently with their sons. Fathers are especially active in such gender-bifurcated socialization of the expression of emotion. They have been found to use more emotion-laden words with their daughters than with their sons and to engage in more negative teasing or aggressive verbal jousting with their sons than with their daughters (Gleason & Greif, 1983; Schell & Gleason, 1989).

So now we have a better developmental understanding of why anger has always been the favorite son of men's limited family of emotions. Through anger—the final common pathway for all their strong feelings—boys, and later men, express their vulnerability and powerlessness in their search for safety. Anger is the stepchild of men's vulnerability and powerlessness in search of legitimate authority. Its true parentage remains too shameful to face—hence, the poorly defined responses of rage, by which men hope to achieve what is in essence the unachievable.[4]

---

[4]This deadly combination of men's Achilles' Heel, including genetic vulnerability, stress-inducing early psychological separation trauma, and a gender role strain code that restricts affective expression (especially of sadness and grief) while reinforcing action and risk orientation, may begin to explain the panoply of biological vulnerabilities of men at midlife and beyond (e.g., cardiovascular and gastrointestinal disturbances). It may also elucidate the health and physician aversion strategies and the health prescription noncompliance behaviors of adult males in our society (see Betcher & Pollack, 1993, pp. 131ff; Chapter 7). This psychologically defensive and physiologically dysfunctional behavior may well be a significant but hidden cost in our health care crisis. Elsewhere I have expressed the notion that type A personality might indeed be "Type M" for men (Oldenberg, 1993; Williams, 1993).

Genetic predisposition combines with cultural socialization patterns to foster an earlier and potentially more hurtful separation paradigm between boys and their parents. Added to my earlier thesis about the unconscious trauma of loss, such an integrated biosocial model becomes a powerful hermeneutic for a new psychoanalytic psychology of men.

If my argument is correct, then, what would a man who as a boy sustained such gender-bifurcated socialization and early psychological hurt look like? In all likelihood, he would be obsessionally concerned with maintaining an independent self and would have a panoply of intrapsychic defenses, such as unconscious anger or rage toward women, condescension toward anyone in a caretaking role, overvaluation of independence, devaluation of the need for connectedness, stoic denial of sadness or pain, with an inability to mourn or grieve loss and a walling-off of the core vulnerable self. Interestingly enough, this is remarkably similar to a description of the prototypical narcissistic personality!

In addition, you would expect that any sense of dependency is quite frightening for such men, especially dependency upon those people with whom he unconsciously experienced the repetition of the "undependable" earlier tie, which had been disrupted. His need to be mirrored and to connect with an idealizable object would exist alongside a terrifying fear of the disruption of these connections. If this is indeed men's dilemma, what is the resolution? I believe change may come in a combination of empathic understanding by others and opportunity for self-repair. From this matrix, transformation may ensue.

Self Psychology

If we are to encourage men to be less walled-off and more empathic, we must in turn be more empathic to men.

We may thank Heinz Kohut (1971, 1977), specifically for his treatment strategy of intervention when the *selfobject* line of development, the so-called narcissistic line, is traumatized or derailed and pathological disorders of narcissism ensue. He argues that the appropriate response is an empathic or "experience-near" understanding of the individual's needs to take in and utilize the other, that is, the selfobject, in a manner that silently performs missing functions within the self—without necessarily acknowledging these significant external contributions. In other words, Kohut accepts that certain people may need to be highly dependent on others in order to fulfill deficits or tolerate conflicts and traumas in their earlier lines of narcissistic or self-development, while never consciously acknowledging such dependency. Such individuals are all too often unempathically experienced as being cold and uncaring by those around them, while they may consider themselves extremely autonomous, rigidly independent, and self-sufficient!

Kohut rejects a unidimensional, autonomy-based, separation-oriented pathway to mental health. He argues persuasively for dual developmental lines: of (1) self and (2) self-with-others. According to Kohut, narcissistic/self concerns are never really abandoned or supplanted in later relationships. Rather, self-interest and interest in other selves develop along separate axes, what I've termed elsewhere parallel but interactive lines of development (Pollack, 1982). From this perspective, earlier forms of narcissistic involvement may mature and be transformed into later self-interests such as vicarious introspection, creativity, work, or humor but will not necessarily blossom into overt relational activity.

Essential to Kohut's theory is the concept of the *selfobject*. The selfobject is a person who is so significant to one's functioning that he or she (i.e., the selfobject) is experienced as part of one's self. The expected control over the selfobject, therefore, is usually closer to the sense of control an individual expects to have over his or her own body or mind than to the type of control one normally expects to have over others (Kohut & Wolf, 1978). Kohut describes two types of selfobjects in early development: "Those [selfobjects] who respond to and confirm the child's innate sense of vigor, greatness and perfection; and those to whom the child can look up and with whom he can merge as an image of calmness, infallibility, omnipotence" (Kohut & Wolf, 1978, p. 414). The first type of selfobject responds to the child's grandiose self and needs for recognition and gives rise to a mirroring transference. The second ministers to the vulnerable child's need for omnipotent soothing and develops into an idealizing transference. It should be stressed that the use of these selfobjects is developmentally phase-appropriate and an outgrowth of legitimate needs to utilize relational connections with others to build internal self-structures. It follows that a normative model of self-development would need to dramatically redefine autonomy and recast self-sufficiency as existing within a context of ongoing relational interactions, for both men and women. Such a redefinition also provides a new framework for understanding and transforming the specific forms of dysfunction that emerge when optimal development goes awry.

The Balancing Act: The "I" and the "We"

Although much of the psychological critique of human development has focused on the differential pathways for men and women along the axes of independent identity, aloneness or autonomy versus connectedness or affiliation, bifurcated along gender lines (Chodorow, 1978, 1989; Gilligan, 1982), there is reason to suspect that a *balance*, within each gender, between the capacity for I-ness and We-ness (following George Klein's concepts) is a better predictor of mental health and of the capacity to sustain intimate relationships (Klein, 1976; Pollack, 1982, 1990, in press). The findings of the Boston University Parenthood and Pregnancy (BUPP) project provide empirical support for a model of healthy emotional development for men that requires a gender-specific balance between the capacity for autonomy and affiliation, between separateness and relatedness—I-ness and We-ness.

The BUPP project was a longitudinal developmental study of 90 couples first seen during the expectancy period of the birth of the indexed child. Women were seen, in individual interviews, close to the beginning of their pregnancy (half of the sample with a first child) and with their husbands later during the gestational period. Entire families (mother, father, and indexed child) were studied at birth and then one, two, and five years later. Data were collected from home visits, naturalistic and structured observations, semistructured interviews, paper and pencil scales, and child assessments. Standardized clinical ratings derived from interaction observations, and video/audiotaped segments of play, interview, and so on, also were utilized in complex time-linked statistical analyses. (Details of the larger study may be found in Fedele, Golding, Grossman, & Pollack, 1988; Grossman, Eichler, & Winnickoff, 1980; and Pollack. & Grossman, 1985.) Among the issues explored were the nonparent-to-parent transition, marital couples' needs/satisfaction, men's and women's changing sense of self, children's affective and cognitive functioning/development, the quality of parenting, and general adaption (Fedele et al., 1988; Grossman, Pollack, & Golding, 1988; Grossman, Pollack, Golding, & Fedele, 1987; Pollack & Grossman, 1985; see also Pollack, in press).

One of the most robust findings from the BUPP was the predictive power of autonomy scores and affiliation scores during the cross-section of the life cycle that was studied, as well as the necessary dialectical and developmental balance between the capacity to remain related and connected to significant others and the capacity to maintain a sense of self-focused interest and achievement. For both men and women it was achieving this healthy balance between autonomous functioning and affiliative relatedness that was predictive of marital satisfaction, "good-enough" fathering, general parental capacity, children's positive mood, and family adaptation (Grossman et al., 1987; Grossman et al., 1988; Pollack & Grossman, 1985; Pollack, 1982, 1983).

These findings stand in contrast to traditional views of autonomy as an alternative to or opposite of affiliation and relatedness (Erikson, 1963). The perspective offered here is one of a *dialectic* (Grossman et al., 1988; Pollack, 1990): Autonomy is related to but not defined solely by participation in separate activities, and affiliation is not just a matter of engaging in relationships. Gerald Stechler and Samuel Kaplan (1980), two child psychoanalysts who built on the work of George Klein, defined the beginning sense of self in children and its later integrated form in adults as a combination of two apparently disparate aspects that must be integrated into one identity. They conceptualized two poles within one cohesive self, the first experienced as an autonomous center of activity, the other experienced as part of a transcendent unit. They called the autonomous pole the "I" component and the more affiliative pole the "We" component. I agree with Stechler and Kaplan that the self can simultaneously be separate from and part of an entity greater than itself. In our research, when we talk about autonomy, we are referring to the sense of the "I" within the self, and when we talk about affiliation, we are referring to the sense of the "We" embedded within an independent self (Grossman, Pollack, & Golding, 1988; Pollack, 1982).

Although the autonomy-affiliation balance was important for women as well as men, men's definition of what was affiliative and what was autonomous differed radically from women's. Any attempt to measure these two concepts required awareness of these basic differences. For example, the men in the study would often show a strong proclivity to be close to their children but would express closeness by attention, physical play, or teaching. Women appeared to be more comfortable holding and hugging their children. We felt, however, that both of these types of interactions were evidence of affiliative capacities. Indeed, the children's responsiveness to these very different parenting styles corroborated this (Pollack & Grossman, 1985).

Given the unique nature of men's state of affiliation, it was necessary to develop gender-specific scales to measure these constructs. Not merely an artifact of one empirical study, this finding has been replicated by other major research groups on empathy (Hoffman, 1977; Lennon & Eisenberg, 1987), substantiating the gender-specific nature of such concepts as self-sufficiency, warmth, empathy, relatedness, and so on. (See also Pollack, 1982, 1983, for a full discussion.) Rather than creating a rigid gender-linked dichotomy between capacities for relatedness and self-sufficiency, I-ness or We-ness (i.e., the "independent man" versus the "interdependent woman"), the empirical data suggest a basis for recasting these functions along the lines of a balance, incorporating the recognition that there may indeed be, at times, a *his* relatedness and a *hers* relatedness, a *hers* autonomy and a *his* autonomy. Psychological well-being, then, is not reflected solely in the achieving of autonomy for men, but rather is a balance of relatedness and independence. Fatherhood both upsets that balance and offers opportunities for its realignment.

Fatherhood: A Second Chance

In reviewing our research from the BUPP project, we found several major trends in healthy couples' negotiations about parenting: One was that, in the traditional family structure of women taking on the primary role of child care, men shy away from competing with this role of primacy with the children. I am not talking here about a dysfunctional setting in which women feel "stuck" with their children and men are off doing something else. Rather, these couples decided on this emotional "division of labor" for their mutual benefit and needs. And when something went wrong in this setup (e.g., the mother became ill or incapacitated), the father was more than ready to step in, give support, and become an alternative nurturer. We described this balance as one of *complementarity*. Perhaps, at times, such complementarities need to be renegotiated, and the possibilities of excluding the man from emotional connection, or abandoning the woman to too much, need to be addressed. Yet such an arrangement can continue to allow the father a significant role in parenting—and a meaningful one for child and mother as well—even though it may not always be the "leading" role. Sometimes, however, unconscious expectations based on deeply ingrained gender roles may impede fathers from taking up their new task of parenting.

In our study, we found that the mother could become an inadvertent *gatekeeper*, keeping her newborn baby from her husband. Her doing so was usually subtle; perhaps she handed the baby to the father at an inopportune moment and then said, "Oh, dear, don't hold her like that," or, "That isn't the way to change a diaper." Often the father, who already felt inadequate, would unconsciously collude by hastily returning the baby to his wife and then backing off. With men and women increasingly invading each other's traditional "turf," it is understandable that women may feel inclined to maintain some control over the household, especially over parenting.

On the father's side, we noticed a parallel unconscious process occurring before the birth of the newborn and continuing into the child's first year; I've called this process *nest-feathering*. The new father often felt that the best way to provide for his wife and child was to work assiduously in order to gain greater income or career status—to "feather the nest" that the young fledgling and mother were placed in. However, we found that what most distressed women in the study was the emotional absence of their husbands during this period. As in the O. Henry story "The Gift of the Magi," the husband was sacrificing for the wife, and the wife for the husband, in ways that were terribly out of sync.

Our advice to these new fathers was that they spend some of their time supporting their wife and newborn by being physically and emotionally present. We suggested to the wives that they try to facilitate their husbands' learning how to take care of a newborn. We believe that men need to accept that their wives can "mentor" them in some nurturing skills. At the same time, they also need their wives to recognize that "male" ways of parenting can be a valuable complement to mothering.

In contradistinction to such complementarity, we found an important result concerning the effect of the quality of the father's time on their interaction with their children. Parenting research has shown that many fathers spend an extremely small period of their day with their children, even if they are "highly" involved (see Grossman et al., 1988). What our findings revealed, however, was that the quantity and quality of time need not be the same. In other words, fathers in our study who were highly involved with their work, were satisfied with that work, and spent a fair amount of time at it could not spend equal amounts of time with their child. However, the quality of the time these "job-satisfied" fathers spent with their child directly and positively affected the child's mental health. Now, a word of caution is in order: I am not saying that fathers can abandon their families and the quality of connection will remain the same. What is clear from our study, however, is that work-invested fathers who care about their children and spend significant time with them—albeit not the same quantity of time as mothers do—can still have an important effect on the emotional well-being of their sons and daughters, owing to the quality of the interaction. Fathers, even actively at-work fathers, do count and indeed do make a big difference! Even if men are not the primary caretakers, they may have an important effect on the mental health of their families and children and, by extension, on their own selves. Often this is a "second chance" for a reparative relationship—and, via this repair, for an enhanced sense of intimacy with themselves, their mates, and their families.

In the interviews with men who were found to be healthy supporters of both autonomy and affiliation in their children, a particular trend was revealed. These men stated that they were invested in learning how to parent correctly and learned to do so from a combination of not only their own memories of parental nurturance but direct observation of their wives. These men often watched their wives parent, viewing them as experts from whom they could learn to be good parents themselves. We understood this to be a form of identification, a process, I think, that offers another chance for repair, especially in the couple's situation. For men, being able to value the tasks that women do traditionally, particularly mothering and child care, and to identify with these nurturing roles helps to dispel at the deepest unconscious layers that fear and dread many men feel about being dependent upon a woman (see Pollack, in press).

Good-Enough Fathering: Fathering as a Developmental Phase

So, one way in which a mutual respect between the genders can be realigned is in the self-reparative role of parenting in men's lives. *Fathering is one of men's greatest opportunities for personal transformation.* The psychoanalyst Theresa Benedek (1959, 1975) created the term "fatherliness," by which she meant an instinctually rooted trait that is characterized by empathic responsiveness to one's children and that she believed originates in a man's earliest psychic memory traces of mother and father. Although Benedek's work was groundbreaking, I prefer to adapt a term that Winnicott (1974) used for mothers: *"good-enough" fathering* (Diamond, 1991; Grossman & Pollack, 1984). This term encompasses both the biological capacities of fatherhood and the overarching, more far-reaching social and intrapsychic constructions of fatherliness that Benedek described. In this term capacity to be both progenitor and protector—not only distantly as a gatherer of food, a hunter, and a warrior but proximally as a nurturant caregiver within a monogamous family system—is all contained.

However, I wish to define good-enough fathering beyond the close-touch world of caring for one's own children, for two reasons. First, a father who cares only for his own children but little at all for other children in the world cannot possibly be inculcating in his family and in himself the kind of reparative experience that was lost for many men in premature separation from a loving connection. This capacity must go beyond selfishness, beyond a narrowly defined family loyalty. Also, there are many men who never have the opportunity to father their own children. Yet there is no reason that this capacity for good-enough fathering cannot emerge within them, and be expressed by them, as well. Here, then, I am referring to a concept that is closest to Erikson's sense of generativity: a caring, supportive, mentoring type of role to younger "others" that for the nurturant older man is experienced as good-enough parenting.

Fathering is a powerful emotional situation for men. Although, historically, research has tended to focus on the absence or loss of the father, the presence of the father and the normative experience of fathering lie at the deepest emotional roots of men's psychosocial being. The research findings of our BUPP project—corroborated now by a number of other innovative interventions (Barnett, Marshall, & Pleck, 1992; Levant, 1990)—suggest that good-enough fathering is not only a salient factor in the healthy development of young boys and girls but an important curative or transforming factor in the mental health of adult men. Contrary to past and popular belief, fatherhood is equally significant to many men as career achievement. Indeed, it appears to have a reverberating impact on their emotional capacities for balance, mental health, and physical well-being. Barnett, Marshall, and Pleck (1992) found that the quality of men's "parental role" was a significant factor in their psychological distress or health; they concluded: "The widely held belief that men's psychological health is primarily determined by their work role is . . . deficient; the quality of men's family roles contributes strongly to their mental health" (p. 366). Barnett and Marshall (1994) found that for married fathers the only factor significantly correlated with their physical health was the quality of their relationships with their children. There was no correlation between the health of these men and their work or marital role. The poet Robert Bly (1986) sums up this transformational matrix in "For My Son Noah, Ten Years Old":

> . . . and slowly the kind man comes closer, loses his rage,
>   sits down at table.
> So I am proud only of those days that pass in undivided
>   tenderness,
> when you sit drawing, or making books, stapled, with
>   messages to the world,
> of coloring a man with fire coming out of his hair.
> Or we sit at a table, with small tea carefully poured.
> So we pass our time together, calm and delighted.[5]

Based upon the results of our own study, I have suggested that men's capacity to achieve a gender-sensitive empathic form of fathering provides the opportunity for a transformation of their self-structure, for two reasons. First, men can recognize the positive impact their emotional commitment has upon the well-being of their children, both girls and boys. They are now able to give their children something they themselves often did not receive from their own fathers (Pollack, in press). This altruistic transformation often enhances men's self-esteem. In addition, it often requires identifying with and internalizing their wives' caretaking capacities, learning from their female partners how to nurture. In so doing, men acknowledge the meaningfulness of women's relational skills and internalize a positive sense of maternal caregiving in a manner that can dramatically undo earlier negative and frightening feelings toward all things feminine and maternal.

Are Men Really That "Bad"?

A plethora of works of popular psychology have focused on men's apparent dysfunction in the arenas of emotional expressiveness, interpersonal mutuality, and intimacy. "Bad," disappointing men are identified and advice is given to women on how to steer between the Scylla and Charybdis of these "intimacy-phobic," "narcissistic," and self-centered "overachievers" who are likely to cause relational pain.

Is it really possible that there are that many bad men out there, or that many women who make so-called foolish choices? Or is it more likely that we have been locked for so long into a cultural stereotype that supports the myth of a fully autonomous man that once it has been debunked, we are

---

[5]Copyright © by Robert Bly. Reprinted by permission.

likely to see the pendulum swing in the other direction and to talk about how aloof, uncaring, unavailable, and unempathic such "alone-men" can be?

As we have seen, it appears that the role of autonomy in human development has been terribly overestimated and misunderstood, for both men and women. Historically, men have been considered by some to be too "well" (i.e., too independent and differentiated) to require any help, intervention, or psychotherapeutic repair. Now it turns out that these men may have been walled-off in a world of defensive self-sufficiency—a pseudoautonomy in which they have been entirely dependent on others for their emotional sustenance—while denying their yearning and need for support. Their isolation in turn has caused confusion and pain, not only for their significant others but also for the men themselves. Autonomy as a sine qua non of mental health has been entirely overrated.

But now, as we come to grips with our criticisms of our present culture as too narcissistic, I believe that men have also been misunderstood—this time by a number of clinicians in particular—as "too sick" to form the relationships required for attachment-oriented, relational psychotherapy.

Requisite Transformations

How can men change? How can they overcome the traumas of premature separation and the losses associated with the shame-based socialization that led to their stoical unresponsiveness? Only the briefest summary is possible here, but it is my argument that men do not have to throw away parts of themselves as much as they need to transform them. The qualities often associated with traditional definitions of masculinity, such as autonomy and aggressiveness, are not in themselves bad except as they become exaggerated, reducing men's complex humanity into an essentialist caricature. Throughout his life, a man has opportunities to grow beyond earlier solutions. He is shaped by biology and his early development, but he need not be enslaved by them. To become as free as possible, however, of the limiting influences of old pain and the overly rigid cultural prescriptions about what it means to be a man requires certain transformations—requisite transformations.

Men's autonomy, sometimes valuable, needs to be tempered, balanced, by the acknowledgment of the importance of connection. Men cannot continue to conduct their lives as if intimate relationships were not all that important. Indeed, men are constantly seeking and yearning to be connected, often with women, but also with fellow men. However, they are terribly frightened by the shameful vulnerability that such connection may bring. Too often the psychology of men has been a means to suppress the feelings—primarily sadness and fear—that such connections elicit and to replace them with a withdrawal or angry frustration that tends to cloud the real issues. Men are not self-sufficient loners who care for no one else. They are frightened searchers, looking to connect but very unsure of what safety net they need should the connection go awry.

My thesis is that, owing to the early, abrupt loss of a man's first love (an emotional trauma) and the shame attending the yearnings to recapture it, a man feels that he must keep a safe distance and deny that he has certain feelings or needs. The adult relationships men and women have with each other, therefore, become polarized—connection and autonomy are seen as the special province of one gender alone. Only when he comes to terms with the wounds caused by these early separations and with the ways he has developed a protective armor can a man be open again to love and to be loved. He must rediscover the submerged peninsulas that once linked him to the mainland.

To accomplish this, a man must be willing to plumb the depths of his own psyche and to revisit the struggles, losses, and traumas that lie at the root of his developmental crisis of self-formation and masculine identity. This cannot be accomplished through the nostalgic drumbeat of primitive masculinity. A weekend workshop or wilderness experience of primitive maleness has value only when it goes beyond playacting and becomes integrated into the meaningful activities and complex relationships of a man's daily life. Genuine change in men must include the capacity to manifest respect for the differences and similarities between themselves and women in our society and to renounce patriarchical or essentialist solutions. The admonition of one respected clinician, the late Dr. Elvin Semrad, to fledgling therapists was that they should help their patients become able to "acknowledge, bear and put into perspective" (see Rako & Mazer, 1980, p. 104) the split-off feelings of traumatic separation and vulnerability from their childhood. He may well have been thinking about what men need to do to mature fully.

Before they can do so, however, men must be able to reach out and acknowledge their need for support. And the support must come from friends, women partners, or psychotherapists (if necessary) who have also achieved an empathic understanding of men's developmental dilemmas. The burdens of masculinity cannot be lifted by stridently insisting that men give up their stoic stance of autonomy, for it is this very underpinning that men continue to need to maintain at all costs. To allow men to save face regarding their earlier traumas, we must realize that they are not bad but sad, and that they require an empathic echo to such sadness in order to create the environment of safety necessary for personal change.

Men are not only able to experience a full range of feelings, including love, sadness, and empathic responsiveness, but they have the inborn bio-genetic equipment to do so. Just as women can compete, men can feel. They are not so much wounded as hurt and experiencing a loss: They have lost the use of the inborn capacity for empathic relatedness that they share with all members of their species, male and female alike (Pollack, in press). As men come to see that they are still yearning to make what is now only half whole again, their anger will be turned into a sense of grief, which is the harbinger of transformation.

Becoming a man should not entail one single rigid pathway, but rather a multitude of possible journeys toward fulfillment. I am suggesting that both men and women become trapped when the personality characteristics necessary for mature involvement in our complex industrialized world become bifurcated along gender lines. It is no more useful for men to be protectors and providers without the capacity for deep empathic feeling or the sharing of sadness with their mates than it is for women to be the nurturant caregivers to a child but to be denied the capacity for achievement at work. The time has come to recognize that what men do well and what women do well are both good!

"Real" Men Versus Real Change

There are two popular schools of thought as to how change for men can come about. I take exception to both. One argues that since women are experts in relationships, they should teach men how to relate and men should follow women's pathways. Although there is much to be gained by each gender respecting the other's skills and capacities—and much that men can learn from women—this alone will not help men understand their own pain or adapt to a changing world. The other argument is that men must eschew the loving and nurturance of women and return to their primitive, essentialist, masculine male roots alone—into a mythos of early "strongmen," "wild men," and cthonic men of steel and iron. Such a return to the archaic or primitive roots of early male development may be correct in identifying the depth of the experience toward which men must grope, but it seems wholly useless as an integrated solution to the complexities of modern adult life in postindustrialized societies—societies that must become more gender-respectful and less gender-phobic.

There must be role functions and identifications for men beyond those of "secondhand" women on the one hand or of strong, "he-man" antiwomen on the other. As I have already stated, deeply ingrained, unconscious models of the masculine self cannot be easily transformed with one workshop, one return to the wilderness for a weekend, or one consciousness-raising event. Neither can women's righteous indignation and demand for change—as rightful as such a clarion call for the dismantling of a dominance-oriented society is—stimulate men, in and of itself, to make the deep personal transformations required to create a society in which there is more genuine balance and respect between both the roles and the psyches of the two genders.

Rather, I believe it is only as men come to see that the present gender role–based expectations for masculinity in our society are impossible to achieve and lead only to pain, loss, and a false, too vulnerable sense of self-esteem that they will then be able to recognize that change is necessary, that there must be a reframing of our concept of what it means to "be a man."

But reaching this point, are we then to once again say that what men have created over centuries and across societies as a "masculine ideology" is entirely worthless, only fit to be scuttled? Or is it possible to look through a more empathic lens at such adaptations to societal demands that manhood be tested? In other words, might not the cross-cultural constructions of masculinity contain some virtues or values worth saving? As we deconstruct the 20th-century gender role straitjacket, can we reconstruct from its elemental components a masculinity worth saving? (See also Chapter 8.)

The Social Construction of "Manhood": The Big Impossible?

David Gilmore (1990), in his review across scores of cultures studied by anthropologists, ranging from preindustrial Western societies to Micronesia and Africa, concludes that while biological maleness (i.e., core gender identity) may be a predestined phenomenon, manhood (gender role) is a culturally constructed concept, and a fragile achievement at that. Manhood often involves a test that must be passed over and over again, leaving the impression that manhood is a "precarious state" painfully achieved and easily lost. Such tests of masculinity are so constantly threatening men with the loss of their sense of identity that one Native American tribe referred to its manhood ritual as the "Big Impossible." Yet Gilmore did not find what he imagined to be conventional wisdom—that women have been more nurturing and protective while men have been more disconnected and uncaring:

> One of my findings . . . is that manhood ideologies always include a criterion of *selfless generosity* even to the point of *sacrifice*. Again and again we find that "real" men are those who give more than they take; they serve others. Real men are generous, even to a fault. . . . Manhood therefore is also a nurturing concept, if we define that term as giving, subventing, or other directed. (pp. 229; my emphasis)

Significantly, then, there are cross-cultural models of male nurturance that have been confused or lost in our industrialized societies. Men help to create new generations, they help to protect and provide for those around them, they promise to take legitimate responsibility for others, and they may rightfully expect a mutual form of authority and respect in turn:

Men nurture their society by shedding their blood, their sweat, and their semen, by bringing home food for both child and mother, by producing children, and by dying if necessary in far away places to provide a safe haven for their people. (p. 230)

Strikingly, however, the personality types and characteristics necessary for this traditional male approach to caregiving are often the mirror opposites of the traditional nurturant "female" personality:

To support his family, the man has to be *distant*, away hunting or fighting wars; to be tender, he must be *tough* enough to fend off enemies. To be generous, he must be *selfish* enough to amass goods, often by defeating other men; to be gentle, he must first be *strong*, even ruthless in confronting enemies; to love, he must be *aggressive* enough to court . . . a wife. (p. 230; my emphasis)

Such a new sociocultural perspective may shed light on a type of "male" empathy, an instrumental, productive, prosocial type of connection between male friends, for example—and a special connection in groups of men—as well as on men's prosocial, empathic role in the world of women (see Pollack, in press). Lest this reconfiguration of what are often seen as male vices into male virtues be viewed as merely an anthropological sleight of hand—holding true only in primitive cultures—the work of the sociologist Robert Weiss (1990) is important to report here. His study of successful America middle-class businessmen points to the possibility of transforming socially constructed male competitiveness into a type of love, protection, and respect.

Weiss studied a representative sample of male professionals utilizing an in-depth, semistructured interview process. He was impressed by these men's capacity to "stay the course," to maintain a sense of commitment to themselves and others. These men had internalized the personality characteristics of "resilience, determination, . . . [and] competence." They were struggling to be "good men" (p. 255). That men's sense of commitment or duty can be distorted into workaholism or patriarchy—such that human values become subservient to perverse or hurtful forms of power—should not cause us to mistrust all men's capacity for taking dutiful responsibility.

My own research on men's capacity, as fathers, for empathic entunement and my critical review of the literature in the field of gender differences in empathy (Pollack, in press) yielded two conclusions. First, there appears to be an inborn physiological capacity to experience vicariously the affective states of another member of the human species, and men and women are equally endowed in this regard. On this, the research sustains Kohut's concept that "the empathic understanding of the experiences of other human beings is as basic (a *human*) . . . endowment . . . as . . . vision, hearing, touch, taste and smell" (1977, p. 144; my emphasis). Second, gender-tracked socialization skills enhance this inborn quality in females while leading to its radical repression in males, creating a proempathic state in girls and an anti-empathic one in boys. Yet even with such rigid socialized repression, the inborn empathic skills and the urge to utilize them remains so strong in boys, and later in adult males, that they continue to manifest themselves in the one arena that is left open to them as socially appropriate: their cognitive capacities for perspective-taking (Hoffman, 1977; Lennon & Eisenberg, 1987). This heavily male-based aspect of empathy, combined with an ethic of justice and fairness (Gilligan, 1982), yields, I believe, men's capacity for prosocial empathic activity, as manifest and sanctioned in our society. This differentiation of the types of empathic responsiveness that are acceptable by gender begins early and dies hard. Indeed, Brody (1985) found that, by elementary school age, girls are already more willing, and boys more reluctant, to report an experience of sadness and fear when hearing stories that evoke such emotions. The fact that boys, and later men, retain the biological vestigial capacity for empathy, despite our attempts to shame it away, is borne out by the earlier study cited by Grief et al. (Brody, in press), who found that fathers—but not mothers—tended to label emotions more frequently when telling a story to young daughters than to young sons. Here we have the reproduction of gender-tracked instruction for empathic capacity.

So men in our society struggle to utilize whatever inborn empathic capacity we fail to socialize out of them as boys. Indeed, one might even argue that men's heroic attempt to maintain the cognitive aspects of empathic connection is evidence of the virtues of masculine empathy rather than merely a manifestation of the deficits of a more sensitive responsiveness or caring.

What Do Men Really Need?

Am I saying, then, that since many of these traditional traits of male gender socialization and identification may be virtues as well as vices, men should cling steadfastly to their emotionally inexpressive, defensively self-sufficient, aggression-dominated, patriarchal, commitment-phobic behaviors? Obviously not.

Rather, I am suggesting that our psychoanalytic (and by extension, psychodynamic) conceptual models of gender development have done both men and women a disservice by hopelessly confusing the binary "bedrock" of core gender identity (i.e., being a "male" or a "female") with the more elastic diversity of gender role alternatives. While *core gender identity* offers few choices, *gender role identity* or identification is a much more complex concept or process: It represents the internalization of unconscious psychic schemas of what "being a man" or "being a woman" means to a particular individual, mediated by the context of their own society, culture, and family. Here we would expect to see the widest range of healthy alternatives or

engendered identities (including so-called heterosexual and homosexual identities) unless a culturally rigid set of standards attempts to channel such normal diversity into a straitjacketed, limited set of societally acceptable norms.
Then we are likely to experience what we have unfortunately seen over the
last century: the utilization of psychoanalysis (a creative theory of unconscious dynamics and human development) as the handmaiden for reduc-
tionistic, essentialist views of masculinity and femininity. This leads in turn
to the muddling of social constructs with biological givens and the use of the
heuristic findings of a developmentally based science as a repressive social
tool for conformity.

Pleck (1981; Chapter 1) has successfully challenged this scientifically
flawed and biased model, but in psychoanalytic psychology's defensive
attempt to fend off the challenge, we have yet to create a coherent alternative
model: a new developmental psychology from within a depth-psychological,
empathic, and psychoanalytic perspective. Feminist critics such as
Chodorow (1978, 1989) and Miller (1976) have rightfully taken to task our
phallocentric models of identity (read as men = healthy, women = depen-
dent/sick). Yet the replacements offered, while appropriately elevating
women's bonded or relational selves to a high level of significance, continue
to unwittingly support a gender-bifurcated and essentialist model of self-
in-relation women versus self-sufficient men. Such a model redresses the
imbalance of the power dialectic but maintains a traditional set of gender
distinctions.

I suggest that we must go beyond this point to lay the foundations of a
new psychoanalytic theory of gender development and identity. We must
create a paradigm that integrates the best elements of psychoanalytic concepts or models of unconscious internalization (an empathic developmental
psychology) with state-of-the-art knowledge of biological processes and the
necessary hermeneutic of an interpersonal and social construction of meaning. Two recent and interesting research findings may point us in the right
direction.

Kyle Pruett (1987) has studied longitudinally a naturally occurring
"experiment of nature": parent-child pairs in which, for a variety of reasons,
the men have become the primary early caretakers. Contrary to collegial
expectations, Pruett has discovered that these fathers are perfectly capable of
nurturant early parenting; that their children do not lose out but gain from
the addition of a primary nurturant father; and that, strikingly, young boys
reared by such fathers appear to have a healthier flexibility in their socialized gender role identity (Pruett, 1987, 1989; quoted in Betcher & Pollack,
1993).

Most empirical research has pointed to men's staggering inability—compared with their female counterparts—to respond empathically to the cries of
young infants. However, these data—which are often used to support a bio-

logical distinction between "natural" mothering and "second-class" fathering—turn out to be dubious. In fact, when a creative research group measured the physiological response rates of heart rhythm and blood pressure of males and females responding to the urgent cries of a young infant, there were no biological or physiological gender differences. Yet the observed behavior continued to show women's movement toward involvement and men's apparent paralysis. So it appears that men and women have a full range of biologically based ("hardwired") empathic capacities for responsiveness that later become skillfully shaped in adult women caretakers and socially suppressed in adult males. One research group concluded: "These findings lend some support to the contention that females are socialized to be more expressive while males are encouraged to deny their feelings and emotions ... and further emphasize that physiological measures may be a truer index of male response to infant signals than behavioral observation or attitudinal measures" (Jones & Thomas, 1989, p. 238). Men therefore, as I have argued above, are not only able to experience a full range of feelings, including love, sadness, and empathic responsiveness, but have the inborn physiological equipment to do so. Just as women can assertively compete, men can nonaggressively feel.

Being a Man

Jewish tradition, like all the cultures and subcultures that Gilmore studied, has a clear boyhood-to-manhood transition in the ritual of the bar mitzvah. Here, the 13-year-old boy is inculcated into the religious world of his elders. But the distinction between becoming a man on the day of the boy's bar mitzvah and being a real man—a *mentsch*—is clear. Freely translated, this word means "man." But to the initiated, it means much more. For being a *mentsch* is more than moving from childhood to manhood: It is a sense of being a full person. In fact, as the term has been adopted into English usage, it has also come to mean "a human being," "a decent and responsible person."

Men are struggling to be decent and responsible. Men are struggling to exist in connection with women and with other men without fear. A new psychoanalytic psychology of men, a reframing of masculinity, would recognize the heroic effort required for such a struggle.

Indeed, we live in a time of fallen heroes. The monuments built of men, by men, and for men are tumbling. Men have been brought to earth, their strengths put in perspective by their flaws. Even their virtues are suspect now as vices: Power has turned out to be oppression, strength rigidity, and self-sufficiency an inability to be emotionally close. If men still appear to be in control, their smug certainty is gone. It is a difficult time to be proud of being a man. In fact, it is a confusing time in which to understand what being a man really is.[6]

Yet to avoid a male backlash, we must replace the fanciful and grandiose notion of distant heroes with the painful realities and sweet successes of everyday life. Barbara Ehrenreich (1990), in critiquing the so-called new man, states:

> So it is not enough, anymore to ask that men become more like women; we should ask instead that they become more like what *both* men and women *might* be. My new man, if I could design one, would be capable of appreciation, sensitivity, intimacy—values that have been for too long, "feminine." But he would also be capable of commitment, to use that much-abused word, and I mean by that commitment not only to friends and family, but to a broad and generous vision of how we might all live together. (p. 137; my emphasis on *both*)

Conclusion

So, in the end, a new psychoanalytic psychology of men must take into account a new psychology of women, and vice versa. As men, we have fallen from high pedestals, and many of us still ache from the thud. We will need to re-create ourselves in a broader, more flexible, less gender-rigid image, but we will need help doing so. As men, we must be sensitive to the needs of women but remain equally sensitive and empathic to the depth of our own selves.

Men can be aided in this process by scholars and clinicians who understand that men's "narcissistic" defenses are not synonymous with "badness" but reflect a traumatic dilemma requiring an affective bridge to greater connection. The fact that men and women speak in different *voices* may often give rise to a cacophony of hurtful and strident anger, but it also offers the possibilities of exciting diversity, a potpourri of intimate excitement. As Narcissus widens the scope of his gaze, and Aristophanes' man finds healthier merger, men may leave their walled-off islands of defensive self-sufficiency and slowly and carefully build bridges of intimacy to the mainland. Then, we may see not only more empathically balanced, stable, engendered selves but also the creation of a more flexible set of internalized object relations, balanced between the "I" (autonomy) and the "We" (affiliation), a set of repaired "connections," for men and women together. In the words of the sage Hillel, "*If not now, then when?*"

---

[6]This idea and several others emerge from my collaboration with Dr. William Betcher. My thanks for his continued input and support (see Betcher & Pollack, 1993).

References

Barnett, R. C., & Marshall, N. L. (1994). *Men, family-role quality, job-role quality, and physical health.*

Barnett, R. C., Marshall, N. L., & Pleck, J. H. (1992). Men's multiple roles and their relationship to men's psychological distress. *Journal of Marriage and the Family, 54,* 358–367.

Benedek, T. (1959). Parenthood as a developmental phase: A contribution to the libido theory. *Journal of the American Psychoanalytic Association, 7,* 389–417.

Benedek, T. (1975). Discussion of parenthood as a developmental phase. *Journal of the American Psychoanalytic Association, 23,* 154–165.

Betcher, R. W., & Pollack, W. S. (1993). *In a time of fallen heroes: The re-creation of masculinity.* New York: Atheneum.

Bly, R. (1986). *Selected poems.* New York: Harper & Row.

Bly, R. (1990). *Iron John.* Reading, MA: Addison-Wesley.

Brody, L. R. (1985). Gender differences in emotional development: A review of theories and research. *Journal of Personality, 53,* 102–149.

Brody, L. R. (1993). On understanding gender differences in the expression of emotion. In S. Ablon, D. Brown, J. Mack, & E. Khantazian (Eds.), *Human feelings: Explorations in affect development and meaning* (pp. 87–121). Hillsdale, NJ: Analytic Press.

Brody, L. R. (in press). Gender, emotional expression and the family. In R. Kavanaugh, B. Zimmerberg-Glick, & S. Fein (Eds.), *Emotion: Interdisciplinary perspectives.* Hillsdale, NJ: Lawrence Erlbaum.

Chodorow, N. (1978). *The reproduction of mothering.* Berkeley: University of California Press.

Chodorow, N. (1989). *Feminism and psychoanalytic theory.* New Haven, CT: Yale University Press.

Cunningham, J., & Shapiro, L. (1984). *Infant affective expression as a function of infant and adult gender.* Unpublished manuscript, Brandeis University, Waltham, MA.

David, D., & Brannon, R. (Eds.). (1976). *The forty-nine percent majority: The male sex role.* Reading, MA: Addison-Wesley.

Diamond, M. (1991). *Fathers and sons: Psychoanalytic perspectives on good-enough fathering throughout the life cycle.* Unpublished manuscript.

Dunn, J., Bretherton, I., & Munn, P. (1987). Conversations about feeling states between mothers and their children. *Developmental Psychology, 23,* 132–139.

Ehrenreich, B. (1990). *The worst years of our lives.* New York: Harper Perennial.

Erikson, E. (1963). *Childhood and society.* New York: Norton.

Fedele, N. M., Golding, E. R., Grossman, F. K., & Pollack, W. S. (1988). Psychological issues in adjustment to first parenthood. In G. Y. Michaels & W. A. Goldberg (Eds.), *The transition to parenthood* (pp. 85–113). New York: Cambridge University Press.

Fivush, R. (1989). Exploring sex differences in the emotional content of mother-child conversations about the past. *Sex Roles, 20,* 675–691.

Freud, S. (1953). The interpretation of dreams. In J. Strachey (Ed. & Trans.), *The standard edition of the complete psychological works of Sigmund Freud* (Vol. 4). London: Hogarth Press. (Original work published 1900.)

Fuchs, D., & Thelen, M. (1988). Children's expected interpersonal consequences of communicating their affective state and reported likelihood of expression. *Child Development, 59,* 1314–1322.

Gilligan, C. (1982). *In a different voice.* Cambridge, MA: Harvard University Press.

Gilmore, D. D. (1990). *Manhood in the making.* New Haven, CT: Yale University Press.

Gleason, J. B. , & Greif, E. G. (1983). Men's speech to young children. In B. Thorne, C. Kramarae, & N. Henley (Eds.), *Language, gender and society* (pp. 140–150). London: Newbury House.

Greenson, R. (1968). Dis-identifying from mother: Its special importance for the boy. *International Journal of Psychoanalysis, 49,* 370–374.

Greif, E., Alvarez, M., & Ulman, K. (1981, April). *Recognizing emotions in other people: Sex differences in socialization.* Paper presented at the biennial meeting of the Society for Research in Child Development, Boston, MA.

Grossman, F. K., Eichler, L., & Winnickoff, S. (1980). *Pregnancy, birth and parenthood.* San Francisco: Jossey-Bass.

Grossman, F., & Pollack, W. (1984, October). *Good enough fathering.* Paper presented at the annual meeting of the National Council on Family Relations, San Francisco.

Grossman, F. K., Pollack, W. S., & Golding, E. (1988). Fathers and children: Predicting the quality and quantity of fathering. *Developmental Psychology, 24,* 82–91.

Grossman, F. K., Pollack, W. S., Golding, E. R., & Fedele; N. M. (1987). Autonomy and affiliation in the transition to parenthood. *Family Relations, 36,* 263–269.

Hoffman, M. L. (1977). Sex differences in empathy and related behaviors. *Psychological Bulletin, 84,* 712–722.

Jones, C. L., & Thomas, S. A. (1989). New fathers' blood pressure and heart rate: Relationships to interaction with their newborn infants. *Nursing Research, 38,* 237–241.

Jordan, J. V., Kaplan, A. G., Baker Miller, J., Stiver, I. P., & Surrey, J. L. (1991). *Women's growth in connection.* New York: Guilford Press.

Jowett, B. (1956). *The symposium of Plato.* New York: Tudor.

Kaplan, J. (Ed.). (1992). *Bartlett's familiar quotations,* 16th ed. Boston: Little, Brown.

Klein, G. S. (1976). *Psychoanalytic theory: An exploration of essentials.* New York: International Universities Press.

Kohut, H. (1971). *The analysis of the self.* New York: International Universities Press.

Kohut, H. (1977). *The restoration of the self.* New York: International Universities Press.

Kohut, H., & Wolf, E. (1978). The disorders of the self and their treatment: An outline. *International Journal of Psychoanalysis, 59,* 413–425.

Lennon, R., & Eisenberg, N. (1987). Gender and age differences in empathy and sympathy. In N. Eisenberg & J. Strayer (Eds.), *Empathy and its development* (pp. 195–217). New York: Cambridge University Press.

Levant, R. F. (1990). Psychological services designed for men: A psychoeducational approach. *Psychotherapy, 27,* 309–315.

Malatesta, C. Z., & Haviland, J. M. (1982). Learning display rules: The socialization of emotion expression in infancy. *Child Development, 53,* 991–1003.

Miller, J. B. (1976). *Toward a new psychology of women.* Boston: Beacon Press.

Modell, A. H. (1976). The "holding environment" and the therapeutic action of psychoanalysis. *Journal of the American Psychoanalytic Association, 24,* 285–308.

Oldenberg, D. (1993, October 12). Men: Getting a life: The movement takes a pragmatic turn. [Interview with William S. Pollack, Ph.D.]. *Washington Post,* p. C5.

Pleck, J. (1981). *The myth of masculinity.* Cambridge, MA: MIT Press.

Pollack, W. S. (1982). *"I"ness and "we"ness: Parallel lines of development.* (Doctoral dissertation, Boston University). *University Microfilms International,* 82–13517.

Pollack, W. S. (1983). Object-relations and self psychology: Researching children and their family systems. *The Psychologist-Psychoanalyst, 4,* 14.

Pollack, W. S. (1990). Men's development and psychotherapy: A psychoanalytic perspective. *Psychotherapy, 27*(3), 316–321.

Pollack, W. S. (1992). Should men treat women? Dilemmas for the male psychotherapist: Psychoanalytic and developmental perspectives. *Ethics and Behavior, 2,* 39–49.

Pollack, W. S. (1992, August). *No man is an island: Reframing the psychology of men.* Paper presented at the centennial meeting of the American Psychological Association, Washington, DC.

Pollack, W. S. (in press). A delicate balance: Fatherhood and psychological transformation—A psychoanalytic perspective. In J. L. Shapiro, M. J. Diamond, & M. Greenberg (Eds.), *Becoming a father: Social, emotional and clinical perspectives.* New York: Springer.

Pollack, W. S., & Grossman, F. K. (1985). Parent-child interaction. In L. L'Labate (Ed.), *The handbook of family psychology and therapy* (pp. 586–622). Homewood, IL: Dorsey.

Pruett, K. D. (1987). *The nurturing father.* New York: Warner Books.

Pruett, K. D. (1989). The nurturing male: A longitudinal study of primary nurturing fathers. In S. H. Cath, A. Gurwitt, & L. Gunsberg (Eds.), *Fathers and their families* (pp. 389–405). Hillsdale, NJ: Analytic Press.

Rako, S. & Mazer, H. (Eds.). (1980). *Semrad: The heart of a therapist.* New York: Jason Aronson.

Ross, J. M. (1982). Oedipus revisited: Laius and the laius complex. *Psychoanalytic Study of the Child* (vol. 37, pp. 169–200). New York: International Universities Press.

Schell, A., & Gleason, J. B. (1989, December). *Gender differences in the acquisition of the vocabulary of emotion.* Paper presented at the annual meeting of the American Association of Applied Linguistics, Washington, DC.

Silverman, D. K. (1987). What are little girls made of? *Psychoanalytic Psychology, 4,* 315–334.

Stechler, G., & Kaplan, S. (1980). The development of the self: A psychoanalytic perspective. *Psychoanalytic Study of the Child* (vol. 35, pp. 85–105). New York: International Universities Press.

Tronick, E. (1989). Emotions and emotional communication in infants. *American Psychologist, 44,* 112–119.

Tronick, E., & Cohn, J. (1989). Infant-mother face-to-face interaction: Age and gender differences in coordination and the occurrence of miscoordination. *Child Development, 60,* 85–92.

Weinberg, M. K. (1992, May). Boys and girls: Sex differences in emotional expressivity and self-regulation during early infancy. In L. J. Bridges (Chair), *Early emotional self-regulation: New approaches to understanding developmental change and individual differences.* Symposium conducted at the International Conference on Infant Studies (ICIS), Miami.

Weiss, R. S. (1990). *Staying the course: The emotional and social lives of men who do well at work*. New York: Fawcett Columbine.

Williams, G. (1993, March). John Wayne disease: Why strong, silent types are weak on life expectancy. [Interview with William S. Pollack, Ph.D.]. *Longevity*, p. 60.

Winnicott, D. W. (1974). *The maturational processes and the facilitating environment*. New York: International Universities Press.

CHAPTER 3

Men's Psychological Development: A Relational Perspective

STEPHEN J. BERGMAN

Introduction

Current theories of male psychological development emphasize the primary importance of the self and fail to describe the whole of men's experience in relationship. Men as well as women are motivated by a primary desire for connection, and it is less accurate and useful to think of "self" than "self-in-relation" as a process. As with women, the sources of men's misery are in disconnections, violations, and dominances and in participation in relationships that are not mutually empowering. However, the specifics of men's development differ in several important ways.

THE RELATIONAL MODEL

For the past 15 years, I've lived with the relational model, watching as my wife, Janet Surrey, every other Monday night, goes off to her "meeting at Jean Baker Miller's house" and sitting in various lecture halls watching this revolutionary work grow. It takes a long time for this theory to sink in, to grasp what is meant by "the relationship," "relational mutuality," and the "movement of relationship." As I began to understand, I had that sense of relief and joy, thinking, "This is true." And in the same way that for women traditional theories of human development, in the light of women's experience, have seemed false and lacking, the traditional theories started to seem false to much of men's experience as I knew it. Nine years ago, Janet and I began to offer workshops—"New Visions of the Female/Male Relationship: Creativity and Empowerment"—and I began to apply a relational approach to male psychological development. My purpose is not to look at all aspects of men's development but to look at men's development in relationship, from a relational perspective.

This work is based on my own experience—that of a middle-class, white, privileged, heterosexual American male—and has limits intrinsic to this viewpoint. In describing general themes in men's experience, I do not imply that they are true for all men. I will be using what I have learned in almost 20 years as a psychiatrist, treating men, women, and couples and using the data from our workshops as well as from my teaching at medical schools, my writing of novels and plays, and, of course, my relationship with Jean Baker Miller, Irene Stiver, and Judy Jordan. Those of you familiar with Janet Surrey's work will hear her voice in much of what follows (Jordan, Kaplan, Miller, Stiver, & Surrey, 1991).

Jean Baker Miller (1983), in a working paper titled "The Construction of Anger in Women and Men," used my first novel, *The House of God* (Shem, 1978), the story of my medical internship, to "illustrate how many emotions—fear, horror, sadness, isolation, and especially pain and hurt—are turned into aggressive actions, even sadism . . . in such a life course the participants are taught an angry denial of reality." At the end of that paper, Jean wrote: "A truly respectful interchange based on the experience of both sexes can lead us along the path of an enlarging dialogue. And I believe that such dialogue is the only path to the survival of us all."

It is in this spirit that I present this work.

As an example of what is often seen in men in relationship, let me quote from my second novel, *Fine* (Shem, 1985). Dr. Fine is an analyst-in-training and is married to Stephanie, who is trying to become a stand-up comic:

> After a while she said: "Tell me, Fine, what are you feeling about us? I need to get in touch with you before I leave."
>
> Fine was full of feeling for his work, and for his internal world, but was startled to find that he did not know what he was feeling for her, his wife. The harder he tried, the more he did not know. Damn, he thought, I'm blocking! "What do you think I'm feeling?"
>
> "I'm not your patient, schmucko, I'm your wife! Just tell me, before I go, where you are with me, okay?"
>
> More blank for her pressure, Fine said: "Don't pressure me."
>
> "Wait—let's not go down this path again—it's so old: I ask, you see it as an attack rather than an invitation, you retreat; I ask again, you withdraw; I feel cut off and frantic, you get comatose and analyze—please, not now—just tell me, simply—I mean with me now, about us—what you feel?"
>
> The word hung on a hook in the air, dropped, balanced, tilted, fell. Fine sensed, in his wife, the same neediness he'd just sensed in his hysteric (patient).

Yet without the luxury of analyzing it, he felt paralyzed. Her asking seemed a demand, and he could sense, in his silence, a chill and dead hollowness. He heard her, knew she cared, and wanted to respond—but could not. Had he terminated analysis prematurely? No, the problem is not men, but her—her neurotic hunger. Distracted by the cries of birds, Fine glanced away, looking out the window at the gulls diving for the garbage thrown from the Hull-Boston commuter ferry. He felt locked into silence.

"You really don't know how to relate, do you, Fine?"

"No," he said, relieved, "I don't. Men don't have the capacity for empathy that women do."

"You're saying men don't know how to relate?"

"Not nearly so well as women."

"How do you know that?"

"I'm expert on empathy—"

"Ha! Haha!" She exploded with laughter. "You? You're the least empathic person I know!"

"Yes," he said, happily. "That's why I'm expert—I can be totally objective about it."

"That's a cop-out, Fine! Some men have empathy, believe me, I know. Men find a way to relate, when they see that their lives depend on it." (p. 77)

Current Theories of Male Development

Most current theories of male development are about a self, not a self-in-relation. Up until recently, most theories of human development have been fashioned by men and gender-blended. Yet in using a relational model of connections, disconnections, and violations to examine male development, it becomes clear that men themselves are fashioned by an event that is profoundly different from that fashioning women: the disconnection from the relationship with mother, and from the whole relational mode, in the name of becoming a man.

Let me comment briefly on current theories of development. Freud suggests that men and women come into the world as isolated selves, with the primary drives of sex and aggression, and that we go through stages of development one after the other, like a train crossing Austria, stopping at the right station at the right time. The withdrawal from and renunciation of mother is framed in the heroic Oedipal stage, primary for establishing a solid, independent gender and sexual identity. Through some tricky theoretical contortions, fear of castration gets twisted into strong male superego. There is talk of "the pre-Oedipal mother," which says something about where the value is placed; if we must use such terms, why "the pre-Oedipal mother" rather than "the post-Jocastal son"? Identification with father comes through competition, fear, and renunciation, not through a wish to connect.

It sets the stage for hierarchy—that is, patriarchy—for dominance, entitlement, ownership of women, and men's fear of men. Identity comes *before* intimacy. Men are taught to fight for power over, and possession of, women, and then, *despite* that context, to relate to them. Given the power of transference, Freud implies that true, intimate relationship is difficult, if not impossible; we are always shouting across an unbridgeable gap.

Erikson and the neo-Freudians are on the same train but extend the line out to adulthood, suggesting we check out who else is at the station when we stop. From basic trust we move to autonomy, industry, and identity, and then, after adolescence, to intimacy driven by sexuality. Only *after* this sexual intimacy do we get to generativity, the participation in the development of others. Only after the self achieves a certain "maturity" can we learn to really relate.

Kernberg (1976) and Mahler (1975), of object relations fame, suggest that we seek objects to satisfy our drives, not for relationship. The key to development is "separation/individuation"—what Mahler calls "hatching" out of a matrix of embeddedness by which a person becomes more internally organized, "field-independent," emotionally controlled, with clear boundaries and an unfolding individuality. Male psychology becomes fixated on achieving a separate and individuated self and what Joe Pleck (1981) calls "male sex role identity." "Self" is based on separation from others and self-other differentiation—self-*versus*-other—which may then become self-*over*-other.

Kohut (1977) and self psychologists hypothesize that we internalize objects to promote narcissistic development. As a child, we need people to nurture, empathize, and mirror us, to "build up" the self. In life we always need holding and self-promotion and buttressing a little, to support the self. Little is said about people nurturing, empowering, or empathizing with *each other*, or building mutual relationships. There is an emphasis on control and power—ego control, control of feelings, a power-control model—and on the basic Western paradigm of comparison, competition, and aggression. Kernberg, Mahler, and Kohut seem to be saying, "Drive your *own* train."

In summary, traditional theories are of "self-out-of-relation," or "self-partly-in-relation." Motivated by sex and aggression, development means learning to be a separate, strikingly impermeable, and static self. A strong identity is necessary for a mature relationship. What is a mature relationship? It may be a deep attachment between self and object, or self and other, it may even be an "intimacy"—a sense of closeness—but it is an intimacy framed by never losing touch with this strong clear vision of self—except perhaps, for temporary lapses during sex. It may be an intimacy, but it is not a mutuality. Growth takes place—in life and psychotherapy—by working to strengthen this sense of self.

Two questions arise: Are these accurate descriptions of the so-called normal process of men's development in current Western culture? Clearly, these theories pay little attention to basic relational questions like, What do we mean by relationship, connection, and mutuality? As a man, trained in the rightness of these theories, I have always felt that while some aspects of them do describe some aspects of men's experience, they are quite superficial and fairly irrelevant to the deeper, more whole levels of my experience. In our workshops, I have realized that other men share this view. I find it curious that theories written mostly by men fail to describe so much of men's authentic experience. Perhaps this failure to write clearly about relationship comes from the difficulty men have in perceiving, understanding, and being in the *process* of relationship. While it is easy for men to envision self, and even self and other, it seems less easy to envision the *relationship* between self and other, with a life of its own, in movement, as a process, arising from and reflecting upon all participants, its realness defined by the qualities inherent in mutual empathic connection. Writing this chapter has helped me to grasp the power of this paradigm shift, how it changes one's perception, understanding, and even language. Recently, using this paradigm in my work with a couple, I was pleased to hear the woman say, "I don't hate him, I hate the *relationship* with him." This way of speaking has the marvelous quality of keeping us in the facts, shifting us away from blame.

The second question is, Are such theories useful in therapy? After almost two decades as a therapist, I have found myself being less concerned in my daily work with penises and castrations and internal objects and narcissistic mirrorings than with the *healing power of mutual relationship*, with men and women both. In my own early training, I came to believe that theories built on images such as "projective identification" were brilliant and crucial. Now I understand that theories can serve as implicit justifications for the distant and relationally unskilled therapist to maintain a self-out-of-relation context with the client. At worst, if used to justify "power-over" actions, they can pave the way for abuse.

Much of what is promoted in these old theories seems inaccurate, irrelevant, worn, and weird. It is time to work toward a new psychology of men.

Male Self-in-Relation Theory

I am suggesting that for men as well as women, there is a *primary desire for connection* with others, and that it is less accurate and useful to think of self than to think of self-in-relation—or even better, movement in relationship—as process. As with women, the seeds of misery in men's lives are planted in disconnection from others, isolation, violation, and dominance and from relationships that are not mutually empowering. To participate in relationships that are not mutual is a source of sadness and rage that even in the dominant gender can lead over a period of time to withdrawal, stagnation, and depression and, characteristically, insecurity, aggression, and violence. Rather than identity *before* intimacy, relationship *informs* identity in a continuous, ongoing process—the more connected, the more powerful. As Surrey (1987) has suggested, the goal of development is the increasing ability to build and enlarge mutually enhancing relationships. As the quality of relationships grow, the individual grows, in life and in psychotherapy.

Not that men's self-in-relation is the same as women's. Let us turn to the differences.

Much evidence, such as that of Daniel Stern (1985), supports the idea that men and women both come into the world not as isolated selves but as selves-in-relation to others, especially to mother. There are biological and hormonal differences between male and female infants, and there is data supporting the existence of sex differences in primitive empathic responses of neonates to other neonates. Yet the first few years of male development are probably quite similar to female development in terms of open emotional connectedness and mutual responsiveness.

There are several implications of this evidence: (1) the experience of this early connectedness *is there* in men; (2) men *do* have a notion of ways of interacting with the world that are grounded in "being-with"; and (3) men's experience of being-with is almost always carried out in a relationship with a woman—at least so far.

While babies are aware of gender identity at about the age of two, and there are some differences in early infancy, male and female development continues in a similar—and connected—manner up until about the age of three. Then, sons and mothers begin to relate to each other in a different way than do daughters and mothers—the "relational context" shifts—and the feelings and impasses that arise around this disconnection have profound implications for the rest of male relational development and for the translation of the dominant male power into the institutions of family and society. Mothers often are startled when their little boys say, as one mother told me, "I can't wait to grow up and not need you." Mothers use the same metaphor over and over to describe this process: "It's as if a wall has gone up between him and me."

Chodorow's (1978) work is relevant here. Having a perspective on self bound by classic psychoanalysis, Chodorow's work describes how, because of developmental differences, women have a looser self than men—as seen, for example, in men's firmer self-boundaries. In Freudian language, she describes the stages of development of these bounded selves, which *then* make different relationships. It is a language of the qualities of self, not of the qualities of relationship. This is very different from the language of the Stone Center, which describes continuous pathways of development based not on self but on connections, and not only on connections but on the *quali-*

ties of those connections that make for healthy growth, centered on the relational idea of mutuality: mutual empathy, mutual authenticity, and mutual empowerment.

This disconnection from the relationship with mother is a primary violation in many men's lives, and a parallel violation in the life of a mother of a son. It is like a big wave, carrying the boy along from then on, a first learning about relationship that colors his learning in other close relationships, not in stages but continuously, in the family and in the culture, with women and men both. Please note that the break is not from "the mother" that traditional theories have described and sometimes exalted, but from a mutually empathic *relationship* that happens to be with mother—from the whole relational mode of being. (For the self-psychological view, see Chapter 2.)

AN AGENT OF DISCONNECTION

Why does this disconnection occur? No one factor brings it about; rather, everything in the culture forces it to come about, in the name of "growth." Prompted by father, and the male image in the culture, the boy is heavily pressured to disconnect, to achieve maleness. Not only is he expected to turn away from mother to do this, and not only is mother told she has to support this turning away, but it is bigger than merely mother: it is a turning away from *the process of connection.* A boy is taught to become an agent of disconnection. The break is not only from connection, from mutual authenticity, but also a break from *being in the process* with a person, who happens to be a woman, and mother at that. From this model, it is clear how "mother blaming" or "the engulfing mother" or "the pre-Oedipal mother" are *not* accurate descriptions of what happens. It is not "separating from the mother," or "disconnecting from the mother," it's *a disconnecting from the very process of growth in relationship,* a learning about *turning away from the whole relational mode.*

This turning-away means that the boy never really learns *how* to do it, how to be in the process with another and grow. Unlike girls, whose relational development is grounded in the practice of attending and responding to others' feeling-states, boys do not get much practice in this arena of empathy (Jordan, 1984). Not knowing how to do it, it soon becomes avoided even more, devalued, and even its existence as a possibility denied. It seems to me that this denial may have much to do with the curious failure of traditional male theorists to speak to the depths of male experience.

A basic quality of this violation of the relational process is a declaration of *difference.* The boy begins to see that he is and must be different from mother, physically, emotionally, in his activities, perceptively, *relationally.* This focus on difference is often a kind of declaration of maleness. Difference implies comparison. Comparison implies better than or worse than and can lead to the idea of one person having power *over* another. If the difference and the conflict over difference cannot be addressed, if the relationship cannot enlarge to encompass difference or engage with difference, the door is opened for the disparagement of mother, and of the relationship with mother, and even of relationship itself.

Little boys soon learn from the culture to compare themselves to others— not only to others' penises (Stiver, 1986)—and with comparison can come competition, aggression, and perhaps violence. Western, middle-class males are often obsessed with comparison and competition. Rather than being encouraged to be in relationship, the emphasis is on becoming someone special. Compare, don't identify. The boy is placed in a terrible bind: on the one hand, he feels the pressure to disconnect for self-achievement (to be especially good at *doing* things or *fixing* things, to be competent in the world); on the other hand, he still has a strong yearning for connection. This "relational paradox" at the heart of normal male development (young boys becoming agents of disconnection to preserve themselves) is different from the "relational paradox" in normal female development described by Gilligan (1982) and Miller (1986) (adolescent girls disconnecting from their authenticity to try to maintain relationship). Becoming someone special often happens *at the expense of* "being-with," or nurturing, others. With a certain inevitability, a boy's life tilts toward trying to become someone special, or toward feeling bad if he does not. His increasing competence at doing things well may even become used in the service of "doing" disconnection well. Over time, becoming a self-in-spite-of-relationship leaves less opportunity to practice relationship. With a growing sense of competence in the world, a boy experiences a parallel sense of incompetence in the process of relationship. This disparity can lead to a sorrowful, enraging, guilty sense of "I'm not enough in relationship." And finally, in a vicious cycle of disengagement and achievement, the "I'm not enough" sense can become an impetus for further striving. The fantasy is that *by* achieving, a man will win love. For example, the "Hi Mom!" syndrome: pro football players on the sidelines after making a great play, when caught by the TV camera, invariably turn, raise an index finger to indicate they are Number One, and shout, "Hi Mom!" Striving can get in the way of living. John Lennon (1980) once said: "Life is what happens to you while you're busy making other plans."

Especially when they are in relationship, some men are in a hurry to get somewhere else, to become something else, as if they need to become something else *in order to be valued* in the relationship they are fleeing to become something else. But no achievement can win love.

From the early differences with mother, conflicts around difference are rarely addressed. Staying connected through conflict can release enormous creative energy. Yet men often wind up being deadly afraid of conflict—perhaps more so than women—so much so that they have to start fights and wars instead of engaging in it relationally. "Troops, not talks."

The boy is taught to disconnect from the relationship with mother and not to share with mother what he feels about disconnecting. More important is the boy (as quoted by Surrey, 1984) "learning not to listen, to shut out my mother's voice so that I would not be distracted from pursuing my own interests." Often the boy is taught not to listen to his mother trying to maintain connection, or to listen with a certain suspicion, and if he does listen, not to *respond* to her. When faced with mother trying to reconnect, the boy is in a terrible conflict. As one of my male patients describes it:

> I remember my mother facing me, asking me something, and my not knowing what to say. And then she got angry, or maybe she started crying. But she kept asking me, and the feeling I had, it was like she was ripping at my heart, my guts. Not only could I not say anything, but I had to steel myself against showing her any reaction. I made my face freeze, showing her no reaction, and tried my hardest not to respond, saying to myself: "Stay like this, and it will be over." I felt like something horrible might happen. I wanted desperately to respond to her, but could not, because if I said anything it would only get worse. I was in the searing spotlight of my mother's love. I froze.

Another of my male patients told me how one day, at about age seven, he was beaten up at school. He walked home along the railroad tracks crying, wanting to tell his mother. But when he walked in the door and she took a look at his face and asked, "What's the matter?" he said, "Nothing." He'd fully intended to tell her, but face to face with her, something about the relational context kept him from telling her.

If the little boy does respond to mother, it's as if he is entering a timeless, scary world where he cannot function as a man. Often the boy gets the message to devalue the mother, and women in general. When I was a boy, one of the worst nicknames you could use on your friends was to call him by his mother's name: "Hi Roz! Hey Myrna!" To be *like* mother is felt as shameful. Connecting with women now feels as if it stands in the way of competence in being a man, and connecting itself starts to feel, by definition, problematic. To whom is the boy to turn?

Father? There is a desperate need at such a time for the boy not to be different from someone but to be *like* someone. Boys are supposed to be able to start to be like father, to connect with father, to have an empathic relationship with a strong and caring father. Yet the disconnection from empathic relationship is an injury from which the father himself is recovering. He too has learned not to listen—or to listen with a certain suspicion—and if he does listen, not to respond. What the father is often worst at teaching—and thinks he values least—is movement in relationship. In studies quoted by Osherson (1987), fathers interacted with their children, in the first three months, an average of 37 seconds per day; at nine months, their interaction is in the range of one hour. Father's role often is to show a son how to become a better agent of disconnection from relationship, especially from that with mother, to "be a big boy, and big boys don't cry." Father may also push mother to disengage. Fathers are often described as "distant" or "absent"—out of relationship—and so remain a mystery. Being mysterious, they can be made larger than life—a "hero," stimulating for a boy the heroic journey—or smaller than life, a "wimp." Rarely are they allowed to be life-sized, merely and authentically human, in Mary Watkins's (personal communication, April 18, 1990) wonderful phrase, "leading normal-sized lives." Father-son is bittersweet (see Levant, Chapter 8).

Making authentic relationships with life-sized fathers is important. There are some wonderful fathers, especially these days, and sometimes the relationship works. Much has been written about father-son relationships recently (for instance, Gerzon, 1982; Nelson, 1988; and Osherson, 1987). Fathers do have special relationships with sons and can teach them how to be effective in the world, play fair, be a team member as well as a leader, uphold moral principles, and form deep bonds with other men and boys, bonds of friendship, loyalty, and love. Yet for all the strengths of the father-son relationship, it is less easy for fathers to interact around emotions, and the process of interaction is quite different from that of mothers and sons, based less on affective give-and-take, continuity, and working through conflict and difference to mutual empowerment. Even when the father-son relationship works, it works in valuing independence and action, in learning to do things out in the world. Often it emphasizes "success" and what a boy does—not who a boy is, rarely who a boy is with others, and almost never who a boy is *mutually* with others.

And while fathers may be able to help consolidate in the boy a sense of maleness and self-worth, based on learning how to relate through sameness, the father may have difficulty in showing his son how to relate, through difference, with mother, with women in general, or even sometimes with other class and ethnic groups.

The boy also learns about relationship from the relationship between mother and father. Not only are we all born into relationship, but we are almost always born into relationships. (Of course, the crucial relationships into which a child is born vary tremendously, family to family and culture to culture.) The boy has an always-present, intense example of the male-female relationship before his eyes. He watches it continuously, observing how the relationship reflects on each participant and moves in time, and he himself participates in the relationship and its reflections. If this main example of how men and women relate is filled with misunderstandings, power struggles, violence, abuse, and unresolved impasses and disconnections, the boy may come to see this as the normal way and/or may come to not expect much in relationship. If a boy feels inadequate in relationship with his mother and with his father separately, and if the mother-father relationship does not appear pleasurable to mimic in action, the boy's quest for self-achievement, out of relationship, may be spurred on. The yearning for both father and mother, and the yearning for relationship in general, may become shut off and denied. Men may wind up unaware of this yearning for connection—or aware only of a dimly sensed yearning for this yearning.

The yearning is not just for connection with others but also for connection with self—"self-empathy," in Jordan's (1984) words. Disconnecting is "learning not to listen" to self and/or other's feeling-states. This may leave the boy less motivated to attend to, or to try to find out about, his own and/or other people's internal worlds—what Surrey calls the "interiority" of experience. Over time, a boy's active curiosity about another person's feeling-states may diminish. The sense of "interiority" itself may become devalued and denied.

OUT IN THE WORLD: CONNECTIONS, DISCONNECTIONS, AND VIOLATIONS

Very often boys find connections out in the world or connect to their own creative fire in isolation. Seven-year-old boys playing together as buddies is a wonderful sight—the enthusiasm between them as they fashion games together, the sense of well-being, the relief at finding a pal. (One of Hollywood's sure moneymakers is the "buddy" story.) Boys find friends and playmates (Harry Stack Sullivan's "chums") and have adventures out in the world. The boys' side of the playground could hardly be more different from the girls', with the boys playing games and sports in leader-follower groups, including the game "war." Gilligan's (1982) work on gender difference in childhood moral reasoning is relevant here. Action is the name of the game. Yet the charm of buddies does not last long: Ask any man about his boyhood and you will hear hair-raising stories filled with incredible cruelty, violence, and daily terror. Boyhood is not a "latency" in any sense of that word.

At worst, in response to the jolt of shifting the relational context from mother-connection to father-disconnection, the boy feels hurt and that something is wrong. Jean Baker Miller points out that anger is often a sign of a person feeling hurt or that something is wrong and that it can be a healthy and motivating force if it can be worked on in relationship (Miller & Surrey, 1990). If it can be worked on with father or mother, it can bring the boy more into relationship. If not, it can turn into aggression and violence, or isolation.

The more isolated boy may turn to the inner world, creating stories or pictures or models. This inner world can be romanticized, as it has been in writers (an acquaintance of Kafka, spotting him at a café, asked, "Mind if I join you?" to which Kafka said, "Yes") and scientists (Einstein, at six, was thought to be retarded; later he would say, "I now bask in the solitude which was so painful in my youth").

No discussion of men's development can ignore male violence or male power. Male violence is epidemic; women are often the victims. In the breakdown of relationship, violence flourishes. The more efficient an agent of disconnection a person becomes, the more potential he holds for violence. What is missing from many theories of male development is a power analysis: men denying they have power over women, and men's reaction to the widespread sexual abuse of girls and women and young boys. A primary violation in women's lives is the early realization that men are strong and can hurt, physically and sexually. Little girls pick up the violence in a lack of connection—as subtle as a look in a man's eyes, a sexual objectification. Little boys often notice this fear in little girls. Boys learn not only to enjoy their physical power but to fear it.

The last thing men can talk about with each other is their feeling about their potential for sexual violence. Often it is not part of their awareness. For example, one day at my swim club I was walking toward the whirlpool wearing only my bathing suit. A woman in the whirlpool turned, saw me, and I saw in her eyes a sudden fear of men, of a man. That look made me realize how deeply women carry this fear, all the time.

While men are taught that they have power and are supposed to act powerfully, men may sense women's fear of it. Men too are afraid of it, in themselves and in other men. In a patriarchy, men may also be victims. Hierarchy means that there is always someone more successful and more powerful. Men are haunted by failure; the biggest winners are potentially the biggest losers. In a power-over model, it is not safe to take an authentic, vulnerable, relational stance. In such systems, relationship can be seen as a threat to power. While a man may find it easy to use power from a narcissistic stance, knocking other people over, it is difficult for him to use power in relationship. Men come to think that sensitivity to the welfare of others drains power and is hazardous. Men may start to conceive that the opposite of vigor and power is wimpiness. The larger struggle is how to express power in relationship.

The question of power in relationship is complex: Physical power, cultural power, and economic power may be more in the province of men, while emotional power and relational power may be more in the province of women.

And so the main arc of men's development: After disconnection from mother, and after engaging in an independence-based relationship with father, the boy makes his way in the world. Boys seek out boy friends, and then girl friends. Mentors come along, usually male, although mentor relationships, mostly being one-way and nonmutual, often end in power-over violations, as often happens between men. Agents of disconnection learn how to disconnect others, and how to twist themselves out of relationship, to "succeed." Men move into marriage and parenthood, which may open them up to the powerful and creative forces of connection that have been masked for years. Some men do seem to get their needs met by women, in traditional marriages, but that is different from participating in a mutual relationship. Moreover, women's needs, in traditional relational structures, are subordinate.

What are the strengths of men-in-relation? In our workshops, women answering that question use phrases such as "caretakers," "deep loyalties," "relationship through action, through projects, through doing," "lifting heavy objects," "rational thinking," "focusing on one thing at a time," "honesty," "directness," "can let things go and move on to other things," "breadwinners," "protectors," "know how to deal with fear," "alliance builders," "not so overwhelmed by feelings," "strategic," "product-makers," "purposeful," "killing spiders," and "frisky about sex."

What are the qualities of male relationship? Although men say they want to be in contact and have love and support and feel that they can love, I think men *do not feel good* about this whole process in the same sense that it does feel good to women—at least not without new learning and practice. For all the reasons I've suggested, men do not engage with pleasure in back-and-forth movement, continuity, interchange, flow, process, bringing out others, mutuality, or dialogue as opposed to debate. There is little holding of the relational moment. While men can feel connection in the moment, they often deflect it—joking, shifting their attention, physicalizing it—breaking the tension of connection, fragmenting the process temporally. Men also tend to fragment work from home, in ways that women do less often. For instance, two breakthroughs in my relationship with Janet were (a) learning to think about her during the day and call her up with no purpose in mind other than to make contact ("I just called to say hello and to stay in touch") and (b) learning to say, "I was thinking about what we were talking about yesterday." My women patients have taught me that women want to feel men are engaged actively and with continuity in the process of relationship.

Men throughout their lives are left with a dim sense of wanting to connect, yes. But actually to be in relationship, to engage in self-with-other experience, is a different thing. What prevents it?

Male Relational Dread

At one point in our workshop, men and women sit facing each other on opposite sides of the room. The men, forced to sit still and interact with the women, are invariably—and almost immediately—surprised to find that they share an unspoken, common, familiar sense in close relationships: the sense of dread. When we asked one man what was wrong, he said, "I'm afraid that *something might happen.*" It is astonishing for men to identify this sense of dread and to discover that it is shared. This realization brings much relief.

Male relational dread is a process. It arises in the intensity of relationship, mostly with women. In the example from *Fine* and in the two clinical vignettes, the man and boy are facing a woman who invites a response from the man on a feeling level, often in this way:

WOMAN: "What are you feeling?"
(*Pause. Silence from the man.*)
WOMAN: "Can you tell me?"
MAN: "I don't know."
WOMAN: "Sure you do. Please, talk to me."

At this point the man may take evasive action, falling silent, changing the subject, yawning, striking out with anger or sarcasm, or making a rapid exit, sometimes into the newspaper. What is going on?

Well, what is going on is a man becoming overwhelmed with a deep sense of dread, a visceral sense, literally in the gut, or heart. Invitation starts to seem like demand, urgency and curiosity like criticism. The more the woman comes forward, offering to explore things relationally, the more the man feels dread and wants to *avoid things relationally*. (Couples and family therapists have described this process but have not described the relational dread.) In the words of a woman friend, women's experience in this process is: "Men don't give women enough information to keep them from going crazy."

What is men's experience in this scene? First of all, men do listen, at least until dread takes over. Second, men do have feelings and are often able to sort out what the feelings are, although this may take some time—that's the "pause." Unfortunately, women often seem to be on a different time, as the man is still sorting out what he feels, she may ask again, "Can you tell me?" This makes the man feel pressure, and his "I don't know"—or even "I don't know, I'll tell you tomorrow"—can be an attempt at buying time to stay focused on what he feels and to say it—in fact, to attempt to stay in relationship. But then when the woman asks again—"Sure you do; please, talk to me," the man's original feeling gets mixed up with the feeling of being under pressure to respond. In this third aspect of relating—response—things really begin to fall apart. Dread starts to take over, rising from the gut, and things get increasingly fuzzy, such that feelings become blurred and homogenized into a wish to escape—even further listening becomes difficult. Note that this is not "the engulfing mother"; rather, it describes *the warp in the relational context*. We are in the wasteland of the negatives of Jean Baker Miller's (1986) five aspects of healthy connection. Things come to a dead stop. The relationship goes flat. The process of dread is relational, not only intrapsychic. While there is, as always, a transferential component, relational dread is not merely a "maternal transference." Dread arises not from the woman reminding the man of his mother but from his being in a relational process where complex things are happening fast on both sides, a dynamic in which one relational style is meeting another, quite different one. At issue is *the process of relationship,* not the person, real or transferential. A man's dread is the result of "negative learnings," over and over again, about the process of relationship. In the previous example of the boy walking up the railroad tracks, it was when he found himself in the process of relationship that his intention to tell of his pain was overwhelmed by his dread.

What are the experiential aspects of this process of relational dread?

1. Inevitability of disaster: Nothing good can come of my going into this, it's just a question of how bad it will be before it's over.
2. Timelessness: It will never be over; an eternity would be too brief.
3. Damage: The damage will be immense, and irreparable.
4. Closeness: The closer I feel to the woman—even, the more I love her—the more intense my dread becomes.
5. Precariousness: Even if it starts to dissipate and clear and feel better, it can turn at any moment back to dread, betraying me.
6. Process: It is a shifting time-warp terrain, a movement in relationship with few fixed landmarks, a way of being in which I, a man, am unsure even of the validity of my perceptions, let alone my "being with" another person while I'm in it. In this quickly forward-moving process, I can't find a firm foothold in myself, and I'm scared something out of control may happen. It seems that male perceptivity and "set" have become more attuned to stasis than movement. The concept and practice of process has been made difficult for men.
7. Guilt: I am not enough. I have not been enough in these relationships before, I feel I have let women down all along, and am guilty about that.
8. Denial and fear of aggression: If I am trapped, pushed too far, and unable to withdraw or leave, I might panic and get violent and hurt someone, as I have done in the past, either by disconnecting or by taking physical action. Rather than engage in this conflict, I'd better leave or be nice. As one man said in our workshop: "I feel like I'm all dressed up in my power with nowhere to go." As a woman patient of mine put it: "He wants it nice; I want it real."
9. Incompetence and shame: All my life I have been taught that I have to be competent in the world, and in this I don't feel competent. She is better at this than I am, verbally and relationally—not only does she know the territory in general better, but she seems to know *me* better than I know myself. I could focus on one thing at a time, but this is many things, all mixed together, and vague things at that. From a workshop: "She insists we talk about violence and patriarchy and our relationship, all at once! It's baffling!"

   I'm ashamed at my incompetence—I ought to be able to function in this, but cannot. I ought to be able to take action, to *fix* the flat tire of this relationship. And before I can say anything, I have to be *sure* of what I am going to say. Usually I can go off by myself and get sure first, but here I cannot, I have to be accurate. Here again, a gender difference: When something goes wrong in relationship, women often feel, "I am wrong"; men feel, "I should be able to fix it" (see also Chapter 4).

10. Paralysis: As each of these things comes up, my dread is redoubled. Trying to fix things, under the pressure of feeling I *have* to fix things, fast, I fumble things even more. From our workshops it has become clear that it is men's feeling that they have to fix the relational impasse that may prevent them from responding at all, or even from acknowledging the impasse: If I can't fix it, I won't say anything at all. And fix it *well:* In one workshop, when the men started to talk about their experience, a woman responded enthusiastically, "A+!" At that, all of us men fell silent, withdrawing—it was male dread in action. As the women, curious, moved forward relationally, asking questions about the men's experience, the men felt and described the women's questions as "bullets," "arrows," or "darts." The men—sometimes with good reason—did not trust the women to let go of their images of men and to accept male vulnerability.

And so, through these various aspects of dread, even though a man may desperately want connection, he again becomes an agent of disconnection. Men often respond by putting a stop to the process—withdrawing, striking out, tuning out, changing the subject, joking, being nice, falling silent. Men also resort to "station identification"—talking at some length about themselves and where they place themselves in the world, their status: "I'm senior vice-president at ———," etc. Under the influence of alcohol or drugs, violence may be the response. Women feel shut out. In the words of one woman:

> When you want to talk about it, they get this glazed look, they look at you like you're a vegetable in a market. When you keep at it, they start to look at you like you're the enemy. You say, "Yoo-hoo, it's me—remember me? Your friend? How did I get to be the enemy? I mean things were fine—what happened?" It makes me feel like a Martian in relation to men. But it makes me feel sorry for them, too.

Another woman put it this way: "It's like when you're pedaling fast on your bicycle and suddenly the chain slips off, and you're left pedaling hard, going nowhere."

In our workshops, while men start out with the dread that "something might happen," women start out with *curiosity* about what men have to say about male experience, they *hope* "something might happen." Again, stasis as opposed to process, a classic impasse. Deborah Tannan (1990) describes the verbal impasses between men and women brilliantly and with scrupulous fairness. Yet if the goal of talking is the caretaking and growth of the relationship, it is not accurate to portray men and women as having separate but equal skill and power. They rarely do.

Culturally, men may come to sense that facing into things with others is futile. I am amazed, in teaching medical students, that by their final year they have bought the notion that facing pain and suffering with patients is draining and must be avoided, even though this is what they went into medicine to do. The process of male relational dread, repeated over and over through men's development, works against male growth-in-relationship. Men's curiosity about relationship—even men's curiosity about other people—can become deadened.

THE POTENTIAL FOR GROWTH AT MIDLIFE

Often, self-out-of-relation serves men well in the world through their twenties, and perhaps their thirties, when relationships become more complex—as long as no major life-crisis happens to strike. And yet, if, as in relational theory, connection is primary to healthy growth and isolation is the killer, the "normal" male way takes men only so far, petering out in the voguish "midlife crisis" in the late thirties and early forties, when men start to fall apart. We men are told to create our lives, our work—even, in a sense, our loves—in isolation, and then our isolation kills us. In midlife men may sense a loss of meaning, an emptiness, loneliness, failure, rage, sadness—all leading to further isolation, stagnation and stasis, and depression. Suddenly, for such men, trying to make deep and meaningful connection with others becomes very important, even as important as their work. If at that time a man cannot open up to exploring the possibility of connection, he may revert to old ways of "relating": buying a sports car, dating a 20-year-old, trying to be virile and powerful. Terrible things may happen: drink or drugs, harmful affairs, workaholism, suicide, neglect and violation of loved ones—and if in positions of power, neglect and violation of other members of society or of other nations. In this crisis, men may use sexuality to try to connect; they can be surprised to find that women may need connection to be fully sexual.

On the other hand, if at that more receptive time of men's lives the yearning for connection is nurtured, amazing things can happen: They may go into therapy, where they may begin to address the relational conflicts and differences instead of stopping them; they may try to reconnect with their children, wives, fathers, and mothers (roughly in that order); and they may try to deal with their abuse of substances by joining Alcoholics Anonymous or similar groups. In a *mutual* help organization such as AA, in my experience, the men who make it are those who, despite almost everything in their nature calling them to stay isolated, go *against* their nature and move toward others, asking for help. (One of AA's slogans is "Identify, don't compare.") By caring for sick and suffering parents, spouses, children, or others, men may open more fully to attending and responding to feelings, empathically and mutually. Men may also turn to spiritual pursuits, even have spiritual awakenings. Tremendous creativity and power-*with*-others can be unleashed to replace power-over. Priorities can shift: Men who have always had vague or hidden concerns about the wholeness of life on the planet can start joining with others in peace or ecological movements. All this can happen.

And yet, however much a man may seek out others, in a nagging, subtle way he may still be seeking to have his own needs met, rather than learning the shift to engaging in mutuality—mutual empathy, empowerment, and authenticity. Moving toward connection with a new openness may inflame the process of relational dread, for the quest for connection is almost always for connection with women. At this time of life, men find that women's power is exactly what they desire: *relational* power, power-with. Not only do women seem to know how to connect, but they also seek it out and actually *enjoy* it. All the old feelings can arise, with new ones added, such as anger at feeling vulnerable to women's emotional and relational power. Men may experience women as so powerful in relationship that they may not be able to figure out what women mean when they complain of being victims; men can feel overpowered and victimized too—something women may find hard to understand. In any nonmutual, power-over system, each participant—even the privileged and dominant—feels like a victim sometimes. And yet, as one man said in our workshop, "Men want relationship, sure, but the bottom line is we don't want to give up our power to get it."

Summary

I believe that it is possible for men to participate in non-self-centered, mutual relationships and to grow in connection. Vast numbers of men now are trying to do this. I believe we are talking here about the creative spirit—a genderless spirit—as evidenced in relationship: collaborative, co-creative, at work together. As a writer, I have come to believe that the creative process is a non-ego, non-self-limited state. This is much the same process that takes place in successful psychotherapy, or in any other healing encounter in life. This creative process can be nonverbal and is seen in times of awe, love, shock, sorrow, and enlightenment. Men desperately want this quality of self-in-relation and in dark times kill themselves or destroy others over their failure to get it. It is not that we men do not have this yearning, it is that the yearning is tied up with our dread. Many of us want to move from the comparative, competitive mind to the relational mind. There is a real split now in men, reflecting the split in the world: between those who would keep on with the old, outdated institutions that are destroying our planet and those who, at a grass-roots level, in relationships and groups, are taking action to change things. The key is in traveling the mutual and creative way—letting self be created in relationship—that is at the heart of all healthy human growth.

What about men's relationships with men? From the 1960s on, women have gotten together with women, and the effect has been truly revolutionary, transforming world consciousness—not only about women's experience but, for the first time in history, about the prevalence of childhood sexual abuse—and shifting attention to women's strengths, which had been seen as weaknesses. Lately, mirroring this process, many of what have been seen as men's strengths are being revealed as weaknesses: competitiveness and aggressiveness, independence and separateness and self-sufficiency, non-emotionality, the ability to block things out and not be affected or deterred from one's goal, toughness. Men are now getting together with men. This is of value, and I applaud the sharing of grief and loss and the healing of male-male wounds that can take place. Yet there are disturbing concerns. Men have been getting together with men for thousands of years—it's the most usual thing for men to do, however current the focus. Of the various different groupings of human beings, however, men alone in groups have proven historically the most dangerous. Two aspects of modern male groups concern me.

First is the idea popularized by Robert Bly that America in the 1980s was populated by "soft males," and his assertion that "we're ready to start seeing the wildman and to put his powerful dark energy to use" (Nelson, 1988, p. 11). While this "dark energy" may help men in "finding a strong and caring father," it has not aided the paradigm shift to finding strong and caring *relationships*, to the two-way, mutual process at the core of healthy growth.

Much of the writing on men's psychological development has focused on the old issues of men's "role" and men's "identity." (See, for example, Pleck's [1981] thorough critique of male sex role identity theory.) Seldom is the question framed in the relational way: What are men's relational roles or relational identities? Often when this question is raised, men, feeling criticized and defensive, say, "But I have good relationships with men—my friend and I can be out fishing for a whole day and not talk much, but it's a good relationship." And yet these same men, when asked, admit that "with my wife it's different—both of us can really open up and talk. I feel she really understands me." When this happens—and it is almost always with a woman—men recognize how good it feels to be in mutual empathic relationship. This desire for mutuality may be hard to bring to the surface of men's awareness and may come out directly only when it is irretrievably lost, or when men, almost despite themselves, find themselves experiencing it, or when they see women having it with their women friends, see that it is missing in their own lives, and sense a deep lonely yearning for connection. It is crucial at this moment in history that we men not let our dread deny us the opportunity to learn, from women and men both.

The part mutuality plays in male-male relationships has not been addressed. Jean Baker Miller, in her paper "What Do We Mean by Relationships?" (1986), lists five aspects of healthy connection: "increased zest, increased sense of self-worth, increased knowledge of self and other, increased empowerment of all parties to act, and a desire for more connection." Men often say that an example of good male relationship is a sports team, which may in fact exhibit these five qualities. Yet team relationships are limited in continuity—conversations tend not to continue after the game is over—and by the team purpose in being formed: to perform a task, with competence, against another team. Also, a team usually has a captain and a hierarchical structure; many connections and conversations happen in the service of carrying out orders given by the teammate with the expertise or power. The back-and-forth flow of dialogue, which more easily generates a sense of mutuality, may be missing. Also missing may be dialogue around feelings. Studies quoted by Tannen (1990) suggest that from an early age conversation reflects tremendous gender differences in such elements of interaction as eye contact, the give-and-take of dialogue, and *mutual* exploration of experience.

I must emphasize again that I am not talking about all men, at all times, in all cultures. Some men are quite able to be in relationship mutually, and some women are quite unable. And yet there are patterns and facts that, in general, are undeniable: When we speak about relationship as mutual—in terms of mutual empathy (in Surrey's [1984] words, "'feeling seen' by the other and seeing the other and sensing the other 'feeling seen'"), mutual authenticity, and mutual empowerment—the process of caring for the relationship and participating actively and with active curiosity in the development of other people in relationship, the genders are not of equal skill and motivation. We men are not taught to be caretakers of relational processes and contexts in the way that women are. This does not mean that men have not been taught to be caretakers in other ways—men have numerous and clear strengths, which I have elaborated in detail. From our workshops, we have seen that when men are motivated, they can learn to participate in the relational process in mutual ways. However, if the focus is on mutual relationship, we men have a lot to learn.

Often men will respond to these ideas by saying: "We men relate, it's just different from the way women do it. Women are not better at it—why should we try to do it their way? You're asking that we men become like women. You want the *feminization* of relationship."

This is not what is being suggested here. Men have strengths, as mentioned above, but we have yet to see men's strengths brought fully into relationship. This process has not been taught or valued in us. We men need to break out of the tired concept of separation/individuation and strong independent male role and identity as prelude to relationship and learn about mutual relationship, which means not only developing it in ourselves but fostering it in others. What is being suggested here is not the "feminization" of men but the "relationalization" of all, men and women both. If, in our culture, this process is called "feminization," we are all in big trouble.

The second aspect of modern male groups that concerns me is that sending men off into the woods alone, à la Bly, will not, by itself, lead to something new; we must also bring men back into relationship with women. In our workshops, we first split the men and women into gender groups. In my work with the men, it is clear that they are comfortable with each other—there is a lot of laughing and finding common experience. It is in the next step, when the genders face each other across the room, that the conflicts through difference arise, the feelings deepen, and the vital work—inevitably moving through the process of male dread and female anger, toward mutuality—gets done. Men blossom in the workshop. Usually they have been brought by women, and being there under duress, they start out skeptical and negative. By the end the women are amazed at how intelligent, sensitive, and actively perceptive men are about relationships—but men blossom only after being forced to face their common *and* individual differences in relationship with women.

No amount of us men learning how to be warriors alone together or jumping out of airplanes alone together or seeing our fathers as human-sized will help us learn to relate to women, or perhaps even learn what is meant by "mutual." Male-male work, if it stays male-male, may fragment energy and deflect power, seeding violence and destruction in the process.

The missing piece, the learning and empowering piece, is to do that which is *new* to our age: bringing men and women back from their enclaves into the creative space called relationship.

The key to this is working, in the present, on the energy contained in the events of that fork in the past, when most of us men—not by choice, mind you—faced with profound difference and the conflict engendered in that difference, rather than walking through it with others and finding the creative power in that conflict and difference and moving into a power-with way of living, deflected the conflict, polarized the difference, set the obsessions of comparison running in our heads, and hurried on full tilt toward the vague rewards we were promised somewhere else than in the mutual relationship that had nourished us, much as it had nourished our sisters. And yet it is a miracle of human evolution that it is always in the present moment, and that when people truly get together, *it can help.* The experience of connecting mutually is there in men and women both, and for both it is deeply linked with the relationship with a woman. Both men and women have experienced violations that interfere with healthy mutual relationships. The creative energy that can be liberated when men and women work with conflict and difference is profound. It seems to me that the real hope for living in harmony and wholeness in the world is that liberation. After all, "something might happen." In shifting the paradigm from self/other to relationship, we are entering the realm of the common good. From there, it is a short step to global awareness and action.

References

Chodorow, N. (1978). *The reproduction of mothering.* Berkeley: University of California Press.

Erikson, E. (1963). *Childhood and society.* New York: Norton.

Gerzon, M. (1982). *A choice of heroes.* Boston: Houghton Mifflin.

Gilligan, C. (1982). *In a different voice.* Cambridge, MA: Harvard University Press.

Jordan, J. (1984). *Empathy and self-boundaries* (Stone Center Working Paper Series, Work in Progress No. 16). Wellesley, MA: Wellesley College, Stone Center.

Jordan, J., Kaplan, S., Miller, J., Stiver, I., & Surrey, J. (1991). *Women's growth in connection.* New York: Guilford Press.

Kernberg, O. (1976). *Object-relations theory and clinical psychoanalysis.* New York: Jason Aronson.

Kohut, H. (1977). *The restoration of the self.* New York: International Universities Press.

Lennon, J. (1980). "Beautiful Boy." *Double Fantasy* [sound recording]. David Geffen Co./Lenono Music (BMI).

Mahler, M. (1975). *The psychological birth of the human infant.* New York: Basic Books.

Miller, J. B. (1983). *The construction of anger in women and men* (Stone Center Working Paper Series, Work in Progress No. 4). Wellesley, MA: Wellesley College, Stone Center.

Miller, J. B. (1986). *What do we mean by relationships?* (Stone Center Working Paper Series, Work in Progress No. 22). Wellesley, MA: Wellesley College, Stone Center.

Miller, J. B., & Surrey, J. (1990). *Revisioning women's anger: The personal and the global* (Stone Center Working Paper Series, Work in Progress No. 43). Wellesley, MA: Wellesley College, Stone Center.

Nelson, J. B. (1988). *The intimate connection.* Philadelphia: Westminster Press.

Osherson, S. (1987). *Finding our fathers.* New York: Fawcett Columbine.

Pleck, J. (1981). *The myth of masculinity.* Cambridge, MA: MIT Press.

Shem, S. (1978). *The house of God.* New York: Dell.

Shem, S. (1985). *Fine.* New York: Dell.

Stern, D. (1985). *The interpersonal world of the infant.* New York: Basic Books.

Stiver, I. (1986). *Beyond the Oedipus complex: Mothers and daughters* (Stone Center Working Paper Series, Work in Progress No. 26). Wellesley, MA: Wellesley College, Stone Center.

Surrey, J. (1984). *The "self-in-relation": A theory of women's development* (Stone Center Working Paper Series, Work in Progress No. 13). Wellesley, MA: Wellesley College, Stone Center.

Surrey, J. (1987). *Relationship and empowerment* (Stone Center Working Paper Series, Work in Progress No. 30). Wellesley MA: Wellesley College, Stone Center.

Tannen, D. (1990). *You just don't understand.* New York: Morrow.

CHAPTER 4

Male Development and the Transformation of Shame

STEVEN KRUGMAN

Introduction

Knowledge follows the need to know; all interest is somehow subjective and personal. Thus, "when an analyst publishes a 'psychoanalytic' book he reveals a fragment of himself" (McDougal, 1987, p. 1). So, too, in my writing about men and shame, why is it I have needed to know so much about this feeling called shame?[1]

I could tell you about the many facets of my own shame, which began as an uncomfortable self-consciousness about myself as shy and my body as chubby. Later I struggled with intensely disquieting feelings toward my parents—I was embarrassed by them and their behavior. My mother's anxiety about my growing independence caused me humiliation on more than one occasion. For a time my family's blue-collar values in a white-collar community were a source of shame; I experienced considerable envy of my affluent peers. As an adolescent, I worried about the adequacy of my physique, my athletic abilities, and my sexuality. The fear that I didn't (or wouldn't) measure up I now recognize as shame. Later, as cancer consumed my proud father's body and spirit, I saw and felt his shame at being helpless to stop the relentless progress of the disease that daily diminished him.

My developmental encounters with shameful feelings and their related states have been part and parcel of my growing up to become the kind of man I can like, respect, and be proud of. Part of this process involved the discovery that talking about the things I feel bad about leaves me feeling less bad. But first I needed to overcome my fear that to admit to shame is in itself

[1] I would like to express my appreciation to Lisa Machoian, M.A., Martin Krugman, Ph.D., and Anne Alonso, Ph.D., for their support and assistance in the preparation of this chapter.

shameful. (Even writing these words, with full confidence that they describe a near-universal set of concerns, I wonder whether others will patronize my confession and secretly look down on me as flawed, and whether the man I wanted to be could really have had feelings such as these.) Still, I began to recognize that acknowledging feelings related to shame, rather than driving others away, draws them in and opens dialogue with both men and women. Indeed, other men—even the unlikely ones—welcome the opportunity to let down their bravura and talk about feeling afraid or unsure. Personally, I learned that acknowledging and sharing shameful secrets diminishes self-hatred and facilitates connections with others.

One irony in this process of self-development was that my own psycho-analytic psychotherapy focused almost exclusively on classic Oedipal concerns—competition with my father for my mother's love. There was little or no recognition of my other anxieties related to fears and ambivalence regarding independence and worries about adequacy. Morrison (1989, p. x) writes of a similar experience.

When I began to read the emerging shame literature, I knew I had identified an important context for my own developmental experience. Many disparate pieces fell together. My feelings throughout childhood, along with my desire for a safer encounter with my therapist, took on a different meaning. It was not guilt I felt at wanting my father's wife, but shame over needing more contact and reassurance from him and others in the process of becoming a man. Recognizing the pivotal role of shame in my own life gave me a framework for talking about my intuitive and successful work with many men in psychotherapy. Men were more likely to stay in treatment if I remembered that humiliation was always close at hand, an ever-present danger to their newly exposed, often fragile, selves. I found that I modified my therapeutic stance to minimize narcissistic injury and to avoid leaving them feeling isolated and under scrutiny for their faults.

The convergence of personal knowledge, therapeutic experience, and theoretical development leads to the need for a revised view of shame's role in male development. This view has two critical elements: one, understanding how shame functions and facilitates the integration of self, both with itself and with the social world; and two, recognizing and understanding that shame states are particularly problematic for males. The development of this perspective leads to a reconsideration of the function of shame in the management of interpersonal aggression and intimacy.

Shame in Men's Lives

Shame plays a prominent but unspoken role in men's lives. Nearly all men have deep personal knowledge of shame but go to great lengths to avoid letting it show or be known. Indeed, male culture is shame-phobic (Wright, 1987). Shame is a familiar childhood experience. It can begin with being teased for playing a girls' game or for being "chicken," and it becomes the companion of every soldier who, facing battle, dreads his own terror and the possibility that his unmanly fear will cause him to act like a coward. Boy culture is competitive, insensitive, and often cruel. Being chosen last, or not at all, is a vivid memory for many men. Being picked on, afraid to fight, or forced to fight generates a welter of intense feelings, with shame at the core. "Talking trash," "doing the dozens," and "sounding out others" show boys teasing and jostling each other in mock verbal combat so they can learn to "take it" and "give it" without being "gotten to" (de Jong, 1993). Such "combat" is vital preparation for young adult manhood. The emergence of sexuality and bodily concerns brings with it a host of shame-related experiences, from the embarrassment of premature ejaculation to fears of being "too small" or not being able to "get it up."

Feelings of inadequacy and inferiority, of emotional neediness and insecurity, are part of every man's experience. Pleck (1981; Chapter 1) argues that rigid, narrow gender norms, which reflect a traditional and idealized notion of masculinity, generate "sex role strain." Every man experiences feelings of inadequacy and inferiority and a sense of neediness and insecurity. These standards leave many boys and men feeling that they do not "measure up," that they do not fit into the male world. For minority males, coping with the stigma of racism and discrimination adds an additional burden of socially induced shame to the normative quantum of shame that is every man's. Social stigma also compounds the developmental burden for gay males, whose atypical gender experience generates significant shame, self-hatred, and despair (see Chapter 11).

Shame signals vulnerability, difference, exposure, and loss of control. When the process of shame socialization is adaptive, boys learn how to manage themselves in relation to authority, peers, and intimate others. But when it is disrupted by developmental and gender role pressures or by psychological trauma, males have a particularly difficult time integrating shame-based experience. Male gender role strain (Pleck, 1981) expresses itself in a variety of ways. In discussing shame in male development, it is useful to recognize that (a) shame is an innate response tendency that (b) has the adaptive function of sensitizing the individual to his or her status/connection with others; that (c) shame functions in normal and pathological development; and that (d) shame plays a formidable and problematic role in normative male development. The *normative* male stance refers to common and nonpathological tendencies among men in response to socialization expectations. Normative male socialization relies heavily on the aversive power of shame to shape acceptable male behavior and attitudes and leaves many boys extremely shame-sensitive. It tends not to foster the maturation and integration of shame responses. Alongside the many ways in which boys and men respond adaptively and creatively to the evolving demands of contemporary life are male tendencies toward social and emotional isolation, patterns of compulsive work and substance abuse, and an alarming growth in the use of aggression to handle social and emotional conflict.

When the integrative and socializing functions of shame are inhibited, exaggerated, or otherwise derailed, boys compensate by masking their insecurities, creating the appearance of control, and developing substitute behaviors that externalize their concerns. Boys who endure significant loss and disruption of family life are likely to develop pervasive characterological rigidities to cope with a faltering sense of self and an unstable sense of male identity. When shame is undischarged and unconscious, dysfunctional character disorders may arise.

Male difficulties with intimacy and with parenting—especially following divorce—can be usefully understood in terms of how hard it is to handle vulnerable and exposed states that generate shameful feelings. Alcohol—which disinhibits and, in a sense, dissolves acute shame—is a gender-linked response to the pressures that arise from close contact with important others or from perfectionistic demands upon the self. Compulsive patterns of behavior, such as workaholism, overcommitment to exercise routines, gambling, or perverse sexuality, derive their considerable power from their effectiveness in minimizing and controlling shameful states of feeling, often by numbing and dissociating the painful affect. Domestic violence—particularly wife battering—is in large measure a shame-driven interpersonal pattern in which feelings of dependency, abandonment anxiety, and humiliation threaten men with psychological disorganization (Lansky, 1992).

CONTEMPORARY SHAME THEORY

Emerging shame theory offers a unique vantage point from which to better understand the contemporary male predicament. A revised view of shame and its role in self-regulation and social integration sheds light on the male struggle to cope with feelings and experiences of psychological vulnerability, on the one hand, and aggression, on the other. The male predicament can be expressed in terms of a polarity. One pole is deeply rooted in traditional "social representations" (Campbell, 1993) that orient males toward issues of aggression and competition with other males. To succeed in this realm, psychological vulnerabilities of all kinds must be mastered and controlled, including feelings associated with early developmental anxiety states: separation anxiety, dependent yearnings, and fears of injury and danger. The lessons of male socialization teach that these self-experiences must be concealed from other males to inhibit scapegoating and aggression and to maintain status in the group. Ultimately, the best way to conceal vulnerability is to conceal it from oneself. Shame avoidance accomplishes both. At the other pole rests the pressure of these very same needs and the wish to be nurtured, to be free of fear, and to be safely connected and well regarded. To complicate matters further, males of all ages find themselves adapting to a changing reality in which they are encouraged, even required, to draw upon psychological knowledge and interpersonal skills based in these highly conflictual needs. Failure to integrate shame-based experiences inhibits the development of these attitudes and skills.

The male role in American society is undergoing a slow transformation, as has occurred during other epochs in our cultural history (Rotundo, 1993). Whereas traditional role divisions between males and females allowed for relatively clear expectations that were shared throughout the culture, contemporary expectations with respect to gender roles are far more diverse. Economic and social realities increasingly require most men to redefine their historical identification with work and share their status as wage earners with their wives. Increasingly, men are asked to develop the skills necessary to participate more fully as fathers and householders. As the world of work demands less physical strength and endurance, men need to rely increasingly on social and communication skills.

The growing diversity of social life confronts many young males with significant developmental challenges. In many households, mothers are the de facto head of household, and sons grow into manhood without an intimate experience of their father at home. Father absence complicates the secure attainment of gender role. Increased diversity in social life has also opened the doors to recognition of homosexuality as a reality in a significant minority of the male population. This change has required that all men confront traditional homophobic attitudes and anxieties.

Pleck (1981) argues that role strain results from the cultural expectation that males conform to an impossibly narrow definition of masculinity. The reality of "many masculinities" is obscured by the dominant masculine ideology. Role strain, in my view, also arises from the discrepancy between traditional standards and contemporary expectations. Shame, at one level, arises when the self feels inadequate in relation to a valued goal or ideal. In this sense, role strain generates shame affect as males fail to live up to the cultural and peer group standards they have internalized. Changes in role expectations alluded to here raise powerful conflicts with respect to adequacy, dependency, vulnerability, and exposure. Each of these "states" stimulates shame responses of varying degrees. For example, the shame attached to feeling too dependent on others may signal a man to "look cool" (Chapter 11), to withdraw, to hide, or to compensate with work, alcohol, or other self-regulating solutions. Sometimes shame over feeling inadequate and fearful inhibits asking for help or paying a visit to the doctor. Shame-based reactions are also intrinsic to domestic and community violence. Men typically resort to abusive force against a partner or a child when threatened with humiliation or abandonment. Loss of face or being "dissed" is a frequently given explanation for black-on-black youth homicide. Humiliated fury has the capacity to transform helplessness and inadequacy into a sense of triumph, remorse, and guilt (Lansky, 1992).

Shame plays an adaptive role in psychological growth, in large part by facilitating the integration of the self into the social world. While shame's aversive qualities are widely recognized, its adaptive functions—particularly in the development of the gendered self—are not so well recognized. To better understand how male development, particularly in Western culture, runs into difficulty in just those areas of self and other where shame management is required, the adaptive and normative function of shame must be understood.

SHAME: DEVELOPMENT OF THE CONSTRUCT

There is broad agreement (see Nathanson, 1987a; Morrison, 1989; Lewis, 1992) that the core shame experience includes the following components:

1. A powerful psychophysiological component that includes autonomic arousal (e.g., blushing, sweating): A sequence of body movements is widely recognized as signaling shame: eyes turned away, head lowered, upper body turned away. (This postural sequence can be considered a "shame signature.") The action initiated by the affect is hiding, then fight-flight (Scheff, 1987).
2. Negative self-appraisal, resulting in lowered self-esteem: The self is judged as unacceptable, inferior, inadequate, small, dirty, and so on (Wurmser, 1981).
3. Heightened self-consciousness and loss of smooth, uninterrupted preconscious processes of memory, speech, and motor coordination (Izard, 1977).

Ekman (1993) proposes that affects be viewed as a family of emotions, related cognitions, and action sequences. The shame family includes mortification, humiliation, shame, and embarrassment. Efforts to cope with shame, such as humiliated fury, envy, contempt, "by-passed" shame, and guilt, as well as a variety of perverse scenarios in which early humiliations are re-enacted, can be understood as shame-related variants.

There has been a continuous but minor interest in shame among psychoanalytic writers since Freud, although his own views of shame's importance were quite ambivalent and unresolved. While he recognized that shame was a "primary symptom of defense" (1896/1962, p. 169), he also viewed it as a "feminine emotion par excellence" (1933/1964, p. 132). In this early theory, shame was viewed as a less evolved affect that, with maturity, would be replaced by guilt. Guilt was thought to reflect a more evolved and internalized state of conflict, whereas shame was seen as tied to external prohibitions. Though psychoanalysts maintained a consistent interest (e.g., Piers & Singer, 1953), contemporary shame theory did not begin to emerge until the 1970s and 1980s, stimulated by the work of Helen Block Lewis (1971), Leon Wurmser (1981), Donald Nathanson (1987a), and Andrew Morrison (1989), among others. This revitalized interest in the affect parallels the ascendancy of self psychology (Kohut, 1971) and the breakdown of a sense of homogeneous American culture; as a result of the latter, guilt, once tied to a set of broadly accepted ethical and moral standards, lost much of its power to inhibit and constrain social and personal behavior (Lasch, 1978). In this regard, Michael Lewis (1992) suggests that shame, more than sex or aggression, is responsible for controlling the development of our modern psychic course.

Helen Block Lewis's (1971) seminal work began with the observation that while shame states in psychotherapy are ubiquitous, they are also largely unrecognized and unacknowledged. She postulated that undischarged shame experiences not only are responsible for treatment failures but play a powerful role in symptom formation. Block Lewis also concluded that shame is an emotion more commonly experienced by women because of its connection to interpersonal acceptance and rejection, and because of the centrality of relationships to women's self-esteem and gender role identity. By contrast, because men are more likely to function in competitive and aggressive modes and to place less value on close relationships, they experience less shame and more guilt.

While the relationship of shame and guilt to gender is still under investigation (Harder, 1990), I believe that shame is far more prevalent in the male experience than Block Lewis recognized, although it manifests itself in rather different ways than it does in the lives of women. By taking a developmental perspective on the question of shame and male gender, I will show that the male predicament is shaped to an important degree by the ways shame affects are integrated and socialized into the developing male self.

Though a sense of self and "objective self awareness" (Lewis, 1992) is prerequisite for a mature sense of shame, developmental evidence suggests that shame, as a response tendency, is part of the innate human affective core. Tomkins (1982, 1987) theorized that shame's innate function is to reduce the infant's or child's interest in, or excitement about, someone or something that is inappropriate, unwelcome, or no longer available. In his view, shame enables the person to brake the affective movement toward a desired but unavailable object. The innatist argument (Broucek, 1982; Nathanson, 1987; Tomkins, 1987) is anchored in the "shame signature." Nathanson cites observations of children in experimental situations that reveal the characteristic postural responses to the loss of mother's interest: "Some children will cry in distress, but many will slump down in the chair with a sudden loss of body tonus, turning the head downward and to the side, averting their eyes from the mother's face" (1987, p. 21). Along these same lines, Broucek (1982) argues that the "stranger anxiety" displayed by 8- to 12-month-old infants is actually a prototypical shame state that arises as the infant experiences itself appraised by someone unfamiliar.

From a functionalist perspective, shame is a response tendency that is intrinsically linked to the attachment system and serves as a regulator of intersubjective contact. Shame signals the need to cover up, both physically and emotionally. It informs us about personal and interpersonal boundaries and shapes concepts of privacy, modesty, tact, and deference. It also provides the emerging self with powerful feedback about the self in relation to its own internalized ideals and with vital information about its exposure to, and acceptance by, others.

As self-awareness develops, shame functions as an internal gauge of our own adequacy, goodness, cleanliness, and worthiness. Shame also serves as a primary channel by which external social expectations and the appraisal of others are internalized. It therefore supports and regulates the integration of the individual into his or her social group (Scheff, 1987). Theoretical differences notwithstanding, there is widespread agreement that the shame response is part of the child's emotional repertoire within the second year of life, accompanying the emergence of objective self-awareness and the consolidation of core gender identity. With the achievement of a self-referential perspective, the child has achieved the cognitive capacity to perceive and internalize norms, expectations, and ideals. The cognitive developmental perspective is, in a sense, implicit in the psychoanalytic view that shame and guilt are the self-conscious moral emotions. The ideal self/superego structures are, for psychodynamic theories, the cognitive structures that represent internalized social standards. Shame arises when there is a negative discrepancy between ideal and real self-experience.

The Ideal Self

With the achievement of "core gender identity" (Stoller, 1968), the child establishes a basic orientation and sense of self that includes his or her biological sex, identification by others as a boy or a girl (which typically involves naming), and early gender-related experiences (Ogden, 1989; Tabin, 1985). Subsequent development of gender role identity involves the internalization of many different types of input. The locus of much of this internalization is the "ideal self."[2]

Shame may begin as self-consciousness under the gaze of the other, but the internalization of gender role and other parental aspirations soon allows shame to function as an independent internal guide and reference. The ongoing process of internalization and structuralization supports psychological autonomy and physical independence. The internalization of gender role models informs the boy as to how boys are expected to behave in most situations. Identification with superheroes or superstars, for example, bolsters the boy's immature self as he makes his first forays into the world of peers and adults. It also communicates in stereotypic form expectations that males are to be powerful, brave, and fearless. In the course of development, shame can become a well-tuned signal system that provides the increasingly independent child with vital information about other people's boundaries and limits, as well as his own personal risk of exposure and vulnerability. In the course of maturation, the ideal self continues to provide adults with a "fluid shape" of phase-appropriate "ideals" against which to measure themselves (Morrison, 1989).

THE TRANSFORMATION OF SHAME

Among the most fascinating and perplexing qualities of shame is its capacity for transformation and disguise. Shame is a form of painful self-awareness. The feeling that one is being negatively evaluated by the other is central to the experience. The impulse to hide is the action associated with the feeling. The importance of shame in human adaptation is underscored by the enduring character of memory for embarrassing moments and by how slow we are to forget the sharp sting of humiliation. Izard (1977) comments that shame produces a higher degree of intrapsychic working-through than other affects, usually in the form of intense ruminative ideation. We consciously remember and say to ourselves, "I can't believe what I did." "If only I had . . . next time I'll. . . ."

At the same time, not all shame is easily remembered. Most shame experience consists of private, often silent and unconscious judgments rendered against the self. While such judgments may have their origins in the nonaccepting behaviors of significant others, before too long they are completely

[2]The "ideal self" is conceptually related to both psychoanalytic model of the ego ideal and superego and to self psychological models (Morrison, 1989). Though not unimportant, the metatheoretical discussion of the various conceptualizations would take this discussion too far afield. For current purposes, the "ideal self" serves to designate the internal psychological repository of external standards (typically in their "idealized" forms) against which the self evaluates itself. The "ideal self" is conceived of as the internal representation of parental expectations and identifications with external models (as well as with internal states) and is the repository of gender role instructions. It is also closely related to the child's experience of the "ideal state of feeling," based on bodily experiences, as well as complex reactions to others of the same and opposite sex.

internalized. These internalizations form the basis for the negative evaluation and objectification of self associated with shame. From a psychodynamic perspective, unconscious and undischarged shame states are among
the most powerful forces generating psychological conflict and symptom
formation. In the course of development, shame affects may evolve in a variety of ways. Optimal outcome involves the transformation of shame into signal affects. For many males, disruptions in the maturation of the shame
response generate less integrated and more dysfunctional adaptations.

Shame as a Signal

When shame is integrated into the developing self it evolves into "signal
affect" (Severino, McNutt, & Feder, 1987) and serves as a stimulus to adaptation. It comes to function as an invisible sensitivity to shifts in exposure,
acceptance, and threat to the self or others. Mastery consists of transforming
the affect from the undifferentiated and overwhelming experiences of early
childhood into weaker, more differentiated signals. These serve to alert us
and help us anticipate situations in which stronger affects are likely to arise
unless adaptive action is taken. Whereas the young child experiences affects,
particularly negative ones, with great sweeping intensity, the older child has
already learned to modulate his or her affective response to a wide range of
situational challenges. The disappointed and shameful feelings that small
children may feel as mother turns and walks away from their outstretched
hands may, in time, come to signal the child to prepare to be left alone. Similarly, the tease that sends a five-year-old rushing from the room in tears may
eventually stimulate a range of self-protective and defensive countershaming, counteraggressive responses.

It is within this context that male problems with shame arise. As a result of
developmental and socialization pressures (discussed later in this chapter),
many men remain extremely reactive to shame experiences. Rather than being
able to tolerate and modulate shame states, males are likely to react with
avoidance, compensatory behaviors, and primitive fight-flight responses. For
males subject to the discontinuities of development and pressures from gender role socialization, shame, or even the possibility of shame, challenges the
security of the male sense of self. In the face of shame, males are more likely to
rely on developmentally immature mechanisms of defense such as denial,
projection, splitting, and acting out (Valliant, 1977). As a result, shame states
remain unmodulated and unintegrated and threaten the integrity of the male
self. Vulnerable and needful feelings are minimized and denied, normatively
hidden behind a "cool pose" (Chapter 11) or some other hypermasculine
stance. When verbal retorts fail, shame triggers rageful feelings that lead to
violent action. Alcohol and drug abuse are prominent, if maladaptive, male
solutions to the pressure of undischarged shame.

Managing Shame

To fully appreciate the role of shame in men's lives, let us consider that shame states not only manifest in the familiar forms of embarrassment and humiliation but also appear as shame equivalents. Block Lewis (1971) characterized as "overt, undifferentiated shame" the familiar intense and self-conscious experience typically associated with shame. This familiar manifestation of shame leaves us wishing to hide and unable to think clearly, speak coherently, or move with grace. At the same time, through her careful analysis of psychotherapy transcripts, she recognized an important alternative form of shame, which she called "by-passed shame." In this manifestation, the affect is by-passed in the sense that it is isolated or dissociated from the experience in an effort to manage the shame experience. The affective component is reduced to nothing more than a "twinge" of discomfort while the cognitive component is amplified. (Levant, in his discussion of alexithymia in Chapter 8, makes a similar observation about the affective component of the experience.) The self is objectified and seen from the perspective of the other; self-consciousness is extreme and takes the form of "How am I doing?" or, "How do I look?" By-passed shame protects the self from being overwhelmed by feeling. In this culture, men are less likely than women to experience and report overt shame, but more likely to "objectify" themselves and project critical qualities onto the other. This analysis is also helpful in clarifying a long-standing confusion about shame and guilt.

Shame and Guilt

At the simplest level, shame is the affect that arises when the self fails to live up to its own ideals, resulting in feelings of unworthiness and inadequacy. It is internal, immediate, and subjective. Shame tends to involve the whole self in a self-reflexive way. By contrast, guilt arises later than shame in a developmental sense. Guilt contains more cognitive content and less affective arousal. It is more likely to be connected to a specific action and to be experienced in terms of more external and possibly more objective standards. It reflects an awareness of having acted badly, broken a law, hurt another. "As guilt invites confession and forgiveness, shame generates concealment out of a fear of rendering the self unacceptable" (Thrane, 1979, cited in Morrison, 1989, p. 2).

It is likely that guilt is actually a shame derivative. Tomkins (1981) viewed guilt as a cognitive elaboration on underlying shame affect. Guilt, in a sense, is a form of by-passed shame. The affect is isolated and reduced, while the cognitive and self-conscious components are heightened and externalized. Experientially, shame and guilt frequently co-occur. It is not surprising that they are often poorly differentiated from one another. Guilt often brings with it a sense of shame; the specific guilt-inducing transgression also stimulates feelings of shame over the failure of the self. Block Lewis (1971) observed that shame can often be discovered "under guilt." Thus, "having transgressed, I feel guilty for having wronged another and ashamed of myself for having failed to behave better." The transformation of shame into guilt by focusing on a transgression of a particular standard protects the self by externalizing and localizing the concern. While it is probably true that for most of us guilt is a more comfortable emotion than shame, it is undeniably so for men.

Other Shame Management Strategies

At times, however, because shame affects can be so intense and can generate corrosive, self-annihilating cognitive activity, shame states can feel intolerable. This is particularly so at the extreme levels characteristic of immature and unmodulated shame experiences. Protection of the self in the face of threatened loss of cohesion and disorganization becomes a psychological priority. For example, intense shame is frequently associated with rage responses. Rage is linked to narcissistic injury and is a common male response to humiliation. Piers and Singer (1953) described a cycle of shame and guilt, while Scheff (1987) has researched "spirals of shame-rage." Central to both cases is the observation that passivity induces shame, which in turn generates narcissistic rage, which then produces guilt. This sequence underlies many types of domestic violence and may generate the interminable quarrels common to conflictual marriages and dysfunctional families.

Shame may also appear as contempt. Morrison (1983) observes: "Like rage, contempt frequently functions as a mechanism for ridding the self of unbearable shame, in this case by projecting the shame out of the self into another person" (pp. 104–105).

Gender guides the selection of certain developmental pathways. Males are consistently found to have a proclivity toward externalization (Cicchetti & Toth, 1991) and toward objectification. Both "strategies" serve to protect the vulnerable self by shifting the focus from the self per se to either its activities and accomplishments, on the one hand, or its objectified or externalized appearance, on the other hand. The previous distinctions between undifferentiated and by-passed shame reflect the tension between internalization and externalization. Likewise, the use of contempt (i.e., the projection of shame onto the other), as well as the shame-rage-guilt cycle, represent externalization strategies favored by males.

Objectification

Kinston (1983), writing from an object relational perspective, proposed that shame can be managed by transforming the self into an "object" that reflects parental wishes. Thus, as the boy reveals his "subjective" self, his spontaneous inclinations and desires, he receives the subtle and not-so-subtle message that his parents are not interested and not accepting of his "true" sense of himself. Instead, they signal what they wish him to be and the parts of him they wish to see. Shame arises as the boy surrenders, and hides, his own subjective self and fashions an objective self to secure parental love and acceptance. The psychological movement wherein the boy abandons his "real" self for a "false" but acceptable one is, according to Kinston, the etiology of the shame experience. The real self has become secret, while the "self as object" can be manipulated in all manner of ways. However, once the transformation is complete and a "permanent state of object narcissism" (p. 222) is achieved, the boy has rendered himself immune to conscious shame. In the fullest extension of this process, the boy has, in a sense, become "shameless."

Kinston's model captures important facets of male adaptation to vulnerability. Making the self and the other into objects is descriptive of many of the ways in which men take control of their feelings and confront painful, even frightening situations. The objectification of the self means that the other's view of me, "how I look," is more important than my own experience. This shift enables males to override feelings of vulnerability and fear and to behave in ways commensurate with gender role expectations. The objectification of the other facilitates treating them in a shameless way. The extremes of this process can be seen in the transformation of the enemy into an inhuman object, the treatment of women as sexual objects, and even the part objectification of the male body as "stud," "workhorse," or "man of steel." In these instances, shame-based prohibitions are disconnected and cease to inhibit behavior.

SHAME AND GENDER

Gender, as a social category, links the child's biological sex to his or her familial and social role. It is one of the fundamental categories of experience around which the self is organized.

> All known languages include terms to distinguish boys from girls and men from women. All known societies differentiate to some degree the roles that are assigned to the two sexes. Belief systems accrue to gender in the form of stereotypes and culturally coded expectations. (Maccoby, 1988, p. 755)

Culturally prescribed gender differences exist for most significant domains of experience. Examples are ubiquitous: Boys in this culture have less permission to acknowledge and express most affects, with the exception of anger (Brody, 1985; Izard, 1977); boys are more likely to engage in rough-and-tumble play and to play win-lose games (Campbell, 1993; Friedman, 1988); boys are expected to be more socially assertive and to take sexual initiative (Maccoby, 1988). Whereas "gender identity" is an aspect of one's core sense of the self as male or female, culturally prescibed differences constitute "gender role identity" and are acquired through identification, social modeling, and role instruction (see Chapter 2). Gender role instructions provide the developing child with some of the earliest information about what is desirable and acceptable to important others (cf. Ley & Carter, 1989). Anthropologists have long recognized that shaming is a primary socialization strategy utilized by all cultures to inculcate and reinforce the integration of personal and social behavior (Braithwaite, 1989). Shame's responsiveness to social cues makes it a uniquely suited vehicle for the integration of the developing self into the family and society. It is one of the ways in which the external world becomes part of our internal world.

It is the thesis of this chapter that shame-related processes operate differently in male and female development, and that these differences have important social and emotional consequences (Block Lewis, 1987). Shame is intrinsically involved in guiding and reinforcing the acquisition of gender-related traits and behaviors. Socialization norms facilitate female tolerance and acknowledgment of shame, while male norms deny its motivational importance and inhibit its adaptive transformation. With the consolidation of gender role identity, shame sensitivities are heightened for those aspects of gender role identity most salient to the boy or girl. Thus, for boys, the potential for shame attaches to any and all aspects of gender expectations, but most particularly in relation to issues concerning independence from mother and being aggressively adequate as a male among other males.

Shame historically has been associated with female experience. Block Lewis (1971) concluded that shame is a prominent feature in women's development as a result of their greater "sociability" and the importance of relationships to women's self-esteem. More recently, however, clinical observers have recognized that "men and women cope with assaults on their self esteem in different ways. Women are more apt to experience them consciously and directly, while men are more prone to deny and defend against lowered self esteem through narcissistic behavior" (Wright, O'Leary, & Balkin, 1989, p. 226). These different constellations of self-experience and behavior arise because affective vulnerability, particularly in the presence of others, has different meanings for women and men.

For shame to undergo the adaptive transformation from a primary, unmodulated affect with deep visceral connections to fight-flight reactions into a mature and subtle signal affect, certain developmental conditions must exist (see below). It is my observation that male gender role socialization mitigates against the transformation and integration of shame into the adult male self. As a result, males are characteristically extremely sensitive and reactive to shame states.

THE ADAPTIVE FUNCTIONS OF SHAME

Shame, as a source of interpersonal and intrapsychic feedback, plays an important adaptive role in the development of the self. Its contributions to the development of autonomy, the integration of narcissism, and the creation of intrapsychic and interpersonal boundaries are singular. Failures in the transformation of shame from traumalike intensity to low-intensity signals interfere with these developmental processes and leave males particularly vulnerable to further disturbances of self in these domains.

Adaptive transformation and integration of shame takes place when vulnerable aspects of the self are exposed to significant others in the context of an accepting relationship in which affect tolerance is encouraged and modeled and children feel safe enough to speak about their fears and insecurities. In families characterized by "good-enough" parenting and a moderate degree of emotional containment, shame affects rarely rise to levels of intensity that threaten psychological organization. Under these circumstances, the affect is modulated to the point where shame signals appear occasionally and are of low intensity and limited duration. They are more likely to dissipate and resolve than to remain active and compelling. The impulse toward hiding and isolation is reduced and underlying fears of abandonment are not activated. Children are able to resolve shame states to the degree that they have developed an internalized capacity to soothe themselves and to feel confident in their connection to family and community. When shame is successfully integrated as a self-affect, boys learn modesty and tact, are appropriately deferential, and are responsive to emotional signals within the self and coming from others. Good shame socialization protects the child from too much exposure of either vulnerability or narcissistic exhibitionism. At a social level, the shame potential of situations can be anticipated and adapted to rather than denied or avoided. Finally, and of particular importance for males, effective shame socialization buffers and attenuates the link between emotional vulnerability and aggression. In its modulated form, shame is less likely to threaten identity or interpersonal connectedness and is therefore less likely to generate an impulsive (e.g., fight-flight) or compulsive (e.g., substance abuse, workaholism) solution. This process provides the emerging self with a silent and sophisticated signal system attuned to subtle changes in interpersonal vulnerability and exposure.

When these conditions are absent to one degree or another, shame states are amplified rather than diminished. As the "holding environment" becomes increasingly unsafe, shame threatens self-cohesion and triggers immature mechanisms of adaptation, such as splitting, denial, projection, impulsivity, and depression. The threat of psychological disorganization and loss of impulse control makes shame-laden encounters aversive. They are avoided or "managed," and as a result, shame intensity is not diminished with expo-sure, nor are shame regulation skills acquired.

Male Dilemmas in the Transformation of Shame

Several prominent features of male development mitigate against the suc-cessful transformation of shame into signal affect and the eventual integra-tion of shame into male gender role identity. These factors include: the process of disidentification and the struggle for psychological autonomy; problematic identification with shaming and absent caretakers; male sex role stereotypes and ideologies that deny vulnerability; and the inclination within the male subculture toward action and doing and away from affect tolerance, self-exposure, and relating.

DISIDENTIFICATION AND THE STRUGGLE FOR PSYCHOLOGICAL AUTONOMY

> There is a constantly recurring notion that real manhood is differ-ent from simple anatomical maleness, that it is not a natural condi-tion that comes about spontaneously through biological matura-tion but rather is a precarious or artificial state that boys must win against powerful odds. (Gilmore, 1990, p. 11)

The process by which boys move toward psychological autonomy and develop a sturdy sense of male identity is a difficult one. Shame affects, which are stimulated during this period of separation/individuation, gener-ate psychological structures that guard vulnerable self-experiences related to dependency needs and feelings of inadequacy, inferiority, and fear. The structures common to developing males include varying degrees of narcis-sistic defense against further exposure. These defensive adaptations mitigate against future shame tolerance and integration.

The transition from primary identification with mother toward a fuller identification with father and male peers often leaves boys feeling vulnera-ble and inadequate on both fronts. This process of identity formation has been discussed in terms of "disidentification" (Greenson, 1968)[3] and "dis-continuity" (Chodorow, 1989). In both versions, the boy's dilemma involves the need to move away from the anchoring maternal connection and toward an often uncertain and, at times, unavailable connection with a paternal fig-ure. For many, this normative transition constitutes a premature loss of

---

[3]The "disidentification" hypothesis, though widely used (see, for example, Hudson & Jacot, *The Way Men Think*, 1991), remains an unsatisfactory formulation of the developmen-tal sequence by which boys develop maternal and paternal introjects. In Chapter 2, Pollack raises these concerns and proposes alternative approaches.

maternal nurturance and protection. In Chapter 2, Pollack characterizes this as a "traumatic abrogation of the holding environment," while Wright (1987) hypothesized a "shame-inducing traumatic separation." Furthermore, the developmental discontinuity for the boy brings with it an awareness of being different from the mother. The experience of being different from and less than the other is fertile ground for shame. The boy's primitive envy (a shame-related affect) of mother's power is embedded in an unconscious struggle for internal differentiation and the dread of being engulfed or swallowed. His residual awareness of his dependent needs leaves him feeling little and babyish. The boy's consciously available shame is connected with infantile wishes to be nurtured and protected. Intense feelings toward mother must be repressed; their emergence threatens the fragile sense of maleness. As Campbell (1993) and others have observed, being male often reduces to "not being female."

The conflict over unresolved dependent yearnings is likely to lay the groundwork for the narcissistic adaptations commonly seen among adult males. The boy's consolidation of his gender role identity and sense of self seems to require that he distance himself from mother and much that is associated with her. The associated loss of comfort and security generates varying degrees of narcissistic defense. The male stance takes shape around the denial of the impact of the loss, and the subsequent inversion of the issue by diminishing the importance of these needs. Strong affects like shame and sadness, as well as unresolved dependent yearnings, threaten to break through the boy's newly gained but still fragile composure. As a clinical observer, I find there is considerable reason to believe that a boy's identity development and later character is marked by this structural fault line. Shame arising either from dependent yearnings or from fears of aggression is potentially disorganizing. Masking and avoiding are primary shame management strategies aimed at protecting underlying sensitivities. When maternal attachments are troubled, boys are more likely to develop patterns of attachment characterized by intense ambivalence, hostility, disorganization, and avoidance (Carlson, Cicchetti, Barnett, & Braunwald, 1989). Obviously, none of these adaptations facilitates further working through of vulnerable states, either by exposing them or talking about them in safe and containing relationships. Instead, boys who are uncertain as to their connection to their mothers, threatened by regressive wishes, and anxious about the judgments of more distant fathers, struggle to prove themselves in gender-approved modes of behavior, often adopting stereotypic roles and behaviors.

Cultural expectations, carried over into the family, further exacerbate these tensions. Boys are expected to move quickly toward psychological autonomy and physical independence. At the level of the peer group and in the culture as well, there is considerable discomfort with male dependency needs. Male gender "ideology" can be seen as overemphasizing autonomy at the expense of connection and relatedness (see Chapters 2 and 3). As above, shame over dependent wishes is difficult to reconcile with the "all-boy" ideals promoted in the culture and rewarded by peers.

PROBLEMATIC IDENTIFICATIONS

Another significant impediment to the development of mature shame responses in males is the variety of problematic identifications boys encounter in family life. Shame, as we have seen, arises when the self experiences itself as deficient in some important feature of identity. This may come to pass either because grandiose ideals dwarf the real self and generate painful feelings of failure and inadequacy or as a direct result of being shamed by an important person in the child's life.

Extrapolating from population studies of child maltreatment and familial alcoholism, we can estimate that upwards of 20% of boys grow up in a family in which physical violence, sexual abuse, or alcoholism are present. In families whose parents or other caretakers are likely sources of shame and shaming, boys are continuously exposed to extreme degrees of shame affect. When parental dysfunction has inhibited the development of reliable and soothing internal objects of identification, it can be difficult to contain and modulate affective intensity. In the face of potentially overwhelming shame and, at times, physical danger, the self must adopt extreme protective measures. When parents are the source of shame, either through physical or sexual abuse, through neglect, or through disdain, boys quickly withdraw emotionally and learn to protect themselves by masking their true feelings. Narcissistic defenses arise under these circumstances and are aimed at warding off the pain of rejection and concomitant threats to self-esteem and self-cohesion. When mother has been humiliated by father, boys frequently develop identifications with each parent in a partial way. Often there is a conscious identification with the victimized mother, with the boy seeing himself as her protector, accompanied by an unconscious identification with father's aggression and inadequacy.

Conflict between parents impacts profoundly on boys and their developing sense of identity (Block, 1983). Consciously, the boy may identify with his humiliated mother and fantasize heroic protection of her, while feeling ashamed of his helplessness to rescue her. Unconsciously, he is prone to identify with his aggressor father, while also feeling ashamed of abandoning his mother. When family conflict is high, shaming and blaming between the parents is a common, if pathological, mode of distance regulation and self-management (Lansky, 1992). Boys often suffer split loyalties and may be emotionally destabilized by the conflict. Traumatically induced shame may be of such intensity and duration that it promotes dissociative reactions and a propensity toward humiliated fury. With dissociative and rage reactions tied to shame states, it is little wonder that boys in such circumstances have little opportunity to modulate and integrate shame experience. Parents in these families model shaming and countershaming in lieu of conflict resolution; they also may model the use of violence as a resolution to unpleasant feelings (Malatesta-Magai, 1991).

The boy's development of a secure sense of his own maleness is facilitated and buffered by the presence of an available and responsive father or father figure. A "good-enough" male presence in the life of a boy may help make the transition from maternal safety to paternal identification more a shifting of emphasis than a precarious leap. When the transition is continuous, affects of loss and abandonment do not rise to disorganizing proportions and are less likely to be shame-inducing. With an absent, unavailable, or hostile father, the transitional steps toward a secure male identification are more problematic. The loss of father through divorce, death, or emotional unavailability seems to leave boys and young men with more vulnerable senses of self and more defensiveness with respect to their male identifications. These circumstances generate multiple layers of shame. The absence of a positive male object of identification sensitizes the boy's awareness of his attachment to his mother, on the one hand, and his own insufficient sense of masculinity, on the other. His identification with a failed or vulnerable father may leave the boy ashamed of both his father and himself. In divorce, boys are often caught in their identification with the discredited and, at times, maligned ex-husband. The boy's discomfort with his own awareness of need and vulnerability leads to masking, compensation, and, at times, decompensation. Increased aggressiveness, often toward women, is one of the consequences of shame-laden identity conflicts. Without a secure anchoring male identification, boys gravitate toward signs and symbols of male gender roles—often in its stereotypic forms. Violent action becomes an alternative to a secure sense of male identity.

Even in a relatively more normative environment, fathers may shame their sons in the course of teaching "manliness." Osherson (1992) describes an all too familiar situation in which a small boy who has hurt himself seeks comfort from his parents. His father minimizes the injury and rejects the boy's wish to be comforted; the mother opens her arms to him. The father's tough-minded response leaves the boy feeling small and ashamed of his neediness, but his mother's open acceptance of his need makes him feel infantile, particularly in front of his father. Caught in an impossible dilemma, he bolts from the house and hides in shame. The father embodies and instructs his son in how males are expected to deal with hurt and their needs for succor. The denial of need becomes part of the psychological movement away from the maternal connection and toward traditional male identification.

GENDER ROLE STEREOTYPES ENCOURAGE DENIAL OF VULNERABILITY

The connection among shame states, gender role instructions regarding the denial of vulnerability, and the assumption of masks and poses that represent invulnerability is neither accidental nor incidental. The modern male role requires boys and men to prepare for two eventualities: In one, the self must be prepared to fight (e.g., as a soldier or protector) and to cope with fears and anxieties related to mortal combat, even if they do not actually have to fight; in the other, the self must be interpersonally connected, be responsive to others in a tactful and empathic manner, and integrate competitive strivings with cooperative aims. In the first instance, gender role models, instruction, and experience mobilize shame to encourage masking of vulnerability and suppression of fear and anxiety. For men to fight and win, their vulnerabilities must be contained, denied, and hidden. Gender-linked shame socialization reinforces self-control in the face of aggression and labels as "cowardly" male behavior that shows too much fear and retreats from the battle. Desertion in the face of combat is punishable by death. To achieve compliance with this gender-linked mission, shame must be avoided at all costs, and emotional vulnerabilities that might lead to shame are to be avoided. In the second instance, however, the achievement of sociability—connection with others—requires that shame be tolerated and modulated so that vulnerable states can be integrated into the self and its relationships and narcissistic ambitions can be integrated into a realistic sense of self in the world. In a sense, males are caught in a double bind with respect to shame socialization. The preparation for the possibility of aggressive encounter requires rigid, shame-based defenses to contain fear and anxiety and mask vulnerability. By contrast, the need for connection and belonging requires a more flexible, more tolerant stance in relation to the experience of shame in daily life.

The male predicament leaves boys fearful of being too close and too dependent on their mothers and unable to acknowledge their fears and inadequacies to their fathers or their peers. In response, boys erect rigid internal and external defenses against the experience of shame. Boys are discouraged from open acknowledgment of doubts, insecurities, and fears. Fears of self-disclosure and the secrets of one's shameful inferiorities—physical, sexual, emotional—breed social and emotional isolation. In their mutual silence about their common concerns, they lose the opportunity for social amelioration and modulation of shameful experience. Instead, normative doubts become fearful secrets. Too often young males fail, because of unmodulated shame reactivity, to learn about mutuality, gradual self-disclosure, negotiation, and acknowledgment of needs (see Chapter 8).

Boys seek out superheroes, athletes, and other male figures who represent invulnerability of one kind or another. As objects of fantasy, heroes ranging from Superman through Rambo appeal to the boy's wish to be invulnerable, all-powerful, and irresistible. Males learn that aggressive postures, which mask underlying uncertainties regarding their attachment and dependency needs, are rewarded by peers and manifest as attitudes and stances like "machismo" and the "cool pose" (Chapter 11). They serve to hide and deny underlying need states and communicate readiness to respond aggressively to threats to self-esteem. Aggressive retaliation is one of the gender-endorsed means of managing humiliation and restoring the shamefully exposed self.

To the degree that boys believe that parents, peers, and others expect them to be tough competitors in all domains, they are less likely to connect with peers or share their unguarded selves. Male norms press boys toward aggressive competition with other boys. Social expectations reinforce and reward these tendencies. Boys come to believe that high self-esteem can be had by being competitive and aggressive toward others. Yet the underside of aggression is in every man's experience as well. In every competition, there is a defeat, someone loses. The shame of not wanting to compete also diminishes self-esteem. For men who subscribe to these norms, either consciously or unconsciously, failure to live up to them, to embody them, can be humiliating and, as a result, isolating.

MALE SUBCULTURE IS INCLINED TOWARD ACTION AND AWAY FROM RELATING

The cumulative effect of the interaction between developmental deviations and socialization expectations leaves many boys and young males isolated with their doubts and insecurities and highly reactive to shame states. Internally aware of the painful gap between their ideal and actual selves, situations and relationships that threaten to reveal their felt sense of inadequacy are increasingly avoided or managed. The transformation of shame from an intense affective response into an integrated signal affect requires that potentially shaming encounters or experiences be tolerated, acknowledged among accepting others, and put into words. Male subcultural norms do not facilitate this process. As we have seen, shame avoidance is a crucial part of the way males learn to manage themselves in relation to the threat of aggression. The optimal desensitization of shameful experiences requires exposure to them rather than avoidance, which, if anything, amplifies the power of the avoidant response. Shame's link to action, by virtue of its psychobiological connection to autonomic arousal and the fight-flight emergency response, short-circuits the opportunity to develop affect tolerance. Intense shame states—with their evocations of vulnerability, exposure, and inadequacy—threaten the psychological coherence of many males. The resulting states of feeling are unbearable and promote impulsive solutions. Hypermasculine overcompensation, obsessive compulsive rigidities, and other strategies arise to manage and ward off feelings of fraudulence, contempt, and self-loathing. Substance abuse is a common maladaptive solution to the failure to live up to internalized gender role ideals.

Social representations of maleness and femaleness (Campbell, 1993) are split along gender lines with respect to instrumental and expressive behaviors (see Chapters 2 and 8). The male gender role is associated with externalization and action solutions to emotional situations. Movement toward action deflects attention from the self to the action or the achievement. Males are doers and problem-solvers, not talkers. Women's greater sociability and readiness to put feelings into words makes their shame modulation and integration more likely. Men, lacking experience in speaking of their vulnerability and shame, are much less likely to find ways of modulating and integrating shame-producing experience except in relation to women—who then become privy to their vulnerabilities and both "indispensable" as well as threatening to male well-being.

IMPACT ON ADAPTIVE DEVELOPMENT

These four factors—disidentification and the struggle for psychological autonomy, problematic identification with shaming and/or absent caretakers, sex role stereotypes and ideologies that deny vulnerability, and the inclination toward action and away from affect tolerance, self-exposure, and relating—which are intrinsic to the process of male development in this culture, often preclude the evolution of the shame response. As a consequence, they also interfere with the achievement of psychological autonomy, the integration of narcissistic aims and ambitions, the formation of psychological boundaries, and the management of aggression, since each of these accomplishments relies heavily on shame-based feedback for its consolidation and maturation. When developmental and socialization factors contribute to the short-circuiting of shame's evolution, these aspects of self-development are adversely impacted. Thus, for example, the development of psychological autonomy relies on shame signals, first to monitor the security of the emotional bond with the caretaker as the child moves away from his caretakers, and second, to provide internalized signals and standards for independent behavior. Similarly, the integration of narcissistic aims and ambitions relies upon shame-based feedback, related to comparison of self with others, to help modulate ideals into realistic standards.

Psychological Autonomy

In the case of psychological autonomy, when separation from maternal support has been premature, boys are left with both deep and unresolved dependent yearnings and narcissistic defenses against acknowledging their need. This all too common eventuality (Chodorow, 1989; Greenson, 1968; Chapter 2; Wright, 1987) leaves males deeply conflicted about intimacy, sexuality, and their feelings toward women (Hudson & Jacot, 1991). Shame over unmet needs leads to deep conflicts over dependency needs and to fears (and wishes) of engulfment by women. As a result of feeling vulnerable in their need, shame-as-humiliation remains close at hand and can easily become humiliated fury and rage at women who are seen as controlling and withholding. The ongoing and conflictual presence of the little boy inside many grown men leads to problematic marital and parenting experiences in which unacceptable dependency needs are consciously denied and then enacted in a variety of ways.

Narcissism

In the case of ordinary narcissism, or "normal infantile narcissism" (Kernberg, 1986), shame, in manageable doses, accompanies the failures of daily life as well as the disappointments secondary to the inevitable deidealization of the self and parental figures. At adaptive levels, normal shame signals generated by these tolerable failures alert the boy to the nature and source of his "failures." Nathanson (1987c) observes that shame signals provide critical information to help with the integration of fantasy and reality. He views the family's use of shame signals as instrumental in helping the child learn to regulate exposure, grandiosity, and self-presentation and to develop a realistic sense of perspective vis-à-vis the self in the world. (Braithwaite [1989] terms this "reintegrative shaming" [p. 5].) Unintegrated and unresolved narcissistic dilemmas leave many men unable to tolerate failure. Narcissistic defenses come into existence to protect the vulnerable self whenever nonacceptance threatens during the course of development. Compensatory narcissism results in a splitting of the self into a "false," "objective," or compliant self and a secret "grandiose" self. At a normative level, narcissistic character styles are prevalent among men and are associated with self-involvement, self-importance, and emotional distance. Such males typically have difficulty taking the needs of others into account. Problems of intimacy and parenting, along with social and emotional isolation, stem from narcissistic unavailability.

Boundaries

Boundary formation is another aspect of self-development in which shame plays a prominent role. "Shame guards the separate, private self with its boundaries and prevents intrusion and merger. It guarantees the self's integrity" (Wurmser, 1981, p. 65). In Erikson's (1965) view, shame and doubt are intimately connected with the child's struggle to control bladder and bowel functions. Shame helps us learn when to hold on and when to let go, when to cover up and when to close down. With the beginnings of increased self-control come privacy and the emergence of a private secret self (Lewis, 1992, p. 99). Shame is one of the great shapers of interpersonal experience. To the degree that a boy has been well socialized in his family, he will be able to move off into the world of others secure in his sense that he can "stand on his own" and not "lose control" of himself and suffer humiliation and isolation. To the extent that his boundaries are stable, reliable, and, at the same time, flexible, he is likely to feel internally cohesive and interpersonally secure. Male gender norms value "firm boundaries," which in turn support cultural expectations that males will control their internal emotional reactions and their external behavior. It is expected that they will be "objective" and not let feelings "get in the way of" making "rational decisions." By contrast, when internal and external boundaries are not well made (i.e., they are either too porous or, as in males, often too rigid), self-regulation is difficult. Such individuals are often vulnerable to extreme states of emotional instability and reactivity, on the one hand, and isolation and distance, on the other.

Too much shaming over failure, inadequacy, or aggression at home inhibits the boy's initiative, willingness to disclose, and interpersonal confidence. Boys with excessive shame sensitivity find themselves scapegoated, too vulnerable, and overpressured from the ever-present danger of humiliation. When boys are unable to contain their competitive anxieties, they may be exposed to provocation, ridicule, and possible loss of control. When unstable boundaries prevail, intimacy and commitment are problematic, giving way to intrusive and engulfing relationships, fears and wishes to merge, and defensive efforts to shore up weak or nonexistent boundaries. Extreme patterns of shaming interfere with impulse regulation, the capacity for empathy, and the development of tact and other forms of interpersonal respect. Training in affect integration and shame avoidance at home equips a young boy for the external world: He will be neither too vulnerable and revealed in his inadequacies nor narcissistically arrogant and intrusive.

Aggression

Among other adaptive benefits, well-socialized shame responses facilitate the mediation of conflict without recourse to violence. This takes place in several ways. Shame awareness allows the male to mediate his discomfort over exposure, containing and attenuating his shame response so that it does not trigger an impulsive solution to unbearable feeling. Breaking eye contact (e.g., "Who do you think you're looking at, bud?") enables boys and men to avoid the threat of violence. Learning to mask one's emotions often gives males increased control in interpersonal situations. Looking composed or in charge (e.g., "macho") suppresses other feelings and diminishes the experience of vulnerability. In the world of males, too much exposure of self, especially of vulnerable feelings, invites possible ridicule and attack. One function of shame integration promotes the development of words and nonthreatening gestures, which are then available to mediate transactions involving dominance and competition. Also, the male who has adapted a mediated stance toward his own vulnerability is likely to be aware of the other's and be able to accurately monitor rising threat.

Stigma

Stigma is social shame, the shame of membership in a scorned group. While it is not intrinsic to the process of male development, it exerts a profound influence on the lives of minority men of color and gay men. For them, stigmatization adds a layer of negative self-awareness that becomes an inevitable part of their individual and group identities. Racism and homophobia arise out of fear of the "other." Although each of these prejudices has its own sources and complexities, they both reflect the social use of shame to manage threatening differences. For the individual man of color, or for the homosexual man, the stigma of prejudice magnifies the feelings of difference, deficiency, and inferiority that make the normative burden of shame integration exceptionally problematic. Stigma, with all its implications for prejudice, discrimination, ostracization, and danger, prompts hiding and withdrawal and the creation of false selves of various forms. Being "in the closet" for gay men, living in ghettoized conditions for blacks, "passing" by disguising one's identity, are social manifestations of stigmatization. Self-hatred, compensatory pride, and reactive aggression, which are among the psychological responses to this pernicious form of internalized shame, are activated and amplified under circumstances of nonacceptance. The social stigma associated with devalued group identities heightens the experience of vulnerability and sensitivity, while further impeding the integration of shame-based character development.

Shame and Male Psychopathology

Shame has been identified by Block Lewis (1971), Morrison (1989), Lansky (1992), and others as playing a significant role in symptom formation. Block Lewis's original research developed connections between what she termed "undischarged shame," low self-esteem, and depression in women. The central argument of this chapter includes a recognition that unmodulated and unintegrated shame experiences in men's lives lead to the development of not only "normative" dysfunctions but also more severe types of character pathology, including some of the most malignant forms of narcissism and

sociopathy. When the emerging male self is overwhelmed by the shame arising from disruptions in the early parenting environment, certain characteristic patterns of behavior and protective defensive structures come into being.

NARCISSISTIC CHARACTER PATHOLOGY

Narcissistic personality traits and disorders are primarily shame management strategies. They involve the development of psychological barriers,
often referred to as "walls," "shells," or "fronts," that seal off the vulnerable
self, protecting it from further injury. Boys respond to the early threat of
excessive exposure to unresponsive, hostile, or rejecting caretakers by constructing such barriers, also known as character defenses. In adulthood, certain individuals manifest these as patterns of extreme self-centeredness,
grandiosity, and contempt for others. In a certain respect, this form of the
disorder is a caricature of the male gender role stereotype: emotionally
unflappable, powerful, and in control. The self is presented as invulnerable
and with no need for the other; intimacy is not possible.

The denial of shame is central to the success of this adaptation, which is
accomplished by the presentation of the grandiose aspects of the self. The
inferior self, demeaned and helpless, is either deeply hidden or projected
onto the other, who, in turn, feels devalued or denigrated. A second type of
narcissistic adaptation has been called a "dissociated type of narcissistic disorder" (Reich, 1960, p. 218; see also O'Leary & Wright, 1986, p. 331). In this
manifestation, the narcissism of the self is projected out onto idealized others, while the individual consciously identifies with the shameful diminished self. While this type of narcissistic adaptation is commonly seen in
women, it is also characteristic of males who have grown up in maltreating
families. With the other empowered or idealized at the expense of the self,
scapegoating and sadomasochistic relationships are common.

BORDERLINE AND POST-TRAUMATIC PERSONALITY ORGANIZATION

In still more hostile and unpredictable environments, the level of psychological danger (and frequently physical danger) generates more extreme
characterological adaptations. While the borderline personality disorder
diagnosis is often associated with women (Cleary, 1987), males also develop
borderline personality disorders in response to unstable and traumatizing
family experience. Boys growing up in abusive environments develop
poorly regulated and volatile emotional states, internalize split and problematic parental introjects, and end up with very unstable self-concepts. They
typically split their identifications with parental figures. Mother may be idealized as a martyred saint, on the one side, while experienced as a manipula-

tive "bitch" on the other; father is seen as a no-good son-of-a-gun while secretly perceived as a tragic soul. Parts of the self are connected to each. Boys often fantasize magical escapes and heroic interventions in the violence or the pain of family life: They save the good mother from the evil father. At the same time, in a hostile environment, the boy's identification with maternal vulnerability is intolerable. In its place arises a mixed identification with father, the aggressor. This identification is also split between the father's power and control, on the one side, and his despicable loss of control on the other. The boy's identification with the aggressive part helps him manage his self-esteem and protects him from feeling overwhelmed by trauma-related affects and memories. To manage the depression and mood instability that frequently accompany these conditions, males often become drug- and alcohol-involved and lead impulse-ridden lives. Many are in endless flight from their profound feelings of unworthiness, lack of self-control, and humiliating desperation.

IMPULSIVE AND VIOLENT SOLUTIONS

Lansky (1992) observes that men who have difficulty maintaining a stable sense of psychological boundaries with others often become pathologically dependent on others, usually women, for purposes of self-regulation. For such men, their collusive dependence secures them and enrages them. In their lives, shame is either a "signal of danger to meaningful bonding . . . [or] . . . the breakdown of the capacity to bond" (p. 208). It is the ever-present threat to self-cohesion and the dread of annihilation anxiety that leads to blaming (as a means of distance regulation) and to violence as well. While not all battering between couples can be subsumed within this model, a powerful case can be made for it being a basic paradigm. Thus, the attachment to their partner binds abandonment fears and sustains a sense of self-worth. As differences emerge between the partners, or when children compete for attention, narcissistically vulnerable men feel threatened by the loss of internal organization and self-cohesion. They experience profound shame over their need and fragility. Fragmentation anxiety triggers primitive defenses. Impulsive action shifts the focus from the failing needy self to the aggressive act and accompanying remorse (Lansky, 1992; Walker, 1985). Guilt over having been aggressive is preeminently more tolerable than shame. Emotional equilibrium, along with psychological distance, is reestablished. The battering of a spouse, or the physical or sexual abuse of a child, often originates in such shame-anxiety sequences (Krugman, 1987).

Fratricidal behavior, which makes violence the leading cause of death among black and Hispanic males under 25, is an extremely complex and overdetermined social tragedy (APA, 1993). At a fundamental level, however, many of the murderous transactions are structured around insults, loss of face, and being "dissed" (disrespected). Impulsive violence in retaliation for shaming transactions serves to ward off fragmentation and depression by discharging rage and fear. In communities where economic disenfranchisement and racial stigma leave males with no other sources of esteem and status, gang membership and personal pride are among the psychological resources that buoy the self. Threats to these threaten self-coherence. Violence restores pride and heightens the bond among gang members, while identification with the victims and feelings about murderous acts are dissociated and numbed.

ANTISOCIAL PERSONALITY DISORDERS

These disorders are among the most malignant varieties of male narcissism, and this diagnosis is given to men two to three times as often as it is given to women (Cleary, 1987). They reflect extreme defensive efforts to cope with severe helplessness and dependency. Chronic disappointment, indifference, and humiliation in early childhood leave such men with "a chronic sense of emptiness, a sense of being alone" (Kernberg, 1992, p. 222). As distinct from other narcissistic personality disorders, antisocial men have little or "no capacity for loyalty to or concern for others or for feeling guilty" (p. 222). Viewed from our current perspective, repeated early experiences of helplessness and unresponsiveness stimulate the development of massive narcissistic defensive structures and preclude the development of normal shame. In the most extreme instances, when the lack of emotional attachment to caretakers is profound or perverted by cruelty, shame does not develop as a self-regulating affect.

Narcissistic personality disorders of all kinds are typically characterized by significant "super-ego pathology" (Kernberg, 1992, p. 222): The shame response is dissociated from conscious experience. Such men are extremely devaluing of others, manipulative, and riddled with envy. When discomforting feelings arise in relation to others, their response to the disquietude is to go into action by lying, stealing, swindling, being sexually promiscuous, assaulting, or even murdering. Such men are said to act without remorse for the injury or harm they do to others. Shame has ceased to play its inhibitory function. Yet while shamelessness may characterize much of their predatory behavior, shame continues to play a role in the scenarios being enacted and is often intrinsic to the antisocial sequence. For those men whose shame has been dissociated from the rage it evoked, the possibility of retaliation is alluring if not compelling. As with the perversions, the actions of antisocial men often involve victims in a routinized, even compulsive manner. Con artists, power rapists, and serial killers often act out sadomasochistic scenarios. Shame is undeniably present. The "mark" is taken advantage of by the con man. He or she will be left humiliated and angry. Power rapists are sexually aroused by the humiliation of their victims. Serial killers often kill prostitutes. Murderous rage, typically dissociated, follows the humiliation of having needed so debased a creature as a prostitute to gratify a repugnant bodily need. Shame is everywhere.

PERVERSIONS

The perversions are another type of narcissistic transformation of shame that, historically, has been viewed as a form of male psychopathology (Kaplan, 1991). Perversions in men (e.g., pedophilia, sadomasochism, exhibitionism, voyeurism) are attempts to solve a particular type of problem involving a fragile and profoundly insecure masculine identification. Like the classic narcissistic presentation, perverse behaviors are at times almost literal caricatures of prescribed sex role behaviors. Perversions function to maintain intrapsychic boundaries and self-cohesion in the face of fears of engulfment and wishes to merge with an all-powerful other. By focusing on a ritualized sadomasochistic scenario, or by enacting some secret behavior or fantasy, the man in question can maintain his sense of separateness and control. The act itself typically involves a scenario in which embarrassment, shame, or humiliation is induced or endured. The man's own shame over his vulnerability and need are split off and denied during the act. At the same time, his need for, and dependence upon, these rigid scenarios is itself shame-inducing. Perversions, like addictions and compulsions, are embedded in layers of shame. Surely they are among the most privately guarded secrets, and most individuals would be mortified were they to be known.

MALE DEPRESSION AND SUICIDE

Male vulnerability to depression is poorly understood. Depression is a universal response to early loss, "traumatic abrogation of the holding environment" (Chapter 2), and to the experience of physical and sexual abuse. It is also a common reaction to gender role failure, whether as a breadwinner, a husband, or a father. Lansky (1992), reflecting on his clinical experience with psychiatrically impaired fathers, writes:

> These men will talk about almost anything rather than admit the[ir] failures at fathering. They complain of "voices" or of suicidality. They admit to substance abuse, domestic violence, even homicide. . . . But they will do almost anything rather than face . . . these failures and the confirmation of the fact that their children are truly ashamed of them. (p. 8)

Depression may also follow experiences with loss of health and robustness. Men who are recovering from cardiac surgery are at extremely high risk for depressive reactions, which in turn may impede recovery. Similarly, many men who have experienced testicular or prostate cancer struggle with depression over both symbolic and real loss of the potency that has been a component of their male gender identity (Reiker, 1993).

Suicidality, which is strongly linked to depression, is a significant mental health concern among depressed men. Men commit suicide nearly four times more often than women (Fawcett, Clark, & Busch, 1993). White male adolescents have the highest suicide rate of any group. Lansky (1992) writes that "suicidal crises . . . reflect narcissistic breakdown, collapse and exposure. It is important to realize that we are dealing with by-passed shame" (p. 199). As in other situations, males, when faced with unbearable shame, move into action to discharge the tension and escape the profound sense of despair. Suicide, like domestic violence and assaults on peers, is an attempt to transform the helpless passivity that threatens their core identification as male.

SUBSTANCE ABUSE AND COMPULSIVE BEHAVIORS

Male intolerance for shame states may suggest some of the reasons fewer men report depression. Unable to bear the depressive experience, men turn to alcohol and drug abuse in great numbers. Indeed, epidemiological data reveal that men abuse alcohol at four to five times the rate of women and abuse drugs almost twice as often. Levy and Dykin (1989) report that "strong correlations have been shown between alcohol abuse and major depression, especially among men" (p. 1464). Additional findings link high rates of suicidal ideation and behavior to substance abuse among men. Alcohol use and abuse among men serves several aims. It dissolves shame, at least temporarily, and softens the harsh superego criticism (Horowitz, 1981) that chastises the self for its failures. For men, drinking facilitates interpersonal connections and self-disclosures that are otherwise hard to make, particularly with other men. When parents—or more likely, fathers—modeled alcohol-dependent behavior, the adult male child of an alcoholic family retains his connection and membership in his family system by drinking. Such modeling is a kind of "identification with the aggressor," with the goal of disavowing the shameful and often enraging impact of parental alcoholism.

Addiction to substances, as well as other compulsive behaviors (e.g., gambling), serves self-regulatory functions (e.g., self-soothing and self-coherence). The individual becomes involved with a substance or a behavior as a substitute for, and symbolic gratification of, his dependent yearnings. The dependency is shifted to the substance or the behavior. Should attention be drawn to the dependent/addictive relationship, the resulting shame may be profound. Not surprisingly, these behaviors are carried out in secret and elaborately protected with lies and deceptions that, in themselves, become obsessive-compulsive routines. Many characteristic male behaviors comprise these patterns to ward off guilt over aggressive impulses and shame over dependent longings and to hide from criticism and further shame. Guilt and aggression are often more prominent in the self-presentation. Below the surface of the guilt, one often discovers massive and unacknowledged shame.

Summary

I have made a complex and, at times, speculative argument about the nature of shame and its role in male gender development. In concluding, it seems worthwhile to briefly summarize the argument before discussing some of the implications.

In contrast to the minimal role assigned the shame family of experience by traditional psychoanalytic and other clinical observers, I have presented a view of shame as a primary self affect, one that is deeply embedded in the development of both self-esteem and gender identity. According to this view, shame, like other affects, has the potential to be transformed from the global intensity of early childhood into sophisticated and subtle affective signals. Such modulation provides continuous "background" information about how the self fits or fails to fit into its interpersonal environment. As such, shame is seen as playing a normative and adaptive role, although its motivational power is derived from its attention-getting aversive sting.

Cultures routinely rely on shame-based sanctions to motivate gender role acquisition and conformity among males and females. Insofar as males and females are expected to learn different roles and reactions with respect to many physical, emotional, and interpersonal dimensions, what is shameful is, to a significant degree, different for males and females.

Males and females have different gender experiences with shame. Females have more direct experiences with it, are more familiar with it and its nuances, and are better able to integrate it into ongoing relationships without becoming psychologically disorganized by it. Females do, however, suffer considerably more depression as a function of shame sensitivity.

I have identified four factors inherent in male development and socialization that contribute to the difficulty males have in expanding their adaptive utilization of shame-based experiences: (1) the process of disidentification and the struggle for psychological autonomy, (2) problematic identification with shaming and/or absent caretakers, (3) sex role stereotypes and ideologies that deny vulnerability, and (4) the inclination toward action and away from affect tolerance, self-exposure, and relating. These normative barriers to more mature shame socialization leave males, in contrast to females, more likely to experience shame states as threatening to their sense of psychological organization and gender identity. Males are socialized to avoid shame and go to great lengths to do so. As a result, the male relationship to shame often remains relatively undeveloped, immature, and reactive. Rather than being modulated and transformed into an adaptive signal to guide interpersonal relations, shame remains closely tied to impulsivity and fight-flight behaviors. Indeed, unacknowledged and unmanaged shame experiences in men have been linked to dysfunctional adaptations such as tendencies toward social and emotional isolation and over reliance on aggression to solve problems. These tendencies are relatively normative and should be seen as extensions of socially reinforced gender norms. Other behaviors, such as substance abuse, impulsive and antisocial behavior, and perverse sexuality, are clearly dysfunctional, although they too take their shape from gender role instructions.

CONCLUSIONS

> At a time when women, with good reason, are asking men to make known their most guarded feelings, when [women] want them to love and raise babies, and remember [their] birthdays, it is also required that they be the ones to rescue people in a burning building, and startle the dragons when they are heard in the dark. (Emerson, 1985, p. 14)

The contemporary American male finds himself in a dilemma rooted in contradictory gender role expectations (Betcher & Pollack, 1993; Pleck, 1981). Traditional social representations of masculinity, as well as contemporary gender role expectations, include deep concerns about aggression and managing the threat of aggression from other males by controlling (denying) one's own fears and concealing signs of emotional and physical vulnerability. As long as gender role norms and expectations include a significant connection between being male and being aggressive, shame socialization is likely to serve as a vehicle through which males are taught to suppress and contain their vulnerabilities. As long as males must be prepared to serve as soldiers, or in other ways as guardians, shame affects will be mobilized during childhood and adolescence to support boys in coping with emotional and physical threat, in conformity with peer group expectations.

At the same time, more contemporary gender role expectations reflect changing social and economic role relationships in the family and workplace. These expectations put pressure on males to be more collaborative and less competitive in their modes of interaction, and more aware of and responsive to emotional needs, their own and others'. These changes include interpersonal as well as intrapsychic pressures to be more communicative in intimate relationships, to be more involved as nurturing parents, and to be able to function effectively in nonhierarchical, team-based work environments.

The analysis presented here argues that (1) shame has a functional role to play in ensuring that boys and girls learn and adhere to the gender roles that will support their membership in their families and society, and that (2) shame has its roots in both the early parental environment and the peer group. To lessen the burden of shame in men's lives, the social reality in which boys continue to be raised largely by their mothers and other women, with men placed at a distance from the parenting process, needs to become one in which fathers are more present parents. Furthermore, social and cultural efforts to modify rigid gender role expectations and reinforce gender role flexibility with respect to behavior and feelings can lessen, to some degree, the impact of shame when boys do not conform to traditional expectations. Social modeling of an increased range of acceptable male behaviors by prominent and estimable figures supports this direction. At the same time, deep issues related to safety and acceptance within the peer group can only be addressed at that level. Educational programs aimed at building self-esteem and mutual regard based on nonaggressive, nonhierarchical challenges have the potential to generate alternative models.

Structural factors based in economic and family life, however, remain the anchor points to the developmental process. Paternal involvement requires economic support for intact families. The shame of the unemployed father is difficult to mediate or compensate. The cycle is pernicious with respect to the management of self-esteem, shame, and violence. Flight from the shame of the disabled family and unworthy father leads to the peer group, as does the defiant retreat from a rejecting, hostile, and racist society. There, unreconstructed male norms for status and power predominate. The role and function of shame in male development reflects, and is responsive to, these social and emotional realities of male experience. To change the one requires that the other change as well.

Gender role norms are widely understood to be socially constructed. This is not to say that they are either superficial or easily modified. Gilmore (1990) observes that gender roles tend to be more extreme as a function of the harshness of the economic conditions facing a society. The dual realities of the male gender role must be kept in mind as we consider the double bind in which we place our sons when we expect them to have the heart of a warrior and the soul of a poet.

References

American Psychological Association (APA) Commission on Violence and Youth. (1993). *Violence and youth: Psychology's response.* Washington, DC: American Psychological Association Press.

Betcher, W., & Pollack, W. (1993). *In a time of fallen heroes: The re-creation of masculinity.* New York: Atheneum.

Block, J. (1983). Differential premises arising from differential socialization of the sexes: Some conjectures. *Child Development, 54*, 1335–1354.

Block Lewis, H. (1971). *Shame and guilt in neurosis.* Hillsdale, NJ: Lawrence Erlbaum.

Block Lewis, H. (Ed.). (1987). The role of shame in depression over the life span. *The role of shame in symptom formation.* Hillsdale, NJ: Lawrence Erlbaum.

Braithwaite, J. (1989). *Crime, shame and reintegration.* Cambridge, Eng.: Cambridge University Press.

Brody, L. (1985). Gender differences in emotional development: A review of themes and research. *Journal of Personality, 53*(2), 102–149.

Broucek, F. J. (1982). Shame and its relationship to early narcissistic developments. *International Journal of Psychoanalysis, 63*, 369–378.

Campbell, A. (1993). *Men, women and aggression.* New York: Basic Books.

Carlson, V., Cicchetti, D., Barnett, D., & Braunwald, K. (1989). Disorganized/disorientated attachment relationships in maltreated infants. *Developmental Psychology, 25*(4), 525–531.

Chodorow, N. (1989). *Feminism and psychoanalytic theory.* New Haven, CT: Yale University Press.

Cicchetti, D., & Toth, S. L. (Eds.) (1991). *Internalizing and externalizing expressions of dysfunction: Rochester symposium on developmental psychopathology.* Hillsdale, NJ: Lawrence Erlbaum.

Cleary, P. D. (1987). Gender differences in stress-related disorders. In R. C. Barnett, L. Biener, & G. K. Baruch (Eds.), *Gender and stress* (pp. 39–72). New York: Free Press.

De Jong, P. (1993, June 6). Talking trash. *New York Times Sunday Magazine,* pp. 30–38.

Ekman, P. (1993). Facial expression and emotion. *American Psychologist, 48*(4), 384–392.

Emerson, G. (1985). *Some American men.* New York: Simon & Schuster.

Erikson, E. (1965). *Childhood and society.* Middlesex, Eng.: Penguin Books.

Fawcett, J., Clark, D.C., & Busch, K.A. (1993). Assessing and treating the patient at risk for suicide. *Psychiatric Annals 23*(5), 244–255.

Freud, S. (1962). Further remarks on the neuro-psychoses of defense. In J. Strachey (Ed. and Trans.), *The standard edition of the complete psychological work of Sigmund Freud* (Vol. 3, pp. 159–185). London: Hogarth Press. (Original work published 1896.)

Freud, S. (1964). New introductory lectures on psychoanalysis. In J. Strachey (Ed. & Trans.), *The standard edition of the complete psychological works of Sigmund Freud* (Vol. 22, pp. 3–183). London: Hogarth Press. (Original work published 1933.)

Friedman, R. C. (1988). *Male homosexuality: A contemporary psychoanalytic perspective.* New Haven, CT: Yale University Press.

Gilmore, D. D. (1990). *Manhood in the making: Cultural concepts of masculinity.* New Haven, CT: Yale University Press.

Greenson, R. R. (1968). Dis-identifying from mother: Its special importance for the boy. *International Journal of Psychoanalysis, 49*, 370–374.

Harder, D. (1990). Comment on Wright, O'Leary, and Balkin. *Psychoanalytic Psychology, 7*(2), 285–289.

Horowitz, M. (1981). Self-righteous rage and the attribution of blame. *Archives of General Psychiatry, 38*, 1233–1237.

Hudson, L., and Jacot, B. (1991). *The way men think: Intellect, intimacy, and the erotic imagination*. New Haven, CT: Yale University Press.

Izard, C. (1977). *Human emotions*. New York: Plenum.

Kaplan, D. L. (1991). *Female perversions: The temptations of Emma Bovary*. New York: Doubleday.

Kernberg, O. (1986). Narcissistic personality disorder. In A. M. Cooper, A. J. Frances, & M. H. Sacks (Eds.), *The personality disorders and neuroses* (pp. 219–230). New York: Basic Books.

Kernberg, O. (1992). *Aggression in personality disorders and perversions*. New Haven, CT: Yale University Press.

Kinston, W. (1983). A theoretical context for shame. *International Journal of Psychoanalysis, 64,* 213–226.

Kohut, H. (1971). *The analysis of the self*. New York: International Universities Press.

Krugman, S. (1987). Trauma in the family: Perspectives on the intergenerational transmission of violence. In B. A. van der Kolk (Ed.), *Psychological trauma* (pp. 127–151). Washington, DC: American Psychiatric Press.

Lansky, M. R. (1992). *Fathers who fail: Shame and psychopathology in the family system*. Hillsdale, NJ: Analytic Press.

Lasch, C. (1978). *The culture of narcissism*. New York: Norton.

Levy, J. C., & Dykin, E. Y. (1989). Suicidality, depression and substance abuse in adolescence. *American Journal of Psychiatry, 146*(11), 1462–1467.

Lewis, M. (1992). *Shame: The exposed self*. New York: Free Press.

Ley, G. D., & Carter, D. B. (1989). Gender schema, gender constancy, and gender-role knowledge: The roles of cognitive factors in preschoolers' gender-role stereotype attributions. *Developmental Psychology, 25*(3), 444–449.

Maccoby, E. (1988). Gender as a social category. *Developmental Psychology, 24*(6), 775–765.

Malatesta-Magai, C. (1991). Emotional socialization: Its role in personality and developmental psychpathology. In D. Cicchetti & S. L. Toth (Eds.), *Internalizing and externalizing expressions of dysfunction: Rochester symposium on developmental psychopathology*. Hillsdale, NJ: Lawrence Erlbaum.

McDougal, J. (1987). *Plea for a measure of abnormality*. New York: Brunner/Mazel.

Morrison, A. P. (1983). Shame, the ideal self, and narcissism. *Contemporary Psychoanalysis, 19,* 295–318.

Morrison, A. P. (1989). *Shame: The under side of narcissism*. Hillsdale, NJ: Analytic Press.

Nathanson, D. L. (Ed.). (1987a). *The many faces of shame*. New York: Guilford Press.

Nathanson, D. L. (1987b). A timetable for shame. In D. L. Nathanson (Ed.), *The many faces of shame* (pp. 1–63). New York: Guilford Press.

Nathanson, D. L. (1987c). Shaming systems in couples, families and institutions. In D. L. Nathanson (Ed.), *The many faces of shame* (pp. 246–270). New York: Guilford Press.

Ogden, T. H. (1989). *The primitive edge of experience*. Northvale, NJ: Jason Aronson.

O'Leary, J., & Wright, F. (1986). Shame and gender: Issues in pathological narcissism. *Psychoanalytic Psychology, 3*(4), 327–339.

Osherson, S. (1992). *Wrestling with love: How men struggle with intimacy, women, children, parents and each other*. New York: Ballantine.

Piers, G., & Singer, M. B. (1953). *Shame and guilt*. New York: Norton.

Pleck, J. H. (1981). *The myth of masculinity*. Cambridge, MA: MIT Press.

Reich, A. (1960). Pathological forms of self esteem regulation. *Psychoanalytic study of the child* (vol. 15, pp. 215–232). New York: International Universities Press.

Rieker, P. (1993, April 13). *Psychological strategies for recovery from testicular and prostate cancer*. Paper presented at conference, "Male Response to Traumatic Exposure," Boston.

Rotundo, E. A. (1993). *American manhood: Transformations in masculinity from the revolution to the modern era*. New York: Basic Books.

Scheff, T. J. (1987). Shame and conformity: The deference-emotion system. *American Sociological Review, 53*, 395–406.

Severino, S. K., McNutt, E. R., & Feder, S. L. (1987). Shame and the development of autonomy. *Journal of the American Academy of Psychoanalysis, 15*(1), 93–106.

Stoller, R. J. (1968). *Sex and gender: On the development of masculinity and feminity*. New York: Science House.

Tabin, J. K. (1985). *On the way to self: Ego and early development*. New York: Columbia University Press.

Thrane, G. (1979). Shame and the construction of the self. *Annual of Psychoanalysis, 7*, 321–324.

Tomkins, S. S. (1981). The quest for primary motives: biography and autobiography of an idea. *Journal of Personality and Social Psychology 44*, 306–329.

Tomkins, S. S. (1982). Affect theory. In P. Ekman (Ed.), *Emotion in the human face* (2nd ed., pp. 353–395). Cambridge, Eng.: Cambridge University Press.

Tomkins, S. S. (1987). Shame. In D. L. Nathanson (Ed.), *The many faces of shame* (pp. 133–161). New York: Norton.

Valliant, G. E. (1977). *Adaptation to life*. Boston: Little, Brown.

Walker, L. (1985). What counselors should know about battered women. In D. J. Sonkin, D. Martin, & L. Walker (Eds.), *The male batterer: A treatment approach* (pp. 150–165). New York: Springer.

Wright, F. (1987). Men, shame and antisocial behavior: A psychodynamic perspective. *Group, 11*(4), 238–246.

Wright, F., O'Leary, J., & Balkin, J. (1989). Shame, guilt, narcissism and depression: Correlates and sex differences. *Psychoanalytic Psychology, 6*(2), 217–230.

Wurmser, L. (1981). *The mask of shame*. Baltimore: Johns Hopkins University Press.

PART II

RESEARCH

CHAPTER 5

Masculinity Ideologies: A Review of Research Instrumentation on Men and Masculinities

EDWARD H. THOMPSON, JR., AND
JOSEPH H. PLECK

FROM THEIR INCEPTION, the social sciences have predominantly provided information about men and male experience. Although social scientific research has traditionally emphasized males, it has not studied men *as men*. Most often, research has treated men as if they had no gender (Kimmel & Messner, 1989). In much the same way that men were thought of as genderless, many schools of thought implicitly generalized from male experience and ignored female experience entirely. However, the work of gender studies scholars over the last 30 years has revealed gender to be a social construction and system of power relations of profound influence. Ironically, we now know far more about womanhood, femininity, and women's experiences than we know about manhood, masculinity, and men's experiences. In recent years, a research interest in men, masculinity standards, and the male experience has arisen. Two notable facts are apparent. This new approach explicitly investigates males as one of two genders and their life opportunities and social experience as systematically different from women's. Second, a number of important instruments and measures have been developed to chart public attitudes toward men and to systematically document how males experience their gender.

An earlier version of this chapter appeared as "Men and Masculinities: Scales for Masculinity Ideology and Masculinity-Related Constructs," *Sex Roles, 27* (December 1992), 573–607. Published by permission of Plenum Publishing.

This chapter contributes to the study of men's lives in two ways. First, we present the concept of "masculinity ideology" as a better way to conceptualize the existing research that addresses attitudes toward men and male roles. Next, we review the 18 extant scales developed in the last three decades that are dedicated to mapping masculinity ideologies or displaying the profound influence of one of these ideologies. Three of the measures were published in the late 1970s, and the remainder have been developed since. We limited the review to (1) attitude measures that tap ideologies about men and masculinities and (2) inventories that reveal how males personally experience their gender, excluding measures that tap gender orientation.

Theoretical Distinctions

Three theoretical concerns are basic to what follows. First is the distinction between gender ideology and gender orientation, a fundamental distinction underlying our classification of measures. Next, conscious of the diversity of gender ideologies, we separate ideologies that focus on men from those that address women and those that address gender relations. Third, because the social meaning of masculinity varies and competing masculinities coexist, we distinguish between the measures that assume a single standard of masculinity and those that recognize more than one version of masculinity.

Distinguishing Gender Ideology from Gender Orientation

As a context for easily recognizing the common underpinning to the measures we review, several preliminary conceptual issues need to be addressed. To begin, we believe parallel but dissimilar conceptualizations of masculinity emerged as research interests in men's experience became more extensive. At the most general level, there appear to be two quite different approaches to masculinity: (1) *trait* perspectives—exemplified by the "male sex role identity" model and conceptualizations of androgyny (see Pleck, 1981, for a more extensive discussion)—view masculinity as a psychologically (or biologically) based characteristic, and (2) *normative* perspectives—exemplified by the "social constructionist" model and conceptualizations of gender as an integral part of any social group's system of power relations—view masculinity as a culturally based ideology scripting gender relations, attitudes, and beliefs. The trait approach presumes that masculinity is rooted in actual differences between men and women and primarily analyzes the personality (e.g., Spence & Helmreich's [1978] Personal Attributes Questionnaire [PAQ]) and behavioral attributes (e.g, Snell's [1989] Masculine Behavior Scale) more often associated with men than women.[1] This approach makes masculinity an individual property. Masculinity is the gender orientation attributed to many but not all men, and it is assessed with self-concept ratings. Men who possess particular personality attributes and behavioral tendencies are referred to as "masculine." To illustrate the trait approach, a "traditional" male possesses the characteristics expected in men and thus *has* masculinity. A "nontraditional" male reveals other traits and is missing something. The heart of masculinity is, therefore, located in the men.

By contrast, the traditional male, viewed in normative terms, is one who endorses the ideology that men *should* have sex-specific characteristics (and women should not). The normative approach views masculinity as a component of a broader gender ideology that recommends the values, traits, and behaviors the members of a group believe a person should have as a man or woman. Masculinity, viewed from a normative approach, is a socially constructed gender ideal for men and for male roles. Investigations using a normative approach typically study what people believe manhood to be, how institutions maintain different masculinity standards, and what consequences arise when one masculinity standard is endorsed rather than another.

Prior theoretical analyses of masculinity generally did not distinguish clearly between the trait and normative approaches but blended elements of the two together (e.g., Brannon, 1976; Pleck, 1976). The distinction we wish to draw between trait-based approaches to gender orientation and normative approaches to gender ideology is not without controversy (cf. Archer [1989, 1990] and McCreary [1990] for debate about whether gender orientation and gender attitudes are conceptually or empirically distinct). However, we adopted this essential distinction as a basis for classifying the masculinity-related assessment instruments currently available in the literature. Instruments designed from a trait perspective to assess men's gender orientation were excluded from this review. They have been comprehensively reviewed elsewhere (Beere, 1979, 1990; Lenney, 1991) and critiqued on methodological (Deaux, 1984; Pedhazur & Tetenbaum, 1979; Taylor & Hall, 1982) and conceptual grounds (Connell, 1987; Pleck, 1981; West & Zimmerman, 1987).

The two groups of measures we review either tap the beliefs and attitudes people maintain about men and their gender or index men's gendered expe-

[1]It should be noted that Spence's and Bem's current intepretations of what their instruments assess differ from how these authors originally presented the scales. Janet Spence's most recent work describes the dimensions assessed as "instrumental" and "expressive" traits stereotypically associated with one sex more than the other (Spence, Losoff, & Robbins, 1991). She continues to accept the idea that the PAQ measures traits but thinks the traits should not be labeled masculine and feminine. By comparison, Sandra Bem (1981) continues to accept the labels masculine and feminine but currently argues that the BSRI does not assess personality "traits" but rather cognitive "schema" related to gender. Despite these reconceptualizations, most research employing the PAQ and BSRI interprets the measures as operationalizing traits or traitlike personality dispositions.

riences. Although the developers of the first group of scales might not recognize their work under the rubric "masculinity ideologies," these instruments were designed to index the extent to which individuals endorse the ideas and beliefs that serve to justify gender scripts and gender relations. The second group of measures shift the focus to how men individually experience gender. Some of these instruments assess personal application of a masculinity standard, and others assess conflict or stress related to a masculinity.

DISTINGUISHING AMONG GENDER IDEOLOGIES

The array of beliefs and attitudes individuals hold about men, women, and gender relations do not make up a single, tidy set. Gender-related attitudes have a wide variety of subjects: For example, there are attitudes toward gender relations, attitudes toward women, attitudes toward feminism and feminist goals, attitudes toward "sex role" traditionality, attitudes toward men, and attitudes toward masculinity. Thus, gender-related attitude scales also can have a wide variety of objects. We conceptualize attitudes toward men and masculinities as expressing distinct ideologies that can differ from the attitudes someone holds toward women or gender relations in general. Thompson and Pleck (1986) observed in their study of undergraduates' gender-related ideologies that endorsement of a masculinity ideology was empirically distinct from attitudes toward women or attitudes toward gender relations, as did Pleck, Sonenstein, and Ku (1993a) in a national sample of adolescent males, and Gradman (1990) in a sample of older men. The various gender ideologies are certainly connected, yet an individual can hold a progressive attitude toward women (e.g., believing that working mothers' employment is quite acceptable) while simultaneously holding a conservative attitude toward men (e.g., believing that men should remain the primary family breadwinner).

Most gender-related ideology scales focus on women and their behavior, or on gender relations, or on both (see Beere, 1990). Fewer focus on men and their relations with others. Unfortunately, many researchers are unfamiliar with the masculinity ideology measures and thus are likely to use ill-suited gender ideology measures to attempt to define attitudes to men and manhood. The first 11 measures we review were all designed to tap respondents' attitudes toward the rights and responsibilities of men.

To tap masculinity ideologies, the content of scale items should concern gender expectations *without* making a comparison between men and women (e.g., "A young man should be physically tougher than his sister, even if he is not big"). The rationale for this criterion is that to understand public attitudes toward masculinities, ideally these ideologies would be assessed independently of attitudes about women or attitudes toward men compared with women.

It might be argued that even when item wording refers only to men living up to male standards, some degree of comparison with females is always implicit. This may be true to some degree. It is nonetheless desirable to use items that focus on men and masculinity standards to the greatest degree possible. Items explicitly comparing the sexes (e.g., "Swearing and obscenity are more repulsive in the speech of a woman than of a man," the first item in Spence, Helmreich, & Stapp's [1973] widely used Attitudes Toward Women Scale [AWS], short form) are logically difficult to interpret as assessing the attitudes held toward one gender independently of attitudes about the other. Conceptually, items making simultaneous assessments of men and women are measuring *gender attitudes* in general. Thus, many scales labeled as assessing attitudes toward women or attitudes toward men may actually assess the broader construct of gender attitudes (e.g., of the 25 items in the short form of the AWS, 15 explicitly compare the sexes, and several others do so implicitly). When researchers developed these gender attitude scales, many believed the variance in gender ideology concerned only women's rights and roles, whereas men's rights and roles were assumed to be invariant, a fixed standard against which attitudes toward women could be compared.

The beliefs and values underlying masculinity ideologies are most often assessed by agreement or disagreement with third-person statements. However, they may also be assessed with first-person statements (e.g., "I would be more comfortable with a male boss than a female boss"). In some instances, deciding whether a first-person item is better classified as assessing the respondent's gender orientation or masculinity ideology may be difficult. We made decisions based on our judgment of the author's intent.

Assessment of attitudes toward masculinities can take two forms. Some items assess prescriptive statements (beliefs about what men *should* be like), and some items assess descriptive statements (beliefs about what men *actually are* like). Both categories of beliefs about men are important. The former are normative statements and are more closely linked with ideology, whereas descriptive beliefs about men are more closely linked with stereotypes. However important the distinction between norms and stereotypes, the masculinity ideology measures reviewed here generally mix both kinds of perceptions together. Thus, it is not possible to draw any conclusions from the present evidence about how differing attitudes toward masculinities compare or about the relative importance of normative beliefs versus descriptive beliefs. This analysis remains for future research.

Assessing a Single Norm for Male Standards?

The third interpretive issue concerns whether the measures of masculinity ideology assume the existence of multiple types of masculinity or one dominant form of masculinity. Critical voices have argued that although many in the gender field accept the idea of *the* male role and its complement, *the* female role, as generalized prescriptions for men and women this assumption is problematic. Studying the male role does not lend itself to an unambiguous understanding of men. Unlike most roles, such as father, telephone lineman, or husband, "the male role" has no specific organizational context or location (West & Zimmerman, 1987). It is thought of as a synthesis of the multiple roles men perform and as a compendium of the varied expectations men face as men. (See Deaux, Winston, Crowley, & Lewis's 1985 study of the relative homogeneity of the male stereotype, and Edwards's 1992 argument that broad cognitive categories, such as "men," do not capture the commonly made distinctions within.) Second, research informs us that, in key respects, men in diverse racial-ethnic groups may define standards for males differently (Baca-Zinn, 1984; Cazenave & Leon, 1987; Franklin, 1988).

Third, items in masculinity ideology scales receive varying levels of endorsement (Downs & Engleson, 1984; Pleck et al., 1993a; Thompson & Pleck, 1986). Rather than signifying that these items simply have dissimilar threshold levels in the assessment of a single masculinity standard, this variance across items may actually indicate that multiple, different standards are held by different subgroups. Finally, but not the least important, the image of a single standard of masculinity is apolitical and ignores the pervasive imbalance of power among different men or within gender relations (Connell, 1987; Morgan, 1990). Being a man changes from one generation to the next, and the expectations differ for men of different racial, ethnic, and religious groups, as well as social classes.

In our view, studies assessing beliefs and attitudes about men, as well as investigations of men's gender-related stress and conflicts, ought not assume that all social groups, cultures, subcultures, and periods have the same male standards. In recognition of the multiplicity of conceptions of masculinity, we generally use the term "ideologies" rather then "ideology," or male "standards" rather than "standard." Scholars have also argued that the term "masculinities" needs to be used rather than "masculinity" (Brod, 1987; Connell, 1987; Hearn & Morgan, 1990; Kimmel & Messner, 1989; Segal, 1990). Historically, Green (1946), Hacker (1957), and Komarovsky (1973) were perhaps the earliest to argue that multiple masculinities coexist and often conflict. We anticipate that the social forces affecting men's experiences will be differentially salient for men of different ages, cohorts, classes, races, sexual preferences, and regions. We also assume that some expectations and social forces will be a common denominator in men's lives (cf. Gilmore, 1990).

Many of the attitudinal measures we review include multiple dimensions. One might argue that these scales therefore do not assume a single masculinity standard. Comparing different groups or cultures on their profiles of these multidimensional instruments would empirically document the extent to which different masculinity standards are endorsed to different degrees by these groups or cultures. Others might argue, however, that these scales still assume one monolithic male role, albeit with component dimensions. Throughout our review, we identify which masculinity ideology measures involve multiple subscales, and which measures assume single versus multiple masculinities.

Measures Reviewed

We include in this review only instrumentation that has been peer-reviewed, is relatively recent in development, and is accessible. Thus, excluded from the review are the early generation of attitude measures, such as the Anti-femininity in Men Scale (Allen, 1954). Also excluded are the measures designed expressly to illustrate gender stereotypes, such as the Sex Role Stereotype Questionnaire (Rosenkrantz, Vogel, Bee, & Broverman, 1968). Nor, as stated above, did we consider the widely used measures of gender orientation, such as the Bem Sex Role Inventory (BSRI) (Bem, 1974) and the Personal Attributes Questionnaire (PAQ) (Spence & Helmreich, 1978), or the lessor-known measures of gender orientation, such as the Boyhood Gender Conformity Scale (BGCS) (Hockenberry & Billingham, 1987) and the Masculine Behavior Scale (MBS) (Snell, 1989). Neither measures of gender stereotypes nor measures of gender orientation describe masculinity ideologies or how a male believes a masculinity ideology affects him. Therefore, this review is restricted to the relatively new instruments assessing masculinity ideologies and how men experience their gender.

The first group of masculinity-related measures reviewed are the instruments assessing attitudes about men or masculinity standards in relatively pure form, that is, with either no items or only a few tapping gender orientation. The second group comprises seven other masculinity-related instruments assessing how males experience their gender. The measures reviewed were identified in a literature search of two databases, *PsychInfo*, since 1967, and *PsycLIT*, since 1974. One unpublished scale not used in later published work (Falkenberg, Hindman, & Masey, 1983, cited in Beere, 1990, pp. 426–427) was not included in this review because it has not been used by others, nor has the article presenting it been subjected to peer review.[2] The research studies employing the instruments reviewed here were located primarily using the *Social Science Citations Index* and by contacting scale authors.

[2]Promising new work by Beth Willinger is also not included. Her work examines men's masculinity ideology across different cohorts of young men, based on a new scale she has developed. She can be reached at the Newcomb Center for Research on Women, Tulane University, New Orleans, LA 70118.

MEASURES OF MASCULINITY IDEOLOGY

Eleven instruments measuring masculinity ideologies were located and are listed in Table 5.1 (pp. 138–39). The scales are arranged chronologically. They focus on gender-related attitudes and values, and they generally do not include items that tap gender orientation. However, many of these scales do include items comparing the sexes or concerning gender relations. Some scales also include items assessing attitudes and beliefs about women. Inclusion of these types of items is noted in the table. Three other general concerns served as guides to systematically evaluate the scales and are summarized in the table: We were interested in whether the authors assessed only a single form of masculinity ideology, in whether subscales were identified, and in the psychometric properties of the scale and subscales.

Macho Scale

Villemez and Touhey's (1977) Macho Scale (MS) is a 28-item self-report measure of individual differences in endorsement of sexist attitudes and discriminatory practices. The scale includes a number of items assessing attitudes toward men, but 25% of the items compare the sexes to tap gender attitudes generally (e.g., "Parents usually maintain stricter control over their daughters than their sons, and they should"). For another 46% of the items, a female noun or pronoun is central, and thus the items measure attitudes about women. For example, one statement reads, "Women who try to be independent of their families are just hurting themselves." Basically, the MS presents both first- and third-person declarative statements to index beliefs about the appropriate behavior for men *and* women (e.g., "A wife who becomes a mother has no more reason to give up her career than a husband who becomes a father," or, "I would be more comfortable with a male boss than a female boss"). Given the content of the items, the MS is fundamentally a measure of attitudes toward antifemininity and patriarchal ideology. It is not strictly a masculinity ideology measure tapping attitudes toward men and masculinity.

The MS has been used for more than a decade (Anderson, 1978; Barrish & Welch, 1980; Brinkerhoff & MacKie, 1985; Downs & Engleson, 1982; Gayton, Sawyer, Baird, & Ozmon, 1982). According to Downs and Engleson, the MS is limited to measuring the power dimension associated with traditional, sexist gender relations. Mazer and Percival (1989) concur, finding that the more sexist subjects were, the more tolerant they were of sexual harassment. Even if limited to measuring a power dimension, Villemez and Touhey's 28-item scale, or Brinkerhoff and MacKie's 18-item adaptation, makes a valuable contribution to the measurement of sexist attitudes by including items about men.

Attitudes Toward the Male Role Scale

Doyle and Moore (1978) developed the 45-item Attitudes Toward the Male Role (AMR) scale to index the appropriate behavior for men. Their conceptual model assumed a universal standard of masculinity, but their design of the AMR includes five distinct segments within men's lives: male dominance, vocational pursuits, sexuality, emotionality, and relations with women and other men. All but one of the items in the AMR has a male noun leading the sentence (Gackenbach & Auerbach, 1985, p. 241). Statements addressing masculinity norms and values are included in the scale (e.g., "A man who cries in front of a woman is making a fool of himself"). The AMR includes both descriptive and prescriptive statements; nearly one-third of the items are descriptive stereotypes about men's lives (e.g., "Men are naturally better drivers than women"), whereas the remainder are the prescriptive "should" statements. However, one-third of the items also require comparing men with women (e.g., "Men are more decisive in crisis situations than women," or, "Men are inclined by nature to be more truthful and direct than women"). With these items, the AMR taps attitudes toward men in comparison with women, and it is difficult to know if one type of gender ideology is being measured more than another. For example, moderate correlations were also found between the AMR and Villemez and Touhey's (1977) MS ($r = .72$, Downs and Engleson, 1982) and Spence and Helmreich's (1972) AWS ($r = .64$ for men and $r = .76$ for women, Doyle & Moore, 1978; $r = .66$, Gackenbach & Auerbach, 1985). The AMR is a general-purpose measure of gender attitudes, not of masculinity ideology explicitly. The scale highlights the expectations men face, and its comparative items tap attitudes toward gender relations and attitudes toward women.

Attitude Toward Masculinity Transcendence Scale

The 46-item Attitude Toward Masculinity Transcendence Scale (ATMTS), developed by Moreland and Van Tuinen (1978), is a general-purpose inventory of the values behind changing masculinities. The ATMTS is based on comparing gender-"transcendent" male behavior with stereotypically masculine behavior (such as outlined by Brannon, 1976). Four aspects of the emerging norms for men and their gender relations were conceptualized: dominance transcendence, homophobia transcendence, nontraditional activities, and acceptance of the new woman. The scale includes some descriptive stereotypes (e.g., "A successful sex life in marriage depends mostly on the man"), but most ATMTS items are prescriptive statements ("Male children should be discouraged from developing interest in traditionally feminine pursuits"). The scale also includes both first- and third-person presentations of norms and values. All but one of the items has the male pronoun leading

TABLE 5.1

Measures of Masculinity Ideology

Authors/Scale	No. of Items	Some Items Compare Sexes	Some Items Measure Attitudes Toward Women	Some Items Measure Gender Orientation	Scale Suggests One Masculinity	Information on Validity[a]	Reliabilities	Sample Size	Subscales[b]
Villemez & Touhey, 1977 Macho Scale (MS)	28	Yes	Yes	No	Yes	Yes	α = (n/a) 2-wk = .91[c]	347—MF	None
Doyle & Moore, 1978 Attitudes Toward the Male Role (AMR)	45	Yes	No	No	Yes	Yes	α = .90 8-wk = .87[c]	1,533—M 1,370—F	None
Moreland & Van Tuinen, 1978 Attitude Toward Masculinity Transcendence Scale (ATMTS)	46	Yes	No	No	No	Yes	α = .94[c]	236—M 176—F	4
Downs & Engleson, 1982 Attitudes Toward Men Scale (AMS)	34	Yes	Yes	No	Yes	Yes	α = .87[c] 2-wk = .92[c]	245—M 361—F	None
Bunting & Reeves, 1983 Macho Scale	15	Yes	Yes	Yes	Yes	Yes	α = (n/a)	197—M	None
Iazzo, 1983 Attitudes Toward Men Scale (AMS)	32	No	No	No	Yes	Yes	α = .79	104—F	4
Brannon & Juni, 1984 Brannon Masculinity Scale (BMS)	110	No	No	No	Yes	Yes	α = .95 4-wk = .92	864—MF	7
Thompson & Pleck, 1986 Male Role Norms Scale (MRNS)	26	No	No	No	Yes	Yes	α = .86	1,510—MF	3

TABLE 5.1 *(continued)*
Measures of Masculinity Ideology

Authors/Scale	No. of Items	Some Items Compare Sexes	Some Items Measure Attitudes Toward Women	Some Items Measure Gender Orientation	Scale Suggests One Masculinity	Information on Validity[a]	Reliabilities	Sample Size	Subscales[b]
Snell, Belk, & Hawkins, 1986a Stereotypes About Male Sexuality Scale (SAMSS)	60	No	No	No	Yes	No	α = (n/a)	27 — M 74 — F	10
Levant et al., 1992 Male Role Norms Inventory (MRNI)	58	No	No	No	No	No	α = .93	287 — MF	7
Pleck, Sonenstein, & Ku, 1993a Male Role Attitudes Scale (MRAS)	8	No	No	No	Yes	Yes	α = .56	1,880 — M	None

[a]See text for validity information.

[b]See text for list of subscales, number of items in each, and alpha coefficients when available.

[c]Reliability coefficient is an average of multiple samples.

or anchoring the statement, yet five items (11%) contrast men to women (e.g., "Men should have less responsibility for child rearing than women").

The ATMTS was designed to measure competing masculinity standards. Unlike many other instruments in which rejection of the "traditional" masculinity script cannot be interpreted as endorsement of a "progressive" ideology, the ATMTS directly taps attitudes toward a nontraditional gender script. However, no empirically reliable factor structure corresponding to the original conceptualization of dominance transcendence, homophobia transcendence, and tolerance of nontraditional activities was found. This lead Moreland and Van Tuinen to suggest that the ATMTS is best considered a unidimensional instrument, and that it has good internal consistency. The final 46-item version of the ATMTS is correlated with the AWS ($r = .62$, Harren, Kass, Tinsley, & Moreland, 1979). The masculinity norms and values tapped by the ATMTS were predictive of decision-making style and satisfaction with career-related decisions (Harren et al., 1978, 1979), perceived and received social support (Burda & Vaux, 1987), and a profeminist position (Buhrke, 1988).

Attitudes Toward Men Scale

Downs and Engleson (1982) developed the 34-item Attitudes Toward Men Scale (AMS) with undergraduates as well as elementary and secondary school teachers in master's degree programs. Like its complement, the Attitudes Toward Women Scale (AWS) (Spence & Helmreich, 1972), the AMS was designed to measure public attitudes toward the roles and status of men. The scale appraises *the* male role as contrasted to *the* female role. Both descriptive stereotypes and prescriptive norms are included in the AMS, and they address men's sexuality, occupational and recreational interests, domestic skills, relationships with women, power-seeking, and emotionality. Each item is worded as a declaration, but not all items assess attitudes toward men separately from attitudes toward women. For example, one item is "Women are more content than men," and another reads, "Women are more comfortable with other women than men are with other men." Eight of the 34 items (24%) have a female noun leading the sentence, and many others examine attitudes toward men and masculinities comparatively. Only 16 items (47%) comment solely on men and masculinities (e.g., "Single fathers are competent to rear children," and, "It is ridiculous for men to stay home and keep house").

Construct validity is supported by the predicted differences in gender and age—males and younger undergraduates were more traditional—by correlations with men's negative attitudes toward seeking help for psychological problems (Good, Dell, & Mintz, 1989), and by correlations with Villemez and Touhey's (1977) MS ($r = .66$), Doyle and Moore's (1978) AMR ($r = .67$), and

Spence and Helmreich's (1972) AWS (r = .84 for men, .57 for women). It is not related to gender orientation as measured by Spence and Helmreich's (1978) Personal Attributes Questionnaire (PAQ). Thus, similar to the AWS, the AMS measures gender attitudes broadly and does not directly tap a gender ideology that specifically concerns men and masculinities.

Macho Scale

Some authors view extreme forms of masculine behavior (or "hypermasculinity") as abnormal or pathological (e.g., Broude, 1990; Glass, 1984). Bunting and Reeves's (1983) 15-item self-report Macho Scale aims to adapt this idea to the assessment of masculinities. The conceptualization of masculinity standards introduced by Brannon (1976) was used as a guide to operationalize a hypermasculinity ideology. The scale is intended for only male respondents. Most items assess the reaction of the respondent to gender violations (e.g., "It irritates me to see a man acting in a way to get sympathy"). The instrument includes both descriptive and prescriptive beliefs about males, as well as a mix of stereotyped beliefs about women (e.g., "There are some jobs that women should not have"). Four (27%) are self-descriptive (e.g., "I am usually able to express my innermost feelings to someone") and assess gender orientation. Because a female pronoun is the primary referent of five items (33%), the Macho Scale does not always assess attitudes toward men and masculinity separately from attitudes about appropriate gender relations or attitudes toward women. This mixing of different types of items limits the scale's usefulness. In many ways, the Macho Scale simultaneously assesses masculinity beliefs, gender attitudes in general, and attitudes toward women. Another limitation of the Macho Scale is that the wording of items best speaks to the unmarried (e.g., "I try not to date a female that is taller than I"). Nonetheless, Bunting and Reeves found that among male undergraduates a "macho" ideology was predictably correlated with an attitudinal tolerance of rape.

Attitudes Toward Men Scale

The 32-item Attitudes Toward Men Scale (AMS) (Iazzo, 1983) was developed to determine the attitudes that *women* have about men. Iazzo's scale encompasses four major domains: marriage and parenthood (13 items, e.g., "Most fathers want very much to be close to their children," α = .85); sexuality (7 items, e.g., "The male body is visually unappealing," α = .73); work (4 items, e.g., "It is important to a man that he provide for his family," α = .60); and physical and personality attributes (8 items, e.g., "A man's independence is to be admired," α = .69). All items are descriptive; all have a male noun as the anchor; and no item directly compares men with women.

Several items do assess attitudes toward women indirectly (e.g., "Most husbands consider their wives to be weak and witless creatures"). Iazzo provided some information on the criterion validity of the AMS. Groups of women predicted to hold less favorable attitudes toward men, specifically rape victims, battered wives, and women active in the National Organization of Women (NOW), did indeed hold less favorable attitudes than other women. This pattern suggests that women's attitudes toward men could be more a function of experience than of belief in cultural scripts. Research that examines the construct and discriminant validity of the AMS is needed.

Brannon Masculinity Scale

The 110-item Brannon Masculinity Scale (BMS) was developed by Brannon and Juni (1984; Brannon, 1985) to measure individuals' approval of the norms and values that define *the* male role. The BMS is based on Brannon's (1976) analysis of American culture's "blueprint" of what a man is supposed to be, want, and succeed in doing. This conceptualization presumes that masculinity centers on four themes. Most pivotal, the No Sissy Stuff standard contains two 16-item subscales: avoiding femininity (e.g., "It bothers me when a man does something that I consider 'feminine'") and concealing emotions (e.g., "When a man is feeling a little pain he should try not to let it show very much"). The Big Wheel standard is described with two subscales: being the breadwinner (15 items, e.g., "Success in his work has to be a man's central goal in this life") and being admired and respected (16 items, e.g., "It's essential for a man to have the respect and admiration of everyone who knows him"). The Sturdy Oak standard is also represented by two 16-item subscales: toughness (e.g., "I like for a man to look somewhat tough") and the male machine ("A man should always try to project an air of confidence even if he doesn't really feel confident inside"). Brannon's last masculinity standard, Give 'em Hell, is described in one violence and adventure subscale (15 items, e.g., "A real man enjoys a bit of danger now and then"). All items have a male noun anchoring the sentence. A few items concern gender relations, though they do not compare the sexes (e.g., "A man always deserves the respect of his wife and children"). The BMS contains declarations, presented in both the first and third persons that tap agreement with masculinity norms. Scoring reflects an individual's endorsement of a "traditional" masculinity (Brannon & Juni, 1984; Brannon, Juni, & Grady, undated). Highly correlated with the full scale ($r = .89$), the 58-item short form is more frequently used (Barnett & Baruch, 1987; Baruch & Barnett, 1986; Good, Braverman, & O'Neil, 1991; Thompson, Grisanti, & Pleck, 1985). Brannon and Juni report that the short form may provide an acceptable overall assessment of a traditional masculinity ideology, but they believe it cannot provide separate subscale scores. Subscales should be drawn from the 110-item version, as Rieker, Edbril, and Garnick (1985) did.

Major strengths of the approach taken by Brannon include the scope of the masculinity standards included and the effort to assess attitudes toward the expectations men face without direct comparison with women. The latter is especially noteworthy, because the scale is based on a model of masculinity that defines the male role as distinct from the female role. As many components of masculinity ideology as the BMS taps, using it provides little information about attitudes toward male privilege, men's rights, or men's sexuality.

Male Role Norms Scale

The 26-item Male Role Norms Scale (MRNS) (Thompson & Pleck, 1986) reveals a "traditional" masculinity ideology. The MRNS was derived empirically by factor-analyzing the short form of the Brannon Masculinity Scale. The MRNS reduces the number of basic dimensions underpinning traditional masculinity to three: status norms (11 items, $\alpha = .81$), toughness norms (8 items, $\alpha = .74$), and antifemininity norms (7 items, $\alpha = .76$). Like the BMS, the MRNS measures one ideology and is uncontaminated by items that measure attitudes toward women or toward gender attitudes in general. Combining multiple samples of college students ($N = 1,510$), the alpha for the scale is .86.

The MRNS was related ($r = .44$ for undergraduate males, $r = .55$ for undergraduate females, Thompson, 1990) to the 15-item AWS, which assesses attitudes toward men, women, and gender relations, and the Sex-Role Egalitarianism Scale ($r = -.33$, Sinn, 1993). By contrast, Desnoyers (1988) found the MRNS only moderately correlated with attitudes toward women when the latter were measured by single declarative belief statements such as, "By nature women are happiest when they are making a home and caring for children" ($r = .27$), or, "It is insulting to women to have the 'obey' clause remain in marriage vows" ($r = -.18$). Thompson and Pleck (1986) also noted that the subscales were differentially and only modestly correlated with single-item measures of attitudes toward women: For example, opposition to the Equal Rights Amendment was not related to endorsing status norms, only to toughness ($r = .35$) and antifemininity ($r = .25$) norms.

Construct validity of the MRNS has been supported in studies of adolescent and adult males. The MRNS held a near-zero correlation ($r = .07$) with the M scale of the Bem Sex Role Inventory in one study (Thompson, 1990), and a sufficiently small correlation in another ($r = .26$, Sinn, 1993). Sinn affirmed the discriminant validity of the MRNS in factor analyses with items from the BSRI and regression analyses predicting homophobia and adversarial views of sexual relationships. In discriminant analysis, the MRNS predicted intimates' use of psychologically coercive behavior when gender orientation and attitudes toward women were statistically controlled (Thompson, 1990). The antifemininity subscale successfully predicted which adult men seeking help for psychological problems would drop out of therapy sooner (Riley, 1990).

Variations of the MRNS have emerged. Stark (1991) extracted three items from each subscale. Masculinity ideology more strongly predicted a lower level of same-sex intimacy and greater homophobia than another measure of attitudes toward equality. Like Stark, Gradman (1990) modified the MRNS for his study of older men's transition to retirement. He extracted the three items with the largest loadings from each subscale and modified the items to make them more acceptable to older men (e.g., "sexual partner" was changed to "wife"). Retired men versus those still working did not differ in their endorsement of the traditional masculinity ideology, and endorsement of this gender ideology was unrelated to the older men's gender orientation (the M scale of the PAQ) or well-being.

The brevity of the MRNS, its construct validity, and evidence of its discriminant validity in relation to gender orientation or other gender attitudes are its improvements. The MRNS provides a short measure of attitudes toward three standards within the traditional masculinity ideology. Its limitations, however, are like those of the BMS: The MRNS presents one version of masculinity, provides little information about attitudes toward male privilege, and abridges the range of masculinity standards.

Stereotypes About Male Sexuality Scale

The 60-item Stereotypes About Male Sexuality Scale (SAMSS) (Snell, Belk, & Hawkins, 1986a, 1986b) is a self-report instrument designed to index attitudes toward 10 stereotypes about male sexuality: (1) men should not have certain feelings; (2) sex equals performance; (3) men must orchestrate sex; (4) men are always ready for sex; (5) all physical contact leads to sex; (6) sex equals intercourse; (7) sex requires erection; (8) sex requires orgasm; (9) sex is spontaneous; and (10) men are sexually knowledgeable. Each stereotype is evaluated with six declarative statements about men (e.g., "Lack of an erection will always spoil sex for a man," or, "Most men don't want to assume a passive role in sex"). Some statements are descriptive stereotypes and others are prescriptive norms, but the content of the statements consistently addresses attitudes toward men. Only the reliability estimates for the 10 subscales were reported (alphas range from .63 to .93, average .80); apparently the authors did not intend to use a summary score. Snell and his colleagues (1986b, 1988) provide some information on construct validity. However, the gender-specific correlations were based on 25 to 27 college males and 69 to 74 college females. The strength of the SAMSS is that it broadens the scope of attitudes toward masculinity to include sexual behavior, an area omitted in many other scales. Construct validity, however, still needs to be established in larger, more diverse samples.

Male Role Norms Inventory

The 58-item Male Role Norms Inventory (MRNI) (Levant et al., 1992) is composed of both normative and nontraditional statements about *the* male role. The authors theorized seven normative standards: avoidance of femininity (8 items, e.g., "Boys should prefer to play with trucks rather than dolls"), homophobia (5 items, e.g., "A man should be able to openly show affection to another man"), achievement/status (10 items, e.g., "It's not important for men to strive to reach the top"), attitudes toward sex (10 items, e.g., "A man doesn't need to have an erection in order to enjoy sex"), restrictive emotionality (10 items, e.g., "A man should never reveal worries to others"), self-reliance (7 items, e.g., "A man should never count on someone else to get the job done"), and aggression (8 items, e.g., "A man should not force the issue if another man takes his parking space").

Confirmatory factor analysis indicated that the MRNI consists of three rather than seven dimensions. These factors present masculinity norms that are being rejected and those that are still thought to regulate behavior. The first consists of items from the femininity avoidance, homophobia, achievement/status, attitudes toward sex, and restrictive emotionality subscales ($\alpha = .93$). The second matched the conceptually derived self-reliance subscale ($\alpha = .62$), and the third matched the aggression subscale ($\alpha = .48$). The content of the MRNI is largely prescriptive statements about appropriate behavior for men. It is noteworthy that the authors found evidence that age, marital status, and gender affect attitudes toward the masculinity norms.

Broadening the scope of the measured, traditional masculinity norms to explicitly include sexuality is a major strength of this approach. The MRNI also effectively used both normative and nontraditional statements and thus clearly permits the interpretation that rejection of "traditional" masculinity favors a "progressive" masculinity. Although seven types of norms were not empirically confirmed, the instrument may provide reliable subscales. What is now needed is research that attests to the MRNI's construct and discriminant validities.

Male Role Attitudes Scale

Pleck, Sonenstein, and Ku's (1993a, 1993b, 1993c, in press) eight-item Male Role Attitudes Scale (MRAS) uses seven items from the MRNS (Thompson and Pleck, 1986) and an item concerning sexuality from Snell et al.'s (1986a) SAMSS ("Men are always ready for sex"). Item wording was simplified or otherwise modified for adolescent males (e.g., "A guy will lose respect if he talks about his problems"). Like the BMS and MRNS (on whose items it draws), the MRAS uses only items that examine the perceived importance of men fulfilling traditional masculinity standards. Analyses to detect differential correlates of traditional masculinity attitudes among white, black, and Hispanic adolescent males have been conducted, and little evidence of differential relationships was found (Pleck et al., 1993a, 1993b).

Pleck et al. (1993b, in press) observed that, in a national sample of adolescent males, endorsement of the traditional masculinity ideology tapped in the MRAS is associated with school difficulties, alcohol and drug use, delinquency, and coercive sexual behavior. Elsewhere, Pleck et al. (1993a) reported that upholding a traditional masculinity ideology is linked to a negative attitude toward male responsibility for contraception, less consistent use of condoms, more sexual partners, and a belief that relationships between men and women are inherently adversarial. The traditional masculinity ideology indexed in the MRAS predicted condom use in analyses that statistically controlled for more global attitudes toward gender, suggesting that the MRAS has discriminant validity. Using the same data, Marsiglio (1993a, 1993b) found that the MRAS was associated with male pride in making a partner pregnant and predicted heterosexual adolescent males' homophobic views and willingness to befriend a gay. Pleck et al. (1993c) conducted a more extensive discriminant validity analysis, which established that the MRAS is independent of attitudes about women. In addition, although the MRAS is linked to beliefs about gender relations, it has differential correlates with measures of homophobic attitude toward male homosexuals and of male procreative beliefs.

The construct validity of the MRAS and the evidence of its discriminant validity in relation to gender attitudes more generally are its particular advantages. Noteworthy is the finding that the MRAS and its component items have similar correlates among male adolescents in diverse racial-ethnic groups. The small number of items in the scale makes it efficient to administer. However, perhaps because of this, the MRAS's internal reliability is lower than that of any other scale reviewed here ($\alpha = .56$). Its developers hold that while it assesses only one of many possible standards of masculinity, it does not theoretically assume that only one standard or one masculinity exists. "Use of a masculinity ideology scale does not necessitate a theoretical assumption that there is one universal, unvarying standard of masculinity. Rather, the argument is that there is a *particular* social construction of masculinity that has been widely (though not universally) prevalent in the contemporary U.S., which theorists have argued has various kinds of negative concomitants" (Pleck et al., 1993b, p. 91). Critics may still object that the MRAS and similar scales nonetheless present a single standard.

MEASURES FOR MASCULINITY-RELATED CONSTRUCTS

Conceptually distinct from measures of gender orientation, seven other scales were designed to reveal men's experience with gender, particularly as defined by traditional masculinity (see Table 5.2). We have ordered the scales in the table chronologically. The first three include items assessing support of a masculinity ideology. These three masculinity inventories include first-person accounts of personal applications of masculinity standards, a dimension very close to gender orientation. The remaining four instruments assess the level of personal conflict or stress aroused by masculinity standards.

Traditional-Liberated Content Scale

The 29-item Traditional-Liberated Content Scale (TLCS) was designed to identify men's gender traditionalism or liberalism and is inappropriate for women (Biggs & Fiebert, 1984; Fiebert, 1983). Based upon a study of 277 adult men, the TLCS indexes how men behave and feel in four key social relations: their relationships with women, relationships with children, relationships with other men, and involvements at work. The TLCS is made up of two subscales that separately measure "liberated" or emerging views (15 items) and traditional views (14 items). First-person statements comprise 60% of the liberated and 58% of the traditional items; they basically assess men's degree of comfort with masculinity standards (e.g., "I would be flattered if a woman asked me out for a date," or, "I would not feel uncomfortable having a homosexual as a friend"). The remainder of the items are prescriptive attitudinal statements (e.g., "Lack of job success does not mean a man is a failure in life," or, "Every boy should be tough enough to defend himself in a fight"). Two of the prescriptive items in each subscale (or about one-eighth of the items), however, examine men's attitudes about women rather than men.

The scale's content validity has received some support (Fiebert & Vera, 1985; Vera & Fiebert, 1987). The TLCS offers a relatively short measure of individual differences in men's evaluation of themselves as "traditional" or not. A drawback, however, is that the nearly equal representation of self-representational and attitudinal items creates a problem of interpretation. Another concern is that its discriminant validity and other psychometric properties have not been well established.

Hypermasculinity Inventory

Mosher and Sirkin (1984; Mosher & Tomkins, 1988) argue that rigid conformity to traditional masculinity or overcompensation to these gender

TABLE 5.2
Measures for Masculinity-Related Constructs

Authors/Scale	No. of Items	Some Items Compare Sexes	Some Items Measure Attitudes Toward Women	Some Items Measure Gender Orientation	Scale Suggests One Masculinity	Information on Validity[a]	Reliabilities	Sample Size	Subscales[b]
Fiebert (& Biggs), 1984 Traditional-Liberated Content Scale (TLCS)	29	Yes	Yes	No	No	Yes	α = (n/a) 3-wk = .88[c]	277—M	2
Mosher & Sirkin, 1984 Hypermasculinity Inventory (HI)	30	No	Yes	Indirectly	Yes	Yes	α = .89	135—M	3
Snell, 1986 Masculine Role Inventory (MRI)	30	No	No	Yes	Yes	Yes	α = (n/a)[d]	729—MF	3
O'Neil et al., 1986 Gender Role Conflict Scale (GRCS-I)	37	No	No	No	No	Yes	α = (n/a)[d] 4-wk = .79[c]	527—M	4
Gender Role Conflict Scale (GRCS-II)	16	No	No	No	No	Yes	α = (n/a)[d] 4-wk = .80[c]	527—M	4
Eisler & Skidmore, 1987 Masculine Gender Role Stress (MGRS)	40	No	No	No	No	Yes	α = .90s 2-wk = .93	150—M	5
O'Neil et al., 1993 Gender Role Journey Measure (GRJM)	34	Yes	Yes	No	No	Yes	α = .90s[d] 2-wk = .70s	563—F 315—M	3

[a] See text for information on validity.

[b] See text for list of subscales, number of items in each, and alpha coefficients when available.

[c] Reliability coefficient is an average of multiple samples.

[d] Internal consistency estimate for full scale was not reported; however, alphas for subscales are summarized in text.

expectations can manifest itself in a "macho personality" characterized by socially callous attitudes, violence, and aggression. Drawing from psychoanalytic theory and a view of the male role as the antithesis of the female role, the authors' Hypermasculinity Inventory (HI) measures three components of the macho personality construct that arise from the macho male cultural script—calloused attitudes toward sex, seeing violence as manly, and seeing danger as exciting. Ten items for each dimension make up this 30-item scale. Items are presented as "forced choices." Such a choice is believed to better mirror real-life situations. Each pair consists of one macho alternative. Two examples read as follows:

a. Lesbians have chosen a particular life style and should be respected for it.
b. The only thing a lesbian needs is a good, stiff cock.

a. After I've gone through a really dangerous experience my knees feel weak and I shake all over.
b. After I've been through a really dangerous experience I feel high.

The HI determines the "macho syndrome" by revealing a respondent's attitudes toward women as well as toward masculinity. Several items would seem to approximate trait-measures of gender orientation (e.g., "When I am bored I watch TV or read a book," versus, "When I am bored I look for excitement"). The forced-choice format and the extremity of the content measured led us to classify many items as indirect measures of gender orientation. Factor analysis revealed the single, predominant, latent variable ("macho") was relatively homogeneous.

Since items in the HI tap both gender attitudes and gender orientation, it is not surprising that the macho personality pattern is empirically associated with attitude measures such as the AWS, with gender orientation measures such as the M scale of the BSRI, and with measures relevant to both attitudes and orientation, such as acceptance of callous sex (including rape of both wives and strangers), rape proclivity, frequency of alcohol consumption and drug use, self-disclosure, aggressive behavior, assaultiveness, violent behavior, negative contraceptive attitude and use, sexual experience, and history of sexual coercion (Archer & Rhodes, 1989; Exner, 1985; Koralewski & Conger, 1992; Mobayed, 1990; Mosher & Anderson, 1986; Mosher & Sirkin, 1984; Smeaton & Byrne, 1987; Sullivan & Mosher, 1990). Unique aspects of the HI include its focus on hypermasculinity, the distinct content domains measured, and its forced-choice format. A major strength of the HI is its established construct validity, which links societal norms to individual behavior. One limitation, however, is that scale items define the macho personality in homophobic terms; thus, the scale may be limited to heterosexuals. Second, the scale also includes items that assess gender orientation indirectly and attitudes toward women directly. Last, hypermasculinity represents an extreme. It is a distal indicator of the possible effects of the social forces scripting men's behavior, and thus the scale may be relevant only to the extremes in male behavior.

Masculine Role Inventory

The self-report Masculine Role Inventory (MRI) (Snell, 1986) was designed to measure men's (and women's) agreement with three standards of masculinity: success preoccupation, restricted emotionality, and inhibited affection. The items associated with each subscale were empirically derived. Snell reported that five items make up the success preoccupation subscale. Thirteen items define the restrictive emotionality factor, and seven items define the inhibited affection subscale. The MRI includes both first-person statements of conformity to stereotypical norms (e.g., "I avoid discussing my feelings because others might think I am weak") and third-person endorsements of stereotypes (e.g., "People who cry will not get anywhere in the working world"). The descriptive stereotypes focus on masculinity standards without explicit comparison between genders. However, the nearly equal representation of self-representational and attitudinal items creates a problem of interpretation.

All available research with the MRI reports that respondents received the full 30-item scale, but only the 25 items that define subscale scores are used in analyses. Perhaps using the total score could mask different patterns of approval. Construct validity has been partly established. Sex differences were found for the two emotionality subscales but not for success preoccupation. The subscales are differentially and predictably associated with gender orientation, elevated levels of negative life experiences, alcohol and drug use, self-disclosure, and use of avoidance strategies in intimate relationships (Belk & Snell, 1988; Snell, Belk, & Hawkins, 1986b, 1987). Newcomb (1990) selected four items with the largest factor loadings from each of the three subscales and interpreted them (with reverse scoring) as assessing "commitment to communality." He confirmed his construct with confirmatory factor analysis and found it associated with individuals' intimate/familial support network.

Gender Role Conflict Scales

O'Neil and his colleagues (O'Neil, 1981, 1982; Chapter 6; O'Neil, Helms, Gable, David, & Wrightsman, 1986) suggest a different approach to studying the traditional expectations men face. They introduce the construct "gender role conflict." This form of conflict is defined as a psychological state arising from the inherently contradictory and unrealistic messages within and across the standards of masculinity. Gender role conflict exists when masculinity standards result in personal restriction and devaluation. The Gender Role Conflict Scale-I (GRCS-I) was developed as an inventory of men's reactions to the gender expectations routinely faced. The GRCS-I is a 37-item, self-report scale examining men's concerns with success, power, and competition (13 items, α = .85; e.g., "Moving up the career ladder is important to me"); restrictive emotionality (10 items, α = .82; e.g., "Telling my partner my feelings about him/her during sex is difficult for me"); restrictive affectionate behavior between men (8 items, α = .83; e.g., "Hugging other men is difficult for me"); and the conflicts in work/family relations (6 items, α = .72; e.g., "My needs to work or study keep me from my family or leisure more than I would like"). This four-factor structure was confirmed in three other college student samples (Good et al., 1991). All items use the first-person voice; all are worded to tap the individual's anxiety and distress; and most of the items imply gender role conflict rather than state it directly. Test-retest reliabilities over a four-week period ranged from .72 to .86 for each factor.

Validity was established for the GRCS-I and its subscales in a number of studies (Campbell & Snow, 1992; Davis, 1987; Good & Mintz, 1990; Good et al., 1991; Kaplan, 1992; O'Neil et al., 1986; Robertson & Fitzgerald, 1992; Sharpe & Heppner, 1991; Sinn, 1993; Stillson, O'Neil, & Owen, 1991). Some baseline information on how race and class may construct men's experience of the four patterns of gender role conflict also have been reported (Berlin, 1988; Kim, 1990; Stillson, O'Neil, & Owen, 1991). The gender role conflict construct provides an important link between societal norms scripting traditional masculinities and individuals' adaptation. Distinctive features of the approach taken by O'Neil and his colleagues for the GRCS-I include its implicit use of the appraisal model of stress (Lazarus & Folkman, 1984) and the establishment of construct validity in relation to indicators of psychological well-being. The GRCS-I readily complements masculinity ideology measures and could be used in conjunction with them. One limitation is the narrow range of types of gender role conflict in the GRCS-I; it excludes nontraditional masculinity standards, such as men actively participating in family life or men engaging women as equals and sharing power.

A second GRCS instrument, designated GRCS-II, measures men's degree of comfort in concrete situations that might entail gender role conflict (O'Neil et al., 1986). For example:

> "There's a guy you've idolized since grade school. He's three years older than you are. In high school he was the star quarterback, valedictorian, and very active in the Young Methodist Fellowship. Last year he graduated from college. You have just learned he is a homosexual. How much conflict do you feel between your admiration for this person and the fact that he is a homosexual?"

Empirically derived, 16 situations like the example above are tapped by the GRCS-II. The 16 comprise 4 empirically distinct domains: success, power, and competition (6 situations, $\alpha = .79$); homophobia (4 situations, $\alpha = .78$); lack of emotional response (3 situations, $\alpha = .85$); and public embarrassment from gender role deviance (3 situations, $\alpha = .83$). Four-week test-retest relia- bilities ranged from .79 to .85. Men with a masculine gender orientation (measured by the PAQ) had higher homophobia scores than other men (O'Neil et al., 1986). No other published research has used the GRCS-II, thus no additional information is available on its validity.

Masculine Gender Role Stress Scale

Drawing explicitly on the cognitive stress model (Lazarus & Folkman, 1984), Eisler and his colleagues' 40-item Masculine Gender Role Stress (MGRS) Scale (Eisler and Skidmore, 1987; Chapter 7) measures the way indi- viduals appraise five types of situations that are common to men's lives and hypothetically more stressful for men than for women: situations that demonstrate physical inadequacy (9 items; e.g., "Feeling that you are not in good physical condition"); expressing "tender" emotions (7 items; e.g., "Telling your spouse that you love her"); placing men in subordination to women (9 items; e.g., "Being out performed at work by a woman"); threaten- ing a male's intellectual control (7 items; e.g., "Having to ask for directions when you are lost"); and revealing performance failures in work and sex (8 items; e.g., "Being unemployed").

In samples of college students, the MGRS Scale has demonstrated a high degree of internal consistency and test-retest reliability (Eisler, Skidmore, & Ward, 1988; Skidmore, 1988). As evidence of the scale's construct validity, the MGRS has been predictably correlated with a range of different con- cerns, from men's endorsement of a traditional masculinity ideology to their adverse health habits to their cardiovascular reactivity to situation stress (Eisler & Blalock, 1991; Eisler & Skidmore, 1987; Eisler et al., 1988; Lash, Eisler, & Schulman, 1990; Lash, Gillespie, Eisler, & Southard, 1991; Saurer & Eisler, 1990; Thompson, 1991). Strengths of this measure include its explicit use of the stress-appraisal model, the scope of the gender-relevant situations in the scale, and its discriminant validity in relation to measures of gender role orientation. The explicit focus on men's gender-related stresses and the finding that masculine gender role stress is independent of gender orienta- tion (Eisler & Skidmore, 1987; Thompson, 1991) are especially noteworthy. Interestingly, Gillespie and Eisler (1992) have recently published a parallel measure for women's gender-related stresses.

Gender Role Journey Measure

Working from a framework that examines what arises from gender social- ization, O'Neil, Egan, Owen, and McBride (1993) have constructed a 34-item scale to assess men's (and women's) stage of gender development. The Gender Role Journey Measure (GRJM) is rooted in the notion that an individual's internalized gender ideology can change, progressing systematically, stage by stage, from endorsing traditional, sex-segregated social worlds to viewing self and the world in less restrictive and sexist ways. The transitions can arise from normal developmental processes (e.g., aging) and from experience (e.g., encounters with sexism). The end point is a gendered consciousness that promotes social change. O'Neil et al. (1993) built empirically the self-report GRJM to reliably measure three (of the five conceptual) stages: acceptance of traditional gender roles (10 items, $\alpha = .87$; e.g., "Men should make the major money decisions for the family," and, "Feminists have caused the problems between men and women"); gender role ambivalence, confusion, anger, and fear (11 items, $\alpha = .76$; e.g., "I sometimes feel confused about gender roles"); and personal-professional activism (13 items, $\alpha = .89$; e.g., "I use my knowledge about sexism to make a difference in my life"). This three-stage structure essentially collapsed into the middle dimension the middle-level developmental issues that were originally conceptualized. All but seven items use the first-person voice to tap the individual's endorsement of values and beliefs representative of the different phases of gender development; the remaining seven are third-person declarative gender stereotypes. Because the GRJM is as appropriate for women as men, female pronouns anchor some items, male pronouns anchor others, and, most often, first-person assessments of gender experiences characterize each item.

Construct validity was determined (O'Neil et al., 1993) in a sample comprising undergraduates, graduate students, and working adults enrolled in college classes. The GRJM uses only subscale (or stage) scores, and each was predictably related to gender orientation. Persons classified as androgynous on the PAQ were highest on the third stage, personal-professional activism, whereas masculine and undifferentiated persons scored highest on the first stage, acceptance of a traditional gender ideology. Men described as masculine or undifferentiated on the PAQ reported markedly higher acceptance of traditional gender ideology. In effect, the stages of the "gender role journey" are marked by conspicuous gender and gender orientation differences. No other published research has used the GRJM. Thus, perhaps it is premature to address strengths and limitations, yet the GRJM seems to offer the research community a new instrument that is sensitive to multiple masculinities and competing gender ideologies within a life-span perspective.

Conclusions

Visualizing masculinity ideologies as distinct clusters of values and beliefs about how men should be men, distinct from masculine gender orientation, has aided our analysis. We have distinguished among the various gender ideologies—those that invoke standards for men, for women, and for gender relations in general. We have also been sensitized to the prevalence of measures that assess a single masculinity.

This review suggests a number of conclusions regarding currently available masculinity-related measures and the future development of instrumentation in this area. First, the distinction underlying our classification of measures has been that gender orientation and gender ideology are separate constructs. The available evidence affirms this assumption. Whenever the relationship between the constructs was examined, measures of masculinity ideology and gender orientation were basically independent. The M and F scales of the BSRI or PAQ are found strongly correlated with gender ideology in only one empirical study (Villemez & Touhey, 1977). Gender orientation was distinct from Moreland and Van Tuinen's ATMTS, Downs and Engleson's AMS, and Thompson and Pleck's MRNS. Although both the ATMTS and the AMS tap more global gender ideologies as much as they tap masculinity ideology, neither is correlated with gender orientation. Studies using the MRNS also document the independence of masculinity ideology and gender orientation.

Unlike the measures summarized in Table 5.1, the inventories in Table 5.2 were designed to index men's experiences with their gender. Not surprisingly, four of seven were found to be correlated with measures of gender orientation—that is, the M and F scales of the BSRI or PAQ—because they either include items that measure gender orientation (the MRI and HI) or tap gender experiences (GRCS-I and GRJM). Thus, a negative correlation between the F+ scale from the PAQ and both the restrictive emotionality and inhibited affection subscales of Snell et al.'s (1987) MRI is predictable. Similarly, given that "hypermasculinity" was conceptualized as a personality syndrome and the HI includes items that indirectly tap gender orientation, finding a positive correlation between the M scale of the BSRI and the HI (Archer & Rhodes, 1989) is also unsurprising. By not fully separating the MRI and HI from the way gender orientation is measured, both these scales may have limited utility. The observed correlations between M and F gender orientation scales and several subscales of the GRCS-I and GRJM seem to arise for a different reason: Both measures tap individuals' accommodations to and experiences with gender, something measures of gender orientation also do.

Second, there is some evidence that masculinity ideologies that define standards for men *are* distinct from ideologies that set standards for women and gender relations in general. We believe this evidence signals the separateness of a masculinity ideology, even though it could be correlated with measures tapping ideologies about women. Studies that report high correlations between masculinity ideology measures and Spence and Helmreich's

AWS (Archer & Rhodes, 1989; Buhrke, 1988; Downs & Engleson, 1982; Doyle & Moore, 1978; Gackenback & Auerbach, 1985; Gayton et al., 1982; Harren et al., 1979; Stark, 1991; Thompson, 1990) do not necessarily undermine our argument that masculinity ideologies are distinct from ideologies about women and gender relations. It should be recalled that the AWS is not a pure measure of attitudes toward women, since the majority of its items explicitly compare women and men in terms of gender-related characteristics, and many of the measures of masculinity ideology do the same. Studies that have investigated the relationship between masculinity ideology and measures specifically tapping attitudes toward women (e.g., Desnoyers, 1988; Thompson & Pleck, 1986) observe much lower correlations, averaging about .20, and Pleck et al. (1993c) reported a beta of only .04 in multivariate analysis.

Research investigating the correlates of masculinity ideology and masculinity-related constructs should now examine their discriminant validity by determining whether attitudes toward women or gender relations have the same correlates, and whether any relationships found for the former persist when the latter are controlled. Several research studies have established the discriminant validity of a masculinity-related measure this way: Good and Mintz (1990) established the validity of O'Neil et al.'s GRCS-I to predict depression in relation to Downs and Engleson's measure of gender attitudes; Koralewski and Conger (1992) demonstrated that the HI was predictive of level of sexual coerciveness, but the AWS was not; Thompson (1990) affirmed the validity of the MRNS in relation to the AWS in a study of courtship violence; and Pleck et al. (1993a, 1993c) established the discriminant validity of the MRAS in a national sample of adolescent males' sexual attitudes and behavior. Making this type of analysis routine in future research would enhance understanding of which gender ideologies are operative for men in different circumstances.

As much as attitudes toward men and attitudes toward women are conceptually independent, they are very likely to be empirically correlated. When the two are highly correlated, then measures purporting to index masculinity ideology may be of limited research utility because they may not pass the test of discriminant validity. In our judgment, measures intended to assess masculinity ideology and other masculinity-related constructs should include no gender-comparative items. Those that do (four of the measures in Table 5.1) cause problems in interpretation.

Similarly, the general status of instrumentation for the constructs of attitudes toward women and gender relations (these terms are often used interchangeably) needs more attention. The constructs assessed by these measures currently have remarkably little theoretical interest. For example, our literature search revealed only one recent review article on this topic (Del Boca, Ashmore, & McManus, 1986). There has been some interest in gender *stereotypes;* however, with few exceptions, this interest has been methodological in nature or focused on the degree of evaluative favorability-unfavorability of the female compared with the male stereotype, not on stereotypes as normative definitions of female or male behavior (Ashmore, Del Boca, & Wohlers, 1986; Eagly & Mladinic, 1989; Eagly, Mladinic, & Otto, 1991).

Third, O'Neil et al.'s GRCS-I and Eisler and Skidmore's MGRS suggest a promising new approach in masculinity-related measures. These instruments go beyond measuring respondents' endorsement of traditional masculinity standards (from which it may be inferred that male respondents would be motivated to fulfill these standards). They assess directly the extent to which males feel that violating traditional masculinity ideologies is uncomfortable or stressful for them. The construct of men's masculinity conflicts and stresses (which O'Neil et al. call "gender role conflict" and Eisler and Skidmore label "masculine gender role stress") is likely to be a more proximal predictor of males' behavior in some gendered situations than masculinity ideology. Which of the two constructs is most predictive of men's experiences and behavior is largely uncharted and warrants investigation.

Fourth, we want to call attention to the need to validate the masculinity measures with behavioral and biophysiological observations. With few exceptions, validation studies have depended almost exclusively upon other self-report instruments to establish the construct validity and/or discriminant validity of a masculinity instrument. Eisler and his colleagues, for example, have begun to use behavioral and physiological measures (Eisler et al., 1988; Lash et al., 1990, 1991; Watkins, Eisler, Carpenter, Schechtman, & Fisher, 1991) to validate the linkage between masculine gender role stress and personal well-being (e.g., cardiovascular reactivity, elevated systolic and diastolic blood pressure, verbal expression). Rieker et al. (1985) and Riley (1990) were able to show that the masculinity ideology in the BMS and MRNS, respectively, was predictive of sexual impairment among men who survive testis cancer and dropout rates of adult men who seek psychological help for personal problems. Epstein (1991) demonstrated in role-play situations that macho men, as determined by the HI, are less likely to nurture or comfort as fathers taking care of crying infants (lifelike dolls), and more inclined toward anger and instrumental actions such as diapering or placing a bottle in the crib. Aside from these few, other validation studies use self-report measures, which share method variance with the masculinity measure under investigation and reduce the strength of the validity estimate. Like Campbell and Fiske's (1959) call for multimethod-multitrait validation, if instruments determining masculinity ideology and how men experience their gender are to gain a trusted foundation, then what is needed are studies involving behavioral observation measures, clinical standards, and/or third-person reports.

Finally, many existing instruments measuring attitudes toward men and masculinity standards direct attention too narrowly to a single masculinity script. This interpretation of masculinity is implicitly based on a conventional division of labor, contrasted to a single femininity script, and presumed to be heterosexual. The point is, the research community may very well have ignored (and misrepresented) the other masculinities that are found in the culture and in institutions. We are largely unfamiliar with how generation, sexual orientation, class, race, and ethnicity differentially structure the form and content of men's lives and the masculinity ideologies to which they adhere. Studies are needed that try to identify the wide variety of footings that have yielded diversity in men's lives.

Many of the measures reviewed in this article could prove to be of considerable value. By comparing different men's responses to subscales or individual items, these existing measures can be used to identify how different male populations view masculinity. The "matrix of masculinities" (Kimmel & Messner, 1989) that we assume to exist needs to be mapped.

References

Allen, D. (1954). Anti-femininity in men. *American Sociological Review, 19*, 591–593.

Anderson, S. M. (1978). Sex-role typing as related to acceptance of self, acceptance of others, and discriminatory attitudes toward women. *Journal of Research in Personality, 12*, 410–415.

Archer, J. (1989). The relationship between gender-role measures: A review. *British Journal of Social Psychology, 28*, 173–184.

Archer, J. (1990). Gender-stereotypic traits are derived from gender roles: A reply to McCreary. *British Journal of Social Psychology, 29*, 273–277.

Archer, J., & Rhodes, C. (1989). The relationship between gender-related traits and attitudes. *British Journal of Social Psychology, 28*, 149–157.

Ashmore, R. D., Del Boca, F. K., & Wohlers, A. J. (1986). Gender stereotypes. In R. D. Ashmore & F. K. Del Boca (Eds.), *The social psychology of female-male relations: A critical analysis of central concepts* (pp. 69–119). New York: Academic Press.

Baca-Zinn, M. (1984). Chicano men and masculinity. *Journal of Ethnic Studies, 10* (Summer), 29–44.

Barnett, R. C., & Baruch, G. K. (1987). Determinants of fathers' participation in family work. *Journal of Marriage and the Family, 49*, 29–40.

Barrish, G., & Welch, M. R. (1980). Student religiosity and discriminatory attitudes toward women. *Sociological Analysis, 41*, 66–73.

Baruch, G. K., & Barnett, R. C. (1986). Fathers' participation in family work and children's sex-role attitudes. *Child Development, 57*, 1210–1223.

Beere, C. A. (1979). *Women and women's issues: A handbook of tests and measures.* San Francisco: Jossey-Bass.

Beere, C. A. (1990). *Gender roles: A handbook of tests and measures.* Westport, CT: Greenwood Press.

Belk, S. S., & Snell, W. E. (1988). Avoidance strategy use in intimate relationships. *Journal of Social and Clinical Psychology, 7*, 80–96.

Bem, S. (1974). The measurement of psychological androgyny. *Journal of Consulting and Clinical Psychology, 42*, 165–174.

Bem, S. (1981). Gender schema theory: A cognitive account of sex-typing. *Psychological Review, 88*, 354–364.

Berlin, C. (1988). *Gender role conflict, future time perspective, and contraceptive behavior among unmarried black, white, and Hispanic adolescent fathers and their nonfather peers.* Unpublished doctoral dissertation, New York University.

Biggs, P., & Fiebert, M. S. (1984). A factor-analytic study of American male attitudes. *Journal of Psychology, 116*, 113–116.

Brannon, R. (1976). The male sex role: Our culture's blueprint for manhood, what it's done for us lately. In D. David & R. Brannon (Eds.), *The forty-nine percent majority: The male sex role* (pp. 1–49). Reading, MA: Addison-Wesley.

Brannon, R. (1985). A scale for measuring attitudes toward masculinity. In A. Sargent (Ed.), *Beyond sex roles* (2nd ed., pp. 110–116). St. Paul, MN: West.

Brannon, R., & Juni, S. (1984). A scale for measuring attitudes toward masculinity. *JSAS Catalog of Selected Documents in Psychology, 14*, 6. (Ms. 2012)

Brannon, R., Juni, S., & Grady, K. (undated). *A scale for measuring attitudes toward masculinity.* Unpublished manuscript.

Brinkerhoff, M. D., & MacKie, M. (1985). Religion and gender: A comparison of Canadian and American student attitudes. *Journal of Marriage and the Family, 47*, 415–429.

Brod, H. (1987). *The making of masculinities: The new men's studies.* Boston: Allen & Unwin.

Broude, G. J. (1990). Protest masculinity: A further look at the cause and the concept. *Ethos, 18*, 103–122.

Buhrke, R. A. (1988). Factor dimensions across different measures of sex role ideology. *Sex Roles, 18*, 309–321.

Bunting, A. B., & Reeves, J. B. (1983). Perceived male sex orientation and beliefs about rape. *Deviant Behavior, 4*, 281–295.

Burda, P. C., & Vaux, A. C. (1987). The social support process in men: Overcoming sex-role obstacles. *Human Relations, 40*, 31–44.

Campbell, D. T., & Fiske, D. W. (1959). Convergent and discriminant validation by the multitrait-multimethod matrix. *Psychological Bulletin, 56*, 81–105.

Campbell, J. L., & Snow, B. M. (1992). Gender role conflict and family environment as predictors of men's marital satisfaction. *Journal of Family Psychology, 6*, 84–87.

Cazenave, N., & Leon, G. (1987). Men's work and family roles and characteristics: Race, gender and class perceptions of college students. In M. Kimmel (Ed.), *Changing men: New directions in research on men and masculinity* (pp. 244–262). Newbury Park, CA: Sage.

Connell, R. (1987). *Gender and power.* Stanford, CA: Stanford University Press.

Davis, F. (1987). *Antecedents and consequents of gender role conflict: An empirical validation of sex role strain analysis.* Unpublished doctoral dissertation, Ohio State University.

Deaux, K. (1984). From individual differences to social categories: Analysis of a decade's research on gender. *American Psychologist, 39*, 105–116.

Deaux, K., Winston, W., Crowley, M., & Lewis, L. L. (1985). Level of categorization and content of gender stereotypes. *Social Cognition, 3,* 145–167.

Del Boca, F. K., Ashmore, R. D., & McManus, M. A. (1986). Gender-related attitudes. In R. D. Ashmore & F. K. Del Boca (Eds.), *The social psychology of female-male relations: A critical analysis of central concepts* (pp. 121–163). New York: Academic Press.

Desnoyers, R. M. (1988). *The role of religiosity in male sex role attitudes.* Unpublished honor's thesis, Holy Cross College, Worcester, MA.

Downs, A. C., & Engleson, S. A. (1982). The Attitudes Toward Men Scale (AMS): An analysis of the role and status of men and masculinity. *JSAS Catalog of Selected Documents in Psychology, 12,* 45. (Ms. 2502)

Doyle, J. A., & Moore, R. J. (1978). Attitudes Toward the Male Role Scale: An objective instrument to measure attitudes toward the male's sex role in contemporary society. *JSAS Catalog of Selected Documents in Psychology, 8,* 35–36. (Ms. 1678)

Eagly, A. H., & Mladinic, A. (1989). Gender stereotypes and attitudes toward women and men. *Personality and Social Psychology Bulletin, 15,* 543–558.

Eagly, A. H., Mladinic, A., & Otto, S. (1991). Are women evaluated more favorably than men? *Psychology of Women Quarterly, 15,* 203–216.

Edwards, G. H. (1992). The structure and content of the male gender role stereotype: An exploration of subtypes. *Sex Roles, 27,* 533–551.

Eisler, R. M., & Blalock, J. A. (1991). Masculine gender role stress: Implications for the assessment of men. *Clinical Psychology Review, 11,* 45–60.

Eisler, R. M., & Skidmore, J. R. (1987). Masculine gender role stress: Scale development and component factors in the appraisal of stressful situations. *Behavior Modification, 11,* 123–136.

Eisler, R. M., Skidmore, J. R., & Ward, C. H. (1988). Masculine gender-role stress: Predictor of anger, anxiety, and health-risk behaviors. *Journal of Personality Assessment, 52,* 133–141.

Epstein, R. J. (1991). *Macho personality and the punitive socialization of distress in infants.* Unpublished doctoral dissertation, University of Connecticut.

Exner, T. (1985). *Hypermasculinity and male contraceptive attitude and behavior.* Unpublished doctoral dissertation, University of Connecticut.

Falkenberg, S. D., Hindman, C. D., & Masey, D. (1983). *Measuring attitudes toward males in society.* Paper presented at the meeting of the Southeastern Psychological Association, Atlanta. (ERIC Document Reproduction Service No. ED 233 287)

Fiebert, M. S. (1983). Measuring traditional and liberal males' attitudes. *Perceptual and Motor Skills, 56,* 83–86.

Fiebert, M. S., & Vera, W. (1985). Test-retest reliability of a male sex-role attitude survey: The Traditional-Liberated Content Scale. *Perceptual and Motor Skills, 60,* 66.

Franklin, C. W. (1988). *Men and society.* Chicago: Nelson-Hall.

Gackenbach, J. I., & Auerbach, S. M. (1985). Sex-role attitudes and perceptual learning. *Journal of Social Psychology, 125,* 233–243.

Gayton, W. F., Sawyer, B. L., Baird, J. G., & Ozmon, K. L. (1982). Further validation of a new measure of machismo. *Psychological Reports, 51,* 820–822.

Gillespie, B. L., & Eisler, R. M. (1992). Development of the feminine gender role stress scale: A cognitive-behavioral measure of stress, appraisal, and coping for women. *Behavior Modification, 16,* 426–438.

Gilmore, D. L. (1990). *Manhood in the making: Cultural concepts of masculinity.* New Haven, CT: Yale University Press.

Glass, L. L. (1984). Man's man/ladies' man: Motifs of hypermasculinity. *Psychiatry, 47,* 260–278.

Good, G. E., Braverman, D., & O'Neil, J. M. (1991, August). *Gender role conflict scale: Construct validity and reliability.* Paper presented at the annual meeting of the American Psychological Association, San Francisco.

Good, G. E., Dell, D. M., & Mintz, L. B. (1989). Male role and gender role conflict: Relations to help-seeking in men. *Journal of Counseling Psychology, 36,* 295–300.

Good, G. E., & Mintz, L. B. (1990). Gender role conflict and depression in college men: Evidence from compounded risk. *Journal of Counseling and Development, 69,* 17–20.

Gradman, T. J. (1990). *Does work make the man: Masculine identity and work identity during the transition to retirement.* Santa Monica, CA: The RAND Corp.

Green, A. (1946). The male middle class child and neurosis. *American Sociological Review, 11,* 31–41.

Hacker, H. (1957). The new burdens of masculinity. *Marriage and Family Living, 19,* 227–233.

Harren, V. A., Kass, R. A., Tinsley, H. E. A., & Moreland, J. R. (1978). Influence of sex role attitudes and cognitive styles on career decision making. *Journal of Counseling Psychology, 25,* 390–398.

Harren, V. A., Kass, R. A., Tinsley, H. E. A., & Moreland, J. R. (1979). Influence of gender, sex role attitudes, and cognitive complexity on gender-dominant career choices. *Journal of Counseling Psychology, 26,* 227–234.

Hearn, J., & Morgan, D. (1990). *Men, masculinities, and social theory.* Boston: Unwin Hyman.

Hockenberry, S. L., & Billingham, R. E. (1987). Sexual orientation and boyhood gender conformity: Development of the Boyhood Gender Conformity Scale (BGCS). *Archives of Sexual Behavior, 16,* 475–492.

Iazzo, A. (1983). The construction and validation of the Attitudes Toward Men Scale. *Psychological Record, 33,* 371–378.

Kaplan, R. (1992). *Normative masculinity and sexual aggression among college males.* Unpublished doctoral dissertation, University of Connecticut.

Kim, E. J. (1990). *Asian American men: Gender role conflict and acculturation.* Unpublished doctoral dissertation, University of Southern California.

Kimmel, M. S., & Messner, M. A. (1989). Introduction. In M. Kimmel & M. Messner (Eds.), *Men's lives* (pp. 1–13). New York: Macmillan.

Komarovsky, M. (1973). Cultural contradictions and sex roles: The masculine case. *American Journal of Sociology, 78,* 873–884.

Koralewski, M. A., & Conger, J. C. (1992). The assessment of social skills among sexually coercive college males. *Journal of Sex Research, 29,* 169–188.

Lash, S. J., Eisler, R. M., & Schulman, R. S. (1990). Cardiovascular reactivity to stress in men: Effects of masculine gender role stress appraisal and masculine performance challenge. *Behavior Modification, 14,* 3–20.

Lash, S. J., Gillespie, B. L., Eisler, R. M., & Southard, D. R. (1991). Sex differences in cardiovascular reactivity: Effects of the gender relevance of the stressor. *Health Psychology, 10,* 392–398.

Lazarus, R., & Folkman, S. (1984). *Stress, appraisal, and coping.* New York: Springer.

Lenney, E. (1991). Sex roles: The measurement of masculinity, femininity, and androgyny. In J. P. Robinson, P. R. Shaver, & L. S. Wrightsman (Eds.), *Measures of personality and social psychological attitudes* (pp. 573–660). New York: Academic Press.

Levant, R. F., Hirsch, L., Celentano, E., Cozza, T., Hill, S., MacEachern, M., Marty, N., & Schnedeker, J. (1992). The male role: An investigation of contemporary norms. *Journal of Mental Health Counseling, 14,* 325–337.

Marsiglio, W. (1993a). Adolescent males' orientation toward paternity and contraception. *Family Planning Perspectives, 25*(1), 22–31.

Marsiglio, W. (1993b). Attitudes toward homosexual activity and gays as friends: A national survey of heterosexual 15- to 19-year-old males. *Journal of Sex Research, 30,* 12–17.

Mazer, D. B., & Percival, E. F. (1989). Ideology or experience? The relationships among perceptions, attitudes, and experiences of sexual harassment in university students. *Sex Roles, 20,* 135–147.

McCreary, D. R. (1990). Multidimensionality and the measurement of gender role attributes: A comment on Archer. *British Journal of Social Psychology, 29,* 265–272.

Mobayed, C. P. (1990). *Hypermasculinity as a predictor of self-disclosure in males: A sequential analysis.* Unpublished doctoral dissertation, University of Connecticut.

Moreland, J., & Van Tuinen, M. (1978). *The Attitude Toward Masculinity Transcendence Scale.* Paper presented at the Department of Psychology, Ohio State University.

Morgan, D. H. J. (1990). Issues of critical sociological theory: Men in families. In J. Sprey (Ed.), *Fashioning family theory: New approaches* (pp. 67–106). Newbury Park, CA: Sage.

Mosher, D. L., & Anderson, R. D. (1986). Macho personality, sexual aggression, and reactions to guided imagery of realistic rape. *Journal of Research in Personality, 20,* 77–94.

Mosher, D. L., & Sirkin, M. (1984). Measuring a macho personality constellation. *Journal of Research in Personality, 18,* 150–163.

Mosher, D. L., & Tomkins, S. S. (1988). Scripting the macho man: Hypermasculine socialization and enculturation. *Journal of Sex Research, 25,* 60–84.

Newcomb, M. D. (1990). Social support by many other names: Towards a unified conceptualization. *Journal of Social and Personal Relationships, 7,* 479–494.

O'Neil, J. (1981). Patterns of gender-role conflict and strain: Sexism and fear of femininity in men's lives. *Personnel and Guidance Journal, 60,* 203–210.

O'Neil, J. (1982). Gender-role conflict and strain in men's lives. In K. Solomon & N. Levy (Eds.), *Men in transition* (pp. 5–44). New York: Plenum.

O'Neil, J. M., Egan, J., Owen, S. V., & McBride, V. (1993). The Gender Role Journey Measure: Scale development and psychometric evaluation. *Sex Roles, 28,* 167–185.

O'Neil, J. M., Helms, B. J., Gable, R. K., David, L., & Wrightsman, L. S. (1986). Gender-Role Conflict Scale: College men's fear of femininity. *Sex Roles, 14,* 335–350.

Pedhazur, E. J., & Tetenbaum, T. J. (1979). Bem Sex Role Inventory: A theoretical and methodological critique. *Journal of Personality and Social Psychology, 37,* 996–1016.

Pleck, J. H. (1976). The male sex role: Definitions, problems, and sources of change. *Journal of Social Issues, 32*(3), 155–164.

Pleck, J. H. (1981). *The myth of masculinity.* Cambridge, MA: MIT Press.

Pleck, J. H., Sonenstein, F. L., & Ku, L. C. (1993a). Masculinity ideology: Its impact on adolescent males' heterosexual relationships. *Journal of Social Issues, 49*(3), 11–29.

Pleck, J. H., Sonenstein, F. L., & Ku, L. C. (1993b). Masculinity ideology and its correlates. In S. Oskamp & M. Costanzo (Eds.), *Gender issues in social psychology* (pp.
85–110). Newbury Park, CA: Sage.

Pleck, J. H., Sonenstein, F. L., & Ku, L. C. (1993c). *Attitudes toward male roles: A discriminant validity analysis.* Unpublished paper, Wellesley College Center for Research
on Women.

Pleck, J. H., Sonenstein, F. L., & Ku, L. C. (in press). Problem behaviors and masculinity ideology in adolescent males. In R. Ketterlinus & M. Lamb (Eds.), *Adolescent
problem behaviors.* Hillsdale, NJ: Lawrence Erlbaum.

Rieker, P. P., Edbril, S. D., & Garnick, M. B. (1985). Curative testis cancer therapy: Psychosocial sequelae. *Journal of Clinical Oncology, 3,* 1117–1126.

Riley, D. P. (1990). *Men's endorsement of male sex-role norms and time spent in psychotherapeutic treatment.* Unpublished doctoral dissertation, Boston University.

Robertson, J. M., & Fitzgerald, L. F. (1992). Overcoming the masculine mystique: Preferences for alternative forms of assistance among men who avoid counseling. *Journal of Counseling Psychology, 39,* 240–246.

Rosenkrantz, P., Vogel, S., Bee, H., Broverman, I., & Broverman, D. (1968). Sex-role
stereotypes and self-concepts among college students. *Journal of Consulting and
Clinical Psychology, 32,* 287–295.

Saurer, M. K., & Eisler, R. M. (1990). The role of masculine gender role stress in
expressivity and social support network factors. *Sex Roles, 23,* 261–271.

Segal, L. (1990). *Slow motion: Changing masculinities, changing men.* New Brunswick,
NJ: Rutgers University Press.

Sharpe, M. J., & Heppner, P. P. (1991). Gender role, gender role conflict, and psychological well-being in men. *Journal of Counseling Psychology, 38,* 323–330.

Sinn, J. S. (1993). *Masculinity ideology: Establishing convergent and discriminant validity.*
Unpublished master's thesis, Old Dominion University.

Skidmore, J. R. (1988). *Cardiovascular reactivity in men as a function of masculine gender
role stress, Type A behavior, and hostility.* Unpublished doctoral dissertation, Virginia
Polytechnic Institute and State University.

Smeaton, G., & Byrne, D. (1987). The effects of R-rated violence and erotica, individual differences, and victim characteristics on acquaintance rape proclivity. *Journal
of Research in Personality, 21,* 171–184.

Snell, W. E. (1986). The Masculine Role Inventory: Components and correlates. *Sex
Roles, 15,* 443–455.

Snell, W. E. (1989). Development and validation of the masculine behavior scale: A
measure of behaviors stereotypically attributed to males and females. *Sex Roles, 21,*
749–767.

Snell, W. E., Belk, S. S., & Hawkins, R. C. (1986a). The Stereotypes About Male Sexuality Scale (SAMSS): Components, correlates, antecedents, consequences and counselor bias. *Social and Behavioral Sciences Documents, 16,* 9. (Ms. 2746)

Snell, W. E., Belk, S. S., & Hawkins, R. C. (1986b). The masculine role as a moderator
of stress-distress relationships. *Sex Roles, 15,* 359–366.

Snell, W. E., Belk, S. S., & Hawkins, R. C. (1987). Alcohol and drug use in stressful
times: The influence of the masculine role and sex-related personality attributes.
Sex Roles, 16, 359–373.

Snell, W. E., Hawkins, R. C., & Belk, S. S. (1988). Stereotypes about male sexuality and the use of social influence strategies in intimate relationships. *Journal of Social and Clinical Psychology, 7,* 42–48.

Spence, J. T., & Helmreich, R. (1972). The Attitudes Toward Women Scale: An objective instrument to measure attitudes toward the rights and roles of women in contemporary society. *JSAS Catalog of Selected Documents in Psychology, 2,* 66. (Ms. 153)

Spence, J. T., & Helmreich, R. (1978). *Masculinity and femininity: Their psychological dimensions, correlates, and antecedents.* Austin: University of Texas Press.

Spence, J. T., Helmreich, R., & Stapp, J. (1973). A short version of the Attitudes Toward Women Scale (AWS). *Bulletin of the Psychonomic Society, 2,* 219–220.

Spence, J. T., Losoff, M., & Robbins, A. S. (1991). Sexually aggressive tactics in dating relationships: Personality and attitudinal correlates. *Journal of Social and Clinical Psychology, 10,* 289–304.

Stark, L. P. (1991). Traditional gender role beliefs and individual outcomes: An exploratory analysis. *Sex Roles, 24,* 639–650.

Stillson, R. W., O'Neil, J. M., & Owen, S. V. (1991). Predictors of adult men's gender-role conflict: Race, class, unemployment, age, instrumentality-expressiveness, and personal strain. *Journal of Counseling Psychology, 38,* 458–464.

Sullivan, J. P., & Mosher, D. L. (1990). Acceptance of guided imagery of marital rape as a function of macho personality. *Violence and Victims, 5,* 275–286.

Taylor, M. C., & Hall, J. A. (1982). Psychological androgyny: Theories, methods, and conclusions. *Psychological Bulletin, 92,* 347–366.

Thompson, E. H. (1990). Courtship violence and the male role. *Men's Studies Review, 7,* 1, 4–13.

Thompson, E. H. (1991, August). *Men's gender role conflicts and strain: The dilemma of traditional men.* Paper presented at the meeting of the American Sociological Association, Cincinnati.

Thompson, E. H., Grisanti, C., & Pleck, J. H. (1985). Attitudes toward the male role and their correlates. *Sex Roles, 13,* 413–427.

Thompson, E. H., & Pleck, J. H. (1986). The structure of male role norms. *American Behavioral Scientist, 29,* 531–543.

Vera, W., & Fiebert, M. S. (1987). Validity of an instrument measuring male attitudes: The Traditional-Liberated Content Scale. *Perceptual and Motor Skills, 65,* 437–438.

Villemez, W. J., & Touhey, J. C. (1977). A measure of individual differences in sex stereotyping and sex discrimination: The Macho Scale. *Psychological Reports, 41,* 411–415.

Watkins, P. L., Eisler, R. M., Carpenter, L., Schechtman, K. B., & Fisher, E. B. (1991). Psychosocial and physiological correlates of male gender role stress among employed adults. *Behavioral Medicine, 17,* 86–90.

West, C., & Zimmerman, D. (1987). Doing gender. *Gender and Society, 1,* 125–151.

CHAPTER 6

Fifteen Years of Theory and Research on Men's Gender Role Conflict: New Paradigms for Empirical Research

JAMES M. O'NEIL, GLENN E. GOOD, AND SARAH HOLMES

THIS CHAPTER REVIEWS empirical research on men's gender role conflict. Over the last 20 years, empirical research on men's problems has lagged far behind theory and the popular literature. Consequently, little is known about men's gender roles from a scientific perspective. This lack of knowledge has been evident when leaders of the various men's movements have appeared on national talk shows. Overall, these leaders have represented the various men's movements adequately, given our limited knowledge about men's lives. Typically, they are asked difficult and sometimes unanswerable questions about men. In 30-second sound bytes, these talk-show guests are asked to respond to some complex questions: Why are men so unhappy and seeking liberation in the men's movements? Why do men have so many problems with women in intimate and work relationships? Why do men communicate differently than women and not express many feelings? How can we get men to change? Why do men work so much and die earlier than women? Why do men avoid domestic work and fathering roles? Why are men violent? Why do men molest children, fear homosexuals, and become addicted or sexually dysfunctional? Why do men harass, rape, and batter women?

Information about the Gender Role Conflict Scale and the test manual can be obtained by writing James M. O'Neil, School of Family Studies, U-Box 58, University of Connecticut, Storrs, CT 06269-2058. Parts of this chapter were presented at the 102nd annual convention of the American Psychological Association, August 1994, in Los Angeles. The authors thank the many colleagues from across the country who have used the GRCS in their research. The results reported in this chapter would not have been possible without their scholarly efforts. The statistical consultation of Dr. Steve Owen, University of Connecticut, is acknowledged and appreciated in the development of the GRSC-I. The authors also appreciate the helpful comments and critique of the chapter from Dr. Larry Wrightsman, at the University of Kansas, Ann R. Fischer at the University of Missouri at Columbia, and Dr. Ron Levant and Dr. William Pollack, editors of this volume.

Talk-show guests are rarely able to give answers based on established theories or empirical research. The limited answers given reflect how little we know about men's gender roles over the life span and how neglected this concern has been in psychology. Even less is known about men of different ages and from different races, ethnic backgrounds, class levels, and sexual orientations. Theory and empirical research on men is still in its early stages of development. Finding out how men think, feel, and experience their lives is a priority for the new psychology of men.

This chapter reviews a program of research created in the late 1970s to empirically assess men's lives in the context of gender role conflict. Even though this chapter reviews research data, it should be useful to readers who want to know what men report about their conflict with their gender roles. A brief history of the research program is given below.

The Development of the Gender Role Conflict Concept: Background

In the mid-1970s, I [James O'Neil] was integrating feminist literature on women's gender role socialization into the courses I taught. One day in the fall of 1977, I was hurriedly leaving my lecture on women's gender role development when I was suddenly stopped by Jan Muchow, a graduate student in the class. Jan emotionally said, "When are you men going to seriously examine your own gender role issues, rather than solely focusing on women's development?" I stopped, put my lecture notes down, and listened. Jan then gave an eloquent 30-minute justification for the comprehensive study of men and masculinity. It was another good example of "the student teaching the teacher." Having already started my reading on men's liberation (David & Brannon, 1976; Farrell, 1974; Fasteau, 1974; Pleck & Sawyer, 1974), I acknowledged that, indeed, she was right, a new psychology of men was needed.

Furthermore, I was having increasing difficulty with a few radical feminist women who believed that "all men are oppressors" and exclusively blamed *all* men for the pervasive sexism against women in American society. During those days, the verbal attacks on men (i.e., male-bashing) were less subtle than today. However, I did not have adequate answers to the many good questions that even moderate feminists were asking. I knew there must be a reason why men were sexist and why sex discrimination was so widespread. I felt that it was more complex than reducing all men to innate oppressors and misogynists. I reasoned that there must be something in the political or family system that contributed to sexism against women. Part of my problem was that I had no conception of how patriarchy worked. I had a very limited knowledge of how men were socialized to restrictive gender roles. Furthermore, I did not fully understand how sexism was a political reality in my own life.

These political and personal issues and my encounter with Jan Muchow signaled a turning point in my study of gender roles. From that time on, men's gender role conflict became a major part of my research program. I wanted to find or create theory and research that explained how sexism and gender role socialization interact to produce oppression for *both* sexes. During those early days, I felt that both sexes were victims of sexism. Women's victimization was easily documented, but men as victims was harder to conceptualize. The gender role conflict construct was one way to conceptualize about sexism against men. This chapter summarizes the concepts and research developed on men's gender role conflict over these last 15 years. Those heated discussions with colleagues and students in the 1970s were the primary stimuli for creating research on men's gender role conflict.

The specific purposes of this chapter are: (a) to define gender role conflict and related concepts; (b) to review the evolution of gender role conflict theory as it relates to men's gender role development; (c) to review the psychometric development of the Gender Role Conflict Scale (GRCS) (O'Neil, Helms, Gable, David, & Wrightsman, 1986), a scale designed to measure men's conflict with their gender roles; (d) to review the empirical research completed on the GRCS; and (e) to present a research paradigm for future research on the gender role conflict theory. The chapter will be useful to researchers, therapists, educators, and other audiences seeking information about the scientific study of men's gender role conflict.

The literature reviewed does not include other relevant research programs on related topics (Brannon, 1985; Brannon & Juni, 1984; Eisler & Skidmore, 1987; Chapter 7; Levant et al., 1992; Mosher & Sirkin, 1984; Snell, 1986; Thompson, Grisanti, & Pleck, 1985). Readers are encouraged to review these other research programs as evidence of an accumulating database on men's lives.

Gender Role Conflict Theory and Related Concepts

DEFINITION OF GENDER ROLE CONFLICT

A series of theoretical and research papers present the basic constructs of gender role conflict theory (O'Neil, 1981a, 1981b, 1982, 1990; O'Neil & Egan, 1992a, 1992b, 1992c; O'Neil, Egan, Owen, & Murry, 1993; O'Neil & Fishman, 1992; O'Neil, Fishman, & Kinsella-Shaw, 1987; O'Neil et al., 1986). Readers are referred to these earlier papers for complete summaries. Only an overall summary is given below.

Gender role conflict is a psychological state in which socialized gender roles have negative consequences on the person or others. Gender role conflict occurs when rigid, sexist, or restrictive gender roles result in personal restriction, devaluation, or violation of others or self. The ultimate outcome of this kind of conflict is a restriction of the human potential of the person experiencing the conflict or a restriction of another's potential.

Gender role conflict is a multidimensional and complex concept. How gender roles are learned, internalized, and experienced, from early childhood to late adulthood, is very complex and idiosyncratic. Therefore, gender role conflict is quite individualized. There are generational, racial, sexual orientation, class, age, and ethnic differences in the experience of gender role conflict. Overall, gender role conflict implies cognitive, emotional, unconscious, or behavorial problems caused by the socialized gender roles learned in sexist and patriarchial societies.

Gender role conflict operates at four overlapping and complex levels: cognitions, affective experiences, behaviors, and unconscious experiences. Gender role conflict experienced on a cognitive level emanates from restrictive ways individuals think about the gender roles of masculinity and femininity. Stereotyped attitudes and worldviews about men and women result from this cognitive restriction. Gender role conflict experienced on an affective level emanates from deep emotional turmoil about masculine and feminine gender roles. Gender role conflict experienced on a behavioral level is the actual conflict experienced with masculinity-femininity as we act, react, and interact with ourselves and others. Gender role conflict as an unconscious phenomenon represents the intrapsychic and repressed conflicts with masculinity-femininity that are beyond our conscious awareness. Assessing and understanding these different levels of gender role conflict as they operate simultaneously in people's lives is a complex undertaking.

Men experience gender role conflict directly or indirectly in six contexts: when they (1) deviate from or violate gender role norms (Pleck, 1981); (2) try to meet or fail to meet gender role norms of masculinity; (3) experience discrepancies between their real self-concept and their ideal self-concept, based on gender role stereotypes (Garnets & Pleck, 1979); (4) personally devalue, restrict, or violate themselves (O'Neil, 1990; O'Neil, Fishman, & Kinsella-Shaw, 1987); (5) experience personal devaluations, restrictions, or violations from others (O'Neil, 1990; O'Neil et al., 1987); and (6) personally devalue, restrict, or violate others because of gender role stereotypes (O'Neil, 1990; O'Neil et al., 1987).

These six contexts and the four levels of gender role conflict mentioned above provide a conceptual foundation for individuals' personal experiences of the conflict. Personal experiences of gender role conflict are situational and therefore complex. A diagnostic schema has been developed (O'Neil, 1990; O'Neil & Egan, 1992a) that details three personal experiences of gender role conflict in three situational contexts. The overlapping contexts include gender role conflict *within oneself*, gender role conflict *caused by others*, and gender role conflict *expressed toward others.* These contexts imply that gender role conflict can be experienced internally by a person, stimulated by other people's conflict, or expressed toward others.

Personal experiences of gender role conflict are defined as the negative consequences of gender role in terms of gender role devaluations, restrictions, and violations (O'Neil, 1990; O'Neil & Egan, 1992a; O'Neil et al., 1987). When individuals are personally devalued, restricted, or violated because of sexism and gender role conflict, psychological and physical health may be at risk. For example, a man who conforms to the masculine norms of emotional inexpressiveness may be at greater risk for health problems and a variety of psychological ailments, including depression and anxiety. On the other hand, men who freely express emotions may be devalued by others because emotionality has been stereotypically defined as feminine.

Cognitions, emotions, behaviors, or unconscious processes may interact, causing a person to feel bad about him- or herself or producing negative relations with others. Some of the personal outcomes of gender role conflict may include anxiety, depression, low self-esteem, and stress. Some of the interpersonal outcomes may include limited intimacy, unhappiness in relationships, work conflicts, power and control issues in relationships, and even physical and sexual assault. Most of the research presented in this chapter focuses on men's gender role conflict *within themselves* and *expressed toward others.*

RESOLVING GENDER ROLE CONFLICT: THE GENDER ROLE JOURNEY AND GENDER ROLE TRANSITIONS

Limited literature exists on how gender role conflict is resolved and how gender roles change over the life span. Clearly, many more men and women are attempting to liberate themselves from the bondage of patriarchy through personal, professional, and political action. The literature that does exist addresses the relationship between gender role change and ego development (Block, 1973, 1984), life stages (Rebecca, Hefner, & Olenshanky, 1976), gender polarities (Levinson, Darrow, Klein, Levinson, & McKee, 1978), and androgyny (Bem, 1974). Very little is known about the specific processes that individuals experience when they resolve their gender role conflict.

From our perspective, resolving gender role conflict is an ongoing process of consciousness-raising over the life span. We conceive of this process as the gender role journey (O'Neil, in press; O'Neil & Egan, 1992a; O'Neil et al., 1993; O'Neil & Roberts Carroll, 1987, 1988a, 1988b). "Journeying" implies an active exploration of one's gender role socialization and a recognition that sexism has affected one's life. The gender role journey concept has been theoretically defined (O'Neil & Egan, 1992b; O'Neil & Roberts Carroll, 1988b) and empirically derived. Three empirically derived phases of the gender role journey include: (1) acceptance of traditional roles; (2) gender role ambivalence, confusion, anger, and fear; and (3) personal-professional activism (O'Neil et al., 1993). Part of the journey is the process of gaining an understanding of how gender role conflict develops in the family and from other socialization experiences in society. Furthermore, "journeying" implies identifying gender role transitions as they occur in life and reexamining gender role themes (O'Neil & Egan, 1992b; O'Neil & Fishman, 1992; O'Neil et al., 1987). Gender role transitions are events and nonevents in a person's gender role development that produce profound changes in his or her gender role values and self-assumptions. In an earlier paper, 30 gender role transitions for men were operationally defined over 6 life stages, from early childhood to old age (O'Neil & Egan, 1992c). During gender role transitions, the person demonstrates, reevaluates, or integrates new and old conceptions of masculinity and femininity. Certain gender role themes are redefined (e.g., power, control, success, sexuality, and parenting) as the gender role transition occurs (O'Neil & Fishman, 1992). For example, a man at midlife may realize that he cannot be completely fulfilled by career success. This may lead him to redefine his success in the context of equally important aspects of life, including family relationships and intimacy.

Resolving gender role transitions and conflicts can occur through operationally defined transformational processes (O'Neil & Egan, 1992c). First, there is the shift in the person's psychological defense system about sexism and recognition of deep emotions about one's personal gender role. Second, false assumptions or illusions about gender roles are confronted through readings, experiential learning, or personal dialogue. Third, this new learning may produce an expanded internal dialogue as the person recognizes and works with his or her gender role conflict. Fourth, this intense dialogue may produce "psychological warfare" within the person as he or she struggles with the old self and the new, emerging gender role identity. Lastly, resolving gender role conflicts and making gender role transitions may require the manipulation and creation of healthy symbols of masculinity and femininity that transcend the traditional stereotypes. Discussion of what constitutes healthy conceptions of masculinity is beginning to emerge in the literature (Good, 1992; Good & Mintz, 1993), but clearly much more work needs to be done. The psychology of women and the new psychology of men are beginning to address this transformational process in the context of therapy, consciousness-raising, and experiential workshops.

For example, gender role conflict and the gender role journey metaphor have been used in academic classes and workshops (Egan, 1990, 1992; Egan & O'Neil, 1993; O'Neil, in press; O'Neil & Roberts Carroll, 1987, 1988a, 1988b), in campus programs (Braverman, O'Neil, & Owen, 1992; Croteau & Burda, 1983), and with resources to teach others about men (Gertner, 1994;

Harris, 1991). We now turn to describing the gradual emergence of the gender role conflict theory over the last 15 years.

Development of Gender Role Conflict Theory, 1979–1994

The gender role conflict construct has evolved from early theorizing to formal conceptualization to empirical testing. The only scholarly conceptualization in the 1970s related to gender role conflict was Garnets and Pleck's (1979) sex role strain analysis. This framework was the primary conceptualization that prompted the gender role conflict construct. Garnets and Pleck's sex role strain analysis defined sex role strain as an intrapsychic process that leads to poor psychological adjustment, particularly low self-esteem. Sex role strain was defined as "discrepancies between an individual's perception of her or his personal characteristics and her or his standards for herself or himself deriving from sex role norms" (pp. 274–275). According to these authors, sex role strain occurs when there are "discrepancies between real self and that aspect of the ideal self-concept rooted in sex role norms" (p. 276). Sex role strain implied that the violation of gender roles leads to negative psychological consequences.

Garnets and Pleck's overall sex role strain analysis was an important contribution to the psychology of gender roles. Yet the model did not specify the precise patterns of sex role conflicts that occur when discrepancies exist between a person's real and ideal self-concept. Operational definitions of men's and women's sex role conflicts were needed if empirical research was to verify the strain and conflict hypothesized by Garnets and Pleck.

In 1979 our research team searched the psychological and sociological literature for patterns of men and women's sex role strain. We found much literature on role strain but only two studies that associated it with men's gender roles (Komarovsky, 1976; Levinson et al., 1978). We concluded that operationally defined patterns of sex role conflict did not currently exist for either men or women. Furthermore, few models existed that explained how men's socialization to their masculinity affected their personal and work lives. A large gap also existed between men's problems identified in the popular literature (David & Brannon, 1976; Farrell, 1974; Fasteau, 1974; Goldberg, 1977; Nichols, 1975; Pleck & Sawyer, 1974) and any empirical evidence for men's gender role conflict. We conceptualized theoretical models of men's sex role conflicts based on this literature review and our own clinical experience with men (O'Neil, 1979, 1980, 1981a, 1981b, 1982).

In the first theoretical summary of men's sex role conflicts, the complex factors affecting men's socialization were critically reviewed (O'Neil, 1981a). Additionally, 17 psychological patterns to men's sex role conflicts and 24 psychological effects were enumerated in men's interpersonal, career, family, and health lives. The outcome of this first literature review was the theoretical foundation for men's sex role conflicts. Next, the 17 patterns of sex role conflict were reduced to 6 major patterns of gender role conflict (O'Neil, 1981b, 1982). At this time, we changed the term "sex role conflict" to "gender role conflict," based on Unger's (1979) differentiation between sex and gender role.

We theorized that men's socialization and the "Masculine Mystique and Value System" produce the fear of femininity in men's lives (O'Neil, 1981a, 1981b, 1982). We proposed that the fear of femininity produces six patterns of gender role conflict, including: restrictive emotionality; socialized control, power, and competition; homophobia; restrictive sexual and affectionate behavior; obsession with achievement and success; and health care problems. Additionally, we hypothesized that these six patterns of gender role conflict interact with personal and institutional aspects of sexism. In other words, how men are socialized produces sexist attitudes and behavior that explains much of the personal and institutional sexism in society.

Then, in 1981, Joseph Pleck's seminal book, *The Myth of Masculinity*, was published. This book provided a much more comprehensive base for the sex role strain paradigm and the patterns of gender role conflict that we were developing. Pleck's book quickly became the primary scholarly resource that criticized the masculine sex role identity paradigm and replaced it with a sex role strain paradigm. Pleck specified 10 propositions about sex role strain that extended the earlier sex role strain analysis (Garnets & Pleck, 1979). These propositions stated that gender roles are defined by gender role stereotypes, are contradictory and inconsistent, and are violated by many individuals. Additionally, Pleck proposed that violating gender role stereotypes is common and can lead to social condemnation. Furthermore, he posited that overconformity to the stereotypes can have more severe consequences for males than females. The sex role strain paradigm also includes the hypothesis that characteristics of prescribed gender roles are psychologically dysfunctional and that both sexes experience sex role strain in work and family roles. Finally, Pleck proposed that historical change causes sex role strain. Currently, Pleck has renamed the sex role strain paradigm the gender role strain paradigm (see Chapter 1). We will use this new term throughout the rest of the chapter.

While Pleck was writing *The Myth of Masculinity* (between 1978 and 1980), our research program was finalizing the six patterns of men's gender role conflict (O'Neil, 1979, 1980, 1981b, 1982). Pleck's 10 propositions and gender role strain paradigm gave our work conceptual clarity. For example, Pleck's Proposition 8, that "certain characteristics prescribed by sex roles are psychologically dysfunctional" (1981, p. 9), was theoretically relevant to our work. Our gender role conflict model specified the kind of stereotyped masculinity that can produce dysfunction. We defined the negative aspects of the masculine stereotype as the Masculine Mystique and Value System (O'Neil, 1981a, 1981b, 1982). The Masculine Mystique and Value System was defined as a complex set of values and beliefs that define optimal masculinity. These values, learned during early socialization, are based on rigid stereotypes and beliefs about men, masculinity, and femininity (see O'Neil, 1981a, 1981b, 1982, for the specific beliefs).

Additionally, Pleck's Propositions 2, 4, and 5 indicated that gender roles are contradictory and inconsistent and that violating them leads to social condemnation, negative psychological consequences, dysfunction, and severe problems for males. These propositions provided an important premise for the gender role conflict construct. First, we identified the biological and psychological factors affecting men's gender role socialization that contribute to men's gender role conflict (O'Neil, 1981a, 1982). We also discussed how this socialization produces sexist attitudes and behaviors that could explain many aspects of personal and institutional sexism (O'Neil, 1981b). In this way, Pleck's gender role strain paradigm was extended to the politics of sexism in society. We went on to specify patterns of gender role conflict that might emerge when men experience gender roles in contradictory or inconsistent ways. More specifically, the six patterns of gender role conflict constituted some of the operationally defined patterns of gender role strain in Pleck's paradigm. Our work focused on the outcome of gender role strain when a person adheres to gender roles or violates them. We discussed men's gender role conflict in the context of how gender role conflict and sexism interact, affecting people's relationships with each other (O'Neil, 1981a, 1981b; O'Neil et al., 1987).

Moving beyond the six patterns, we discussed how to assess gender role conflict in terms of gender role devaluations, restrictions, and violations in three contexts: within the self, from others, and toward others (O'Neil, 1990). In the late 1980s and early 1990s, we provided ways to resolve gender role conflict by identifying gender role transitions and themes (O'Neil & Egan, 1992c; O'Neil & Fishman, 1992; O'Neil et al., 1987) and through the gender role journey metaphor (O'Neil & Egan 1992b; O'Neil et al., 1993; O'Neil & Roberts Carroll, 1987). Most recently, we have extended gender role conflict to its relationship with patriarchy, power abuses, and psychological violence (O'Neil, 1991, 1992; O'Neil & Egan, 1992). Finally, in January 1995, a special section of the *Journal of Counseling Psychology* will be devoted to men's gender role conflict. Two major papers have been prepared for publication (Cournoyer & Mahalik, in press; Good, Robertson, et al., in press), and one reaction paper suggests future directions and implications (Heppner, in press).

In the early 1980s, we had a conceptualization of gender role conflict but no way to scientifically test it. With the encouragement and support of Lawrence Wrightsman, an eminent social psychologist at the University of

Kansas, and with Nancy Betz's gracious offer to help collect data at Ohio State University, the measurement of the gender role conflict construct began in the fall of 1981.

Description and Development of the Gender Role Conflict Scale (I and II)

The Gender Role Conflict Scale (GRCS) emanated from the theoretical propositions about men's gender role conflict as reviewed above. There were two separate scales. GRCS-I assessed men's personal gender role attitudes, behaviors, and conflicts. GRCS-II assessed men's degree of comfort or conflict in specific gender role conflict situations. The specific item reduction procedures for developing the scale are found elsewhere (Beere, 1990; O'Neil et al., 1986) and only partially reviewed below.

The GRCS-I was developed as a 37-item measure that assesses directly or indirectly men's conflicts with their gender roles. Respondents are asked to report the degree to which they agree or disagree with statements, using a six-point Likert-type scale ranging from "strongly agree" (6) to "strongly disagree" (1). Examples of items include: "I have difficulty expressing my tender feelings," "I strive to be more successful than others," and, "Finding time to relax is difficult for me." Each item assesses one of the four gender role conflict patterns. Higher scores reflect an expression of greater gender role conflict.

The GRCS-II was developed as a 16-item measure that assesses the degree of comfort or conflict an individual experiences in specific gender role conflict situations. Respondents are asked to rate their degree of comfort or conflict, using a four-point Likert scale ranging from "very much conflict—very uncomfortable" (4) to "no conflict—very comfortable" (1). Examples of items include:

1. "Your best friend has just lost his job at the factory where he works. He is obviously upset, afraid, and angry, but he has his emotions hidden. How comfortable/uncomfortable are you with responding to your friend's intense emotions?"
2. "There's a guy you've idolized since grade school. He's three years older than you are. In high school he was the star quarterback, valedictorian, and very active in the Young Methodist Fellowship. Last year, he graduated from college. You have just learned he is a homosexual. How much conflict do you feel between your admiration for this person and the fact that he is a homosexual?"

Each item assesses one of the four gender role conflict patterns. A high score reflects and assumes an expression of gender role conflict.

Initial Construct Validity of GRCS-I and GRCS-II

The original GRCS-I had 85 items reflecting one of the six patterns of gender role conflict. A common factor analysis with oblique rotation yielded the most meaningful factor solution for the GRCS-I. Four factors that accounted for 36% of the total variance were identified. These factors were labeled Success, Power, and Competition (13 items), Restrictive Emotionality (10 items), Restrictive and Affectionate Behavior Between Men (8 items), and Conflict Between Work and Family Relations (6 items). To be retained, items were required to have a factor loading of .30 or greater, to not cross-load on other factors, and to have a standard deviation of at least 1.00 on a six-point scale. Assessments of the factor reliabilities yielded internal consistency estimates using alpha coefficients that ranged from .75 to .85. Four-week test-retest reliabilities for the factors ranged from .72 to .86.

The original GRCS-II had 51 items reflecting one of the patterns of gender role conflict. Using the same procedures and criteria as for GRCS-I, 16 items met the criteria. The four factors meeting this criteria were Success, Power, and Competition (6 items), Homophobia (4 items), Lack of Emotional Response (3 items), and Public Embarrassment from Gender Role Deviance (3 items). These four factors explained 48% of the variance. Assessment of the scale's reliabilities found internal consistency scores using alpha coefficients ranging from .59 to .76. Four-week test-retest reliabilities ranged from .78 to .85.

The lower internal consistency reliabilities for two of the GRCS-II factors (Lack of Emotional Response [.51] and public embarrassment from Gender Role Deviance [.59] required that further research be conducted. Consequently, GRCS-II has been unavailable for research use. Only the original study (O'Neil et al., 1986) and one other analysis (O'Neil, Helms, Gable, Stillson, David, & Wrightsman, 1984) have reported data on the situational aspects of gender role conflict assessed in GRCS-II. Further development and refinement of GRCS-II is currently under way.

Figure 6.1 depicts the gender role conflict theory described earlier and the empirically derived patterns of gender role conflict for the GRCS-I. Men's gender role socialization, the Masculine Mystique and Value System, and fear of femininity are hypothesized to be related to the four patterns of gender role conflict. These patterns are directly related to personal and institutional sexism. The remainder of this chapter exclusively focuses on the empirically derived gender role conflict patterns of GRCS-I shown in Figure 6.1. The gender role conflict patterns are defined in the following way:

1. *Success:* Persistent worries about personal achievement, competence, failure, status, upward mobility and wealth, and career success.
   Power: Obtaining authority, dominance, influence, or ascendancy over others.

FIGURE 6.1
Emperically Derived Patterns of Gender Role Conflict—GRCS-I

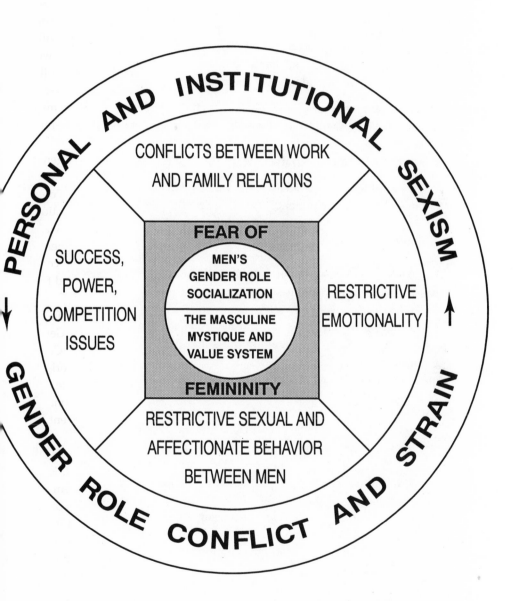

Competition: Striving against others to gain something or the comparison of self with others to establish one's superiority in a given situation.

2. *Restrictive Emotionality:* Having difficulty and fears about expressing one's feelings and difficulty finding words to express basic emotions.

3. *Restrictive Affectionate Behavior Between Men:* Having limited ways to express one's feelings and thoughts with other men and difficulty touching other men.

4. *Conflicts Between Work and Family Relations:* Experiencing difficulties balancing work-school and family relations, resulting in health problems, overwork, stress, and a lack of leisure and relaxation.

The remainder of the chapter reviews 35 studies that have used the GRCS-I to assess these four empirically derived patterns of gender role conflict.

Construct Validity and Reliability Research on GRCS-I

Five additional factor analyses or validity studies have been completed on the GRCS-I (Braverman, 1990; Chamberlin, 1994; Chartier, Graff, & Arnold, 1986; Good, Robertson, O'Neil, Fitzgerald, Stevens, DeBord, Bartels, & Braverman, in press; Mendelson, 1988). These five studies found a factor structure similar to the one reported in the original factor analysis (O'Neil et al., 1986). Two of these validity studies (Chamberlin, 1994; Mendelson, 1988) were with adult men, suggesting that the GRCS-I has some initial validity for older men as well as college-age men. Recently, Betz and Fitzgerald (1993) have advocated that a confirmatory factor analysis be done on the GRCS-I. Good, Robertson, et al. (in press) have recently shown that the factor structure is similar to the original factor structure using the more rigorous confirmatory factor analysis.

O'Neil and Owen (1994) summarize 11 studies that have calculated internal consistencies on the GRCS-I (Arnold, 1983; Chamberlin, 1994; Chartier et al., 1986; Cournoyer, 1993; Good, Dell, & Mintz, 1989; Good, Robertson, et al., in press; Hayes, 1985; Horhoruw, 1991; Kaplan, 1992; Kim, 1990; Mendelson, 1988). All of these studies provided similiar or better internal consistency reliabilities than the original study (O'Neil et al., 1986). To provide an overall summary of the GRCS-I's internal consistency, average reliabilities across the 11 studies were calculated using z transformations. For the Success, Power, and Competition factor, the alpha ranged from .83 to .89, with an average of .86. For the Restrictive Emotionality factor, alphas ranged from .81 to .91, with the average being .84. For the Restrictive Affectionate Behavior Between Men factor, the alphas ranged from .82 to .88, with an average of .84. For the Conflict Between Work and Family Relations factor, the alpha ranged from .73 to .87, with an average of .80. For the seven studies in which GRCS-I total score alphas were calculated, the alphas ranged from .75 to .90, with an average of .88.

Betz and Fitzgerald (1993) have recently questioned whether the items of the gender role conflict factors relate to men's actual conflict with their gender roles, as well as whether some of the items assess conflict, defined as the result of two competing response tendencies. Clarification about these questions and item content is found below.

The GRCS-I items were first generated from the negative assumptions and stereotypes of the Masculine Mystique and Value System (see O'Neil, 1981a, 1981b, 1982). Each item reflected a direct or indirect negative consequence of deviating from or conforming to these stereotyped values. Furthermore, gender role conflict was construed as complex thoughts, feelings, and behaviors within a man caused by gender role socialization and sexism. Gender role conflict was also hypothesized to be stimulated by others and expressed toward others (O'Neil, 1990; O'Neil & Egan, 1992a). A careful examination of the GRCS-I indicates that 25 items primarily reflect conflict within a man, 9 items reflect conflict expressed toward others, and 3 items reflect conflict stimulated by others.

Consequently, gender role conflict is defined as more than the result of two competing response tendencies, avoidance tendencies, or unambivalent approaches within a man, as suggested by Betz and Fitzgerald (1993). Their useful critique stimulates more elaboration on the item content. A careful perusal of the GRCS-I items reflect men's gender role conflict when they (1) try to meet the masculine stereotypes and norms to avoid appearing feminine; (2) fear not meeting the masculine stereotypes and norms and/or perceive a discrepancy between real and ideal gender role concept; (3) fear or experience self-devaluation, self-restriction, or self-violation when adhering to or violating expected gender role norms of masculinity; (4) fear devaluation, restriction, or violation from others when deviating or violating the gender role norms of masculinity; (5) fear devaluation, restriction, or violation from others when they deviate or violate gender role norms of masculinity. Betz and Fitzgerald's (1993) labeling of the items has prompted the above clarification. Most of the items reflect actual restrictions of behavior that cause conflict, fears of not meeting the stereotypic norms of masculinity and appearing feminine, self-devaluation, self-restriction, and self-violation, or fears of being devalued, restricted, or violated by others.

POPULATIONS ASSESSED BY THE GRCS-I

The GRCS-I has been used with numerous samples since its development. The early studies were completed with college students in the United States and Canada (Chartier et al., 1986; O'Neil et al., 1986). Numerous studies have assessed college-age men's gender role conflict (Archer, Murphy, Foos, Jensen, & Morgan, 1985; Braverman, 1990; Davis, 1988; Good, 1987; Good et al., 1989; Good & Mintz, 1990; Kaplan, 1992; Rhoades, 1985; Sharpe & Heppner, 1991).

In the late 1980s and early 1990s, studies assessed adult men across the life cycle. Studies have also been completed on married adult men (Campbell & Snow, 1992), adult engineers (Mendelson, 1988), adult white-collar men (Cournoyer, 1994; Cournoyer & Mahalik, in press; O'Neil, Owen, Holmes, Dolgopolov, & Slastenin, 1994; Sharpe, 1993), black and Hispanic men (Stillson, O'Neil, & Owen, 1991), and recently separated men (Nahon, 1992). Four studies compared men at different ages and life stages (Cournoyer, 1994; Cournoyer & Mahalik, in press; Mendelson, 1987; Stillson et al., 1991). Numerous studies have focused on special groups of men based on race, ethnicity, nationality, and class. Stillson et al. (1991) assessed adult men's gender role conflict from different races and classes. Kim (1990) gathered data on an Asian-American sample of Japanese-American, Korean-American, and Chinese-American college students. Black, white, and Hispanic unmarried fathers and their nonfather peers have been assessed (Berlin, 1988). Horhoruw (1991) assessed a group of Indonesian men, and three studies have used the GRCS-I with Canadian college students (Arnold, 1983; Chartier & Arnold, 1985; Chartier et al., 1986). O'Neil et al. (1994) used a sample of Russian men and compared them with American men. Other studies have assessed counselors in training (Hayes, 1985), counseling center clients (Good, Robertson, et al., in press), alcoholic men (Moore, 1993), fraternity men (Braverman, 1990; Rounds, 1994), airline pilots (Chamberlin, 1994), and adolescent sex offenders, adolescents in custody, and high school nonoffenders (Walls, 1991). These studies demonstrate that a wide variety of samples have been used in studying men's gender role conflict.

GRCS-I's Relation to Other Gender Role Measures

The relation of GRCS-I to other gender role measures has received some attention. In addition to the initial validity study of GRCS-I (O'Neil et al., 1986), two studies have assessed the relationship between the Personal Attributes Questionnaire (PAQ) (Spence & Helmreich, 1978) and the GRCS-I (Sharpe, 1993; Sharpe & Heppner, 1991). In both studies, it was hypothesized that the Masculinity subscale would positively correlate with the GRCS-I and the Femininity subscale would negatively correlate with the GRCS-I. In both studies, the PAQ Masculinity subscale did not significantly correlate with the GRCS-I as a whole. However, the Masculinity subscale was significantly and positively correlated *only* with the Success, Power, and Competition factor. In the first study, the Femininity subscale was negatively correlated with the GRCS-I subscales of Success, Power, and Competition and Restrictive Emotionality (Sharpe & Heppner, 1991). In the second study, the Femininity subscale also negatively correlated with Restrictive Emotionality and Restrictive Affectionate Behavior Between Men (Sharpe, 1993). In both studies, the authors indicated that the PAQ and GRCS-I do not have a substantial amount of overlap and thus measure different constructs. In another study, Chartier and Arnold (1985) also found significant negative correlations between GRCS-I and PAQ Masculinity and Femininity subscales.

The GRCS-I has also been correlated with other measures related to men. Two studies found the GRCS-I to be uncorrelated with two early measures of men's attitudes and roles. Moore (1993) found the GRCS-I to be negatively correlated with the Attitudes Toward the Male Role Scale (AMR) (Doyle & Moore, 1978). Good and Mintz (1990) found the Attitudes Toward Men Scale (AMS) (Downs & Engelson, 1982) to also be negatively correlated with the GRCS-I. These results suggest that these early scales do not have much in common with the gender role conflict construct. Good, Robertson, et al. (in press) found the Brannon Masculinity Scale (BMS) (Brannon, 1985; Brannon & Juni, 1984) to be correlated with all subscales of the GRCS-I except the Conflict Between Work and Family Relations Subscale. Moore's (1993) small sample experimental study found the GRCS-I to be correlated with the Masculine Gender Role Stress Scale (MGRS) (Eisler & Skidmore, 1987), which is a similiar measure of gender role conflict.

SUMMARY OF PSYCHOMETRIC EVIDENCE ON GRCS-I

Considerable evidence supports the psychometric properties of the GRCS-I. Namely, the validity of the scale and its four subscales has been supported by evidence of a stable factor structure across numerous samples, using both exploratory and confirmatory factor analyses (Good, Robertson, et al., in press; O'Neil et al., 1986). Also, the GRCS-I has demonstrated convergent validity with some of the other masculinity measures as well as measures of men's conflicts and stress. The GRCS-I has demonstrated freedom from socially-desirable-responses consistency for the total scale and subscales (Good, Robertson, et al., in press). The Conflict Between Work and Family Relations factor has been shown to be the weakest factor psychometrically and therefore may require further item development and empirical testing. In sum, the GRCS-I appears to warrant the increasing attention that it is receiving in the psychological literature (Beere, 1990; Betz & Fitzgerald, 1993; Good, Robertson, et al., in press; Thompson, Pleck, & Ferrera, 1992).

Empirical Research Completed on GRCS-I, 1985–1995

Thirty-five studies used the GRCS-I from 1985 to 1995. This section summarizes the results of these studies and the part gender role conflict theory plays in the following areas: (1) demographic and classification variables; (2) personality variables; (3) positive and negative correlates of psychological health and well-being; (4) relational, interpersonal, and political variables;

and (5) experimental interventions and counseling process studies using GRCS-I.

Table 6.1 (pp. 182–85) lists these studies in alphabetical order by author and date, sample employed, and measures or variables used with the GRCS-I. This table provides more specific information about the samples and measures used than is found in the research review below.

DEMOGRAPHIC AND CLASSIFICATION VARIABLES

Demographic and classification variables include age, life stage, fraternity-nonfraternity status, change over time, race, class, ethnic background, and nationality. In most cases, these variables were used to categorize men into different groups to assess differences in gender role conflict.

Life Stage and Age

Four studies have assessed gender role conflict differences in men at different life stages or ages (Cournoyer, 1994; Cournoyer & Mahalik, in press; Mendelson, 1988; Stillson et al., 1991). Stillson et al. (1991) found no relationship between age or life stage and the patterns of gender role conflict, using Levinson et al.'s (1978) early and middle adulthood periods. Mendelson (1987) assessed undergraduate and adult engineers for differential gender role conflict using Levinson et al.'s (1978) first three life stages: Leaving Family (age 17–22), Getting into the Adult World (age 22–28), Age 30 Transition (age 28–30). Men 22 to 28 years old had significantly less overall gender role conflict than men in the age 17–22 and 28–30 cohorts. Restrictive emotionality was significantly higher for the age 28–30 cohort compared with age 22–28 group. Restrictive affectionate behavior between men was significantly higher for the 17- to 22-year-olds than the age 22–28 cohort. Cournoyer (1994) assessed differences in gender role conflict for undergraduate men (17–22 years) and middle-aged men (36–45 years). Undergraduate men reported significantly more conflict with success, power, and competition issues than did older men. The older men reported more conflicts between work and family relations than did the younger men.

These last two studies indicate that young men in their late teens and early twenties struggle more with showing affectionate behavior to other men and also struggle with conflicts related to success, power, and competition. Men in their late twenties and early thirties tend to struggle more with expressing and receiving emotions from men and also report more conflict between work and family relations. These findings indicate that men in different life stages and ages may be experiencing different patterns of gender role conflict. Further research is needed to better understand how age and stage of life relate to gender role conflict.

Fraternity-Nonfraternity Status and Time

Braverman (1990) studied prospective fraternity students and nonfraternity students for differences in gender role conflict. He also assessed changes in each group's gender role conflict over a 12- to 18-month period. He found initially that prospective fraternity students reported more problems with success, power, and competition compared with actual fraternity members. However, over time, he found that both prospective fraternity members and nonfraternity members reported greater restrictive emotionality and conflict between work and family relations. The important finding is that regardless of fraternity status, all men reported increased gender role conflict the longer they were on campus.

Race and Class

In a recent study, Stillson et al. (1991) used a sample of adult men from different races and classes. Race and class were significantly related to gender role conflict in two ways. First, men from three different races (white, black, and Hispanic) all reported problems with success, power, and competition, restrictive emotionality, and conflicts between work and family relations. Second, lower-class black men—who were both instrumental and inexpressive on the PAQ, exhibiting low psychological strain—reported conflicts with success, power, and competition, but few problems with restrictive emotionality and conflict between work and family relations. These initial results suggest the need for research on the complexity of different race and class variables as they relate to gender role conflict.

Ethnic Background

Kim (1990) studied the gender role conflict and acculturation of Chinese-American, Japanese-American, and Korean-American college students. She found that Chinese-American and Japanese-American men differed significantly in the areas of restrictive emotionality and conflict between work and family relations. More important, she found that the more acculturated men reported significantly higher gender role conflict over success, power, and competition issues, while reporting significantly less conflict with restrictive emotionality.

Nationality

In one of the first cross-cultural assessments, the gender role conflict of American and Russian men was studied (O'Neil et al., 1994). Russian men reported significantly greater gender role conflict than did American men on

TABLE 6.1
Empirical Studies Using the Gender Role Conflict Scale-I, 1984–1994

Author/Date	Sample	Measures or Variables Used with GRCS-I
Archer, Murphy, Foos, Jensen, & Morgan (1985)	College students (N = 417)	Likert items assessing male attitudes toward women and changing roles
Arnold & Chartier (1984)	Canadian college students (N = 146)	Ego Identity Incomplete Sentences Blank (EI-ISB) Intimacy Categories Questionnaire Miller Social Intimacy Scale
Berlin (1988)	Black, white, and Hispanic unmarried fathers and their nonfather peers (N = 181)	Future Time Perspective Inventory Contraceptive Behavior Index
Braverman (1990)	College students (N = 572)	Fraternity vs. nonfraternity status Upper-class student vs. lower-class student
Campbell & Snow (1992)	Married men (N = 70)	Family Adaptability and Cohesion Evaluation Scale III (FACES) Dyadic Adjustment Scale (DAS)
Chamberlin (1994)	Airline pilots (N = 188)	Cockpit Management Attitudes Problem Solving Inventory (PSI) Authoritarianism Personality Scale Least Preferred Coworker Scale
Chartier & Arnold (1985)	Canadian college students (N = 143)	Objective Measure of Ego Identity (OMEI) Erickson's Psychosocial Inventory (EPSI) Intimacy Subscale of EPSI Social Intimacy Scale Personal Attributes Questionnaire (PAQ)
Chartier, Graff, & Arnold (1986)	Canadian college students (N = 555)	Hostility Toward Women Scale
Cournoyer (1994) and Cournoyer & Mahalik (in press)	Adult men, ages 36–45 (N = 98); college men (N = 99)	Coopersmith Self-esteem Inventory (CSI) State Trait Anxiety Inventory (STAI) Beck Depression Inventory (BDI) Miller Social Intimacy Scale (MSIS) Nebraska Scale of Marital Happiness Age
Davis (1987)	Undergraduate men (N = 304)	Rosenberg Self-esteem Scale (RSS) Texas Social Behavior Inventory Jackson Personality Inventory Anxiety Scale Garnets Sex Role Salience Measures
Ducat (1994)	Undergraduate men (N = 69)	Political Gender Gap Scale Attitudes Toward Lesbian and Gay Men Scale Avoiding Femininity subscale of the Brannon Masculinity Scale

Empirical Studies Using the Gender Role Conflict Scale-I, 1984–1994

Author/Date	Sample	Measures or Variables Used with GRCS-I
Gertner (1994)	College students ($N = 30$)	Gender Role Journey Measure (GRJM)
Good, Dell, & Mintz (1989)	College students ($N = 401$)	Attitude Toward Men Scale (ATM) Fisher-Turner Attitudes Toward Seeking Professional Psychological Help Scale (ASPPHS) Help Seeking Attitude and Behavior Scale (HSABS)
Good & Mintz (1990)	College students ($N = 401$)	ATM Center for Epidemiological Depression Scale
Good, Robertson, Fitzgerald, Stevens, & Bartels (1994)	Counseling center clients ($N = 130$)	Symptom Checklist (SCL-90-R)
Good, Robertson, O'Neil, Fitzgerald, DeBord, Bartels, & Braverman (in press)	3 samples of college students ($N = 107$, $N = 555$, $N = 397$)	Brannon Masculinity Scale (BMS) Fear-of-Intimacy Scale Marlowe-Crown Social Desirability Scale
Good & Wood (in press)	College students ($N = 397$)	ASPPHS HSABS Center for Epidemiological Depression Scale
Harris (1991)	Male college students ($N = 142$)	BMS ASPPHS HSABS
Hayes (1985)	Counselor trainees ($N = 96$)	Counselor self-rating scales of traditional and nontraditional male clients
Horhoruw (1991)	Indonesian men ($N = 65$)	Male Friendship Behavior Questionnaire
Kaplan (1992)	College juniors and seniors ($N = 196$)	Sexual Experience Survey (SES) Likelihood to Rape or Force Sex Measure Hypermasculinity Inventory Hostility Toward Women Scale GRJM
Kim (1990)	Chinese-, Japanese-, and Korean-American college men ($N = 125$)	Suinn-Lew Asian Self Identity Acculturation Scale Personal data sheet Ethnic background
Mendelson (1988)	Alumni in their twenties and under-graduate engineers ($N = 303$)	Marlowe-Crowne Social Desirability Scale Age-life stage

TABLE 6.1 *(continued)*
Empirical Studies Using the Gender Role Conflict Scale-I, 1984–1994

Author/Date	Sample	Measures or Variables Used with GRCS-I
Moore (1993)	Nonalcoholic and alcoholic veterans and control group ($N = 64$)	Attitudes Toward the Male Role Scale Emotion Scale Expression of Emotion Scale (EES) Masculine Gender-Role Stress Scale Tennessee Self-concept Scale
Nahon (1992)	Recently separated men ($N = 61$)	Yalom's Curative Factors Questionnaire SCL-90-R Personal Orientation Inventory RSS EES Jourard Self-disclosure Questionnaire
O'Neil, Helms, Gable, David, & Wrightsman (1986)	College students ($N = 527$)	PAQ
O'Neil, Owen, Holmes, Dolgopolov, & Slastenin (1994)	American men ($N = 95$) Russian men ($N = 174$)	Psychological Violence Scale Personal Strain Questionnaire (PSQ) Nationality
Rhoades (1985)	Men in late teens ($N = 170$)	Contraceptive Mutuality Index
Robertson & Fitzgerald (1992)	Male college students ($N = 435$)	UNIACT Technical and Social Service Scales PAQ ASPPHS
Rounds (1994)	College students ($N = 165$)	Inventory of Psychosocial Development (Identity and Intimacy subscales) Expanded PAQ Index of Attitudes Toward Homosexuals
Sharpe (1993)	Adult, married, white-collar men ($N = 88$)	CSI STAI Selye's Stress Symptom Checklist MSIS DAS Inventory of Interpersonal Problems-Intimacy subscale, Social subscale PAQ
Sharpe & Heppner (1991)	Male college students ($N = 190$)	PAQ CSI STAI BDI MSIS Austin Contentment/Distress Measure

TABLE 6.1 *(continued)*
Empirical Studies Using the Gender Role Conflict Scale-I, 1984–1994

Author/Date	Sample	Measures or Variables Used with GRCS-I
Stillson, O'Neil, & Owen (1991)	Adult men of different classes, races, ages, and life stages (*N* = 134)	PAQ PSQ Index of Social Position Age-life stage
Wall (1991)	Adolescent sex offenders, adolescents in custody, and high school nonoffenders (*N* = 60)	Bem Sex Role Inventory UCLA Loneliness Scale (version 3) Attitude Toward Women Scale for Adolescents
Wisch, Mahilik, Hayes, & Nutt (1993)	College students (*N* = 165)	Counselor Rating Form Working Alliance Inventory Sessions Evaluation Questionnaire ASPPHS

success, power, and competition issues and with restrictive affectionate behavior between men. This study demonstrates that ethnic-nationality variables may differentially affect men's gender role conflict but does not explain why these differences exist. In another study, Horhoruw (1991) assessed how Indonesian men's male friendship and confiding behaviors related to gender role conflict. She found that restrictive affectionate behavior between men negatively related to both confiding and expressive behavior between men. For this specific nationality, one of the four patterns of gender role conflict affected male-male friendships.

PERSONALITY VARIABLES

Three personality variables have been correlated with gender role conflict. They include instrumentality-expressiveness from Spence and Helmreich's (1978) Personal Attributes Questionnaire, ego identity, and authoritarianism.

Instrumentality-Expressiveness

Two studies have assessed relationships between the PAQ subscales of instrumentality and expressiveness and gender role conflict (O'Neil et al., 1986; Stillson et al., 1991). O'Neil et al. (1986) found that men who described themselves as expressive, instrumental, both expressive and instrumental, or neither expressive nor instrumental expressed differential degrees of gender role conflict across three of the gender role conflict patterns. For example, men who described themselves as expressive had less difficulty with showing emotions than men who described themselves as instrumental. However, men who were neither expressive nor instrumental reported more difficulty with expressing and receiving emotions. Furthermore, Stillson et al. (1991) found that black men from lower social classes who described themselves as instrumental and inexpressive had greater gender role conflicts with success, power, and competition issues, but not with issues of restrictive emotionality or conflict between work and family relations. In these two studies, the variable of instrumentality-expressiveness appears to be related to differential degrees of gender role conflict.

Ego Identity and Intimacy

Three studies have assessed some aspect of ego identity, intimacy, and gender role conflict (Arnold & Chartier, 1984; Chartier & Arnold, 1985; Rounds, 1994). Chartier and Arnold (1985), using Canadian college students, found that greater gender role conflict was associated with lower ego identity. In a second study, Arnold and Chartier (1984) studied gender role conflict's relationship to ego identity and intimacy with opposite- and same-sex pairs. In opposite-sex relationships, high ego identity and low gender role conflict interacted to predict high intimacy. Furthermore, low ego identity and higher gender role conflict interacted to predict low intimacy. Rounds (1994), using American college students, assessed ego identity and intimacy development and attitudes toward homosexuals. He found that low ego identity scores significantly correlated with the total gender role conflict score and restrictive emotionality. He also found that gender role conflict had a significant and uniquely negative association with ego identity. These studies provide consistent evidence that men with lower ego identity have higher gender role conflict.

Authoritarian Personality Style

Chamberlin (1994) studied airline pilots' authoritarian personality style and gender role conflict. He found that authoritarian personality attributes are highly correlated with gender role conflict patterns in the areas of success, power, and competition; restrictive emotionality; and conflicts between work and family relations. For example, two factors of the authoritarian personality style, men's poor leadership and interpersonal conflict, were related to three of the four patterns of gender role conflict.

POSITIVE AND NEGATIVE CORRELATES OF PSYCHOLOGICAL HEALTH AND WELL-BEING

Numerous gender role conflict studies have been conducted on the positive and negative correlates of psychological health and well-being. Six categories of variables have been studied, including: (1) self-esteem; (2) intimacy; (3) depression; (4) anxiety; (5) personal strain, distress, and stress; and (6) attitudes toward help-seeking. Each of these categories is summarized below.

Self-esteem

Cournoyer (1993) studied the relationship between gender role conflict and self-esteem for both undergraduate and middle-aged men. For the adult sample, the only gender role conflict pattern found to be negatively and significantly associated with self-esteem was restrictive emotionality. This result indicates that adult men with lower self-esteem reported more difficulty in expressing and receiving emotions. For the undergraduate sample, conflicts between work and family relations were significantly and negatively associated with self-esteem.

Using three separate measures of self-esteem, Davis (1987) studied the relationship between gender role conflict and self-esteem in college males. Three of the patterns of gender role conflict (restrictive emotionality, restrictive affectionate behavior between men, and conflict between work and family relations) consistently showed negative correlations with self-esteem. Only the gender role conflict pattern of success, power, and competition failed to show a negative correlation. Sharpe and Heppner (1991) corroborated these results by finding that the same three patterns of gender role conflict correlated negatively and significantly with self-esteem in college students. Sharpe (1993) extended his research to successful middle-aged men who belonged to professional service organizations. He found that self-esteem did not correlate with any of the four patterns of gender role conflict in this sample of successful men.

These results with samples of college men have consistently demonstrated that college men with low self-esteem report greater levels of gender role conflict. For adult men, the relationship between self-esteem and gender role conflict has been documented only with the work-family conflicts. Consequently, more study is needed with adult men to better understand whether there is a relationship between gender role conflict and self-esteem.

Intimacy

Six studies have assessed gender role conflict's relationship to intimacy. Sharpe and Heppner (1991) found that intimacy for college men was negatively related to gender role conflict patterns in the areas of success, power, and competition; restrictive emotionality; and restrictive affectionate behavior between men. This finding indicates that men who were experiencing gender role conflict also had difficulty with intimacy in relationships. Sharpe (1993) used two separate measures of intimacy and obtained mixed results when assessing the relationship of adult men's gender role conflict with intimacy. For the first scale, he found only restrictive emotionality negatively correlated with intimacy. For the second scale, restrictive emotionality and restrictive affectionate behavior between men negatively correlated with intimacy. This finding was also replicated by Good, Robertson, et al. (in press) with college students. Likewise, Cournoyer (1994) found similar results in his study of middle-aged men. Both restrictive emotionality and restrictive affectionate behavior between men negatively correlated to intimacy. For Cournoyer's undergraduate sample of men, only restrictive emotionality significantly and negatively correlated to intimacy. Rounds (1994) assessed college students and found gender role conflict to be correlated negatively with a measure of intimacy.

Chartier and Arnold (1985) assessed the relationship between gender role conflict and global intimacy, same-sex intimacy, and opposite-sex intimacy. All analyses indicated that gender role conflict and intimacy were negatively correlated. This result indicated that men with higher gender role conflict had lower global intimacy. In another study of men in same-sex relationships, high gender role conflict predicted lower intimacy and low gender role conflict predicted higher intimacy (Arnold & Chartier, 1984). The results of the six intimacy studies indicate that gender role conflict and intimacy are related. Restrictive emotionality and restrictive affectionate behavior between men are the most consistent patterns being reported.

Anxiety

Four studies have assessed the relationship between gender role conflict and anxiety (Davis, 1987; Cournoyer, 1994; Sharpe, 1993; Sharpe & Heppner, 1991). Davis (1987), assessing college students, found all subscales of the gender role conflict scale to be significantly correlated with anxiety measures. Also using college students, Sharpe and Heppner (1991) found that restrictive emotionality, restrictive affectionate behavior between men, and conflict between work and family relations all correlated positively with anxiety. Cournoyer (1994) assessed relationships between anxiety and gender role conflict for undergraduate and middle-aged men. For undergraduate men, success, power, and competition; restrictive emotionality; and conflict between work and family relations were all significantly associated with anxiety. For the middle-aged men, only restrictive emotionality and conflict between work and family relations were significantly associated with anxiety. Using only successful adult men, Sharpe (1993) found only conflict between work and family relations correlated with anxiety. These results show undergraduate men's anxiety was consistently related to all patterns of gender role conflict, but with adult men only work-family conflicts and restrictive emotionality are related to anxiety.

Depression

Five studies have assessed the relationship between depression and gender role conflict (Cournoyer, 1994; Good & Mintz, 1990; Good & Wood, in press; Sharpe, 1993; Sharpe & Heppner, 1991). Using college students, Good and Mintz (1990) found all four of the GRCS-I factors significantly correlated with depression. Sharpe and Heppner (1991), also using college students, found only restrictive emotionality and conflict between work and family relations correlated significantly with depression. Cournoyer (1994) found college men's depression significantly correlated with success, power, and competition and with conflict between work and family relations. Similarly, Good and Wood (in press) found that a factor labeled "achievement based masculinity," comprising two of the GRCS-I's subscales (Success, Power, and Competition and Conflict Between Work and Family Relations), was highly predictive of men's depression. However, with middle-aged men, Cournoyer (1994) found only restrictive emotionality significantly correlated with depression. Finally, Sharpe (1993), using white, successful adults, failed to find any relationships between gender role conflict and depression. Overall, these studies demonstrate that among college men, depression is associated with a variety of gender role conflict patterns. Among successful adult men, the relationship between depression and gender role conflict is less strong and convincing.

Personal Strain, Stress, and Problem-Solving

Four studies have assessed gender role conflict in relationship to men's personal strain, stress, and problem-solving (Chamberlin, 1994; Good, Robertson, et al., in press; Sharpe, 1993; Stillson et al., 1991). Using canonical correlations, Stillson et al. (1991) found two significant relationships between men's strain and gender role conflict. First, adult men from three different races, who expressed low vocational but high physical strain, reported significant degrees of gender role conflict, including issues of restrictive emotionality, conflict between work and family relations, and success, power, and competition. Second, lower-class black men who were highly instrumental, inexpressive, and low on psychological strain reported high success, power, and competition conflicts and few problems with restrictive emotionality or conflict between work and family relations. In another study, Sharpe (1993) assessed the relationship between adult men's stress and gender role conflict. Conflict Between Work and Family Relations was the only subscale correlated with personal stress. The overall results of these two studies provide some initial evidence that adult men's strain and gender role conflict are related. The relationships are complex, and not all of the gender role conflict patterns are consistently found in the two studies completed.

In the only study relating gender role conflict to a clinical sample, Good,

Robertson, et al. (in press) studied counseling center clients' gender role conflict and psychological distress. They found a significant correlation between global psychological distress and gender role conflict. Furthermore, gender role conflict was significantly related to depression, anxiety, somatization, interpersonal sensitivities, as well as the more severe symptoms of paranoia, psychoticism, and obsessive-compulsivity.

Chamberlin (1994) assessed the relationship between problem-solving and gender role conflict with airline pilots. The overall GRCS-I scores correlated positively with the three problem-solving subscales of Confidence, Approach/Avoidance, and Personal Control. Restrictive emotionality correlated with all three aspects of problem-solving. Success, power, and competition correlated positively with problems of personal control. Restrictive affectionate behavior between men positively correlated with approach/avoidance and personal control. Using canonical correlation, Chamberlin (1994) provided evidence for a relationship between high restrictive emotionality and difficulties with problem-solving confidence and problem-solving approach/avoidance. All of these positive correlations indicate that greater gender role conflict was associated with less effective problem-solving appraisal for men.

Attitudes Toward Help-Seeking

Four studies have assessed gender role conflict's relationship to help-seeking (Good et al., 1989; Good & Wood, in press; Robertson & Fitzgerald, 1992; Wisch, Mahalik, Hayes, & Nutt, 1993). Using canonical correlation and regression analyses, Good et al. (1989) found significant relationships between restrictive emotionality and restrictive affectionate behavior between men and negative help-seeking attitudes. Robertson and Fitzgerald (1992) assessed whether success, power, and competition and restrictive emotionality were related to negative views of help-seeking. They found a significant relationship between these patterns of gender role conflict and negative attitudes toward help-seeking. Furthermore, they found that men who scored higher on gender role conflict were significantly more likely to prefer a nontraditional counseling brochure (i.e., describing workshops, classes, etc.) over a brochure describing traditional counseling center helping formats (i.e., direct service counseling). Wisch et al. (1993) found that undergraduate men with lower gender role conflict expressed more willingness to seek psychological help than men with higher gender role conflict. Furthermore, men scoring high on gender role conflict who viewed a cognitively focused counseling videotape indicated that they had more positive attitudes toward seeking psychological help than men scoring high on gender role conflict who viewed the more affectively focused videotape. Finally, Good and Wood (in press) found that restrictive-based aspects of gender role conflict (i.e., restrictive emotionality, restrictive affectionate behavior between men, and success, power, and competition) accounted for one-quarter of men's attitudes toward seeking professional psychological assistance. In summary, the results of these four studies indicate strong evidence for the relationship between men's gender role conflict and negative attitudes toward help-seeking.

RELATIONAL, INTERPERSONAL, AND POLITICAL VARIABLES

The relational and interpersonal variables empirically related to gender role conflict so far include marital satisfaction, attitudes toward homosexuals and contraceptive use, and sexual aggression toward women. The political variables identify men's attitudes toward such issues as war, the environment, and gays in the military.

Marital and Relationship Satisfaction

Four studies have assessed the relationship between men's gender role conflict and marital or relationship satisfaction. Cournoyer (1994) correlated the GRCS-I with marital happiness in adult men. He found restrictive emotionality correlated negatively with marital happiness. In a study with college students, Sharpe and Heppner (1991) found relationship satisfaction correlated negatively with conflict between work and family relations. Sharpe (1993) assessed married men and found that relationship satisfaction correlated negatively with restrictive emotionality. Campbell and Snow (1992) also found that married men's restrictive emotionality and conflict between work and family relations negatively related to marital satisfaction. These four studies provide initial evidence that the gender role conflict patterns of restrictive emotionality and conflict between work and family relations relate to marital unhappiness or relationship dissatisfaction for both college and adult men.

Contraceptive Use

Two studies have related men's use of contraceptives with patterns of gender role conflict. Berlin (1988) and Rhoades (1985) studied white and minority men's contraceptive behavior and gender role conflict. Both studies found that restrictive affectionate behavior between men was correlated with less positive attitudes toward using contraceptives.

Attitudes Toward Homosexuals and Women

Four studies have assessed the relationship between men's gender role conflict and attitudes toward homosexuals and women. Rounds (1994) assessed college men's gender role conflict and attitudes toward homosexuals. Gender role conflict was significantly related to negative attitudes and intolerance toward homosexuals. Only conflict between work and family relations did not positively correlate with negative attitudes toward homosexuals. Ducat (1994) found that the gender role conflict patterns of success, power, and competition and restrictive and affectionate behavior between men significantly correlated with negative attitudes toward lesbians and gay men.

Chartier et al. (1986) found positive correlations between the GRCS-I total score and the total scores on a measure of hostility toward women. Additionally, they found that men with the highest gender role conflict scored significantly higher on subscales of lack of trust and anger at women. In a more recent study, the relationship between college men's gender role conflict and their sexually aggressive experiences with women and the likelihood of their forcing rape or sex was studied (Kaplan, 1992; Kaplan, O'Neil, & Owen, 1993). This research indicated that the gender role patterns of success, power, and competition, restrictive emotionality, and restrictive affectionate behavior between men were significantly correlated with self-reported sexually aggressive experiences and likelihood of forcing sex from age 14 and over the previous year. Overall, these studies indicate that multiple patterns of gender role conflict are related to negative or hostile attitudes and behaviors toward women and homosexuals.

Political Attitudes and Affiliation

In the only study relating men's political ideology to gender role conflict, Ducat (1994) correlated the GRCS-I with the Political Gender Gap Scale. He found that success, power, and competition and restrictive affectionate behavior between men correlated with prowar attitudes, antienvironmental sentiments, and opposition to gays in the military.

EXPERIMENTAL INTERVENTIONS AND COUNSELING PROCESS STUDIES USING GRCS-I

Four studies have used the GRCS-I as a dependent measure to assess change during a structured intervention to help men change (Harris, 1991; Gertner, 1994; Moore, 1993; Nahon, 1992). Harris (1991) assessed the effectiveness of a psychoeducational intervention designed to change men's attitudes about masculinity and attitudes toward psychological help-seeking. College students received a structured treatment and their gender role conflict was assessed. No significant pretest-posttest changes in gender role conflict scores were found. Nahon (1992) developed a program for recently separated men designed to reduce their gender role conflict and help with their marital transitions. She found no differences in gender role conflict scores in the pregroup, postgroup, or six-week follow-up phases. Moore (1993) compared alcoholics, nonalcoholics, and a control group in a psychoeducational intervention over a four-week period. No significant differences in gender role conflict scores were reported between the treatment and control groups. Gertner (1994) tested the effects of a semester-long men's studies course designed to decrease gender role conflict using a pretest-posttest, control-group design. He found that restrictive emotionality was significantly decreased when comparing the treatment and control groups.

Recently, gender role conflict has been suggested as a relevant variable when conducting counseling/psychotherapy process research (Mintz & O'Neil, 1990). Two studies relevant to understanding client-counselor interactions have been completed (Hayes, 1985; Wisch et al., 1993). Hayes (1985) assessed counselors in training by relating GRCS-I scores to counselor's liking, empathy with, comfort with, and willingness to see a nontraditional male client. One or more of the gender role conflict patterns significantly related to each of these counseling process variables. Restrictive affectionate behavior between men was the most consistent predictor of less positive liking, empathy, and comfort toward the nontraditional male client. Additionally, counselors characterizing themselves as prone to restrictive affectionate behavior between men were more likely to see the nontraditional male client as psychologically maladjusted.

Finally, Wisch et al. (1993) assessed undergraduate men's gender role conflict and evaluation of two 10-minute counseling sessions in terms of counselor's expertness, attractiveness, and trustworthiness. They found that students with lower gender role conflict rated the counselor as more expert and trustworthy, whereas the students with higher gender role conflict rated the counselor as less expert and trustworthy.

Summary of Previous Research on Gender Role Conflict

Research on gender role conflict is in its earliest stages of development. Consequently, much more research is needed before many generalizations about men's gender role conflict are made. The research that does exist indicates that gender role conflict does relate to problem areas of men's mental health, as hypothesized earlier (David & Brannon, 1976; Komarovsky, 1976; Nichols, 1975; O'Neil, 1981a, 1981b, 1982; Pleck, 1981). The 35 studies reviewed suggest that gender role conflict is a documented area of difficulty for men across a number of demographic, psychological, and interpersonal domains.

There is some initial evidence that race, class, stage of life, and ethnic background may be related to varying patterns of gender role conflict. The initial data do suggest that some patterns of gender role conflict are based on men's life stage and age. Studies using the variables of expressiveness, instrumentality, authoritarianism, and ego identity indicate that certain personality characteristics may differentially predict men's gender role conflict.

A strong relationship between low self-esteem and gender role conflict for college men has been documented in three studies. For older men, this relationship is much less clear. Six studies have shown a negative relationship between gender role conflict and intimacy. For college-age men, all the patterns of gender role conflict have been related to lower intimacy. For adult men, restrictive emotionality and restrictive affectionate behavior between men have been correlated with lower intimacy. Four studies have shown positive correlations between anxiety and gender role conflict. Again, for college-age men, all the gender role patterns have been related to anxiety. For adult men, only restrictive emotionality and conflict between work and family relations have been correlated to anxiety. In three studies with college students, gender role conflict and depression were highly correlated to all of the gender role conflict patterns. Only restrictive emotionality has correlated with adult men's depression, and in one study no relationship between gender role conflict and adult men's depression was found (Sharpe, 1993).

Personal strain, stress, and difficulties with problem-solving have been significantly related to adult men's gender role conflict with all patterns except restrictive affectionate behavior between men. No study has directly assessed college men on these variables. But anxiety, as reported earlier, has been consistently related to gender role conflict for college-age men. Four studies have correlated college men's gender role conflict to negative attitudes toward help-seeking. No study has assessed adult men's attitudes toward help-seeking and gender role conflict.

There is accumulating evidence that gender role conflict is related to men's difficulties in interpersonal relationships. For adult men, in three studies, restrictive emotionality has been consistently associated with lower marital or relationship happiness. Additionally, conflict between work and family relations has been associated with lower relationship happiness for both adult and college-age men. In a cross-cultural sample, restrictive affectionate behavior between men has been shown to be related to less confiding-expressive behaviors between men. Two studies have linked restrictive affectionate behavior between men to men's negative attitudes toward contraceptive use. One study found that three of the four patterns of gender role conflict were related to negative attitudes toward homosexuals. Another study found gender role conflict to be associated with hostility toward women. Finally, in one study, three of the four gender role conflict patterns have been associated with past sexual aggression toward women.

Four studies have used the GRCS-I as dependent variables in experimental designs. In three of the four studies, the treatments failed to indicate significant changes in men's gender role conflict. Only Gertner's (1994) men's studies treatment demonstrated that the patterns of restrictive emotionality can be changed over a semester time period. Two studies have found that patterns of gender role conflict may influence either counselor or client attitudes toward counseling process or outcome variables.

A RESEARCH PARADIGM TO EXPAND GENDER ROLE CONFLICT RESEARCH

The results of the previous empirical research provide a context to project a more elaborate paradigm for future research on gender role conflict. Figure 6.2 provides a research paradigm representing the past and future variables to be tested in the gender role conflict research program. The three rectangular boxes at the top of the diagram represent the precursor variables to men's gender role conflict. As shown by the horizontal arrows, personal and institutional sexism and patriarchy directly contribute to men's gender role socialization and the Masculine Mystique and Value System. These political, social-familial, and personal components of men's gender roles are directly related to the four empirically derived patterns of gender role conflict, as shown by the vertical arrows. The gender role conflict patterns shown at the bottom of Figure 6.2 are: (1) success, power, and competition, (2) restrictive emotionality, (3) restrictive affectionate behavior between men, and (4) conflict between work and family relations. These relationships between sexism-patriarchy, men's gender role socialization, and the sexist values of the Masculine Mystique and Value System and the patterns of gender role conflict represent the early theory underlying the gender role conflict construct (O'Neil, 1981a, 1981b, 1982; O'Neil et al., 1986).

The research reviewed in this chapter has explored some of the tested variables that relate to gender role conflict theory. Figure 6.2 extends the already tested variables by suggesting additional variables to be tested in the future. What is new in Figure 6.2 are the four different kinds of variables to be tested with the gender role conflict construct. Shown at the top of the figure are: (1) demographic and classification variables, (2) personality or attitudinal variables, and (3) counseling process and outcome variables. For the sake of simplicity, these three categories of variables are suggested as independent variables to be tested with gender role conflict. These three classifications represent potential precursor variables that may explain differential degrees of gender role conflict in men. However, some of these independent variables could easily be used as dependent variables, based on the individual researcher's design or hypotheses.

Enumerated at the bottom of Figure 6.2 are 29 psychological or physical health variables that have been or could be related to the four documented patterns of men's gender role conflict. These variables represent an initial list of problem areas discussed in the new psychology of men and psychology of women literature over the last 20 years. These variables represent possible dependent or criterion variables for future researchers to use with GRCS-I.

FIGURE 6.2 Research Paradigm on Past and Future Variables Related to the Gender Role Conflict Construct

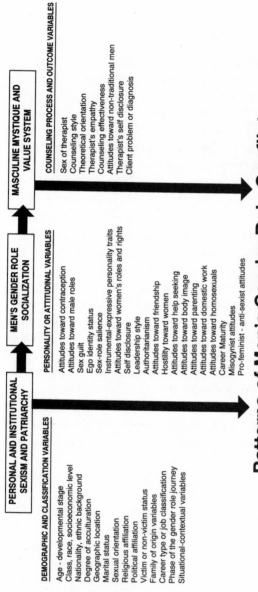

PERSONAL AND INSTITUTIONAL
SEXISM AND PATRIARCHY

MEN'S GENDER ROLE
SOCIALIZATION

MASCULINE MYSTIQUE AND
VALUE SYSTEM

DEMOGRAPHIC AND CLASSIFICATION VARIABLES

Age - developmental stage
Class, race, socioeconomic level
Nationality, ethnic background
Degree of acculturation
Geographic location
Marital status
Sexual orientation
Religious affiliation
Political affiliation
Victim or non-victim status
Family of origin variables
Career type or job classification
Phase of the gender role journey
Situational-contextual variables

PERSONALITY OR ATTITUDINAL VARIABLES

Attitudes toward contraception
Attitudes toward male roles
Sex guilt
Ego identity status
Sex-role salience
Instrumental-expressive personality traits
Attitudes toward women's roles and rights
Self disclosure
Leadership style
Authoritarianism
Attitudes toward friendship
Hostility toward women
Attitudes toward help seeking
Attitudes toward body image
Attitudes toward parenting
Attitudes toward domestic work
Attitudes toward homosexuals
Career Maturity
Misogynist attitudes
Pro-feminist - anti-sexist attitudes

COUNSELING PROCESS AND OUTCOME VARIABLES

Sex of therapist
Counseling style
Theoretical orientation
Therapist's empathy
Counseling effectiveness
Attitudes toward non-traditional men
Therapist's self disclosure
Client problem or diagnosis

Patterns of Men's Gender Role Conflict

SUCCESS, POWER, &
COMPETITION ISSUES

RESTRICTIVE
EMOTIONALITY

RESTRICTIVE & AFFECTIONATE
BEHAVIOR BETWEEN MEN

CONFLICT BETWEEN WORK &
FAMILY RELATIONS

PSYCHOLOGICAL OR PHYSICAL HEALTH VARIABLES

Capacity for intimacy
Depression
Anxiety
Stress
Life and career satisfaction
Self esteem
Counselor bias against men
Type A Behavior
Family Cohesion & parenting
Problem solving skills

Sexual aggression and abuse
Psychological violence
Help seeking behaviors
Rape myths
Family violence
Overwork & workaholic behavior
Marital conflict
Sexual dysfunction
Burn out behaviors
Battering behaviors

Shame and guilt
Alexithymia
Fear of failure
Health Maintenance behavior
Obesity from food abuse
Crime
Violence toward women
Substance abuse
Sexual harassment

This research paradigm provides an arbitrary organizer to help gender role conflict researchers conceptualize their research studies. There may be other ways to conceptualize research studies. For example, therapy supervision, career and work behavior, and family interaction are other areas from which specific variables could be generated. Given the number of variables listed in Figure 6.2, we offer some research priorities that appear most pressing given the past research and men's problems in contemporary society.

RESEARCH PRIORITIES FOR THE GENDER ROLE CONFLICT CONSTRUCT

Other researchers have critiqued the gender role conflict research program (Beere, 1990; Betz & Fitzgerald, 1993; Good, Wallace, & Borst, 1994; Heppner, in press; Thompson et al., 1992). For example, Betz and Fitzgerald (1993) indicated that the "GRCS-I has proven itself to be a heuristic and fruitful contribution to the empirical literature on the male gender role" (p. 360). Thompson et al. (1992) concluded that the "gender role conflict construct provides an important link between societal norms scripting traditional masculinities and individuals' adaptation" (p. 28).

These positive critiques are encouraging, but they should not mask the critical need for further validation of the gender role conflict construct. These critiques definitely do not imply that the validation of the gender role conflict construct is complete. To the contrary, research on gender role conflict is still in its early stages of development. There is still much to test, much to know, and many complicated questions to be answered, as indicated below.

More research is clearly mandated with special groups of men. African-American, Hispanic, Asian, and Caucasian men could be compared, and other groups of men could be studied. More conceptual analyses, like Brooks's (1990) appraisal of veterans' gender role strain, are needed of men who are violent, alcoholic, sexually dysfunctional, suicidal, unemployed, or sexually abusive. There has been no study of gender role conflict in men with disabilities or gay men. More research on men from other countries and nationalities is clearly needed. There is no research on middle school or high school students' gender role conflict. Comparing the degree to which preretired and retired men experience gender role conflict needs to be pursued. Study of men who are antisexist or who hold profeminist attitudes and behaviors may provide important information about how gender role conflict becomes resolved or how men cope with their socialized sexism.

The situational aspects of men's gender role conflict need more study. Men's gender role conflict varies based on situations and environmental cues. Deaux and Major's (1987) timely conceptualization about "putting gender into a context" is directly relevant to gender role conflict. Putting gender role conflict into a context is critical to understanding variation in specific attitudes and behaviors. Identifying high and low sex- or gender-typed situations (e.g., male sporting events or church gatherings) and relating them to gender role conflict might provide more information about the contextual nature of gender role conflict. In this regard, further development of the GRCS-II would help provide more information about the situational nature of gender role conflict.

The research reviewed in this chapter provides initial evidence that there are relationships between men's conflict with their gender roles and some of the psychologically negative outcomes shown at the bottom of Figure 6.2. Gender role conflict has been related to anxiety, depression, lower self-esteem, marital dissatisfaction, stress, negative attitudes toward help-seeking, and sexual coercion. Most of the relationships found are categorized as gender role conflict within the man (i.e, within self). Gender role conflict's effect on others (i.e., as expressed toward others) has much less evidence. The exceptions are the studies on sexual coercion (Kaplan, 1992; Kaplan et al., 1993) and, more indirectly, studies on relationship satisfaction (Campbell & Snow, 1992; Cournoyer, 1994). Future studies could expand the variety of men's problems as they relate to affecting others. More research is needed on the relationship between men's gender role conflict and specific behavior toward women and children and within family life. To what degree are family violence and sexual assault related to gender role conflict? The role that parents and family values play in men's gender role conflict needs to be explored. How much of men's violence that is inflicted on others or themselves relates to patterns of gender role conflict (Kaplan et al., 1993; O'Neil, 1992)?

Studies are particularly needed that assess the direct relationship between men's gender role conflict and actual problem behaviors. Much of the past research has used attitude measures and related them to gender role conflict. For example, studies that assess men's degree of gender role conflict as it relates to behavioral indices of violence toward women, children, and other men are clearly needed. Behavioral measures of men's sexual harassment, homophobia, heterosexism, career conflicts, health problems, addictions, and suicidal behavior would be useful in understanding men's difficulties over the life span. For example, does a man's resistance to getting medical checkups or seeking assistance relate to homophobic attitudes or feelings of loss of control? Also, it may be useful to examine gender role conflict and masculinity ideology in relationship to such factors as level of cognitive complexity, bigotry, and prejudice.

Future empirical studies also need to go beyond one-shot, correlational research designs. These usually prohibit inferences regarding gender role conflict's causative potential or how it changes over time. Therefore, more diverse research designs, such as experimental, longitudinal, qualitative, and latent variable modeling, are needed (Good & Wallace, 1994; Good, Robertson, et al., in press). Well-developed qualitative designs, using established scientific methodologies, are needed to understand the internal, situational, and relational aspects of gender role conflict. It is important that studies use research instruments that have documented reliability and validity. Furthermore, theoretical justification from the emerging psychology of men literature should be consulted as hypotheses are generated.

As reviewed earlier, there is considerable evidence supporting the psychometric properties of the GRCS-I. However, like any scale, more refinement and development is needed. One area for further work is with the generalizability (external validity) of the scale. To date, research specifically focusing on the psychometric properties of the GRCS-I has been primarily with undergraduate college students who were predominantly white and middle class. Chamberlin's (1994) factor analysis of airline pilots is the exception. Construct validity would be extended through factor analytic studies examining men of different ages, racial/ethnic backgrounds, nationalities, social classes, marital statuses, abilities, and sexual orientations. Data from more diverse populations would support the external validity of the GRCS-I for a wider array of men in our society and other countries as well. Lastly, more psychometric work needs to be done on the Conflict Between Work and Family Relations subscale (Good, Robertson, et al., in press). Although the reliability is adequate, there are questions about whether the items fully tap the relationship between men's gender roles and work-family stressors.

RESEARCH ON MEN'S GENDER ROLE CONFLICT: SOME FINAL OBSERVATIONS

We wonder, as we close this chapter, whether the research reviewed here would be of much use to the talk-show guests and their audiences mentioned earlier. Does any of this research help answer those complex questions asked in the introduction? We leave the task of answering that question to you, the critical reader. From the studies reviewed, there is clearly evidence that gender role conflict is related to the "hazards of being male" (Goldberg, 1977; Harrison, 1976). Furthermore, the initial evidence points to gender role conflict being negatively related to men's relationships with women and other men.

During the 1980s, many men felt personally attacked, ridiculed, or blamed for the sexist behavior of men in general. Compassion for men appeared to be mostly compromised by anger and blame. Clearly, the sexist behaviors of individual men require constant attention, as do the injustices imposed by the patriarchal nature of American society. However, as noted at the beginning of the 1990s, "blaming men for sexism and labeling them as oppressors has not resolved the anger between the sexes, advanced equality or decreased the victimization" (O'Neil, 1990, p. 23). Men who are struggling to liberate themselves and others from restrictive notions of gender deserve compassion and support for their efforts, not condemnation. Constructive change will be furthered by both men and women becoming more aware of the deleterious effects of restrictive conceptions of gender roles and sexism on *both sexes.*

The 1990s can and should be a different decade. Without question, the new psychology of men needs to accelerate its efforts to understand how men's sexist socialization victimizes women, children, and other men (O'Neil, 1991, 1992). Furthermore, we need more research on the dangerous effects of sexism on men themselves. Additionally, we need to document how men change their sexist and gender-conflicted behavior. Men who become acutely aware of how the social-political and sexist system contributes to their gender role conflict are the ones who usually attempt to liberate themselves. In this light, the research programs in the new psychology of men hold promise for explaining how restrictive gender roles are psychologically dangerous to both men and women. The research reviewed in this chapter suggests that, indeed, there is enough research evidence to support the ongoing study of men's gender role conflict. Documenting men's personal gender role journeys and promoting empirical research appear to be two excellent directions for the new psychology of men to pursue.

The men's movements are much more diversified than the national media have portrayed them (Brod, 1991, 1992). The effort to liberate men involves more than programs for weekend warriors who beat drums to reclaim their lost masculine psyches. As the chapters in this book demonstrate, serious theory and research is developing in men's studies. Maybe one of the most important things to be said on national television is that many more men are now engaged in a new and serious study of themselves, personally and scientifically. This study holds the promise of changing patriarchial and sexist structures that victimize men, women, and children.

References

Archer, J., Murphy, M., Foos, J., Jensen, R., & Morgan, J. (1985). *Role conflict in college males: Implications for preventive mental health programs.* Unpublished manuscript, University of Florida, Gainesville.

Arnold, W. J. (1983). *Ego identity and fear of femininity in same-sex and opposite-sex intimacy in university males.* Department of Psychology, St. Thomas More College, Saskatoon, Saskatchewan.

Arnold. W. J., & Chartier, B. M. (1984, May). *Identity, fear of femininity and intimacy in males.* Paper presented at the 45th annual convention of the Canadian Psychological Association, Ottawa.

Beere, C. A. (1990). *Gender roles: A handbook of tests and measures.* Westport, CT: Greenwood Press.

Bem. S. L. (1974). The measurement of psychological androgyny. *Journal of Consulting and Clinical Psychology, 42,* 155–162.

Betz, N. E., & Fitzgerald, L. (1993). Individuality and diversity: Theory and research in counseling psychology. *Annual Review of Psychology, 44,* 343–381.

Berlin, C. (1988). Gender role conflict, future time perspective, and contraceptive behavior among unmarried black, white and Hispanic adolescent fathers and their nonfather peers (Doctoral dissertation, New York University). *Dissertation Abstracts International, 49/10,* 2940.

Block, J. H. (1973). Conceptions of sex role: Some cross-cultural and longitudinal perspectives. *American Psychologist, 28,* 512–526.

Block, J. H. (1984). *Sex role identity and ego development.* San Francisco: Jossey-Bass.

Brannon, R. (1985). A scale for measuring attitudes toward masculinity. In A. Sargent (Ed.), *Beyond sex roles* (2nd ed.). St. Paul, MN: West.

Brannon, R., & Juni, S. (1984). A scale for measuring attitudes toward masculinity. *JSAS Catalog of Selected Documents in Psychology, 14,* 6. (Ms. 2012)

Braverman, D. (1990). Gender role conflict in fraternity men (Doctoral dissertation, University of Iowa). *Dissertation Abstracts International, 52/03,* 844.

Braverman, D. G., O'Neil, J. M., & Owen, S. (1992). Systematic programming on men's issues and men's studies on campus. *Journal of College Student Development, 33,* 557–558.

Brod, H. (1991, June). *Enhancing men's and women's lives: Directions for the profeminist men's movements, with a critique of mythopoetic and ultraradical politics.* Keynote address at the 16th National Conference on Men and Masculinity, Tucson, AZ. Published in Institute for the Study of Women and Men, University of Southern California, *Working Papers (1993).*

Brod, H. (1992). The mythopoetic men's movement: A political critique. In C. Hardy (Ed.), *Wingspan: A guide to the men's movement.* New York: St. Martin's.

Brooks, G. R. (1990). Post-Vietnam gender role strain: A needed concept? *Professional Psychology: Research and Practice, 21,* 18–25.

Campbell, J. L., & Snow, B. M. (1992). Gender role conflict and family environment as predictors of men's marital satisfaction. *Journal of Family Psychology, 6,* 84–87.

Chamberlin, W. (1994). Gender role conflict as a predictor of problem solving, leadership style, authoritarian attributes, and conflict management attitudes (Doctoral dissertation, Columbia University). *Dissertation Abstracts International, 55/01,* 0206.

Chartier, B. M., & Arnold, W. J. (1985, June). *Male socialization and the development of identity and intimacy in young college men.* Paper presented at the 46th annual meeting of the Canadian Psychological Association, Halifax, Nova Scotia.

Chartier, B. M., Graff, L. A., & Arnold, W. J. (1986, June). *Male socialization and hostility toward women.* Paper presented at the 47th annual meeting of the Canadian Psychological Association, Toronto.

Cournoyer, R. J. (1994). A developmental study of gender role conflict in men and its changing relationship to psychological well-being (Doctoral dissertation, Boston College). *Dissertation Abstracts International, 54/12,* 6476.

Cournoyer, R. J., & Mahalik, J. R. (in press). A cross-sectional study of gender role conflict examining college-aged and middle-aged men. *Journal of Counseling Psychology.*

Croteau, J. M., & Burda, P. C. (1983). Structured group programming on men's roles: A creative approach to change. *Personnel and Guidance Journal, 62,* 243–245.

David, D. S., & Brannon, R. (1976). *The forty-nine percent majority: The male sex role.* Reading, MA: Addison-Wesley.

Davis, F. (1987). Antecedents and consequences of gender role conflict: An empirical test of sex-role strain analysis (Doctoral dissertation, Ohio State University). *Dissertation Abstracts International, 48/11,* 3443.

Deaux, K., & Major, B. (1987). Putting gender into context: An interactive model of gender-related behavior. *Psychological Review, 94,* 369–389.

Downs, A. C., & Engleson, S. A. (1982). The Attitudes Toward Men Scale (AMS): An analysis of the role and status of men and masculinity. *JSAS Catalog of Selected Documents in Psychology, 12,* 45. (Ms. 2502)

Doyle, J. A., & Moore, R. J. (1978). Attitudes Toward the Male Role scale (AMR): An objective instrument to measure attitudes toward the male's sex role in contemporary society. *JSAS Catalog of Selected Documents in Psychology, 8,* 35–36. (Ms. 1678)

Ducat, S. J. (1994). *Correlates of gender gap in politics: Fear of men's femininity, male gender role conflict, and homophobia* (New College of California, San Francisco). Manuscript submitted for publication.

Egan, J. (1990). *Men and women in organizations: A course of gender role socialization and its impact on adult learners.* Unpublished paper, Asnuntuck Community College, Enfield, CT.

Egan, J. (1992). Gender role development as a function of transition coping skills (Doctoral dissertation, University of Connecticut). *Dissertation Abstracts International, 93/15,* 388.

Egan, J., & O'Neil, J. M. (1993, August). Experimental research and interventions on the gender role journey metaphor. In J. M. O'Neil (Chair), *Research on men's sexual assault and constructive gender role interventions.* Symposium conducted at the meeting of the American Psychological Association, Toronto.

Eisler, R. M., & Skidmore, J. R. (1987). Masculine gender role stress: Scale development and components factors in appraisal of stressful situations. *Behavior Modification, 11,* 123–136.

Farrell, W. (1974). *The liberated man.* New York: Bantam.

Fasteau, M. F. (1974). *The male machine.* New York: McGraw-Hill.

Garnets, L., & Pleck, J. (1979). Sex role identity, androgyny and sex role transcendence: A sex role strain analysis. *Psychology of Women Quarterly, 3,* 270–283.

Gertner, D. M. (1994). Learning men: Effects of a semester academic course in men's studies on gender role conflict and gender role journey of male participants (Doctoral dissertation, University of Northern Colorado). *Dissertation Abstracts International, 55/01,* 0046.

Gertner, D. M., & Harris, J. E. (1993). *Experiencing masculinity: Exercises, activities, and resources for teaching and learning about men.* Available from D. M. Gertner, 922 Madison St., Denver, CO 80206.

Goldberg, H. (1977). *The hazards of being male.* New York: New American Library.

Good, G. (1987). The relationship between help-seeking and attitudes toward the male role (Doctoral dissertation, Ohio State University). *Dissertation Abstracts International, 48/10,* 3110.

Good, G. E. (Chair) (1992, August). Psychology of men: Recognizing and affirming healthy conceptions of masculinity. Symposium conducted at the meeting of the American Psychological Association, Washington, DC.

Good, G. E., Dell, D. M., & Mintz, L. B. (1989). Male role and gender role conflict: Relations to help-seeking in men. *Journal of Counseling Psychology, 36,* 295–300.

Good, G. E., & Mintz, L. B. (1990). Gender role conflict and depression in college men: Evidence for compounded risk. *Journal of Counseling and Development, 69,* 17–20.

Good, G. E., & Mintz, L. M. (1993). Towards healthy conceptions of masculinity: Clarifying the issues. *Journal of Mental Health Counseling, 15,* 403–413.

Good, G. E., Robertson, J. M., Fitzgerald, L. F., Stevens, M., & Bartels, K. (1994, August). The relation between masculine role conflict and psychological distress in male university counseling center clients. In J. Robertson & G. Good (Chairs), *Men, masculinity, and psychological services.* Symposium conducted at the meeting of the American Psychological Association, Los Angeles.

Good, G. E., Robertson, J. M., O'Neil, J. M., Fitzgerald, L. F., Stevens, M., DeBord, K., Bartels, K. M., & Braverman, D. G. (in press). Male gender role conflict: Psychometric issues and relations to psychological distress. *Journal of Counseling Psychology.*

Good, G. E., Wallace, D. L., & Borst, T. S. (1994). Masculinity research: A review and critique. *Applied and Preventive Psychology, 3,* 3–14.

Good, G. E., & Wood, P. K. (in press). Male gender role conflict, depression, and help-seeking: Do college men face double jeopardy? *Journal of Counseling and Development.*

Harris, J. E. (1991). Changing men's male sex role attitude and help-seeking attitudes (Doctoral dissertation, Ohio State University). *Dissertation Abstracts International, 51/10,* 5028.

Harrison, J. (1978). Warning: The male sex role may be dangerous to your health. *Journal of Social Issues, 34*(1), 65–85.

Hayes, M. M. (1985). Counselor sex-role values and effects on attitudes toward, and treatment of nontraditional male clients (Doctoral dissertation, Ohio State University). *Dissertation Abstracts International, 45/09,* 3072.

Heppner, P. P. (in press). On gender role conflict in men: Future directions and implications for counseling. *Journal of Counseling Psychology.*

Horhoruw, M. (1991). *Correlation between gender role conflict and male friendship behavior.* Unpublished thesis. Jakarta, Indonesia.

Kaplan, R. (1992). Normative masculinity and sexual aggression among college males (Doctoral dissertation, University of Connecticut). *Dissertation Abstracts International, 53/08,* 3005.

Kaplan, R., O'Neil, J. M., & Owen, S. (1993, August). Sexist, normative, and progressive masculinity and sexual assault: Empirical research. In J. M. O'Neil (Chair), *Research on men's sexual assault and constructive gender role interventions.* Symposium conducted at the meeting of the American Psychological Association, Toronto.

Kim, E. J. (1990). Asian-American men: Gender role conflict and acculturation (Doctoral dissertation, University of Southern California). *Dissertation Abstracts International, 5/11,* 3635.

Komarovsky, M. (1976). *Dilemmas of masculinity: A study of college youth.* New York: Norton.

Levant, R. F., Hirsch, L., Celentano, E., Cozza, T., Hill, S., MacEachern, M., Marty, N., & Schnedeker, J. (1992). The male role: An investigation of contemporary norms. *Journal of Mental Health Counseling, 14,* 325–337.

Levinson, D. J., Darrow, C. H., Klein, E. B., Levinson, M. H., & McKee, B. (1978). *The seasons of a man's life.* New York: Ballantine.

Mendelson, E. A. (1988). An exploratory investigation of male gender-role development during early adulthood (Doctoral dissertation, University of North Carolina). *Dissertation Abstracts International, 48,* 2119–2120B.

Mintz, L., & O'Neil, J. M. (1990). Sex, gender role, and the process of psychotherapy: Theory and research. *Journal of Counseling and Development, 68,* 381–387.

Moore, C. M. (1993). A study of male sex-role attitudes and self-concept differences between alcoholics and nonalcoholics and the effects of a psychoeducation group on these variables and subsequent relapse rates (Doctoral dissertation, University of Texas–Austin). *Dissertation Abstract International, 54/04,* 2215.

Mosher, D. L., & Sirkin, M. (1984). Measuring a macho personality constellation. *Journal of Research in Personality, 18,* 150–163.

Nahon, D. (1992). The effectiveness of "masculinist" group psychotherapy in the treatment of recently separated men. Doctoral dissertation, University of Montreal.

Nichols, J. (1975). *Men's liberation: A new definition of masculinity.* New York: Penguin.

O'Neil, J. M. (1979, March). The male sex role and the negative consequences of the masculine socialization process: Implications for counselors and counseling psychologists. In M. Scher (Chair), *Counseling men.* Symposium conducted at the meeting of the American College Personnel Association, Los Angeles.

O'Neil, J. M. (1980, September). Sex role conflicts: Psychological outcomes of the masculine socialization process. In J. M. O'Neil (Chair), *Sex role conflicts, sexism, masculinity: Psychological implications for counseling psychologists.* Symposium conducted at the meeting of the American Psychological Association, Montreal.

O'Neil, J. M. (1981a). Male sex-role conflict, sexism, and masculinity: Implications for men, women, and the counseling psychologist. *The Counseling Psychologist, 9,* 61–80.

O'Neil, J. M. (1981b). Patterns of gender role conflict and strain: Sexism and fear of femininity in men's lives. *Personnel and Guidance Journal, 60,* 203–210.

O'Neil, J. M. (1982). Gender role conflict and strain in men's lives: Implications for psychiatrists, psychologists, and other human service providers. In K. Solomon & N. B. Levy (Eds.), *Men in transition: Changing male roles, theory, and therapy.* New York: Plenum.

O'Neil, J. M. (1990). Assessing men's gender role conflict. In D. Moore & F. Leafgren (Eds.), *Men in conflict: Problem solving strategies and interventions.* Alexandria, VA: American Association for Counseling and Development.

O'Neil, J. M. (1991, August). Men and women as victims of sexism: Metaphors for healing. In G. Brooks (Chair), *Practitioners' perspectives on male-female relations in the 90's.* Symposium presented at the American Psychological Association, San Francisco.

O'Neil, J. M. (1992, August). Gender role conflict research: New directions to understand men's violence. In R. Levant (Chair), *Toward a new psychology of men.* Symposium conducted at the 100th annual convention of the American Psychological Association, Washington, DC.

O'Neil, J. M. (in press). The gender role journey workshop (1985–1995): A coeducational group setting exploring sexism and gender role conflict. In M. P. Andronico (Ed.), *Men in group: Realities and insights.* Washington, DC: APA Books.

O'Neil, J. M., & Egan, J. (1992a). Abuses of power against women: Sexism, gender role conflict, and psychological violence. In E. Cook (Ed.), *Women, relationships, and power: Implications for counseling.* Alexandria, VA: American Counseling Association (ACA) Press.

O'Neil, J. M., & Egan, J. (1992b). Men's and women's gender role journey: Metaphor for healing, transition, and transformation. In B. Wainrib (Ed.), *Gender issues across the life cycle.* New York: Springer.

O'Neil, J. M., & Egan, J. (1992c). Men's gender role transitions over the life span: Transformations and fears of femininity. *Journal of Mental Health Counseling, 14,* 305–324.

O'Neil, J. M., Egan, J., Owen, S. V., & Murry, V. M. (1993). The Gender Role Journey Measure: Scale development and psychometric evaluation. *Sex Roles, 28*(3/4), 167–185.

O'Neil, J. M., & Fishman, D. (1992). Adult men's career transitions and gender role themes. In H. D. Leas & Z. B. Leibowitz (Eds.), *Adult career development: Concepts, issues, and practices* (2nd ed.). Alexandria, VA: ACA Press.

O'Neil, J. M., Fishman, D. M., & Kinsella-Shaw, M. (1987). Dual-career couples' career transitions and normative dilemmas: A preliminary assessment model. *The Counseling Psychologist, 15*(1), 50–96.

O'Neil, J. M., Helms, B., Gable, R., David, L., & Wrightsman, L. (1986). Gender Role Conflict Scale: College men's fear of femininity. *Sex Roles, 14*(5/6), 335–350.

O'Neil, J. M., Helms, B., Gable, R., Stillson, R., David, L., & Wrightsman, L. (1984, August). *Data on college men's gender role conflict and strain.* Paper presented at the annual meeting of the American Psychological Association, Toronto. (ERIC Document Reproduction Service No. ED 248448)

O'Neil, J. M., & Owen, S. V. (1994). *The manual for the Gender Role Conflict Scale.* Storrs: School of Family Studies, University of Connecticut.

O'Neil, J. M., Owen, S. V., Holmes, S. E., Dolgopolov, N., & Slastenin, V. (1994, August). Russian-American men's psychological violence toward women: Cross-cultural differences. In J. M. O'Neil & G. Good (Chairs), *Research on men's sexual and psychological assault of women: Programming considerations.* Symposium conducted at the meeting of the American Psychological Association, Los Angeles.

O'Neil, J. M., & Roberts Carroll, M. (1987). *A six-day workshop on gender role conflict and strain: Helping men and women take the gender role journey.* Storrs: University of Connecticut, Department of Educational Psychology, Counseling Psychology Program. (ERIC Document Reproduction Service No. ED 275963)

O'Neil, J. M., & Roberts Carroll, M. (1988a, September). *Evaluation of gender role workshop: Three years of follow-up data.* Paper presented at the 95th convention of the American Psychological Association, New York. (ERIC Document Reproduction Service No. ED 287121)

O'Neil, J. M., & Roberts Carroll, M (1988b). A gender role workshop focused on sexism, gender role conflict, and the gender role journey. *Journal of Counseling and Development, 67,* 193–197.

Pleck, J. (1981). *The myth of masculinity.* Cambridge, MA: MIT Press.

Pleck, J. H., & Sawyer, J. (1974). *Men and masculinity.* Englewood Cliffs, NJ: Prentice-Hall.

Rebecca, M., Hefner, R., & Olenshansky, B. A. (1976). A model of sex-role transcendence. *Journal of Social Issues, 32,* 197–206.

Rhoades, C. (1985). *The effect of gender role pressures on male contraceptive responsibility.* (Available from Stafford County Prenatal and Family Planning Program, Dover, NH)

Robertson, J. M., & Fitzgerald, L. F. (1992). Overcoming the masculine mystique: Preferences for alternative forms of assistance among men who avoid counseling. *Journal of Counseling Psychology, 39,* 240–246.

Rounds, D. (1994). *Predictors of homosexual intolerance on a college campus: Identity, intimacy, attitudes toward homosexuals and gender role conflict.* Unpublished master's thesis, Department of Psychology, University of Connecticut.

Sharpe, M. J. (1993). Gender role and psychological well-being in adult men (Doctoral dissertation, University of Missouri–Columbia). *Dissertation Abstracts International, 54/10,* 5373.

Sharpe, M. J., & Heppner, P. P. (1991). Gender role, gender role conflict, and psychological well-being in men. *Journal of Counseling Psychology, 38,* 323–330.

Snell, W. (1986). The Masculine Role Inventory: Components and correlates. *Sex Roles, 13,* 413–426.

Spence, J. T., & Helmreich, R. L. (1978). *Masculinity and femininity: Their psychological dimensions, correlates, and antecedents.* Austin: University of Texas Press.

Stillson, R., O'Neil, J. M., & Owen, S. V. (1991). Predictors of adult men's gender role conflict: Race, class, unemployment, age, instrumentality-expressiveness, and personal strain. *Journal of Counseling Psychology, 38,* 458–464.

Thompson, E. H., Grisanti, C., & Pleck, J. (1985). Attitudes toward the male role and their correlates. *Sex Roles, 13,* 413–427.

Thompson, E. H., Pleck, J. H., & Ferrera, D. L. (1992). Men and masculinity: Scales for masculinity idealogy and masculinity-related contracts. *Sex Roles, 27*(11/12), 573–607.

Unger, R. K. (1979). Toward a redefinition of sex and gender. *American Psychologist, 34,* 1085–1094.

Walls, D. A. (1991). *Adolescent sexual offenders: Sex role orientation, attitudes toward women, gender role conflict, and loneliness.* Unpublished master's thesis, Middle Tennessee State University, Tennessee.

Wisch, A. F., Mahalik, J., Hayes, J. A., & Nutt, L. (1993, August). *Counseling men: Gender role conflict, problem type, and emotional content.* Paper presented at the 101st meeting of the American Psychological Association, Toronto.

CHAPTER 7

The Relationship Between Masculine Gender Role Stress and Men's Health Risk: The Validation of a Construct

RICHARD M. EISLER

Masculinity and Health

The wisdom of relying on traditional masculine gender role beliefs and behavior patterns to ensure men's health and adjustment to life has only recently been critically examined by mental and medical health researchers. In 1976 the popular writer and psychologist Herb Goldberg was one of the first to warn of the emotional and health "hazards of being male." Others, notably Doyle (1989) and Fasteau (1975), have theorized about the stressful and unhealthy aspects of adherence to traditional masculine imperatives, including competitiveness, a focus on obtaining power and control, and being successful at all costs. O'Neil (1982) has hypothesized that culturally sanctioned homophobia and antifemininity are central underlying precepts of masculinity that have produced stifling conformity in men's roles.

Recent epidemiological data on gender-linked differences between men's and women's health have documented sex differences in "premature mortality" and hazardous lifestyles or behavior patterns for men (Cleary, 1987; Harrison, Chin, & Ficarrotto, 1989). In the United States, women live, on average, about seven years longer than men; the rate of death is higher for men than for women at all ages, and for all leading causes of death (Verbrugge, 1985). Some of the data suggest that gender-related lifestyles may impact the differential death rates. For example, between the ages of 15 and 24, men die at three times the rate of women, largely because of the higher rates of violent death among male youth (Cleary, 1987).

Men have nearly twice the premature death rate of women from coronary artery disease. The reasons for that particular higher mortality rate among men are hotly debated between those advocating a biogenetic etiology and those adhering to a psychosocial perspective. What is not debated is the fact that men are nearly three times as likely to die in motor vehicle accidents and three times as likely as women to actually commit suicide (Waldron & Johnson, 1976). Higher death rates in men by homicide, suicide, and accidents have been attributed by some to the paucity of acceptable masculine alternatives for aggressive behaviors in coping with stress. Additionally, data compiled by Waldron and Johnson (1976) showed that men's death rate from lung cancer is nearly six times that of women, and twice as high from cirrhosis of the liver, suggesting that masculine coping styles that incorporate higher rates of smoking and drinking are added health risk factors for men.

MENTAL HEALTH ISSUES

Large-scale American epidemiological studies conducted by Robins and her colleagues (Robins, Helzer, Weissman, Orvaschel, Gruenberg, Burke, & Regier, 1984) looked at gender differences in vulnerability to psychiatrically diagnosed mental disorders. The results showed that while women are more prone to anxiety disorders and depression, men show more evidence of antisocial personality disorder and alcohol and drug abuse. Also compelling is the evidence that men, compared with women, are far more likely to be involved in violent crime and in spouse or sexual abuse (Widom, 1984). Thus, it appears that our culturally sanctioned masculine coping styles, including repertoires of toughness, combativeness, and reliance on aggressive responses, may have maladaptive consequences for men and their families. In the context of our culture's sports events, military operations, and business competitions, masculine initiative and shows of force are virtuously applauded. In the context of armed robbery, rape, or sexual harassment, masculine imperatives of aggression and daring are clearly less than welcome.

THE CONCEPT OF MASCULINE GENDER ROLE STRESS

A central impetus for the measurement of—and the research on—masculine gender role stress reported in this chapter was my assumption that our dominant culture's requirement that men adhere to several aspects of culturally approved masculine ideology and role behavior may have dysfunctional health consequences for many men and for those with whom they come into contact. Unlike some who write about men's issues, I do not believe there is evidence to conclude that all or even most of our most cherished stereotypic masculine qualities in themselves are necessarily detrimental to men's health. For instance, Cook's (1985) extensive review of research on androgynous, masculine, and feminine characteristics showed that many attributes of traditional masculinity, as opposed to traditional femininity, have positive implications for the psychological adjustment of both men and women.

In this chapter, I (a) discuss the theoretical derivation of the masculine gender role stress construct; (b) detail the empirical development of the Masculine Gender Role Stress Scale (MGRSS); (c) present validation of and research with the MGRSS; and finally, (d) discuss the implications of this research for understanding men's health problems.

Theoretical Notions Underlying Masculine Gender Role Stress

During the last few decades, there has been increasing interest among those doing research on men in viewing "masculinities" as cultural constructions that are imposed on men by particular social groups and organizations rather than as routine outcomes of bio-psycho-social development. For example, Franklin (1988) has pointed out that, traditionally, men, as distinct from women, have *shared* a culturally designed and enforced way of seeing things, planning things, and doing things. That is, many American men, whatever their race, politics, ethnic background, and educational or vocational attainment, may have shared a collective "masculine consciousness" or traditional masculinity that is enacted through commitment to socially prescribed masculine gender roles. For example, many men who differ in race or ethnic background commonly value power and dominance in their relationships, approve of a certain degree of aggression and violence in gaining competitive advantage, and disdain "feminine" strategies for coping with life. This antifeminine imperative for men is often manifested through demeaning the importance or utility of self-disclosing emotion or vulnerability in human relationships. Some questions we might ask at this point are: How do men become so deeply committed to particular masculine gender roles? How do these roles become so pervasive among so many men of different ethnic backgrounds and status?

BEM'S GENDER SCHEMA THEORY

In contrast to her work on androgynous sex roles (1974), Sandra Bem's more recent theoretical work on cognitive processing differences between sex-typed and non-sex-typed persons (1981) has relevance for our notions about gender role stress. Bem (1981) has proposed a cognitive theory of the development of gender schema to explain the pervasiveness of each sex's affinity for masculine versus feminine gender roles and attitudes. She has proposed that sex-typed masculinity and femininity originate from an individual's general readiness to encode and organize information about the world and himself or herself in terms of the culture's definitions of "maleness" and "femaleness." Thus, a person's self-concept becomes interwoven with culturally approved, sex-typed distinctions.

What Bem's (1981) gender schema theory proposes, then, is that sex-typed attitudes and behaviors are learned when one is willing to process information primarily according to society's mandates of what is appropriate for one's own sex and to ignore information associated with the opposite sex. For example, the adults in a child's world seldom note how nurturant a little boy is or how stoic a little girl is. Therefore, the child learns to apply the same gender schema to himself or herself.

The implications of Bem's gender schema theory for development of the masculine gender role stress model are: (a) men and women learn to evaluate their adequacy (as persons) based on their ability to regulate their behavior in accord with their learned masculine or feminine gender schema; (b) this self-propagating developmental process becomes stable at an early age; and (c) some men (and some women) become more highly committed than others to regulating their behavior in accord with masculine (or feminine) socially prescribed schema as a way of assessing their self-worth.

One might raise questions at this point about the problems associated with approaching life from such gender-based schemata. Certainly, men acting in predictably masculine ways and women acting in predictably feminine ways provide a certain stable, if not always comfortable, basis for relationships with both the same and the opposite gender. One has to look no further than the current debate about gay men in the military to note the potential havoc many fear will result if some men fail to think or behave in traditionally accepted masculine ways.

To thoroughly explore the complex questions about the disadvantages of men becoming highly committed to culturally stereotypic masculine attitudes and behaviors would require more space than we have here. Certainly, those men and women who have written about and participated in the women's movement against sexism have felt that rigid gender roles were becoming a problem for us all. However, one of the most influential scholars to portray the stressful and unhealthy implications of traditional masculinity was the psychologist Joseph H. Pleck.

JOSEPH PLECK'S VIEW OF MASCULINITY

In the early 1980s, Pleck critically analyzed what he termed the gender role identification (GRI) paradigm in his book *The Myth of Masculinity* (1981). This paradigm had dominated the social sciences' views of masculine sex typing since the 1930s. According to Pleck, the GRI paradigm held that boys innately need to develop a "masculine" sex role identity to ensure that they develop normally into adult men. From this perspective, mental health problems would arise not from the imposition of culturally inspired gender roles, but rather from the failure of men to learn gender roles appropriate to their biological sex.

To counter the long-held traditional notions that certain features of culturally defined masculinity, such as "dominance," are not only innate but necessary for healthy male development, Pleck (1981) set forth what he termed the gender role strain (GRS) paradigm. Among the assumptions of the GRS paradigm are (a) gender role norms are contradictory and inconsistent; (b) the proportion of individuals who violate traditional gender role norms is high; (c) violating gender role norms leads to social condemnation; (d) violating gender role norms leads to negative and stressful psychological consequences; (e) violating gender role norms has more severe consequences for males than females; and (f) certain consequences prescribed by gender role norms are psychologically dysfunctional. Pleck (1981) also reviewed existing research findings on the effects of gender role violation for men to support his propositions that traditional masculinity often produces deleterious psychological and physical health consequences.

Thus, Pleck's landmark book helped to systematically debunk long-held views that there is something inevitable, natural, or necessary about males developing culturally sanctioned masculine attitudes and role behaviors. On the contrary, the implications of Pleck's work for our notions about masculine gender role stress are that: (a) men have been externally directed by societal expectations to live up to culturally *imposed* definitions of masculinity; (b) the struggle to attain these masculine characteristics may frequently have undesirable consequences for many or even most men; and (c) the routine deployment of masculine strategies for dealing with life's problems may produce dysfunctional solutions and emotional distress for many men.

At this point, we might ask what aspects of traditional masculinity predispose men to being stressed in a manner different from women. Is there something about the way men have been socialized to think and respond differently from women that puts them at greater risk for developing certain types of health problems? How can culturally approved masculine gender role behavior increase or decrease a man's vulnerability to stress? To answer these questions, a measure assessing the kinds of situations that tend to produce more stress in men than in women was needed. But first, a theoretical view of stress that would enable the investigators to focus on gender differences in the cognitive attribution of stress in men compared with women needed to be developed. Richard Lazarus and his colleagues (Lazarus & Folkman, 1984; Lazarus, 1990) provided a model of stress appraisal and coping that we deemed particularly relevant to our development of the notion of masculine gender role stress.

LAZARUS'S THEORY-BASED MEASUREMENT OF STRESS

Over time, the concept of stress has evolved as a bio-psycho-social construct in which psychological and biological factors interact with environmental events to produce physical and psychological disorders (Goldberger & Breznitz, 1982; Neufeld, 1989; Selye, 1978). Modern theories that describe the way stressful situations produce illness are based on the notion that cognition links events to arousal. It is realized that the impacts of environmental events are cognitively modified by our perceptions, anticipations, and beliefs about a situation, as well as by our appraisal of the efficacy of our coping responses to them. According to Lazarus and Folkman (1984), "psychological stress is a particular relationship between the person and the environment that is appraised by the person as taxing or exceeding his or her resources and endangering his or her well being" (p. 19). Thus, the interaction between cognitive appraisals of situations and evaluations of one's ability to psychologically and emotionally manage those situations defines the stress process.

While many factors can influence one's appraisal of a situation as challenging or threatening, one's vulnerability to a stressor is partly related, as Lazarus and Folkman (1984) pointed out, to the strength of one's *commitment* to that event. Therefore, if a man becomes extremely committed to being successful at a particular enterprise, his vulnerability to stress and emotional upset should be proportional to the strength of his commitment.

Masculine Gender Role Stress Paradigm

Borrowing from Bem's theory that gender role schema predispose men to view the world through masculine-tinted cognitive lenses, from Pleck's view that culturally imposed masculinity predisposes men to masculine gender role strain, and from Lazarus and Folkman's views about the roles of cognitive appraisal and commitment in understanding stress, we have developed the following propositions about the masculine gender role stress paradigm to help explain stress arousal and subsequent health problems in men.

1. The sociocultural contingencies that reward masculine attitudes and behaviors while punishing nonmasculine (i.e., feminine) attitudes result in the development of masculine gender role cognitive schema in the vast majority of individuals with XY chromosome patterns. Thus, little boys develop masculine schema that encourage them to attack rather than cry when someone hurts or threatens them, because the former response will be rewarded and the latter will be rejected as unmasculine. This schema is first rewarded by social peers and adults and then operates independently through a self-evaluation process in which a child

says to himself, "This is a good [i.e., strong and masculine] way for me to behave."

2. Masculine schema are then employed by men, in varying degrees, to appraise threats and challenges from the environment as well as to evaluate and guide their choice of coping strategies. Masculine schema are lenses that shape men's appraisals of threat along the lines of traditional masculine gender ideology and also guide the selection of a response from a restricted repertoire of masculine coping behaviors. From this perspective, men are more likely to display aggression when challenged than to employ cooperative or conciliatory responses.

3. Based on their disparate experiences, there are important differences among men as to how *committed* they are to culturally accepted models of masculinity. For a variety of temperamental, psychological, and cultural reasons, men differ in their level of commitment to traditional masculinity and stereotyped masculine behaviors. At one end of the continuum, men may be so committed to masculinity that they behave like certain male firefighters in New York City who, because they believed that women could not possess the skills and abilities essential to working safely with men, harassed female firefighters so that they would quit the department. At the other end of the continuum, men have relinquished their commitment to traditional masculinity by abandoning their careers to stay at home and raise their children.

4. Masculine gender role stress may arise from excessive commitment to and reliance on certain culturally approved masculine schema that limit the range of coping strategies employable in any particular situation. Some men may experience severe stress from losing in a competitive game; others who are less committed to masculine values can cope with the loss more easily, by telling themselves they played well anyway or they got healthy exercise from the competition.

5. Masculine gender role stress may also arise from the belief that one is not living up to culturally sanctioned masculine gender role behavior. Men may experience stress if they feel they have acted in an unmanly or feminine fashion. Many men are doubly stressed by experiencing fear or by feeling that they did not appear successful or tough enough in situations requiring masculine appearances of strength and invincibility.

DEVELOPMENT OF THE MGRSS: ITEM GENERATION

A sentence completion task was used to elicit over 200 items from both male and female undergraduate students for both the Masculine Gender Role Stress Scale (MGRSS) for men and the Feminine Gender Role Stress Scale (FGRSS) for women. Only details regarding the gender role stress measure for men will be reported here for women. (See Gillespie & Eisler, 1992, for a description of the FGRSS.) The sentence completion task was designed to elicit sex-typed appraisals from several hundred college students by asking them to separately list what they felt would be the most difficult or most stressful things associated with being either a man or a woman. Additional items regarding the stressful aspects of being a man or woman were taken from various professional books and journals about gender issues. Based on these data, over 100 different items were written for a preliminary version of the men's MGRSS.

The preliminary items were then given to 25 male and 25 female graduate student and faculty judges in the Psychology Department at Virginia Polytechnic Institute and State University. The judges were asked to give their appraisals of how much stress the situations represented by each item would generally be expected to elicit in men and in women on seven-point intensity scales. The items retained for the initial versions of the MGRSS had to meet two criteria: (1) the average intensity ratings for *both* male and female raters of men's probable stress intensity had to be assessed in the moderate to high range (4.0 or above on the 7.0 scale), and (2) the mean appraisals of *both* male and female raters had to indicate that the item was significantly *more stressful* for men than for women to be retained for the original MGRSS scale. Only 66 items passed this screen.

VALIDATION

The 66-item version of the MGRSS was administered to another sample of 82 male and 91 female psychology undergraduates. It was deemed important to distinguish masculine gender role stress from purely sex-typed masculinity, in line with our earlier notion that not all adherence to masculine norms is stress-producing. For example, measures of sex-typed masculinity typically assess socially desirable masculine attributes, including autonomy, assertiveness, self-confidence, and so on. For this purpose, the measure of sex-typing in Spence and Helmreich's (1978) Personal Attributes Questionnaire (PAQ) was administered.

In addition, we felt it was important for this preliminary validation to determine links between masculine gender role stress, emotions frequently associated with stress—including anger and anxiety—and health risk habits. Thus, Siegel's (1986) Multidimensional Anger Inventory and the State-Trait Anxiety Inventory (Spielberger, Gorsuch, Lushene, Vagg, & Jacobs, 1983) were also included in the battery, as were items adapted from the National Health Information Clearinghouse (1984) instrument, which asks subjects about their health habits, including diet, exercise, smoking, drinking, and seat belt use. The results from administering the MGRSS with the above measures follow.

I have to caution our readers at this point that most of the items for our research with the MGRSS were generated by a young group of predominantly white college males and females who may have differed in their views about gender from other, more diverse educational, ethnic, and cultural groups. Additional validation studies will be needed to compare these results with those of other cultural groups.

Gender, the MGRSS, and Masculinity

Since the MGRSS items were constructed to assess experiences that were more likely to be appraised as stressful for men than for women, it was expected that in a population of "normal" men and women, men would score higher on the preliminary MGRSS than women (Eisler & Skidmore, 1987). This was confirmed in that, on average, men achieved higher MGRSS scores (mean = 265) than women (mean = 240) ($p < .01$).

Previous research had shown that some aspects of culturally sanctioned masculinity (e.g., assertiveness) play a positive role in the healthy adjustment of both men and women, whereas we were selecting MGRSS items to reflect the appraisal of the stress-inducing aspects of masculinity for men. Thus, we were expecting that the MGRSS would have weak associations with measures of sex-typed masculinity. The results confirmed our hope for the MGRSS in that it failed to correlate significantly with the PAQ measure of stereotypic positive masculine traits ($r = .08$).

The MGRSS, Anger, and Anxiety

As expected, the MGRSS had significant correlations with anger and anxiety. In this sample, the MGRSS correlated moderately highly with the Siegel anger inventory (.54), and to a lesser degree with state anxiety (.23) and trait anxiety (.22) scores. Just the opposite pattern was found for women. Their scores on the MGRSS correlated more highly with state anxiety (.40) than with anger (.17). Thus, as expected, men who scored high on appraisal of masculine stress were more prone to anger, while women who indicated such stress manifested their stress responses with elevated state anxiety (Eisler, Skidmore, & Ward, 1988). Additionally, in a recent study, Arrindell, Kolk, Pickersgill, and Hageman (1993) found a very strong relationship between MGRSS scores and the self-reported experience of irrational fears, particularly social fears in men.

Masculinity, the MGRSS, and Health Behaviors

Finally, it was predicted that sex-typed masculinity would have a positive association with psychosocial health and adjustment in men, whereas our MGRSS measure would predict high-risk health habits (smoking and high alcohol consumption) in these same men. Multiple regression and correlation analysis showed that, as expected, the PAQ measure of masculinity was negatively associated with anxiety (r = −.42) and anger (r = −.18), but positively associated with good health habits (r = .29) (Eisler, Skidmore, & Ward, 1988). On the other hand, the MGRSS, as previously indicated, was positively associated with anger and anxiety, but also positively associated, albeit weakly, with high-risk health habits.

Thus, our initial investigations with the preliminary version of the MGRSS indicate that masculine gender role stress is a viable construct conceptually and operationally distinct from sex-typed masculinity per se. For this population, MGRSS scores were higher for men than for women, whereas previous research has shown that more typically women admit to greater distress than do men. Additionally, MGRSS scores, but not masculinity, were associated with higher levels of anger and anxiety in the male samples. This is consistent with research on Type A behavior patterns, which has shown that negative emotional traits, such as impatience and hostility are associated with higher Type A health risk (Price, 1982). Finally, these results suggest that while subjects who score high in socially acceptable masculine traits may not be at especially high risk for health problems, those who score high on the MGRSS are more prone to engage in high-risk health behaviors.

The MGRSS and Health Problems

An additional study with employees of a telephone company was undertaken at Washington University Medical Center to determine the associations between MGRSS scores and various health practices of employed adults (Watkins, Eisler, Carpenter, Schechtman, & Fisher, 1991). The results indicated that high MGRSS scores were moderately associated with Type A coronary-prone behavior, hostility, and elevated blood pressure in both men and women. Also, high-scoring MGRSS participants reported less satisfaction with their lives than low-scoring MGRSS participants. Thus, there was a correlation between masculine gender role stress and cardiovascular health in a population of working adults.

FACTOR ANALYSIS OF THE MGRSS

To further refine the MGRSS scale and also to more specifically examine the meaning of the MGRSS itself, individual items were correlated with the total scale scores, using a new sample of 150 college-age males. Also, with this new sample, factor analytic procedures were employed to determine the underlying structure of the instrument (Eisler & Skidmore, 1987).

From these procedures, the initial 66-item version of the scale was reduced to 40 items, owing to either low intercorrelation with the total scale or weak factor loadings of some items. The 40-item version of the MGRSS has the following five interpretable factors.

1. Physical Inadequacy: This group of nine items reflects fears of an inability to meet masculine standards of physical fitness, in sports rivalries or in sexual prowess.
2. Emotional Inexpressiveness: High stress appraisal ratings on these seven items reflect fears of vulnerability in expressing one's emotions, such as love, weakness, or hurt feelings. These items also reflect fear of dealing with other people's vulnerable feelings.
3. Subordination to Women: These nine items reflect fears of being outperformed by women in activities at which men traditionally are expected to excel. Representative items place the male in the position of being outperformed by women at work or in a sports competition.
4. Intellectual Inferiority: Endorsement of these seven items reflects fear of appraisal as unable to think rationally or to be decisive, or as not smart enough to handle a situation.
5. Performance Failure: These eight items reflect men's fear of failure to meet masculine standards in the arenas of work and sexual adequacy. That these two instrumental situations clustered together reflects men's perception that their feelings about their masculine adequacy connect the two areas.

DISCUSSION

The lack of association between MGRSS scores and the PAQ measure of masculinity and the different pattern of these two instruments' associations with indicators of stress, hostility, anxiety, and health risk behaviors were viewed as supportive of the masculine gender role stress construct. First, it appears that men who score high on socially desirable masculine traits are not necessarily at high risk for psychological difficulties or health problems. Being assertive, being decisive, and having the ability to act independently contribute to positive personal adjustment for both genders. It is therefore a mistake to implicate all dimensions of traditional masculinity as the source of the host of stress and personality disorders that occur in men. However, the findings did support the notion that men's commitment or adherence to some aspects of "culturally approved masculinity" may be unhealthy and stress-producing. This was demonstrated in the associations between MGRSS scores and high levels of anger, greater fears, and a propensity for engaging in higher-risk behaviors. The next question addressed was, What are these areas of masculine commitment that are likely to produce stress and/or behavior problems in men? The five dimensions revealed in the factor analytic study of the MGRSS have provided some suggestions.

First, many men place a great deal of emphasis on being able to prevail in situations that require physical strength and physical fitness. Being perceived as weak or sexually below par is a major threat to self-esteem for many men. Second, men tend to be distressed by women who they perceive to be equal or superior to them in traditional masculine domains such as competitive games or earning capacity. Third, it is important for men to view themselves as supremely decisive and self-assured. Men value acting in a rational as opposed to an emotional manner because the latter is viewed as feminine. Fourth, most men are committed to performing well and being perceived as triumphant in two arenas, work achievement and sexual prowess. Finally, many men feel uncomfortable in situations that require expression of tender (read, feminine) emotions because doing so is perceived as a violation of traditional masculine norms. Unfortunately, some men experience little stress when they express anger and violence, which are often sanctioned by some of our culture's most cherished views of masculinity.

THE MGRSS AND EMOTIONAL EXPRESSIVENESS

Based on our factor analytic study, which showed that both expressing emotion and dealing with the emotions of others were associated with distress in our male samples, we conducted a study looking at the relationship between MGRSS scores and emotional expression in college males who role-played scenes requiring expressions of anger and irritability, on the one hand, and expressions of fear and vulnerability, on the other. Verbal emotional expressions and nonverbal facial expressions were videotaped during the role-plays. Mehrabian's (1972) criteria coding "movements of facial muscles to non-neutral expressions" (p. 195) were used to rate changes in facial expressions.

The results indicated that all males, irrespective of MGRSS scores, showed less facial expressiveness when they were expected to express fear or tenderness than when they were expected to express anger. Second, the high-scoring MGRSS men were less verbally expressive than the low-scorers in situations that required the expression of tender emotions. There were no differences between the high- and low-scoring MGRSS men in the verbal expression of anger. Taken as a whole, these results supported the notion that masculine gender role fears are related to the suppression of emotional expression.

Whether men's socialized tendency to inhibit emotional expression has deleterious health consequences for them has been debated in the popular literature. Recently, Pennebaker and his associates (Pennebaker, Hughes, & O'Heeron, 1987; Pennebaker, Kiecolt-Glaser, & Glaser, 1988) have shown that individuals who do not disclose unpleasant emotions have chronic physiological arousal and poorer immune system functioning. Thus, there is some support for the notion that men, with their greater tendency than women to inhibit feelings of fear or sadness, may be more vulnerable to disorders related to physiological arousal. Should future research with the MGRSS substantiate these findings, it would mean that men highly committed to suppressing their feelings of vulnerability are at greater risk for stress-induced disorders.

The MGRSS and Cardiovascular Reactivity

The previously described research on the development and measurement of masculine gender role stress has provided tentative confirmation of our belief that strong commitment to some aspects of masculinity as prescribed by Western cultures may be unhealthy for men.

The positive associations obtained between MGRSS scores and measures of anger arousal and blood pressure have led us to hypothesize that high MGRSS scores may be associated with the cardiovascular disease process, which has been a leading cause of premature death in male, as compared with female, populations. In this section, I focus on a series of laboratory studies conducted with my student colleagues that have attempted to link gender-related appraisal of stress to the increased incidence of cardiovascular disease in men.

The electronic media and the popular press have often speculated about the relationship between men's economic struggles in the competitive jungles of work and their early demise. It remained for Friedman and Rosenman (1974) to introduce the experimentally verifiable concept of a Type A behavior pattern to postulate linking coronary artery disease in their predominantly male patients to such masculine traits as aggressiveness, competitive drive, and overcommitment to work. Since the development of coronary disease occurs over several decades, designing experimentally sound research that attempts to link it to psychological responses requires that one understand the physiological mechanisms through which behavior patterns may initiate a pathogenic process at the biological level, resulting over time in physical illness.

CARDIOVASCULAR REACTIVITY

Cardiovascular reactivity has received much attention as a potential mechanism for the development of coronary artery disease (Krantz & Manuck, 1984; Manuck, Kaplan, & Clarkson, 1985). According to the cardiovascular reactivity model, chronic and sustained increases in heart rate and blood pressure, activated by high levels of stress through endocrine responses, cause injury to the arterial walls over time. Reviews of the literature on gender differences in cardiovascular reactivity have found that men generally show greater blood pressure reactivity than do women, although the sexes typically do not differ in heart rate responses (Polefrone & Manuck, 1987).

There has been much conjecture that greater cardiovascular reactivity, and hence heart disease, in men as compared with women, is primarily a function of gender-based biological differences, including hormonal differences. However, additional studies (e.g., Van Egeren, 1979) have shown that when women are placed in some kinds of stressful situations, they exhibit similar or even more reactivity than men. Thus, researchers have speculated that gender differences in reactivity to particular situations may sometimes be a function of gender differences in the "cognitive appraisal of these situations as stressful" (Jorgenson & Houston, 1981; Polefrone & Manuck, 1987).

From this perspective, the heightened cardiovascular responses in males to the laboratory stressors of pain or competition measured in previous research may be understood as men's cognitive appraisal of these challenges as particularly threatening to their masculine self-image, whereas women are less threatened because femininity does not demand that women withstand pain or be as competitive as men.

The next section reports on a series of laboratory studies designed to explore the relationship between MGRSS scores and cardiovascular reactivity, and hence the risk of cardiovascular disease. Also, these studies were designed to determine how men's cognitive appraisals of situations containing masculine challenge situations may produce measurable differences from gender-neutral or feminine stressors.

THE MGRSS, STRESS, AND REACTIVITY

The first in a series of laboratory studies was designed to evaluate the association between masculine gender role stress appraisal and cardiovascular reactivity. It was conducted by exposing college men with high, medium, or low MGRSS scores to two types of stressors. The first was a standard laboratory induction of "pain" known as the Cold Pressor Stress Test. The subject was required to place his hand in ice water for a period of several minutes. Physiological measures of cardiovascular response were measured before, during, and after the hand was immersed in the cold water. The magnitude of the increases in blood pressure and heart rate response were employed as measures of the men's reactivity to this painful stressor.

In addition to the physical stress of the cold pressor test, high-, medium-, and low-scoring MGRSS subjects were also subjected to the Masculine Threat Interview, a psychologically stressful interview by a female confederate, who frequently challenged the subject's masculinity. The interviewer asked pointed questions based on the masculine gender role stress factors identified by the MGRSS. For example, subjects were challenged to talk about topics such as their academic performance, problems in dating, and ability to express themselves emotionally.

The results, analyzed by multiple regression, indicated that there was a linear relationship between MGRSS scores and systolic blood pressure reactivity to both the Cold Pressor Stress Test and the Masculine Threat Interview. That is, there was a progressive increase in blood pressure reactivity associated with an increasing MGRSS score. The results for the Cold Pressor Stress Test and the Masculine Threat Interview were virtually indistinguishable. The stress of both pain and psychological threat to self-esteem had very similar effects in producing greatly increased reactivity for the high-scoring MGRSS men compared with low-scorers. Thus, the nature of the challenge, pain, or psychological threat was found to be less important than the subject's tendency to appraise the situation as a threat to his masculine gender role competence as reflected in his MGRSS score.

The MGRSS, Stress, Reactivity, and Masculine Challenge

The previous study suggested that cardiovascular reactivity in men is in part a function of differences in their cognitive appraisals of threats to their masculinity. That is, high-scoring MGRSS men tend to appraise certain situations involving masculine challenge as more stressful and therefore show greater reactivity than their low-scoring counterparts. In the absence of cognitive threats to masculinity, there should be no differences in the stress responses, and hence in the reactivity of high- and low-scoring MGRSS men. However, when presented with clear evidence of masculine challenge, we expected the high-scoring MGRSS men to be more reactive than the low-scorers.

To test these predictions, we exposed both high- and low-scoring MGRSS men to the previously described cold pressor test under different gender-relevant instructions, to either enhance or reduce the "masculine challenge" of the task (Lash, Eisler, & Schulman, 1990). We wanted to determine whether the greater reactivity of the high-scoring MGRSS men was a function of the pain of the cold water immersion itself or of the particular way these men assessed the implied masculine demand characteristics of the situation, as compared with the low-scoring MGRSS men.

To ensure that high- and low-scoring MGRSS men would assess the stressor differently, male groups were exposed to either a high or low masculine challenge cold pressor test that differed only in that we provided a different rationale for performing the task. In the low masculine challenge test, prior to immersion, the men were told that we simply wanted to obtain physiological measures on people who had their hands in cold water. In the high masculine challenge test, prior to immersion, we emphasized that this was a test of endurance, strength, and ability to withstand pain. The results, as expected, indicated that for the low masculine challenge test, there were no differences in the cardiovascular responses of high-scoring as compared with low-scoring MGRSS men. However, for men in the high masculine challenge groups, large differences in reactivity occurred, with high-scoring MGRSS men showing much more blood pressure reactivity both prior to and during immersion in the cold water. That is, high-scoring MGRSS men were more reactive than the low-scorers during both the anticipation of the masculine challenge as well as during exposure to the stressor itself.

Further evidence that gender-determined appraisal plays a role in cardio-vascular reactivity was gathered from additional studies we conducted using both male and female subjects exposed to masculine and feminine challenges (Lash, 1991; Lash, Gillespie, Eisler, & Southard, 1991). In these subsequent investigations, it was found that women were more reactive than men if the situation threatened their adequacy in areas in which females are expected to excel, such as nurturance and child-rearing ability. On the other hand, it was found that men were more reactive than women if the situations contained masculine challenges such as competitiveness or ability to withstand pain.

Discussion

It must be recognized that our studies showing relationships between the MGRSS and masculine challenge and cardiovascular reactivity have uncov-ered far from conclusive evidence linking masculine gender role behavior patterns with the development of coronary artery disease in men. However, I think we have been able to show that some stresses in men are gender-specific, and that by increasing the masculine relevance of tasks, we can increase arousal in susceptible high-scoring MGRSS men. Second, we have shown that in understanding how masculinity predisposes men to appraise and struggle with the environment in certain gender-stereotypic ways, we may better understand the connection between masculine constructions of the self and men's vulnerability to gender-induced health problems.

Conclusions

Our research with the MGRSS has shown that men tend to experience stress arousal when attempting to deal with emotions they feel are more appropriate for women, or when fearing that women may best them in an activity at which men are expected to excel. Men are also likely to experience stress if they appraise themselves as not performing up to manly standards of achievement in the masculine spheres of work and sexual performance. These appraisals result from pressures men tend to place on themselves to conform to outmoded stereotypes, that is, caricatures of traditional masculine roles.

Overall, the studies we have done with the MGRSS, laboratory stressors, and measures of cardiovascular reactivity have supported a cognitively mediated view of stress based on men's diverse commitments to traditional masculine ideology. High-scoring MGRSS men who were highly committed to traditional masculinity were more likely than others to become excessively emotionally aroused, as measured by their blood pressure, when asked to perform tasks at which men are expected to excel, such as the ability to withstand pain. When the same tasks were presented without the stereotypic expectation that a man would suppress feelings of pain, there were no differences in stress arousal between high- and low-scoring MGRSS men. Additionally, when men were presented with tasks at which females were expected to excel (Lash, 1991), men did not show as much reactivity as the women. These results suggest that men and women are socialized to follow gender-segregated patterns of response based on perceived masculine- and feminine-relevant challenges. Men, for example, are more likely to be stressed by perceived inadequacies in the work environment or deficiencies in strength or mental toughness. Women, on the other hand, may be more stressed by feelings of inadequacy in such areas as the family and relationships (Gillespie & Eisler, 1992).

Future researchers into the health and adjustment problems of men, such as heart disease, hypertension, alcoholism, spouse abuse, and sexual harassment, must become more informed about the pressures and influences of socialized masculine gender roles, which promote unhealthy coping behavior. New programs for men might develop, promote, and evaluate psychoeducational programs on alternative roles and decision-making strategies for men that would expand their range of healthy behaviors.

Finally, it must be recognized that most of the research reported on here was done with relatively young, well-educated, predominantly white men. Nevertheless, there is reason to suspect that there are dysfunctional aspects to the masculinities created by men of other ages, races, and cultural groups as well. Much additional work is needed to generalize the suitability of these findings to men of other ages, races, and cultural backgrounds.

References

Arrindell, W. A., Kolk, A. M., Pickersgill, M. J., & Hageman, W. J. (1993). Biological sex, sex role orientation, masculine sex role stress, dissimulation and self-reported fears. *Advances in Behaviour Research and Therapy, 15,* 103–146.

Bem, S. (1974). The measurement of psychological androgyny. *Journal of Consulting and Clinical Psychology, 42,* 155–162.

Bem, S. (1981). Gender schema theory: A cognitive account of sex typing. *Psychological Review, 88,* 354–364.

Cleary, P. D. (1987). Gender differences in stress related disorders. In R. C. Barnett, L. Biener, & G. K. Baruch (Eds.), *Gender and stress* (pp. 39–72). New York: Free Press.

Cook, E. P. (1985). *Psychological androgyny.* New York: Pergamon.

Doyle, J. A. (1989). *The male experience.* Dubuque, IA: William C. Brown.

Eisler, R. M., & Skidmore, J. R. (1987). Masculine gender role stress: Scale development and component factors in the appraisal of stressful situations. *Behavior Modification, 11,* 123–136.

Eisler, R. M., Skidmore, J. R., & Ward, C. H. (1988). Masculine gender-role stress: Predictor of anger, anxiety and health-risk behaviors. *Journal of Personality Assessment, 52,* 133–141.

Fasteau, M. F. (1975). *The male machine.* New York: Dell.

Franklin, C. W. (1988). *Men and society.* Chicago: Nelson-Hall.

Friedman, M., & Rosenman, R. (1974). *Type A behavior and your heart.* Greenwich, CT: Fawcett.

Gillespie, B. L., & Eisler, R. M. (1992). Development of the Feminine Gender Role Stress Scale: A cognitive-behavioral measure of stress, appraisal and coping for women. *Behavior Modification, 16,* 426–438.

Goldberg, H. (1976). *The hazards of being male.* New York: Nash.

Goldberger, L., & Breznitz, S. (Eds.). (1982). *Handbook of stress: Theoretical and clinical aspects.* New York: Free Press.

Harrison, J., Chin, J., & Ficarrotto, T. (1989). Warning: Masculinity may be dangerous to your health. In M. S. Kimmel & M. A. Messner (Eds.), *Men's lives* (pp. 296–309). New York: Macmillan.

Jorgensen, R. S., & Houston, B. K. (1981). Type A behavior patterns, sex differences, and cardiovascular responses to and recovery from stress. *Motivation and Emotion, 5,* 201–214.

Krantz, D. S., & Manuck, S. B. (1984). Acute physiologic reactivity and risk of cardiovascular disease: A review and methodologic critique. *Psychological Bulletin, 96,* 435–464.

Lash, S. J. (1991). *Gender differences in cardiovascular reactivity: Effects of gender relevance of the stressor.* Unpublished doctoral dissertation, Virginia Polytechnic Institute and State University, Blacksburg, VA.

Lash, S. J., Eisler, R. M., & Schulman, R. S. (1990). Cardiovascular reactivity to stress in men. *Behavior Modification, 14,* 3–20.

Lash, S. J., Gillespie, B. L., Eisler, R. M., & Southard, D. R. (1991). Sex differences in cardiovascular reactivity: Effects of the gender relevance of the stressor. *Health Psychology, 6,* 392–398.

Lazarus, R. S. (1990). Theory-based stress measurement. *Psychological Inquiry, 1,* 2–13.

Lazarus, R. S., & Folkman, S. (1984). *Stress, appraisal, and coping.* New York: Springer.

Manuck, S. B., Kaplan, J. R., & Clarkson, T. B. (1985). Stress-induced heart rate reactivity and atherosclerosis in female macaques. *Psychosomatic Medicine, 47,* 90.

Mehrabian, A. (1972). *Nonverbal communication.* Chicago: Aldine.

National Health Information Clearinghouse. (1984). *Health style: A self test.* Washington, DC: U.S. Public Health Service.

Neufeld, R. W. (Ed.). (1989). *Advances in the investigation of psychological stress.* New York: Wiley.

O'Neil, J. M. (1982). Gender role conflict and strain in men's lives: Implications for psychiatrists, psychologists, and other human service providers. In K. Solomon & N. B. Levy (Eds.), *Men in transition: Theory and therapy* (pp. 5–44). New York: Plenum.

Pennebaker, J. W., Hughes, C. F., & O'Heeron, R. C. (1987). The psychophysiology of confession: Linking inhibitory and psychosomatic processes. *Journal of Personality and Social Psychology, 52,* 781–793.

Pennebaker, J. W., Kiecolt-Glaser, J. K., & Glaser, R. (1988). Disclosure of traumas and immune function: Health implications for psychotherapy. *Journal of Consulting and Clinical Psychology, 56,* 239–245.

Pleck, J. (1981). *The myth of masculinity.* Cambridge, MA: MIT Press.

Polefrone, J. M., & Manuck, S. B. (1987). Gender differences in cardiovascular and neuroendocrine response to stressors. In R. Barnett, L. Biener, & G. Baruch (Eds.), *Gender and stress* (pp. 13–38). New York: Free Press.

Price, V. A. (1982) *Type A behavior pattern: A model for research and practice.* New York: Academic Press.

Robins, L. N., Helzer, J. E., Weissman, M. M., Orvaschel, H., Gruenberg, E., Burke, J. D., & Regier, D. A. (1984). Lifetime prevalence of specific psychiatric disorders in three sites. *Archives of General Psychiatry, 41,* 949–958.

Selye, H. (1978). *The stress of life.* New York: McGraw-Hill.

Siegel, J. N. (1986). The Multidimensional Anger Inventory. *Journal of Personality and Social Psychology, 51,* 191–200.

Spence, J. T., & Helmreich, R. L. (1978). *Masculinity and femininity: Their psychological dimensions, correlates, and antecedents.* Austin: University of Texas Press.

Spielberger, C. D., Gorsuch, R. L., Lushene, R., Vagg, P. R., & Jacobs, G. A. (1983). *Manual for the State-Trait Anxiety Inventory (Form Y).* Palo Alto, CA: Consulting Psychologists Press.

Van Egeren, L. F. (1979). Cardiovascular changes during social competition in a mixed motive game. *Journal of Personality and Social Psychology, 37,* 858–864.

Verbrugge, L. M. (1985). Gender and health: An update on hypothesis and evidence. *Journal of Health and Social Behavior, 26,* 156–182.

Waldron, I., & Johnson, S. (1976). Why do women live longer than men? *Journal of Human Stress, 2,* 19–29.

Watkins, P. L., Eisler, R. M., Carpenter, L., Schechtman, K. B., & Fisher, E. B. (1991). Psychosocial and physiological correlates of male gender role stress among employed adults. *Behavioral Medicine, 17,* 86–90.

Widom, C. S. (Ed.). (1984). *Sex roles and psychopathology.* New York: Plenum.

PART III

APPLICATIONS

CHAPTER 8

Toward the Reconstruction of Masculinity

RONALD F. LEVANT

Background and Rationale

THE CRISIS OF MASCULINITY

To many men, particularly midlife men, the question of what it means to be a man today is one of the most persistent unresolved issues in their lives. Raised to be like their fathers, they were mandated to become the good provider for their families and to be strong and silent. They were discouraged from expressing vulnerable and tender emotions and required to put a sharp edge on their masculinity by avoiding anything that hinted of the feminine. Unlike their sisters, they received little if any training in nurturing others and in being sensitive to their needs and empathic with their voice. On the other hand, they received lots of training in problem-solving, logical thinking, risk-taking, staying calm in the face of danger, and assertion and aggression. Finally, they were required at an early age to renounce their dependence on their mothers and accept the pale substitute of their psychologically, if not physically, absent fathers.

For the past two decades, men of this generation have had the experience of attempting to fulfill the requirements of the traditional masculine mandate in the midst of criticism that has been building to a crescendo. Men feel they are being told that what they have been trying to accomplish is irrelevant to the world of today. Since women now work and can earn their own

This chapter is adapted from Ronald Levant, "Toward the Reconstruction of Masculinity," *Journal of Family Psychology*, 5(3/4), 379–402. Copyright © 1992 by the American Psychological Association. Adapted by permission of the publisher.

living, there is no longer as much need for men to be "good providers." Furthermore, society no longer seems to value or even recognize the traditional male way of demonstrating care: through *taking care* of his family and friends, looking out for them, solving their problems, and being one who can be counted on when needed. In its place, men are being asked to take on roles and show care in ways that violate the traditional male code and require skills they do not have, such as nurturing children, revealing weakness, and expressing their most intimate feelings. The net result of this for many men is a loss of self-esteem and an unnerving sense of uncertainty about what it means to be a man.

In Robert Waller's best-selling novel *The Bridges of Madison County* (1992), the male protagonist, the photographer Robert Kincaid, voices his view of the male crisis when he tells his lover, Francesca Johnson, that he is "one of the last cowboys," "a breed of man that's obsolete."

> "In fact, men are outliving their usefulness. All you need is a sperm bank to keep the species going, and those are coming along now. Most men are rotten lovers, women say, so there's not much loss in replacing sex with science." (pp. 100–101)

Kincaid's doubts are on the minds of many men and are being fed by an accelerating condemnation of masculinity in the popular press and electronic media. From comic strips to cable channels, from Bloom County to Oprah Winfrey, men are increasingly the butt of jokes and the target of derision. In fact, it could be said that we have been holding a public seminar on masculinity—or at least on its sexual aspects. This seminar began in 1991 in the broadcasts of Anita Hill's allegations of sexual harassment against Clarence Thomas and the subsequent Senate hearings and continued with the William Kennedy Smith "date rape" trial, Mike Tyson's rape trial, the Tailhook scandal, the Woody Allen mess, Judge Sol Wachter's case, and the allegations against Sen. Bob Packwood.

It has thus become increasingly clear that the social construction of masculinity that has been ascendant in the United States for at least the last 50 years—commonly referred to as "traditional masculinity"—has collapsed.

A RECONSTRUCTION OF MASCULINITY

What is needed? What will help? In this chapter, I propose a reconstruction of masculinity as a possible solution to the male crisis. This reconstruction is based on several principles. First and foremost, it recognizes that *there is a problem*. Although I oppose the shrill condemnation of men we hear in our society today, I feel strongly that the concerns expressed by women about men have basis in fact and that feminists like Dinnerstein (1976) and Ehrenreich (1983) are essentially correct in their analyses of the relationship between gender and power.

Second, this reconstruction *breaks with the essentialist tradition* of viewing gender roles as "inherent"—the notion that there is a historically invariant masculine "essence"—and adopts a social constructionist perspective on masculinity (Kimmel, 1987). Specifically, this reconstruction is based on Pleck's (1981; Chapter 1) critique of the essentialist gender role identity paradigm, and his proposal for an alternative, constructionist perspective, the gender role strain paradigm.

The gender role identity paradigm, which dominated psychological research on masculinity for at least 50 years, assumes that people have an inner psychological need to have a gender role identity and that their personality development hinges on its formation.[1] The extent to which this "inherent" need is met is determined by how completely people embrace their traditional gender role. In this paradigm, the development of appropriate gender role identity is viewed as a failure-prone process; specifically, failure for men to achieve a masculine gender role identity is thought to result in homosexuality, negative attitudes toward women, or hypermasculinity.

In contrast, Pleck's gender role strain paradigm proposes that gender roles are contradictory and inconsistent; that the proportion of persons who violate gender roles is high; that violation of gender roles leads to condemnation and negative psychological consequences; that actual or imagined violation of gender roles leads people to overconform to them; that violating gender roles has more severe consequences for males than for females; and that certain prescribed gender role traits (such as male aggression) can be dysfunctional. In this paradigm, gender roles are defined by gender role stereotypes and norms and are imposed on the developing child by parents, teachers, and peers who subscribe to the prevailing norms and stereotypes.

In keeping with the gender role strain paradigm, this reconstruction avoids the pitfall of creating rigid norms and stereotypes. Unlike the traditional model of masculinity that has held sway for so long, it allows for many versions of masculinity (or "masculinities," following Brod, 1987) in place of a single, unvarying, universal model of masculinity.

Third, this reconstruction strives to *be empathic to men*. In fact, the principle aim of this project is to provide a sense of direction and a set of tools to men who are caught up in the masculinity crisis. While it would be wonderful if all men were to examine traditional masculinity and say, "These stereotypes don't fit our reality, we are better than that, and we must claim the richness of [our] . . . experience," as Doherty (1991, p. 30) suggests, I don't think that is going to happen in the current climate. The collapse of traditional masculinity has resulted in defensiveness and demoralization. To

---

[1] Gender role identity is not the same thing as gender identity—the knowledge that one is male or female—which does seem to be a fundamental requirement for personality integration and seems to be accomplished in all but the tiniest minority of cases.

reach out and be empathic to men, we must remember that for many men the essential dilemma is that much of what they have been taught to value since childhood is either under attack or fully discredited. To help these men come to terms with what must be changed and restore some of their lost pride, the still-valuable aspects of masculinity need to be credited.

Thus, this reconstruction must respond both *affirmatively* to the feminist critique of patriarchy and *empathically* to men. It must also walk the fine line of crediting men for what is valuable about the traditional model of masculinity, on the one hand, and helping men come to terms with what must be changed, on the other hand. Finally, this reconstruction must attempt to inspire men to find the courage to undertake the "modern hero's journey" (Napier, 1991, p. 10), which is an inner pilgrimage, involving confrontation with one's own emotional demons.

In keeping with these aims, this reconstruction identifies the aspects of the traditional male code that are still quite valuable and celebrates them— and targets for change those aspects that are obsolete and dysfunctional.

Some of the positive attributes celebrated here are: a man's willingness to set aside his own needs for the sake of his family; his ability to withstand hardship and pain to protect others; his tendency to take care of people and solve their problems as if they were his own; his way of expressing love by doing things for others; his loyalty, dedication, and commitment; his stick-to-it-ive-ness and will to hang in until a situation is corrected; and his abilities to solve problems, think logically, rely on himself, take risks, stay calm in the face of danger, and assert himself. These traits are expected results of the male gender role socialization process. Attributes of the traditional male code that are still quite valuable, They have been lying around in the dust ever since the edifice of traditional masculinity collapsed. We need to express our appreciation for these traits so that men can regain some of the lost self-esteem and pride associated with being a man.

Then there are the other traits, those parts of the traditional male code that are obsolete or dysfunctional: a relative inability to experience emotional empathy; difficulty in being able to identify and express their own emotional states; a tendency to flip anger into rage, resulting in violence; a tendency to experience sexuality as separated from relationships; difficulties with emotional intimacy; and difficulties in becoming full partners with their wives in maintaining a home and raising children. These traits are also results of the male gender role socialization process. Rectifying them requires learning new skills and doing emotional work.

A recent study suggests that the time may be ripe to undertake this reconstruction of masculinity. Using the Male Role Norms Inventory, Levant et al. (1992) found that their respondents (mostly undergraduates) tended to not endorse many of the norms of traditional masculinity: the requirement to avoid all things feminine; the injunction to restrict one's emotional life; the emphasis on achieving status above all else; nonrelational, objectifying attitudes toward sexuality; and fear and hatred of homosexuals. However, the respondents did endorse the norms of self-reliance and aggression. These results are similar to those of Thompson, Grisanti, and Pleck (1985). Using the Brannon Masculinity Scale (Brannon & Juni, 1984) with a sample of undergraduate males, the investigators found that their respondents tended not to endorse the norms of No Sissy Stuff (avoidance of femininity and concealing emotions) and The Big Wheel (the breadwinner, admired and respected) but did tend to endorse the norms of The Sturdy Oak (toughness, the male machine) and Give 'em Hell (violence and adventure). Although the results of these studies are encouraging, it is still somewhat disheartening to find that both samples endorsed the norm of male aggression.

I need to also point out that for many working-class and lower-class men, the traditional norms may not be changing. For example, Gary Brooks has pointed out in a personal communication (1991) that for the working-class men he sees in the Temple Texas Veterans' Hospital, avoiding all things feminine remains a strong norm.

There are certain limitations to this proposal for the reconstruction of masculinity. My database is derived primarily from clinical and research experience with middle- and upper-middle-class, white, heterosexual men. I have had very limited firsthand clinical or research experience with men of color, men of the lower and upper classes, or gay and bisexual men. Given this database limitation, space limitations, and the fact that issues of ethnocultural and sexual orientation diversity are covered in Part 4 of this volume, this chapter does not take into explicit account the variables of social class, ethnicity, and sexual orientation.

THE NEW MEN

What forms will the new masculinities take? What will the new images look like? Who will be the new role models?

For contemporary men, the John Wayne–Gary Cooper model of masculinity that suited our fathers clearly does not work, but neither does the 1970s "sensitive man" for which Alan Alda served as the caricature. The search for appropriate images of what it means to be a man is a central issue today. The journalist Ellen Goodman (1991) recently nominated Gen. Norman Schwarzkopf to be a model man of the 1990s: "This complicated character seems to synthesize conflicting and changing male images. Introspective but decisive, caring yet competent, one of the guys and a leader. Not stuff that always comes in the same male packages" (p. 22). There is a certain irony in suggesting a military man as a role model to today's midlife men, the Vietnam generation; however, as Goodman points out by contrasting Schwarzkopf with Col. Oliver North, military men come in various shapes and sizes.

However you might feel about Schwarzkopf as a role model, a new combination of values is increasingly in evidence among public figures and opinion-makers. When he was stricken with lymphoma in 1984, Sen. Paul Tsongas left the U.S. Senate because of his concern that his two-year-old daughter might never know her father. President Bill Clinton revealed during his 1992 presidential campaign that his mother was widowed three months before he was born and that his grandfather stepped in to fill the void of the father he never knew; he expressed quite a bit of feeling when making these disclosures. And Sen. Tom Harkin of Iowa spoke openly during the 1992 presidential campaign season of his feelings of sadness and empathy for his brother Frank, who was ridiculed as a child for his deafness. These are significant changes in the posture of public figures, especially when you recall that in 1968 the former senator from Maine, Ed Muskie, saw his presidential ambitions melt in the snow after he cried during an emotional campaign speech.

So what will the new men, the men of the 1990s and beyond, be like? They will subscribe to different mixes of old and new values and exhibit varying combinations of old and new traits. Many will still value strength, self-reliance, and reliability. Many will still show care by doing for others, looking out for them, and solving their problems. Many will still be good at solving problems and being assertive. Many will still be logical and still live by a moral code. But we can hope that fewer will continue to be strangers to emotions. They will have a greater appreciation of their own emotional lives and an ability to express emotions in words. Their emotional lives will also be richer and more complex. Anger will retreat to an appropriate level, and they will be more comfortable with sadness and fear. They will feel less afraid of shame. They will be aware of the emotions of others and adept at reading subtle nuances. They will have a better balance in their lives between work and love. They will be better husbands and lovers because they will be able to experience the true joys of intimacy and will come to prefer that intimacy over unconnected lust. They will be the fathers they wanted for themselves.

Reconstructing Masculinity

Contemporary adult men grew up in an era when traditional masculinity ideology held sway. Consequently, as boys they were reared to fit the traditional male mold. According to the tenets of the gender role strain paradigm (Pleck, 1981; Chapter 1), trying to fit that mold while growing up male was an enormous strain with damaging consequences. In this section, I examine the strain of growing up male through three lenses:

1. I first consider gender role socialization, and the ordeal of male emotional socialization, using the lens of social learning theory;
2. I next discuss associated normative developmental traumas, using the lens of modern psychoanalytic developmental psychology; and
3. I then look at certain additional demanding cultural requirements, using the lens of cultural anthropology.

Along the way, I note those aspects of traditional masculinity that remain valuable, honor them, and discuss in some depth how the dysfunctional aspects of traditional masculinity might be changed.

GENDER ROLE SOCIALIZATION

The gender role strain paradigm (Pleck, 1981; Chapter 1) suggests that, to the extent that parents, teachers, and peers subscribe to traditional gender role ideology, children are socialized accordingly. Prior to the late 1960s, traditional gender role ideology prevailed. Hence, children brought up in the postwar era were reared on gender tracks. In this section, we examine the process and consequences of gender role socialization. The valuable aspects of the male role—those that deserve to be honored—have resulted from gender role socialization, but some of the problems have as well.

To get some idea of how gender-tracked socialization works, think back to how it was in your own childhood. Boys played with mechanical objects, such as cars and trucks, or with very aggressive "dolls," such as military figures or superheroes, and began to develop action-oriented attitudes, while girls played with dolls and dollhouses and started to develop nurturing attitudes. This gender differentiation continued throughout childhood. Boys were allowed to climb trees, roam through the woods in small packs, and come into the house covered head to toe with dirt, activities that girls were not usually allowed to do. On the other hand, boys were not usually asked to mind their younger siblings, nor were they encouraged to offer babysitting services or to enroll in home economics classes. While girls visited nursing homes with their Girl Scout troops, boys shivered in the forests, rubbing sticks together to start a fire.

At a more fundamental level, the current generation of adult men were trained as boys in the skills of instrumental problem-solving, teamwork, risk-taking, maintaining calm in the face of danger, and assertiveness, masculine *action* skills that are still very valuable. On the other hand, boys did not learn certain *emotional* skills which were more the province of girls: the ability to be empathically attuned to the feeling-states of others, the ability to access and to become aware of their own feelings, the ability to experience their own emotions intensely, and the ability to express their feelings through verbalization or through facial activity and other nonverbal means (Brody & Hall, 1993; Osborne, 1991).

The Ordeal of Emotional Socialization

It is not accurate, though, to simply say that boys did not learn these emotional skills. Owing to what seem to be biologically based differences, male infants are more emotional than female infants. That is, boys start out life more emotional than girls. Through the ordeal of emotional socialization, males learn to tune out, stifle, and channel their emotions, whereas the emotion socialization of females encourages their expressivity. Let's look at some of the evidence. Haviland and Malatesta (1981), reviewing data from 12 studies (11 of which were of neonates), concluded that male infants are more emotionally reactive and expressive than their female counterparts: they startle more easily, become excited more quickly, have a lower tolerance for tension and frustration, become distressed more quickly, cry sooner and more often, and fluctuate more rapidly between emotional states. Boys remain more emotional than girls at least until six months of age. Weinberg (1992) found that six-month-old boys exhibit "significantly more joy and anger, more positive vocalizations, fussiness, and crying, [and] more gestural signals directed towards the mother . . . than girls" (p. vii).

How can we account for this "crossover in emotional expression" (Haviland & Malatesta, 1981, p. 16), such that boys start out more emotional than girls but wind up, as adults, much less so? Using a social learning model, Levant and Kopecky (in press) propose that the developmental influences of mothers, fathers, and peer groups result in the suppression and channeling of male emotionality and the encouragement of female emotionality:

1. *Mothers* work harder to manage their more excitable and emotional male infants: They "employ more contingent responding (and particularly contingent smiling) in playing with their sons. Mothers may go to special lengths to ensure that their sons are contented" (Haviland & Malatesta, 1981, p. 202). Mothers also control their own expressivity to "preclude upsetting their [sons'] more fragile emotional equilibria" (Haviland & Malatesta, 1981, p. 202). In contrast, mothers expose their infant daughters to a wider range of emotions than they do their sons (Malatesta, Culver, Tesman, & Shephard, 1989).

2. *Fathers* take an active interest in their children after the 13th month of life (Lamb, 1977) and from that point on socialize their toddler sons and daughters along gender-stereotyped lines (Lamb, Owen, & Chase-Lansdale, 1979; Siegal, 1987). Fathers interact more with infant sons than they do with daughters (Lamb, 1977). With older children, fathers

engage in more verbal roughhousing with sons and tend to speak more about emotions with daughters (Greif, Alvarez, & Ulman, 1981; Schell & Gleason, 1989).

3. Both parents participate in the gender-differentiated *development of language* for emotions. Parents discourage their son's learning to express vulnerable emotions (such as sadness and fear), and while they encourage their daughters to learn to express their vulnerable and caring emotions (such as warmth and affection), they discourage their expression of anger and aggression. It should be noted that females' language superiority also plays a role in their greater ability to express emotions verbally (Brody & Hall, 1993). Dunn, Bretherton, and Munn (1987) found that mothers use more emotion words when speaking with daughters than they do with sons. Fivush (1989) found that mothers speak more about sadness with daughters than with sons and speak about anger only with sons. With daughters, mothers discuss the experience of the emotion, whereas with sons they discuss the "causes and consequences of emotions," thereby helping their sons learn to control their emotions. Greif, Alvarez, and Ulman (1981) had parents "read" stories to their children using wordless books, then videotaped and transcribed their conversations. Mothers talked about anger twice as frequently with sons as compared to daughters. Finally, Fuchs and Thelen (1988) found that school-age sons expect their parents to react negatively to the expression of sadness, whereas school-age daughters expect their mothers to react more positively to the expression of sadness than they would to anger.

4. Sex-segregated *peer groups* complete the job. Young girls typically play with one or two other girls, and their play consists of maintaining the relationship (by minimizing conflict and hostility and maximizing agreement and cooperation) and telling each other secrets, thus fostering their learning skills of empathy, emotional self-awareness, and emotional expressivity. In contrast, young boys typically play in larger groups in structured games in which skills such as learning to play by the rules, teamwork, stoicism, toughness, and competition are learned (Lever, 1976; Maccoby, 1990; Paley, 1984).

The suppression and channeling of male emotionality by mothers, fathers, and peer groups has four major consequences: (1) Men develop a form of empathy that I call "action empathy"; (2) men become strangers to their own emotional life, and most develop at least a mild form of alexithymia ("without words for emotions"); (3) men pour their vulnerable emotions out through the channel of anger ("the male emotional funnel system"—Long, 1987); and (4) men channel their caring emotions through the channel of sexuality.

Action Empathy

Boys do learn a variant of the skill of empathy. Empathy can be defined in cognitive-developmental terms as "interpersonal understanding" (Selman, 1980), a definition that emphasizes the ability to "de-center" from one's own frame of reference and take another person's perspective. In this view, boys can be said to learn action empathy, which can be defined as the ability to see things from another person's point of view and predict what they will *do*. This is in contrast to emotional empathy—taking another person's perspective and being able to know how they *feel*. Action empathy also differs from emotional empathy in terms of its aim: Emotional empathy is usually employed to help another person and is thus prosocial; action empathy is usually (though not always) employed in the service of the self.

Action empathy is usually learned in the gymnasiums and on the playing fields from gym teachers and sports coaches, who put a premium on learning an opponent's general approach, strengths, weaknesses, and body language in order to be able to figure out how he might react in a given situation. It is a valuable skill, and one that helps men function well in their work roles.

Action empathy can also be used as a foundation for teaching emotional empathy. Since action empathy enables men to take another person's perspective, they can then be taught to redirect their examination of the other person's frame of reference from action to feelings. At the Boston University Fatherhood Project, we developed a psychoeducational program for teaching men emotional empathy (Levant & Kelly, 1989). The first step is to develop a vocabulary for emotions, particularly the vulnerable ones (such as hurt, sadness, disappointment, rejection, abandonment, and fear), as well as the caring ones (such as warmth, affection, closeness, appreciation). The men are then taught to read facial gestures, tone of voice, and other types of body language in other people. Finally, men are encouraged to learn to identify the emotions of other people in different situations—in conversations, while observing other people, while watching movies. They are instructed to ask themselves questions during this process, such as, What is he feeling? What does this feel like from his perspective? (For another viewpoint on men's empathy, see Pollack, 1992b.)

Alexithymia

One of the most far-reaching consequences of male gender role socialization is the high incidence among men of at least a mild form of alexithymia—the inability to identify and describe one's feelings in words. The word *alexithymia* is derived from a series of Latin roots: *a*—"without," *lexi*—"word," and *thymia*—"emotions." Alexithymia is a condition originally observed in severely disturbed patients diagnosed with psychosomatic disorders, post-traumatic stress disorder, or chemical dependencies. These patients exhibited a constellation of symptoms, including difficulty identifying and describing their feelings, a concrete and reality-based cognitive style, and impoverished imagination (Krystal, 1982; Sifneos, 1967). Based on clinical observations, I believe that a mild form of alexithymia is very widespread among adult men and that it results from the male emotional socialization ordeal, which requires boys to restrict the expression of their vulnerable and caring emotions and to be emotionally stoic. Not only were boys not encouraged to learn to identify and express their emotions, but more pointedly, they were told not to. They might have been told that "big boys don't cry." In sports, they were told, "No pain, no gain," and were admonished to learn to "play with pain." They were very likely made to feel ashamed of their fear. Such exhortations trained them to be out of touch with their feelings, particularly those feelings on the vulnerable end of the spectrum. As a result of this socialization ordeal, men are often genuinely unaware of their emotions. Lacking this emotional awareness, when asked to identify their feelings, they tend to rely on their cognition and try to logically deduce how they should feel. They cannot do what is so automatic for most women—simply sense inwardly, feel the feeling, and let the verbal description come to mind.

At the Fatherhood Project and in my clinical practice, I developed a psychoeducational approach to teaching the skill of emotional self-awareness in order to help men overcome alexithymia (Levant, 1993a; Levant & Kelly, 1989). Men who are in the presence of an unrecognized emotion often experience only the bodily sensation of its physiological component: tightness in the throat, constriction in the chest, clenching of the gut, antsy feelings in the legs, constriction in the face, difficulty concentrating, and gritting of teeth.

I have found that men tend to respond to this unrecognized emotion in one of four characteristic ways: (1) distraction, a cognitive shift that serves as a "circuit breaker," allowing men to disengage from the bodily discomfort of the unrecognized emotion; (2) the "Rubber Band Syndrome," in which the unrecognized emotion builds and builds until it erupts in an explosion of anger; (3) the "Tin Man" approach, which requires locking up the unrecognized emotion tighter than a drum so that the man no longer feels anything; or (4) the "Mixed Messenger," in which the unrecognized emotion oozes out through the man's nonverbal behavior.

To help men learn the skill of emotional self-awareness, I first work with them to develop a vocabulary for emotions, particularly the vulnerable ones, as well as the caring ones, building on the work in teaching them emotional empathy. I then ask them to keep an emotional response log, noting when they experienced a feeling that they could identify, or a bodily sensation that they became aware of, and what the circumstances were that led up that feeling or sensation. The logs are then discussed in the group or at the next session, with the emphasis on learning how to apply the verbal labels for feelings to emotional states. At the Fatherhood Project, we also taught men to tune in to their feelings through watching and discussing immediate play-backs of role plays in which feelings are engendered. By pointing out the nonverbal cues and asking such questions as "What were your feelings, Don, when you grimaced in that last segment?" fathers learned how to access the ongoing flow of emotions within. The video playback was so effective that we came to refer to it as the "mirror of a man's soul."

The Overdevelopment of Anger and Aggression, the Emotional Funnel System, and the Rubber Band Syndrome

An important corollary of alexithymia is the overdevelopment of anger and aggression. Boys are allowed to feel and become aware of emotions in the anger and rage part of the spectrum, and to behave aggressively, as pre-scribed in the toughness and aggression dimension also known as the "Give 'em Hell" injunction of the male code (David & Brannon, 1976). As argued by Campbell (1993), males and females are socialized to view aggression in very different ways. Whereas females view it "expressively"—"as a tempo-rary loss of control caused by overwhelming pressure and resulting in guilt" (p. viii)—males view it "instrumentally"—as a way of establishing control and gaining one's own ends. Furthermore, as discussed above in relation-ship to the gender-differentiated development of language for emotions, parents discuss anger more often with sons than with daughters. Hence, the expression of anger and aggression is sanctioned for boys. Anger is, in fact, one of the few emotions boys are encouraged to express, and as a conse-quence, the outlawed vulnerable emotions, such as hurt, disappointment, fear, and shame, get funneled into the anger channel. Long (1987) refers to this as "the male emotional funnel system," the final common pathway for all those shameful vulnerable emotions it is too unmanly to express directly.

In addition, owing to the general lack of sensitivity to emotional states that characterizes alexithymia, many men do not recognize anger in its mild forms, such as irritation or annoyance, but detect it only when they are very angry. Consequently, angry outbursts often come too readily in men. Such men are victims of the Rubber Band Syndrome.

At the Fatherhood Project, we developed techniques for anger manage-ment that involve learning to identify both the vulnerable feelings that turn into anger and the incipient and mild stages of anger. Being able to identify these feelings permits one to talk about them, rather than becoming "pos-sessed" by them.

Keeping an emotional response log can be particularly helpful because it provides a means to get a handle on the stages that lead to an eruption. Through keeping such a written record, a man might discover, for example, that his anger proceeds through four distinct stages, each with its own markers, and this information gives him a kind of early warning system. He now knows that Stage 1, inability to focus, signals an incipient annoyance. If he takes action at this stage, he can prevent the emotion from progressing to Stage 2, antsyness; Stage 3, teeth grinding; and Stage 4, eruption.

The Suppression and Channeling of Tender Feelings into Sexuality

Another important corollary of alexithymia is the limitation of the expression of caring emotions. This message often comes from the father, as illustrated in the following anecdote:

> The father drove into the driveway and his children bounded out to greet him. He first hugged and kissed one little daughter, and then hugged and kissed the second daughter. His four-year-old son stood waiting to be hugged and kissed. The father said, "No, Timmy, men don't hug and kiss." Slowly, Timmy got reorganized and offered a stiff manly little hand for a handshake.

Socialization experiences of this type set up barriers to the expression of caring emotions. Later, in adolescence, the caring emotions get channeled into sexuality, which takes the form of unconnected lust—that is, sexuality with no fixed requirement for emotional intimacy (Levant, 1993b). Zilbergeld (1992) describes how teenage boys learn about sex. An absence of realistic, compassionate portrayals of sexuality combined with ubiquitous fantasy images of the woman as sex-object leads to unconnected lust:

> The message is clear: For men sex doesn't have to be connected to anything except lust, and it doesn't matter much toward whom it's directed.... The female in his fantasies is simply a tool to gain release. And then to do it again, and again, and again. Next time it will probably be with a different female. And he certainly doesn't have to like the girl to have sex with her.... Sex is a thing unto itself for adolescent boys, cut off from the rest of their life and centered on their desire for physical release and the need to prove themselves. (pp. 34–35)

In summary, the male emotional socialization process, through the combined influences of mothers, fathers, and peer groups, suppresses and channels natural male emotionality to such an extent that boys grow up to be men who, though skilled in action empathy, cannot readily sense other people's or their own feelings and put them into words and who tend to channel their vulnerable feelings into anger and their caring feelings into sexuality. I have described psychoeducational programs for addressing these effects of the male emotional socialization process by teaching the skills of emotional empathy, emotional self-awareness, and anger management. (See Chapter 10 for a more detailed discussion of the problems associated with aggression and sex.)

NORMATIVE DEVELOPMENTAL TRAUMAS

In this section, using the lens of modern psychoanalytic developmental psychology, I examine certain additional traumas that so reliably occur as a part of male development that they must be considered "normative" (Pollack, 1990, 1992a; Chapter 2): the early separation from mother, and the unavailability of father. Here we will find that men need to undertake emotional work, work that will go much better if they have first developed the skills of emotional empathy and emotional self-awareness described above.

Separation from Mother

The gender role socialization of boys includes the requirement of an early and sharp separation from their mothers during the separation-individuation phase of early childhood. Girls, on the other hand, can prolong the symbiotic attachment with their mothers and avoid experiencing this emotional rupture. As Chodorow (1978) expressed it:

> Boys are more likely to have been pushed out of the preoedipal relationship, and to have had to curtail their primary love and sense of empathic tie with their mother. A boy has been engaged, and required to engage, in a more emphatic individuation and a more defensive firming of experienced ego boundaries. (pp. 166–167)

At an early age, then, boys are given the prize of a sense of themselves as separate individuals; in return, they are required to give up their close attachment to their mothers. Hence, as boys grow up, yearnings for maternal closeness and attachment (which never completely go away) become associated with the fear of losing their sense of themselves as separate. When such yearnings for maternal closeness begin to emerge into awareness, they often bring with them terrifying images of the loss of the sense of identity. Consequently, many adult men feel much safer being alone than being close to someone, a phenomenon that Pollack (1990) has termed "defensive autonomy." This may be experienced as a fear of engulfment, which often motivates the well-known clinical pattern of male distancing in marriage. On the other hand, those yearnings for maternal attachment also get expressed in marriage in the form of the husband's (often unconscious, certainly unacknowledged) dependence on his wife.

Pollack (1991) has referred to the early separation of boys from their mothers as the "traumatic abrogation of the holding environment" (p. 4). This loss of the holding environment, which robs boys of the tranquillity of childhood, is never acknowledged, much less mourned, leaving men vulnerable to developing what Boszormenyi-Nagy and Ulrich (1981) refer to as "destructive entitlement"—the unconscious belief that people in one's adult life are required to make up for what one did not get as a child. Oft-criticized male selfishness may spring from these roots.

Father Absence and "the Wound"

The socialization ordeal for boys also includes the requirement that they identify with their psychologically—sometimes physically—absent, emotionally unavailable fathers. The stress of this ordeal is further complicated by the fact that when the father is available, he is often very demanding of his son. There is a great paradox here, from the father's point of view: Many men feel that their lives will not be complete unless they have a son; when they do have a son, they wind up being very hard on him. Part of this paradox stems from the father's feeling that he must take an active role in enforcing his son's compliance with gender stereotypes.

The difficult father-son relationship leaves a deep impression on a man—referred to as the "wound" in the men's studies literature (Osherson, 1986)—and is manifested in myriad direct and disguised forms of desperately seeking some contact, some closeness, with his father (or his surrogate) or in being furious at him for his failures.

To illustrate, I will describe an experience at the Fatherhood Project that often occurs during the second meeting of a group. One man starts to speak, bottom lip quivering, struggling to maintain control: "You know, the reason why I'm here. I'll tell you. . . . [pause] . . . The reason why I am here is so that my little son Jimmy will not grow up to feel as bad about me as I feel about my own dad." This statement opens the floodgates, and the men pour out their stories and their grief about their own fathers: never knowing their fathers, or how their fathers felt as men, or whether their fathers even liked them, or whether their fathers ever really approved of them. This acutely painful feeling of father loss is very widespread and requires grief work to resolve.

CULTURAL REQUIREMENTS

Having considered the ordeal of gender role socialization and certain normative developmental traumas, we now take a look at the overarching masculinity ideology to which many societies subscribe, an ideology that informs and organizes the socialization practices of parents and peers. In this section, we will consider the cultural requirements for achieving manhood and the role of shame in this process. We will also look at men's propensity for self-sacrifice, discussing the relationship between self-sacrifice and destructive entitlement.

Achieving Manhood

Gilmore (1990) demonstrated that, in most of the cultures he surveyed, ranging from the neolithic to the modern, manhood is viewed as an achieved state, one that requires the passing of a series of tests.[2] The requirements are more severe in societies in which life is harsher. Women are not subjected to such tests, partly because they are under the control of men in most societies.

In most societies, the tests for manhood are never considered finished; it is impossible for a man to feel that he has found a permanent place in the community of men. He believes that he can always slip back over the line, losing his manhood and suffering shame and disgrace by failing the next test. In fact, most men do slip over that line. The consequences for men of violating sex role norms are quite severe (and a fate worse than death in many societies) and usher in enormous shame. Many a man harbors the feeling that he is alone in his shame, that he alone has egregiously violated the male code, that "all those other guys" are doing just fine, and that if anyone knew his secret, he would be completely ostracized.

Shame

This problem of never permanently attaining manhood leaves men with considerable reluctance to violate the male code, lest they be disgraced and overwhelmed with feelings of shame. Krugman (1991) has noted that "male culture can be said to be shame phobic, in that men will go to great lengths to avoid feeling ashamed." Shame thus serves as a powerful cultural mechanism for ensuring compliance with the male code, and hence as a formidable obstacle to change. Therapeutic work must be informed by an awareness of the role of shame in men's lives, and therapists must take pains to avoid shaming male clients (Osherson & Krugman, 1990).

Selfless Generosity, Self-sacrifice, and Entitlement

Gilmore (1990) found one criterion, widespread among many societies, for judging manhood—selfless generosity, to the point of sacrifice. "Real men are those who give more than they take; they serve others. Real men are generous, even to a fault" (p. 229). Selfless generosity is clearly one of the admirable parts of the traditional male code. But male self-sacrifice is often problematic in our society. There are several facets to the problem. First, when self-sacrifice is

---

[2]Gilmore's (1990) core argument, as noted by Pleck (Chapter 1), is a reversion to the gender role identity paradigm (particularly the identity paradigm's notion that achieving a masculine identification is necessary to male personality development), as is evident in the following passage: "The struggle for masculinity is a battle against these regressive wishes and fantasies, a hard-fought renunciation of the longings for the prelapsarian idyll of childhood" (pp. 28–29). However, the ethnographic data that Gilmore presents, including the "contrast cases" of the Semai and the Tahitians, can also support a social constructionist view of gender roles. I have chosen to cite Gilmore's work because it illustrates the power of traditional masculinity ideology and also helps bring to light the dynamics of shame and self-sacrifice.

combined with skill deficits in emotional empathy and emotional self-aware-ness and with defensive autonomy, which together make relationships diffi-cult, workaholism may be the result. Workaholic men often do not know what to do with themselves other than work. Second, self-sacrifice often interacts with the sense of destructive entitlement that results from the traumatic early separation from mother, forming sacrifice-indulge cycles that can occur on a daily basis. For example, consider the man who throws himself into a grueling 14-hour day of work, then comes home to make childlike demands on his fam-ily, is abusive to them, or rewards himself with one indulgence or another. These cycles can also occur over a longer period of time and lie at the heart of object accumulation, nonrelational and addictive sexuality, and chemical dependency. Self-sacrifice carried to extremes also has health consequences. (See Chapter 10 for a more detailed discussion of these problems.)

No Man Is an Island: Challenges for Men in Marriage

Gender role socialization, associated normative developmental traumas, and the cultural requirements described above leave many men unprepared for the world of intimate relationships. Lacking the ability to read their own and other people's emotions, feeling much safer being alone than being close to people, and egged on by a fear of shame, a drive to self-sacrifice, and an overriding commitment to work, many men founder on the shoals of rela-tionship complexity. In this section, we examine only two of the many issues: the division of family labor, and the causes of marital breakdown. (See Chapter 9 for a more detailed discussion of these matters.)

Before discussing these matters, the familiar litany of criticisms of men's difficulties with intimacy must be put into perspective. They should be regarded first from the vantage point of the male role socialization process, which results in differing skill profiles for men and women, skill profiles that put women at an advantage in relationships. Second, traditional male ways of being close, bonded, and intimate should be honored. I am referring to the feeling of "side-by-side intimacy," described by Moore (1991), that two guys might have as they spend a warm summer day together leaning under the hood of a Chevy. Do they feel close? Yes. Would one of them say to the other, "You know, I really feel close to you as we work together replacing the valves on this old heap"? No way!

The Division of Household Labor

In the middle and late 1960s, large-scale time budget studies indicated that husbands' participation in family work (both child care and housework) was quite low (1.1–1.6 hours/day) compared with that of their wives (7.6–8.1

hours/day for housewives and 4.0–4.8 hours/day for employed wives) and that husbands tended to increase their participation only slightly (0.1 hour/day) in response to their wives' employment (Robinson, 1977; Walker & Woods, 1976). Juster and Stafford (1985) found a 20% increase in the amount of time husbands put into family work over the period 1965–81. Douthitt (1989) found additional increases during the 1980s. However, the amount of time husbands spend in family work still remains only about one-third of the total. Moreover, Berardo, Shehan, and Leslie (1987) found that the type of family work men do has shifted from yard and car work to child care and meal preparation, but in the area of child care men still tend to rely on their wives to assign tasks rather then taking responsibility themselves.

Why do men not do more? I have argued elsewhere (Levant, 1990) that one of the major reasons men do not participate more in child care is because of skill deficits, deficits that could be remedied through fatherhood education. But this is clearly not the whole story. When I sit with parents who are in conflict about this issue, it is not too difficult to discern in the father the plaintive voice of a little boy who feels he should not have to do all this women's work and who feels entitled to leave the truly odious jobs to his wife. Once again we come smack up against some of the consequences of the early separation from mother, consequences that require significant emotional work.

There are compelling reasons to address the skill deficits and do the emotional work, reasons having to do not only with men's overloaded wives and conflicted marriages but with their children. It is of the utmost importance for men to get deeply involved in rearing their children so that their sons will not grow up with the same skill lacks and emotional problems and so that their daughters can derive the benefits of being parented by their fathers. It is also important for men themselves. I am referring not only to the obvious notion that if men do this emotional work they will function better in life but also to recent studies indicating that both psychological distress and physical illness may be related to the quality of men's family roles. Gottman (1991) found that husbands who do housework are in better health. Barnett, Marshall, and Pleck (1991) found that the quality of men's marital role and of their parental role are both significant predictors of their psychological distress. And Barnett, Davidson, and Marshall (1991) found that the quality of men's parental role (but not that of their marital role) is a significant predictor of their physical health.

Causes of Marital Breakdown

We now have some pretty good longitudinal data on what causes marital breakdown. The primary factor, based on the research of Markman, Notarius, Gottman, and others, seems to be how couples handle conflict, especially hot conflict with strong negative affect.

A particularly malignant pattern, one that is more predictive of marital breakdown than measures of marital satisfaction (Markman, Duncan, Storaasli, & Howes, 1987), is one in which the wife angrily pursues the resolution of conflicts while the husband withdraws. Floyd and Markman (1983) found that distressed wives distort their perceptions of their husbands' behaviors based on feelings of hostility, whereas husbands in distressed marriages do not attend to the negativity expressed by their wives, suggesting that they are coping by withdrawing. This pattern has been long recognized in the family therapy literature as the end stage of the distancer-pursuer cycle (Fogarty, 1979).

Recent publications make the controversial claim that this cycle may have a biological basis. Gottman and Levenson (1988) and Notarius and Johnson (1982) found that husbands experience conflict (including the anticipation of conflict) with a much higher sympathetic nervous system arousal than do wives and that husbands take much longer to return to baseline. The arousal is distinctly aversive. In situations of low conflict, husbands attempt to prevent the conflict from escalating through positive, reconciling behaviors or by being rational and logical. In situations of high conflict, husbands withdraw as a way of avoiding the arousal.

It is not yet clear what accounts for the greater physiological arousal in men. Is it the result of biological differences, or is it in some way learned? I would advance the hypothesis that men's greater arousal in conflict situations results from the skill deficits (in empathy and emotional self-awareness) and the emotional problems (defensive autonomy, unconscious dependence, destructive entitlement) that result from gender role socialization. In particular, men's relative inability to become aware of and process emotional states would make it very difficult to sort out the feelings they are having, to say nothing of dealing with matters that may be unconscious. It is no wonder that men become overwhelmed by what we have termed the "physiological buzz" (Levant & Kelly, 1989), which may be the same phenomenon as the physiological arousal that Gottman has measured in his laboratory.[3]

Summary

The male role socialization process produces men adept at the skills of provision and protection, such as action empathy, problem-solving, assertiveness,

---

[3]The situation is even more complicated. Jacobson (1983) hypothesized that the wife-demand–husband-withdraw cycle is a function of power differentials within marriage, with husbands having greater power. Christensen and Heavey (1990) attempted to discern whether the demand-withdraw cycle is due to gender differences (resulting from socialization, biology, or both) or to power differences; they found that both factors play a role, the power differential slightly more so.

staying calm under fire, and providing for others, but lacking the ability to know their own emotional life and to be emotionally empathic with others. In addition, men's more severe gender role socialization ordeal and its associated normative developmental traumas and cultural requirements make emotional intimacy threatening to them but leave them with unmet dependency needs; they also become burdened with a sense of entitlement and a longing for their fathers, and at risk for experiencing overwhelming shame.

The reconstruction of masculinity involves several components. First, there is a need to validate the skills men learn and the ways men have of showing care and concern so that they can recapture some of the lost pride of masculinity. Second, men need opportunities to learn some of the skills women learn as girls, particularly emotional empathy, emotional self-awareness, and emotional expressivity. Developing these skills will help balance men's emotional lives, so that the outpouring of vulnerable emotions through the channel of anger, and of caring emotions through the channel of sex, is reduced. Third, aided by these new skills, men need to do the important emotional work that will enable them to come to terms with the loss of mother, the absent father, and the fear of being shamed for not being man enough.

One consequence of doing this work might be moderation of the mandate for self-sacrifice, which may help men put their work in a more balanced perspective. Another consequence might be reduction of sacrifice-indulge cycles, which would be of help to men caught up in the pursuit of money or objects or in addiction to chemicals or sex. A third might be reduction of defensive autonomy and integration of dependency needs, clearing the way for greater emotional intimacy with their wives. A fourth might be reduction of the sense of entitlement, enabling them to be more involved with their children. And finally, a possible result of these consequences would be men's improved health.

References

Barnett, R. C., Davidson, H., & Marshall, N. (1991). Physical symptoms and the interplay of work and family roles. *Health Psychology, 10,* 94–101.

Barnett, R. C., Marshall, N., & Pleck, J. (1991). Men's multiple roles and their relationship to men's psychological distress. *Journal of Marriage and the Family, 54,* 348–367.

Berardo, D. H., Shehan, L. L., & Leslie, G. R. (1987). A residue of tradition: Jobs, careers and spouse time in housework. *Journal of Marriage and the Family, 49,* 381–390.

Boszormenyi-Nagy, I., & Ulrich, D. N. (1981). Contextual family therapy. In A. S. Gurman & D. P. Kniskern (Eds.), *Handbook of family therapy* (pp. 159–186). New York: Brunner/Mazel.

Brannon, R., & Juni, S. (1984). A scale for measuring attitudes about masculinity. *JSAS Catalog of Selected Documents in Psychology, 14,* 6. (Ms. 2012).

Brod, H. (1987). *The making of the masculinities: The new men's studies.* Boston: Unwin Hyman.

Brody, L., & Hall, J. (1993). Gender and emotion. In M. Lewis & J. M. Haviland (Eds.), *Handbook of emotions* (pp. 447–460). New York: Guilford Press.

Campbell, A. (1993). *Men, women and aggression.* New York: Basic Books.

Chodorow, N. (1978). *The reproduction of mothering: Psychoanalysis and the sociology of gender.* Berkeley: University of California Press.

Christensen, A., & Heavey, C. (1990). Gender and social structure in the demand/ withdraw pattern of marital conflict. *Journal of Personality and Social Psychology, 59,* 73–81.

David, D., & Brannon, R. (Eds.). (1976). *The forty-nine percent majority: The male sex role.* Reading, MA: Addison-Wesley.

Dinnerstein, D. (1976). *The mermaid and the minotaur: Sexual arrangements and human malaise.* New York: Harper and Row.

Doherty, W. J. (1991). Beyond reactivity and the deficit model of manhood: A commentary on articles by Napier, Pittman, and Gottman. *Journal of Marital and Family Therapy, 17,* 29–32.

Douthitt, R. A. (1989). The division of labor within homes: Have gender roles changed? *Sex Roles, 20,* 693–704.

Dunn, J., Bretherton, I., & Munn, P. (1987). Conversations about feeling-states between mothers and their children. *Developmental Psychology, 23,* 132–139.

Ehrenreich, B. (1983). *The hearts of men.* New York: Doubleday.

Fivush, R. (1989). Exploring sex differences in the emotional content of mother-child conversations about the past. *Sex Roles, 20,* 675–691.

Floyd, F., & Markman, H. (1983). Observational biases in spouse observation: Toward a cognitive/behavioral model of marriage. *Journal of Consulting and Clinical Psychology, 51,* 450–457.

Fogarty, T. F. (1979). The distancer and the pursuer. *The Family, 7*(1), 11–16.

Fuchs, D., & Thelen, M. (1988). Children's expected interpersonal consequences of communicating their affective state and reported likelihood of expression. *Child Development, 59,* 1314–1322.

Gilmore, D. (1990). *Manhood in the making: Cultural concepts of masculinity.* New Haven, CT: Yale University Press.

Goodman, E. (1991, March 14). A shining (four) star. *Boston Globe,* p. 22.

Gottman, J. (1991). Predicting the longitudinal course of marriages. *Journal of Marital and Family Therapy, 17,* 3–7.

Gottman, J., & Levenson, R. (1988). The social psychophysiology of marriage. In P. Noller & M. A. Fitzpatrick (Eds.), *Perspectives on marital interaction* (pp. 182–200). Clevedon, UK: Multilingual Matters.

Greif, E. B., Alvarez, M., & Ulman, K. (1981, April). *Recognizing emotions in other people: Sex differences in socialization.* Paper presented at the meeting of the Society for Research in Child Development, Boston.

Haviland, J. J., & Malatesta, C. Z. (1981). The development of sex differences in nonverbal signals: Fallacies, facts, and fantasies. In C. Mayo & N. M. Henly (Eds.), *Gender and nonverbal behavior* (pp. 183–208). New York: Springer.

Jacobson, N. S. (1983). Beyond empiricism: The politics of marital therapy. *American Journal of Family Therapy, 11,* 11–24.

Juster, F. T., & Stafford, F. P. (1985) *Time, goods, and well-being.* Ann Arbor, MI: Institute for Social Research.

Kimmel, M. S. (1987). Rethinking "masculinity": New directions for research. In M. S. Kimmel (Ed.), *Changing men: New directions in research on men and masculinity.* Newbury Park, CA: Sage.

Krugman, S. (1991, October). Male vulnerability and the transformation of shame. In W. S. Pollack (Chair), *On men: Redefining roles.* Cambridge Series, Cambridge Hospital/Harvard Medical School, Cambridge, MA.

Krystal, H. (1982). Alexithymia and the effectiveness of psychoanalytic treatment. *International Journal of Psychoanalytic Psychotherapy, 9,* 353–378.

Lamb, M. E. (1977). The development of parental preferences in the first two years of life. *Sex Roles, 3,* 475–497.

Lamb, M. E., Owen, M. J., & Chase-Lansdale, L. (1979). The father-daughter relationship: Past, present, and future. In C. B. Knopp & M. Kirkpatrick (Eds.), *Becoming female* (pp. 89–112). New York: Plenum.

Levant, R. F. (1990). Coping with the new father role. In D. Moore & F. Leafgren (Eds.), *Problem solving strategies and interventions for men in conflict.* Alexandria, VA: American Association for Counseling and Development.

Levant, R. F. (1993a). *Men and psychotherapy: Assessment and treatment of alexithymia in men.* Paper presented at the annual convention of the American Psychological Association, Toronto.

Levant, R. F. (1993b). *Unconnected lust in men.* Paper presented at the annual convention of the American Psychological Association, Toronto.

Levant, R. F., Hirsch, L., Celentano, E., Cozza, T., Hill, S., MacEachern, M., Marty, N., & Schnedeker, J. (1992). The male role: An investigation of norms and stereotypes. *Journal of Mental Health Counseling, 14*(3), 325–377.

Levant, R. F., & Kelly, J. (1989). *Between father and child.* New York: Viking.

Levant, R. F., & Kopecky, G. (in press). *Masculinity, reconstructed.* New York: Dutton.

Lever, J. (1976). Sex differences in the games children play. *Social Work, 23*(4), 78–87.

Long, D. (1987). Working with men who batter. In M. Scher, M. Stevens, G. Good, & G. A. Eichenfield (Eds.), *Handbook of counseling and psychotherapy with men.* (pp. 305–20). Newbury Park, CA: Sage.

Maccoby, E. E. (1990). Gender and relationships: A developmental account. *American Psychologist, 45,* 513–520.

Malatesta, C. Z., Culver, C., Tesman, J., & Shephard, B. (1989). The development of emotion expression during the first two years of life. *Monographs of the Society for Research in Child Development, 50*(1–2, Serial No. 219).

Markman, H. J., Duncan, S. W., Storaasli, R. D., & Howes, P. W. (1987). The prediction and prevention of marital distress: A longitudinal investigation. In K. Hahlweg & M. Goldstein (Eds.), *Understanding major mental disorder: The contribution of family interaction research* (pp. 266–289). New York: Family Process.

Moore, D. (1991). Men and emotions: Teaching men to be more emotionally expressive. In R. Levant (Chair), *Men, emotions, and intimacy.* Symposium conducted at the annual meeting of the American Psychological Association, San Francisco.

Napier, A. (1991). Heroism, men, and marriage. *Journal of Marital and Family Therapy, 17,* 9–16.

Notarius, C. I., & Johnson, J. (1982). Emotional expression in husbands and wives. *Journal of Marriage and the Family, 44,* 483–489.

Osborne, R. W. (1991). Men and intimacy: An empirical review. In R. Levant (Chair), *Men, emotions, and intimacy.* Symposium conducted at the annual meeting of the American Psychological Association, San Francisco.

Osherson, S. (1986). *Finding our fathers: The unfinished business of manhood.* New York: Free Press.

Osherson, S., & Krugman, S. (1990). Men, shame and psychotherapy. *Psychotherapy, 27,* 327–339.

Paley, V. G. (1984). *Boys and girls: Superheroes in the doll corner.* Chicago: University of Chicago Press.

Pleck, J. H. (1981). *The myth of masculinity.* Cambridge, MA: MIT Press.

Pollack, W. S. (1990). Men's development and psychotherapy: A psychoanalytic perspective. *Psychotherapy, 27,* 316–321.

Pollack, W. S. (1991, August). Can men love? In R. Levant (Chair), *Men, emotions, and intimacy.* Symposium conducted at the annual meeting of the American Psychological Association, San Francisco.

Pollack, W. S. (1992a). Should men treat women? Dilemmas for the male psychotherapist: Psychoanalytic and developmental perspectives. *Ethics and Behavior, 2,* 39–49.

Pollack, W. S. (1992b, November). *Men's empathy and empathy for men: Reframing masculinity.* Paper presented at the Cambridge Series, Cambridge Hospital/Harvard Medical School, Cambridge, MA.

Robinson, J. (1977). *How Americans use time: A social-psychological analysis.* New York: Praeger.

Schell, A., & Gleason, J. B. (1989). *Gender differences in the acquisition of the vocabulary of emotion.* Paper presented at the annual meeting of the American Association of Applied Linguistics, Washington, DC.

Selman, R. L. (1980). *The growth of interpersonal understanding: Developmental and clinical analyses.* New York: Academic Press.

Siegal, M. (1987). Are sons and daughters treated more differently by fathers than by mothers? *Developmental Review, 7,* 183–209.

Sifneos, P. E. (1967). Clinical observations on some patients suffering from a variety of psychosomatic diseases. *Proceedings of the Seventh European Conference on Psychosomatic Research* (pp. 27–39). Basel, Switzerland: Kargel.

Thompson, E. H., Jr., Grisanti, C., & Pleck, J. H. (1985). Attitudes toward the male role and their correlates. *Sex Roles, 13,* 483–489.

Walker, K., & Woods, M. (1976). *Time use: A measure of household production of goods and services.* Washington, DC.: American Home Economics Association.

Waller, R. J. (1992). *The bridges of Madison County.* New York: Warner Books.

Weinberg, M. K. (1992). *Sex differences in 6-month-old infants' affect and behavior: Impact on maternal caregiving.* Doctoral dissertation, University of Massachusetts.

Zilbergeld, B. (1992) *The new male sexuality.* New York: Bantam.

CHAPTER 9

Men in Families: Old Constraints, New Possibilities

GARY R. BROOKS AND LUCIA ALBINO GILBERT

Introduction

Masculinity, as a social construct, includes role proscriptions for men in a range of interpersonal contexts. Families are basic social systems that translate cultural expectations to developing males and are social arenas in which these role proscriptions are acted out. This chapter addresses two critical aspects of masculinity in the context of family life—men in heterosexual marriage, and fathering.

Special emphasis is given to marriage and fatherhood as complex and evolving institutions that require new definitions of manhood and call for men to access role behaviors commonly alien to traditional masculinity. After review of the problematic interactions of masculinity and family life, attention is given to prospects for redefining the male role in a way that replaces narrow and crippling definitions of masculinity with a range of "masculinities" that are creative, flexible, and adaptive to ever-changing interpersonal landscapes.

Men and Traditional Marriage

Marriage, as the most intense of male-female relationships, is deeply affected by the larger issues of men's historical views of women and by the historical patterns of female-male relationships. Also, the marital institution itself deserves comment, particularly since researchers have shown it to have differential meaning to women and men, that is, any marital relationship includes a "her" marriage and a "his" marriage (Bernard, 1972).

How a Man Comes to Marriage

A traditional man enters marriage with considerable emotional ambivalence. Marriage is a major step for traditional men, a step made in the face of a heritage of conflictual relations between women and men. To fully appreciate the sometimes enigmatic or problematic behavior of men in marriage, we must understand several important perspectives—psychodynamic perspectives on men's early development, men's studies perspectives on men's childhood socialization and adolescent sexual socialization, feminist perspectives on patriarchy and misogyny, and historical perspectives on the changing nature of marriage as a social institution.

Male Early Development: Psychodynamic Perspectives

Not only are men created inside women's bodies, but as infants they are also dependent on women for physical and emotional survival. During their most vulnerable years, male infants derive their most intense sensual pleasure and emotional security from being held, rocked, and verbally and physically soothed. Typically, these critical developmental needs are met by mothers, creating a situation that some theorists view as inherently problematic for traditional male development (Chodorow, 1978; Pollack, 1990). According to this perspective, the emotional comfort with the mother is only temporary; soon the male child encounters a bewildering conflict between attachment and autonomy. While young girls are freer to connect and identify with their mothers, young boys sense the need to be different from their mothers if they are to accomplish the developmental task of defining themselves as masculine. Rather than relishing the emotional and sensual pleasures of attachment to their mothers, they are compelled to seek a more clearly defined intrapsychic and interpersonal separation. This creates markedly different gender-based developmental themes—girls focus on affection and attachment, and boys focus on separation and autonomy. The picture presented by these developmental theorists is one in which the young male's earliest encounters with a woman are replete with conflict. Drawn to, yet fearful of, mother's love and nurturance, the young boy develops "defensive autonomy" or "pseudo-self-sufficiency" (Pollack, 1990; Chapter 2), as well as "fear of being engulfed" (Chapter 4; Osherson & Krugman, 1990). In far too many cases, this situation is worsened by the relative physical and psychological absence of the father, who is commonly perceived as rejecting and disinterested (Osherson, 1986).

According to this psychodynamic view, the earliest experience of men with women is characterized by a deep emotional conflict—immense desire for nurturance and attachment, coupled with a felt need for separation and autonomy. Any desire for attachment can become shame-inducing, a situation commonly exacerbated by experiences with shaming or rejecting male figures.

Restrictive Early Socialization: Hypermasculinity

Maccoby (1990) observed that the relationship between boys and girls during childhood is largely characterized by "widespread gender segregation," the result of boys' preference for a competitive, rough-and-tumble play style and their "insensitivity to the influence of girls" (p. 515). Although it is unclear whether this segregation is created by biological or social-developmental factors, the results are quite clear—developing males do not learn to interact with, and accommodate, their female peers. They learn to prefer the companionship of other boys and become uneasy in the presence of girls.

Developmental researchers have consistently reported another feature of male socialization that has major implications for intergender relations in adulthood. Numerous researchers have documented that the socialization of young males is far more vigorous and restrictive than it is for young females. O'Neil (1982), in summarizing the research, noted that "boys seem to (a) have a more intensive socialization experience than girls, and (b) experience more pressure to conform to an unclearly defined masculine role" (p. 14). O'Leary and Donahue (1978) reported that (a) males who deviate from stereotypically defined masculine roles are more severely punished than sex role–deviant girls; (b) young men are severely penalized for failure and incompetence; (c) young men who violate traditional norms risk marked devaluation; and (d) early childhood deviation from the prescribed male role works against psychological adjustment.

Young male socialization is not only restrictive, it also demands physical and verbal "toughness." Robert R. Holt, quoted in Miedzian (1991), observed that parents, especially fathers, in their efforts to ensure that their sons grow up to be strong and tough, often overstimulate them from an early age. They "toss them about more and act loud and tough rather than soft and gentle as they do with girls" (p. 46). Holt cited evidence from animal and human studies to outline the consequences for males of this kind of handling. "To take this kind of treatment the organism becomes less sensitive. Part of the callousness, part of the toughness is not being sensitive, not having as much pain sensitivity and not as much general awareness of feelings" (p. 83).

What implications does this intense and restrictive male socialization have for male-female relationships? Obviously, one implication would be that males can be expected to display a generalized pattern of toughness, emotional insensitivity, and a consequent lack of empathy. They can be expected to be resistant to the influence of women. In fact, some have seen such resistance as deeply imbedded in American cultural traditions. Wilkinson (1984), comparing European and American cultures, describes American child-rearing as a process geared toward finding opportunities for natural vigor and expression. "Children should be considerate, get along with others, but not be too angelic, too artificially repressed—boys especially should show a little bit of the rascal, the hellion" (p. 29). Wilkinson also observed "the male assumption that authority, in its taming role, is essentially feminine and schoolmarmish" (p. 29). Echoes of the negative sentiment about women's influence can be found prominently within the mythopoetic branch of the men's movement. Many have noted that its leading spokesman, Robert Bly, is preoccupied with resistance to the "dangers" of feminine influence, fearful that too much of the feminine will rob men of essential maleness.

While resistance to women's influence is troublesome enough, the wider picture makes the issue even more problematic. Resistance to women is only part of the problem—young males are taught to distrust and reject all that is feminine, to avoid anything that smacks of femininity. One of the most peculiar features of the masculine code is that even though it demands rigid adherence to a narrow range of behaviors, it is, at times, oddly vague and inconsistent about what masculine behavior is supposed to look like. In fact, some have noted that "masculine" is often defined less by what it is than by what it is not—that is, not feminine. Young men are sternly admonished to reject femininity and feminine characteristics. David and Brannon's (1976) "No Sissy Stuff," Doyle's (1988) "anti-feminine element of the male role," and O'Donovan's (1988) "femiphobia" all reflect this consistently reported trend in male socialization. "A fundamental guide for men's behavior may be a negative touchstone—anything feminine" (Thompson, Grisanti, & Pleck, 1985, p. 314).

Some observers envision rather extreme consequences resulting from a boy's need to reject femininity. Hartley (1959) stated that "the demeanor of women with whom he is forced to associate is often such that the boy feels that women just don't like boys" (p. 460). Lynn (1966) argued that "since it is the 'girl-like' activities that provoked the punishment administered in efforts to induce sex-typed behavior in boys . . . boys should be expected to generalize and consequently develop hostility toward all females as representatives of the disliked role" (p. 469).

Adolescence and Sexuality

A primary developmental challenge of male adolescence is the need to make the transition from the gender-segregated world of boyhood to a mutually rewarding intergender adult environment. Fueled by social and hormonal pressures, heterosexual male adolescents discover the other gender, which they had previously seen as relatively uninteresting. Unfortunately, teenage boys' lack of prior positive interactions with girls, as well as their massive (mis)education about sexuality, encumbers them with considerable ambivalence about heterosexual relations.

Of all the negative emotional "baggage" (i.e., ambivalence and negative emotional loading) outlined in this section, none is more complex and conflictual than that related to sexuality. In the past two decades, a new body of literature relating to male sexuality (Carnes, 1983; Farrell, 1987; Goldberg, 1976; Gross, 1978; O'Neil, 1982; Zilbergeld, 1978, 1992) has finally incorporated sensitivity to male gender socialization into the discourse, resulting in a rather unsettling conclusion—male sexuality is a tangled mess. Once it may have been possible to think of male-female sexual dysfunction as principally attributable to "frigid" women whose Victorian upbringing caused them to be sexually repressed. In this view, men were seen as naturally healthy and sexually focused, though sometimes in need of technical guidance in "loosening up" their repressed partners. Perhaps one of the finest contributions of recent men's studies literature is the exposure of this outrageously false picture. A consistent issue in the men's literature is the hidden confusion of men in the area of sexuality. For example, according to Solomon (1982), "sexual dysfunction" is one of the six defining features of masculinity. Naturally, since full examination of the complexities of male sexuality could occupy volumes, only a few important points can be made here.

The first issue to address is the commonly held assumption that sex is more important to men than it is to women. "Sex is believed by *both* men and women to be more central, important, urgent, and enjoyable for men than for women" (Gross, 1978, p. 89).

Although there is widespread belief that male sexual preoccupation is biologically based, more evidence points to environmental causes, with socialization playing a major role. Critical here are the messages given to young men about sexual activity. Kanin (1967) observed that adolescent males receive such intense pressure to validate their masculinity through sexual experiences that sex becomes separated from other aspects of social life and an obsessive preoccupation. Young men's ventures into sexual activity are further complicated by a general lack of accurate information, minimal mentoring, and a mythology that lack of information is synonymous with unmanliness.

Unfortunately, as young boys prepare themselves for the sexual quest, young girls are preparing themselves for quite a different experience—to attract, yet control, the sexual overtures of these sexually preoccupied boys. Gagnon and Henderson (1975) commented on this dilemma of differing agendas.

> The young male . . . pushes for more sexual activity when dating . . . conversely, many young females . . . spend a good deal of time preventing sexual intimacy. Therefore, because of earlier differences in learning how to be sexual, males

committed to sexuality, but less trained in affection and love, may interact with females who are committed to love but relatively untrained in sexuality. (p. 38)

Young men and young women tend to view relationships and sexuality quite differently. Peplau, Rubin, and Hill (1977) studied dating couples and found that males reported sex to be a more important aspect of the relationship and that characteristics of the female were better predictors of whether the couples engaged in intercourse. They found that since "virtually every male in the study was highly interested in having sexual intercourse ... women exercised 'negative control,' responding to the male's initiative by either granting or denying his request" (p. 105). Many others have noted this pattern of men being very interested in sexual activity, regardless of relationship issues, and women being more discriminating in their decision to enter sexual activity (Guinsburg, 1973; O'Neil, 1982; Rytting, 1976). Farrell (1987) believes this pattern creates "enormous sexual leverage power" for women over men, a situation that causes men to make exaggerated efforts to win women's attention and "sexual favors." Farrell sees adolescence as a time when young men are taught the "male primary fantasy"—that the most desirable women are those who meet the beauty ideal of the centerfold model. Conversely, women are taught to seek relationships with men who meet the success image. The crux of Farrell's argument is that since many young women may resemble the female of the primary male fantasy (physically appealing), and virtually no young men meet the primary female fantasy (successful), heterosexual men's first significant sexual interactions with women are marked by feelings of inadequacy and sexual powerlessness. As a result, Farrell argues, young men learn to seek women's sexual attention through commitment to achievement and as a result, come to crave, yet resent, the sexual "gifts" of women.

We can easily see that adolescent males are set up to have significant problems around sexuality. Physiological urges and socialization pressures push them to "conquer" women, who are simultaneously being programmed to control the degree of sexual activity. This response, of course, creates psychic distress for young males (as well as for young females) and contributes to the resentful feelings young men have toward young women, who seem determined to prevent males from relieving sexual tension and validating their masculinity. Making physiological matters worse for adolescent males are the rather strong injunctions against the most natural source of physical relief—masturbation. Strong, Wilson, Robbins, and Johns (1981) observed that while masturbation is "the only sexual outlet for many adolescents," it is viewed by most males as "sexual failure." Hence, we hear masturbation described by young males in deprecatory terms ("jacking off, beating your meat"), rather than in positive terms ("pleasuring oneself").

This intergender tension around sexual activity seems to set the stage for significant problems when young men enter marriage. Effective sexual relationships, which by their nature require cooperation and communication, cannot help becoming problematic when sexual activity is structured in an adversarial context (that is, as an interpersonal contest with "winners" and "losers"). Often young men have entered marriage expecting that, by giving up their "freedom," they will be compensated with open access to sexual activity. Unfortunately, this pattern sets men up for a view of sexual activity based on reward and entitlement, rather than one couched in interpersonal understanding and emotional intimacy.

Misogyny in Patriarchal Culture

An inherent feature of patriarchal culture is misogyny, which profoundly affects the ability of men to value and trust women. Men have long been socialized to view women in contradictory ways, ranging from idealization and celebration to distrust, fear, and abnegation. Williams (1977) cataloged some of the many sexist views of women's nature throughout history, including images of woman as "earth mother, temptress-seductress, mystery, and necessary evil." The history of sexist views toward women is well documented in feminist literature and does not require elaboration here. It is critical, however, that emphasis be given to the profound negative impact of sexism and misogyny on the lives of women, as well as on the capacity for men to relate to women as desirable partners. The dilemma of male-female relations is only exacerbated when any of the aforementioned developmental sources of intergender stress is juxtaposed against a culture that offers men easy explanations for their discomfort—"It's those damn women!"

The Institution of Marriage

Thus far, we have examined the multiple aspects of male socialization that influence men entering into a marital relationship. An additional factor that must be appreciated is the traditional man's most common views of the marital institution itself—what does a man expect from marriage? Bernard (1972) pointed out that there are two marriages in every marital union—a "his" marriage and a "her" marriage, and that they do not always coincide. In this section, we look at "his" marriage—the traditional man's most common images, fantasies, and expectations of marriage—and speculate about how his ideas about marriage affect his behavior as a husband.

TRADITIONAL MEN'S PERCEPTION OF MARRIAGE

In the study of traditional men's perceptions of marriage, an intriguing paradox becomes apparent. On the one hand, marriage is seen as malignant, something that should be avoided as long as possible. Oscar Wilde captured this sentiment with his aphorism, "Marriage is a wonderful institution, every woman should be married, but no men." For centuries, men have attacked this institution yet, despite their dominant political position, have not seen the need to dramatically alter it. The historical vitality of the marital institution is testament to its considerable benefit to men. "For centuries men have been told—by other men—that marriage is: no bed of roses, a necessary evil, a noose, a desperate thing, a field of battle, a curse, a school of sincere pretense . . . [however,] contrary to the charges leveled against it, the husbands' marriage, whether they like it or not (and they do), is awfully good for them" (Bernard, 1972, p. 16).

The empirical support for Bernard's assertions is impressive. In general, husbands report being more satisfied with marriage than their wives do (Whitehurst, 1977), enjoy greater health benefits (Gove & Hughes, 1979; Gove & Tudor, 1972), are less likely to seek divorce (Jaffe & Kanter, 1976; Pettit & Bloom, 1984), reenter marriage more quickly and more often after divorce (Nordstrom, 1986), and die sooner after being widowed (Nordstrom, 1986). While many complex factors are at work here, there is dramatic evidence of pronounced ambivalence in men over the marital institution. Men castigate it publicly, but privately they are quite attached to it. To better understand this paradox, additional issues must be explored.

The "Necessity" of Marriage

Clatterbaugh's (1990) description of the "conservative legacy" details the "essentialist" view of the "basic nature" of men and women. Both "moral conservatives" and "social conservatives" view masculinity and femininity as manifestations of intrinsic biological nature. Marriage, from this perspective, has been seen as absolutely necessary for the survival of civilization. One proponent of this view (Gilder, 1973) argued that the male nature is "barbaric" and can only be civilized through marital bonds, which "subordinate male sexual impulses and psychology to long-term horizons of female biology" (p. 24). According to Gilder, women control "the life force in our society and our lives . . . [and determine] the level of happiness, energy, creativity, and solidarity in the nation" (p. 27). According to this perspective, marriage is a trade-off—women hold erotic power over men, with whom they exchange sexual gratification for men's agreement to meet women's demands for monogamy and marriage and to fill the role of provider and protector.

Parallel to Gilder's view of marriage as necessary for men is the view that marriage "saves" men. Durkheim's classic studies of suicide (1951), which showed marriage to have a "salvaging" or "preserving" effect on men, have a modern counterpart in the work of Barnett and Baruch (1987), Gove and

Tudor (1972), and Gove and Hughes (1979), all of whom have shown marriage to have beneficial effects on men's morbidity and mortality.

Marital Services

Traditional males commonly expect marriage to provide "marital support services," that is, someone to clean, cook, and raise children (Nordstrom, 1986). Despite the dramatic increase in women's presence in the workplace, their involvement in domestic chores has not decreased proportionately (Hochschild, 1989). There is evidence that men are doing more domestic labor (Pleck, 1993), and that many of the growing number of men who share marital roles are relatively satisfied (Gilbert, 1985; Robertson & Verschelden, 1993), yet most traditional men still expect women to provide the bulk of household services (just as they continue to expect to be primary breadwinners themselves).

Career and Symbolic Benefits

Most men rely on women to provide domestic services, and many, particularly white-collar men, also expect women to serve the symbolic and real role of "wife." This role calls for the woman to subjugate her activities to the advancement of her husband's career by functioning in a variety of social, technical, and administrative capacities. Additionally, the presence of a "wife" provides important symbolic evidence of a man's psychological maturity: He has advanced to the stage of the male life cycle that Levinson et al. (1978) labeled "settling down." In the words of Danny DeVito's character in the movie *War of the Roses*, "The world can take the measure of a man by his house, his car, his shoes, and his wife."

Emotional Benefits

Marriage is essential to most men as a source of emotional security and as a remedy for emotional deficits. Nordstrom (1986) noted that men report one major benefit of marriage: providing emotional security, a sense of being accepted and emotionally supported. "The marriage and the home are described by the men themselves as a base, a refuge, and a haven" (p. 37).

Marriage is also perceived by many men as a convenient way to alleviate shortcomings in their own emotional skills. Pleck (1980) noted that "in traditional male-female relationships, men experience their emotions vicariously through women. Many men have learned to depend on women to help them express their emotions for them. At an ultimate level, many men are unable to feel emotionally alive except through relationships with women" (p. 421). In Pleck's view, this "emotional expressiveness power" contributes to men's emotional dependence on women and makes men quite fearful of losing a long-standing relationship.

In a similar vein, Doyle's (1989) description of the benefits of marriage for men included "the number of situations in which the wife acts as a kind of socioemotional bridge between her husband and others" (p. 248). In this view, the husband's difficulty in dealing with emotional relations with children, parents, or close friends and his discomfort with certain tender emotions cause him to expect his wife to act as "a personal emissary to convey the husband's feelings to other people" (p. 248).

In addition to getting help with emotional skills, men also rely on marriage to provide the emotional benefit of social companionship. Researchers have consistently found differences between the friendship patterns of the genders. Although men and women report similar numbers of same-sex friendships, there are major qualitative differences. To attain intimate, emotionally disclosing relationships, men are highly dependent on relationships with women (Komarovsky, 1976; Wheeler, Reis, & Nezlek, 1983; Wright & Keple, 1981). After marriage, this dependence becomes more pronounced as men's networks of intimate friendships contract and wives' networks expand or remain the same (Fischer & Phillips, 1982). Tschann (1988) found that married men were much less self-disclosing with same-sex friends than single men, and that "married men work even less at keeping the same-sex relationships intact and growing" (p. 65).

Physical Benefits

Men benefit substantially from marriage in terms of improved physical health. The traditional wife role includes the expectation that she will care for the physical well-being of family members. As a result, "many wives express concern over their husband's physical health, often prompting him to take better care of himself than he would if he were single. . . . For many husbands, the first person they turn to with their aches and pains is the ever-present family nurse, who is expected to make it all better" (Doyle, 1989, p. 249).

There is compelling evidence that marriage provides considerable health benefits to men in the form of significantly lower rates of disease and morbidity (Gove, 1972). Many variables could account for this, including many of those noted earlier. An additional factor may be related to the way many men typically enter the health care system. Traditional masculine values call for men to abuse their bodies and resist most preventive health care practices (Fasteau, 1975; Goldberg, 1976; Harrison, Chin & Ficcarroto, 1989; O'Neil, 1982). Marriage, however, may change this habit: Exposure to women's nurturing roles gives men a face-saving excuse to care for themselves ("I'm fine, but I'll do this for the good of you and the kids").

To this point, we have described a rather peculiar situation. Traditional heterosexual men come to marriage with an abundance of ambivalent feelings toward women, rooted in their psychosocial development, their early masculinity socialization, their adolescent sexual experiences, and their participation in a patriarchal culture. Moreover, they have been encouraged to hold contradictory views toward the institution of marriage—that it is life-saving and necessary, yet enslaving and emasculating. In the midst of this already confusing situation comes a new element—the rapidly changing political and economic environment, with its potential for sweeping changes in the marital institution itself.

The Changing Nature of Marriage

As the previous sections make clear, we have witnessed a profound change in the nature of marriage, a change related to profound changes in how we view women and men as individuals and in relationships (Gilbert, 1993). Unlike in earlier times, many American women and men today assume that women will participate in meaningful paid work, regardless of the nature of their relationships with men. Only 10% of American families fit the traditional model of a wage-earning husband, a homemaker wife, and children. Even among two-parent heterosexual families, the proportion in which the husband is the only wage earner has dropped to 20%; for minority families, the figure is even lower (Spain, 1988; U.S. Department of Labor, 1991). More than half of women return to their jobs within one year of having a child, and 60% of employed men have employed spouses (U.S. Bureau of Labor Statistics, 1991). The average working wife employed full-time contributes approximately 40% of the family's annual income (U.S. Bureau of Labor Statistics, 1991). In addition to staying in the workforce after marriage, women are entering careers in increasing numbers. Thus, a significant proportion of employed women and men become partners in dual-earner relationships, many of which fall into the category of dual-career relationships (Gilbert, 1985, 1993).

Contrary to tradition, then, many partners, male and female alike, view women's employment as salient to their self-concept and life goals, and many men assume that their spouses will pursue paid work regardless of their family situation. Men's declining economic resources and women's increased entitlement to employment appear to have shifted many men away from feeling obligated to fill the traditional "good provider" role long associated with male privilege and power (Bernard, 1981; Gerson, 1993). Contemporary forms of marriage are becoming less characterized by Talcott Parson's notion of gender specification (Parsons & Bales, 1955): women performing expressive roles while men perform instrumental roles. Instead, marriages are increasingly characterized by the assumption that women and men should be free to involve themselves in similar roles and activities because they possess similar attributes, needs, and abilities.

As women's and men's roles have become more convergent, so have the kinds of questions about marriage asked by researchers (Gilbert, 1994). Initially, questions focused on women's changing roles. Guiding these research efforts were the assumptions that traditional roles benefit women and men and that any changes in them would be harmful. Because women's roles began changing in the 1960s and 1970s but men's did not, questions centered on whether women could "do it all" and on how to minimize the potential harm to their traditional responsibilities of caring for husbands and children. Close watch was kept on how women dealt with the stress of their "multiple roles," how their children fared, and how happy their husbands were. Researchers, for example, looked for harm to children and compared children reared in traditional and dual-wage homes; however, results from the many studies conducted showed preschool children to be at no added risk when they receive alternative child or day care instead of parental care for some portion of the day (Hoffman, 1989; Scarr, Phillips, & McCartney, 1990).

As changing social circumstances became more modal and stable, researchers began to recognize that men's self-concepts and roles were also undergoing some modification. Societal changes were seen as presenting both women and men in marriages and in families with new responsibilities, new constraints, and new freedoms with regard to occupational and family life. Recognizing changes in men's experiences was important for two reasons. First, it allowed a shift in assumptions about how to arrange occupational work and family life: No longer were women universally expected to do all the accommodating; instead, arrangements were more commonly worked out between spouses. This shift allowed both women and men to occupy "multiple" roles. Second, an explicit assumption of past research in this area had been that men's traditional roles hold little if any potential harm for men and that any deviation from masculinity ideology would be costly. Recognizing that men who involve themselves in family as well as occupational roles benefit from such involvement called into question assumptions about the correlates of masculinity ideology.

A good deal of research has centered on comparisons of women and men. How much are men doing in the home compared with women? Do women and men cope in different ways? Are there gender differences in marital, occupational, or parenting satisfaction? One major finding is that although inequity remains in participation in home roles, a major gender norm has shifted: Men are now more often expected to participate in family work (Stacey, 1990). A second, and related, major finding is that multiple role involvement benefits both women and men (Barnett & Baruch, 1987; Barnett, Marshall, & Pleck, 1992). Benefits for women include increased self-esteem, better physical and mental health, and enhanced economic independence. For men, benefits include increased emotional involvement and bonding with children, better overall health, and lower levels of psychological distress. These findings support the gender role strain model for masculinity in that societally sanctioned involvement in the caring and expressive aspects of family and marriage broadens men's self-concepts and lowers role strain.

In Chapter 1 of this book, Pleck describes how individuals' endorsement and internalization of masculinity ideology influences their behavior. One does not, however, ascribe to an ideology in a cultural vacuum. Beliefs about the importance of men adhering to culturally defined standards of male behavior go beyond the behaviors of individual women and men to color the implicit and explicit practices of our society. Masculinity ideology has influenced and largely determined the policies provided by employers as well as such long-standing societal practices as expecting employees to act as if they do not have families.

Recognition of this larger influence of gender ideology has led researchers to broaden their investigations of work and family life to include the context of societal norms and practices. Important questions being raised here include, What happens to employees who use family leave or flextime? and, Do men feel pressured to underutilize leave policies or alternative work schedules? This line of research explicitly recognizes that how couples combine work and family and carry out their multiple roles depends on much more than their personal wishes or preferences (Ferree, 1990; Gerson, 1993; Gilbert, 1994).

Division of Household and Family Work

A good deal of attention has been paid to who does what in the home. Despite the many societal changes just described, partners today must still act out their private roles as spouses, parents, and homemakers within the larger world of the "gendered" occupational and institutional structures and policies associated with masculinity ideology and gender roles. Men still earn much more than women on average and hold many more of the policy-making positions in society. Women can more readily and explicitly use family-related employee benefits, such as parental leave and flextime. Moreover, individuals, both female or male, still feel they must accommodate their personal lives to traditional occupational structures if they expect to be rewarded by employers (Gilbert, 1993).

Despite this situation, recent data on the division of domestic labor indicate that the inevitability of a "second shift" for wives is overstated, and that although some wives do face a double day, others are in a more equitable arrangement. Overall, men's participation in family work has continued to increase from 1970 to the present time, more so in parenting than in household work (Blair & Lichter, 1991; Ferree, 1990; Thompson & Walker, 1989). There is also important variation among heterosexual couples. Studies of dual-career and dual-earner families indicate three general marital patterns: conventional, modern, and role-sharing (cf. Dancer & Gilbert, 1993; Gerson, 1993; Gilbert, 1985). In a conventional dual-earner family, both partners are involved in occupational work, but the responsibility for family work (household work and parenting) is retained by the woman, who adds her employment role to her traditional family role. Typically, both partners agree to the premise that work within the home is women's work and that men "help out" as long as doing so does not interfere with their occupational pursuits. The men in these families typically hold traditional views about men's roles, command much higher salaries than their spouse, and see the choice of whether to combine occupational work with family life as belonging to women.

In the modern pattern, parenting is shared by the spouses, but the husband takes less responsibility for household work than does the wife. Characteristic of this pattern may be the husband's motivation to be an active father, a motivation that may or may not be strongly associated with egalitarian views. Commonly, a man wants close relations with his children yet may still see other aspects of family work as more the responsibility of women than men.

The third pattern—the role-sharing, dual-career family—is the most egalitarian and best represents the pattern for which many couples, and female partners in particular, strive. In this variation, both partners actively involve themselves in household work and family life as well as in occupational pursuits. At least one-third of heterosexual dual-earner families fit this variation, although many who are not role-sharing describe their situation as equitable.

Differences among the variations of dual-earner families involve variables associated with individual partners (e.g., a man's need to be dominant or to be nurturing; each partner's abilities, attitudes), employment practices (e.g., provisions for paternity leave, flextime), and social norms (e.g., attitudes toward men who take paternity leave, or toward women or men who are not continuously employed). No pattern seems to guarantee more or less satisfaction, but satisfaction within a particular pattern depends on these factors, especially each partner's perceptions of fairness about the arrangement they have worked out. Also crucial to partners' satisfaction with a particular pattern are the sources of support available to them from friends, relatives, and colleagues, as well as from society at large.

Men and Fathering

Men's fathering behavior is a product of both what is expected and what is possible. Expectations of fatherhood have changed dramatically over the century, and families have faced significant adjustment challenges. Fathering possibilities change also but are subject to complex interactions between many factors, such as men's psychoemotional skills, typical relationship patterns, and sociocultural contexts. In this section, we first explore how the limiting ideas of traditional socialization about acceptable fathering have constrained men's interactions with their children. We then adopt a historical perspective to examine how shifting value systems and sociopolitical variables have impacted the conduct of fathering from the late 1800s to the present. Next, we focus on contemporary culture to see how new definitions of masculinity have removed some traditional constraints, made newer models of fatherhood possible, and produced a wealth of meaningful new research and scholarship about the important role of fathers in children's lives (Bozett & Hanson, 1991; Cath, Gurwitt, & Gunsberg, 1989; Griswold, 1993; Hewlett, 1991; Lamb, 1987; Lewis & O'Brien, 1987; Pruett, 1988; Rotundo, 1993). We also examine how sociopolitical and contextual changes impact contemporary families, thereby encouraging, or impeding, new fathering roles. We conclude with speculations about what changes are necessary to perpetuate the promising trends in men's approaches to the challenges and opportunities of fatherhood.

TRADITIONAL MALE SOCIALIZATION AND FATHERING

Just as traditional gender role socialization sharply distinguishes between acceptable conduct for girls/women and boys/men, it has also assigned markedly different parenting duties to mothers and fathers. As a result, men have strongly identified with certain aspects of fathering and have ignored, delegated, or dismissed others.

Work and the Good Provider Role

Among all the possibilities for the father role, men have most strongly identified with the "good provider" role (Bernard, 1981). Manhood has long been closely tied to the worker role. Likewise, fatherhood has long been closely tied to the good provider role. Of the traditional man, Fasteau (1975) said, "He is functionally designed mostly for work" (p. 1). Of fathers, Brenton (1966) said, "The American male looks to his breadwinner role to confirm his manliness" (p. 93). Vivid testimony to the centrality of this element of the fathering role has been the literature on men's extreme psychological reactions to disability and unemployment—for example, Pleck's (1981) description of "breadwinner suicides." Similarly, men have been described as strongly opposed to women's efforts to share the breadwinning role, sometimes feeling that they are "co-opting the man's passport to masculinity" (Gould, 1974, p. 97). It is primarily through the assumption of this provider role that traditional men feel they are able to demonstrate their loyalty and love for their children. Bernard (1981) said, "The good provider was a 'family man.' He set a good table, provided a decent home, paid the mortgage, bought the shoes, and kept the children well-clothed" (p. 3).

Violence and Protector Roles

Another major element of the traditional male role has been physical strength, aggressiveness, and, when necessary, interpersonal violence. David and Brannon (1976) called this the "Give 'em Hell" feature of the male role; Doyle (1989) labeled it the "aggressive element" of masculinity. This aspect of traditional male socialization translates into dictates for fatherhood as the protector role. Men are raised to view the world as competitive, violent, and unsafe; fathers are far more likely than mothers to view themselves as the immediate agents of physical protection against a range of evil extrafamilial forces. In situations of actual physical danger, such as war, natural disaster, or violent crime, men have traditionally been expected to leave the home to take on the job of protector. Young males commonly rehearse for this adult role through fantasy play as policemen, superheroes, or soldiers. Although white, middle-class American culture has generally moved away from considering physical aggression proof of manhood, this role remains salient in many working-class and ethnic minority subcultures. Cazenave and Leon (1987), Staples (1982), and Majors and Billson (1992) have described how "toughness" and aggressiveness remain important features of black male identity; Mirande (1985) noted how courage, strength, and assertiveness have been critical parts of the machismo of Hispanic men. Ethnic identity and socialization are not the only factors contributing to a subculture's greater emphasis on the protector role. As has been observed by those studying underclass families (Rubin, 1976), life in this socioeconomic niche is commonly more dangerous, lacking the insulating protections of middle- and upper-middle-class life.

Family Leadership, Toughness, and Emotional Stoicism

Another integral feature of the traditional male role is that of emotional toughness and stoicism. Brannon and David (1976) referred to this characterization as "the Sturdy Oak," while Doyle (1989) called it the "self-reliant element." Translated into dictates for fathering, this element of the male role calls for men be emotionally tough family leaders whose priorities are executive leadership, task accomplishment, and strict discipline of children. This role, of course, meshes well with the model of family life in patriarchal culture—rule by the father. Many point to Christianity as a primary basis for this family model, citing the biblical teachings of the Apostle Paul: "Let the woman be subject to their husbands as to the Lord, because the husband is the head of the wife, as Christ is the head of the Church" (quoted in Ruether, 1974, p. 160).

Fathers have generally taken their family leadership role seriously, as illustrated by the developmental research indicating that it usually is the father who is most concerned about children adhering to expected gender roles (Lamb, 1987; O'Neil, 1982; Siegel, 1987).

Closely related to the expectation that men will be emotionally stoic leaders is the expectation that they will reject anything considered "feminine." David and Brannon (1976) called this prescription "No Sissy Stuff"; Doyle called it the "anti-feminine element of the male role." The feminine attributes to be avoided are those of "being warm, open, tender, emotional, and vulnerable" (p. 151). This role mandate translates into a model of fathering that emphasizes discipline of children and encouragement of individual achievement but allows little room for nurturing children and relating to them emotionally. Fathers usually come to their parenting roles with little skill or experience in nurturing others. Most "simply are not prepared for the role" (Levant, 1990, p. 84).

FATHERING IN HISTORICAL PERSPECTIVE

The push for new and broader roles for fathers has been integral to both the contemporary women's movement and the recently emerging men's movement (Shiffman, 1987). However, despite widespread support for what has been referred to as the "new father" (Pleck, 1987) and the "participant father" (Rotundo, 1987), older images of fatherhood have remained dominant. Since one change-resistant force has been essentialist beliefs (the idea that traditional fathering is inherent to men's makeup and unchanging across time), a historical perspective is critical. Doyle (1989) observed that "one of the significant values of a knowledge of the historical perspective is that we see the contemporary male gender for what it really is—a changing social phenomenon" (p. 44).

Many have analyzed changes in fatherhood ideology (Demos, 1986; Griswold, 1993; Pleck, 1987; Rotundo, 1987, 1993), and these analyses have consistently noted certain sociopolitical forces that have shaped modern expectations of men as fathers. Prior to the 18th century, the patriarchal economic system that granted the father ownership and control of all family property made him "a towering figure in the family ... the family's unquestioned ruler" (Rotundo, 1987, p. 65). The principal duties of fathers were preparing children (particularly sons) for life's work and overseeing children's moral and spiritual growth. Because men were thought to have superior reason and to be less susceptible to "passions" and "affections," and women were thought to be indulgent with and excessively fond of children, fathers were viewed as the family's ultimate source of moral teaching and leadership.

Between the early 1800s and the early 1900s, the shift from an agricultural economy to an industrial one produced a major change in fathering as men became physically and psychologically divorced from the mainstream of family life. Maternal responsibility (and blame) for children vastly increased; the fathering role shrunk to little more than the breadwinner aspect. To the family, the father became the "economic specialist, the member of the work world, the producer" (Rotundo, 1987, p. 68). While some degree of emotional involvement with their daughters was allowed, fathers' interactions with their sons were characterized by aloofness and detachment. Sons were expected to learn harsh lessons about the ways of the world.

The period from 1946 to 1965 has been identified by Pleck (1987) as a time when emphasis was placed on the psychological integration of the father as a "sex role model." Though fathers were receiving recognition for the first time as important figures in child development, the attention was negative: It was focused on the extensive emotional damage of father absence.

> According to the [sex role identity] theory, the combination of too much mothering and inadequate fathering led to insecurity in male identity. . . . This conception of father as sex role model served as the equivalent of the much earlier view of the father as moral pedagogue. Healthy sex role identification replaced salvation as the moral imperative. (p. 92)

It was not until the late 1960s and early 1970s that the "new father" model began to gain salience. This new father, or "participant father," has been characterized by the expectation that he will dramatically increase his physical and psychological presence in the family, as well as his emotional immersion in the lives of his children. Essential to this model are beliefs that men are ethically obligated, and intrinsically able, to make parental contributions equivalent to those of mothers. Furthermore, increased participation is seen as reciprocally beneficial—as not only important in the development of children but as a major source of emotional satisfaction and stimulus for developmental growth in many men (Cowan, 1988).

Recent sociopolitical, practical, and psychological factors have encouraged new fathering models. The contemporary women's movement, the gay fathers' movement, the profeminist men's movement, the mythopoetic men's movement, and the fathers' rights movement, despite their substantive philosophical differences (Clatterbaugh, 1990), share the common belief that fathers need to be more involved in the lives of their children. In the psychological realm, the newer developmental theories of Chodorow (1978) and Dinnerstein (1976) push for a much broader role for fathers and suggest that men are impoverished by their limited involvement as fathers. At a practical level, the increasing economic necessity of dual-earner marriages has made it critical that women be freed from exclusive responsibility for child care.

Through this brief historical review, we can see that fathering has not been a stagnant aspect of men's behavior. Rather, it has been an evolving role, shaped over time by shifts in the cultural and sociopolitical climate. Although the climate has recently become more conducive to more participant fathering, no fundamental transformation has yet taken place. Hochschild (1989) and DeVault (1991) have argued that changes in fathering have been minimal and that changes in family roles are moving much too slowly. DeLarossa (1989) differentiated between the "culture" of fatherhood, which has changed significantly, and the "conduct" of fatherhood, which has not. Moreover, others (Ehrenreich, 1983; Faludi, 1991) have noted massive resistance among men to the relationship changes proposed by feminists. Many factors contribute to this resistance. Recent feminist study of the family as a political institution (Thorne & Yalom, 1982; Goldner, 1985, 1988; Hare-Mustin, 1989; Luepnitz, 1988) has enriched the study of family interactions and shown how power, entitlement, and relational politics are fundamental issues that must be understood to fully appreciate why men behave as they do within the family context. Additionally, men's studies perspectives, by illustrating the constraining effects of male socialization, have added further levels of understanding. However, despite obvious reasons for some dissatisfaction with the rate of cultural change, there nevertheless is considerable evidence of change. Pleck (1987, 1993) has acknowledged that though the father-breadwinner model established in the 19th and early 20th centuries remains culturally dominant today, "there is an unmistakable trend toward greater father involvement" (1987, p. 93).

FATHERING IN CONTEMPORARY CULTURE

Men's greater involvement in relationships, caring, and parenting is likely to be the hallmark of the 1990s. The outpouring of new books and studies (e.g., Gerson, 1993; Griswold, 1993) perhaps makes this change self-evident. On Father's Day in recent years, most newspapers have carried stories indicating that for many fathers, roles are shifting.

What kinds of changes are we seeing? Perhaps most dramatic is the increased involvement of divorced fathers, particularly those successfully attaining custody, either jointly or solely. Single fathers are one of the fastest growing segments in the workforce, increasing almost 35% over the past five years (U.S. Bureau of Labor Statistics, 1992). Among married fathers, studies indicate that when both parents of preschoolers are employed, the combined time fathers and mothers spend in direct interaction with their children is about the same as it is in families in which only one spouse is employed (Nock & Kingston, 1991). The difference is that working parents spend more time with children on weekends and plan more of their time with their children. Census data on primary child-care arrangements used by dual-wage families indicate that 17.9% of fathers provide primary care for children under five years of age (Pleck, 1993; U.S. Bureau of Labor Statistics, 1991). Reports from the Department of Labor indicate that increasing numbers of men use vacation and sick days to tend to newborns and other children, refuse long work hours, and seek flexible schedules or family leave (Pleck, 1993). Finally, studies cited earlier (Gerson, 1993; Gilbert, 1985; Pleck, 1987) indicate that men as a group are more involved in parenting than in household work and that nearly two-thirds of fathers in dual-earner families describe themselves as sharing the parenting with their spouses. Men in traditional single-earner families also report increased involvement with children compared with earlier cohort groups.

The motivations for men's increasing involvement in parenting appear to be related to both individual differences and social change. Some men were nurturing and participating parents long before doing so was considered an appropriate and desirable aspect of the fathering role. Thus, to some degree, participation in parenting is motivated by personal preferences and motivations quite independent of changes in gender-role preferences and behaviors. Self-comfort and perceived competence as a parent, for instance, increase men's participation (Crouter, Perry-Jenkins, Huston, & McHale, 1987). Husbands may enjoy being involved in child-rearing or want a closeness with their children that they never had with their own fathers. Or they may be that they simply love children (Gilbert, 1988). Gilbert (1985) reported that fathers whom raters judged to be more involved in parenting rated themselves as closer to their children and rated being a parent and having a sense of family as more important than did those judged to be less involved.

Motivations for involved fathering are also clearly tied to social change. First, the current social milieu appears more accepting of fathers who provide nurturing and hands-on, day-to-day caretaking. Ads in men's magazines and television commercials depict fathers who are actively engaged with children. Some corporations expect men to use family benefit policies. The overall message to men from these many sources is encouragement and permission to involve themselves in loving relationships with their children.

A second aspect of social change is important here as well—the fact that many men are partners in dual-earner families. That is, many men's motivation for participation in parenting is related to their marital and family situation. Regardless of, or in addition to, their personal preferences and motivations, the realities of maintaining family life with two working parents require that husbands engage in parenting activities (and household work).

Employed wives typically push for their husbands' increased participation, particularly if the wives prefer to be employed (Thompson & Walker, 1989). Women who plan to participate in dual-earner marriages expect their spouses to fully involve themselves in parenting (Gilbert, 1993). And one of the best predictors of marital satisfaction in dual-earner families is the perceived parity of the husband's participation in family work (Ferree, 1990; Gilbert, 1993; Thompson & Walker, 1989). Thus, many men no longer have a choice about being an involved father; their role as father is being redefined for them. Being the uninterested, distant, traditional father who *takes* care but does not *give* care is inconsistent with current societal norms and practices and with the expectations of female partners.

Husbands' changing motivations and behaviors about fathering are important to the kinds of family environment experienced by children. How partners relate to one another and to their children communicates a reality associated with gender that children assimilate into their developing self-schemas (Gilbert & Dancer, 1992). For example, in contrast to the more traditional family situations in which work and family roles are assigned along gender lines, men's family participation in dual-earner situations, particularly in role-sharing dual-earner families, reflects a merging of spouses' roles. Similarly, men who actively involve themselves in fathering model less stereotypic male behaviors and provide their children with alternative images of male and female attributes and role-related behaviors (Pruett & Litzenberger, 1992). A case in point is a study by Gilbert et al. (1994) that found a strong positive association between young men's endorsement of role-sharing in their own marriages and rating their own fathers as significantly involved in household work when they were growing up.

Concluding Remarks

A featured article in the January 9, 1994, issue of the *New York Times Book Review* asked, "What do men want?" The article provides a "reading list for the male identity crisis" and in so doing gives readers the impression that reading will be of no help. "The cacophony of voices in the male identity crisis literature is merely a symptom of our times. . . . The time has come for [men] to choose to be something else." Unfortunately, the author believes men have no models to look to "for what it means to really be a man" (Shweder, 1994, p. 3). Interestingly, even at this time of identity crisis, the author appears to fall back on a powerful myth about masculinity—namely, that real men make their own lives. Which brings us to our concluding remarks and their focus on prospects for change in a masculinity ideology that separates men from their families. Perhaps the greatest prospect for change lies in the recognition that despite the prevailing image of men as independent actors in control of their own lives, men too are molded by social forces. Differences in workplace opportunities, in relationships with spouses, and in responsibilities for children influence men in different ways and lead some to adopt relatively traditional family patterns and others to follow more modern ones.

Differences in workplace opportunities are dramatic. Middle-class men in particular can no longer count on the upward mobility characteristic of earlier decades, and they can no longer count on earning more than their spouses. Defining oneself as the good provider has lost much of its social meaning, except perhaps for the very wealthy. This reality may make it easier for some men to embrace broader self-concepts and to move away from a masculinity ideology grounded in stereotypic notions of men and women as opposite sexes. Recent studies indicate that female and male employees hold increasingly similar attitudes toward relocation, business travel, and child care and that family obligations influence the plans and experiences of men as well as women (Zedlick & Mosier, 1990). Combining occupational work and family life across the life cycle is now the norm for both women and men, although it is still somewhat out of step with social institutions and with how we define occupational careers and advance in them. The issues of work and marriage are no longer framed within an either-or paradigm but rather within an integrated one. Facilitating well-being in contemporary marriage requires that we focus on ways to modify structures once viewed as so sacred or so embedded in the social order that they defied change. The kinds of care provided, the definitions of optimal care, and the nature of employers' policies directly influence men's experience of family life in contemporary marriages (Ferree, 1990). Obviously, the more employers' policies reflect a traditional workplace culture in which women with children leave the workplace and men with children are unencumbered by family responsibilities, the more difficult it becomes for men to father and for both partners to parent.

A second prospect for changing aspects of the masculinity ideology that separates men from their families arises out of our understanding of gender processes. Particularly important is recent work on how gender processes are reproduced within the sexes and between the sexes (e.g., Deaux & Major, 1987; Unger, 1990). West and Zimmerman (1987), among others, have helped us to understand the many ways in which the "doing of gender" is an active process engaged in by women and men. Men who feel uncomfortable with their emotions may look to women to express feelings for them. Women who are uncomfortable with power may look to men to use it for them. These kinds of tendencies often reflect how deeply we have internalized societal expectations for women and men and how easily and unconsciously we can play them out in our interactions, particularly when gender is made salient. The doing of gender can occur in relations with colleagues, spouses, and children but is best documented in research with children.

Block (1984) was the first to document how, from an early age, we socialize girls to have "roots" and boys to have "wings." Even today, young boys are not taught the emotional skills of interpersonal sensitivity, empathy, and compassion as consistently and as well as young girls are taught these skills. Young boys are still encouraged to make their own lives, to do whatever they want, and to need no one. For significant value shifts to occur, children need male parents, teachers, and peers who model vulnerability and interpersonal tenderness and female parents, teachers, and peers who openly recognize and accept male emotionality and dependency.

Finally, prospects for positive change depend on our recognition of the considerable diversity among men. We have focused much of our discussion on the heterosexual, dual-earner marital pattern. It is only one of a number of sociocultural patterns influencing men's lives today. For example, the greater acceptance of gay male couples and families is noteworthy and requires more of our attention, as do the complex issues of race, ethnicity, and culture. We could not do justice to this diversity in a single chapter. At the same time, we believe that our focus on the traditional male and on aspects of the masculinity ideology has relevance to many men. We also believe that by working to achieve a better understanding of masculinity ideology, and by changing those aspects that separate men from their families, we will generate substantial benefits to all men and to their families.

References

Barnett, R. C., & Baruch, G. K. (1987). Social roles, gender, and psychological distress. In R. C. Barnett, L. Biener, & G. K. Baruch (Eds.), Gender and stress (pp. 122–143). New York: Free Press.

Barnett, R. C., Marshall, N. L., & Pleck, J. H. (1992). Men's multiple roles and their relationship to men's psychological distress. Journal of Marriage and the Family, 54, 358–367.

Bernard, J. (1972). The future of marriage. New York: World.

Bernard, J. (1981). The good provider role: Its rise and fall. American Psychologist, 36, 1–12.

Blair, S. L., & Lichter, D. T. (1991). Measuring the division of household labor. Journal of Family Issues, 12, 91–113.

Block, J. H. (1984). Sex role identity and ego development. San Francisco: Jossey-Bass.

Bozett, F. W., & Hanson, S. M. H. (1991). Fatherhood and families in cultural context, vol. 6, Focus on men (Springer Series). New York: Springer.

Brenton, M. (1966). The American male. New York: Coward-McCann.

Carnes, P. (1983). Out of the shadows: Understanding sexual addiction. Minneapolis: CompCare.

Cath, S. H., Gurwitt, A., & Gunsberg, L. (Eds.). (1989). *Fathers and their families.* Hillsdale, NJ: Analytic Press.

Cazenave, N., & Leon, G. (1987). Men's work and family roles and characteristics: Race, gender, and class perceptions of college students. In M. S. Kimmel (Ed.), *Changing men: New directions in research on men and masculinity* (pp. 244–262). Beverly Hills, CA: Sage.

Chodorow, N. (1978). *The reproduction of mothering.* Berkeley: University of California Press.

Clatterbaugh, K. (1990). *Contemporary perspectives on masculinity: Men, women, and politics in modern society.* Boulder, CO: Westview.

Cowan, C. (1988). Becoming a father: A time of change, an opportunity for development. In P. Bronstein & C. Cowan (Eds.), *Fatherhood today: Men's changing role in the family* (pp. 13–35). New York: Wiley.

Crouter, A. C., Perry-Jenkins, M., Huston, T. L., & McHale, S. M. (1987). Processes underlying father involvement in dual-earner and single-earner families. *Developmental Psychology, 23,* 431–440.

Dancer, L. S., & Gilbert, L. A. (1993). Spouses' family work participation and its relation to wives' occupational level. *Sex Roles, 28,* 127–146.

David, D. S., & Brannon, R. (1976). *The forty-nine percent majority: The male sex role.* Reading, MA.: Addison-Wesley.

Deaux, K., & Major, B. (1987). Putting gender into context: An interactive model of gender-related behavior. *Psychological Review, 94,* 369–389.

DeLarossa, R. L. (1989). Fatherhood and social change. *Men's Studies Review, 6,* 1, 3–9.

Demos, J. (1986). The changing faces of fatherhood. In J. Demas (Ed.), *Past, present, and personal: The family and the life course in American history* (pp. 41–66). New York: Oxford University Press.

DeVault, M. L. (1991). *Feeding the family: The social organization of caring as gendered work.* Chicago: University of Chicago Press.

Dinnerstein, D. (1976). *The mermaid and the minotaur: Sexual arrangements and human malaise.* New York: Harper & Row.

Doyle, J. A. (1989). *The male experience* (2nd ed.). Dubuque, IA: William C. Brown.

Durkheim, E. (1951). *Suicide* (J. A. Spaulding & G. Simpson, Trans.). New York: Free Press.

Ehrenreich, B. (1983). *The hearts of men: American dreams and the flight from commitment.* Garden City, NY: Anchor.

Faludi, S. (1991). *Backlash: The undeclared war against American women.* New York: Crown.

Farrell, W. T. (1987). *Why men are the way they are.* New York: McGraw-Hill.

Fasteau, M. F. (1975). *The male machine.* New York: Dell.

Ferree, M. M. (1990). Beyond separate spheres: Feminism and family research. *Journal of Marriage and the Family, 52,* 866–884.

Fischer, C. S., & Phillips, S. L. (1982). Who is alone? Social characteristics of people with small networks. In L. A. Peplau & D. Perlman (Eds.), *Loneliness: A sourcebook of current theory, research, and therapy.* New York: Wiley Interscience.

Gagnon, J., & Henderson, B. (1975). *Human sexuality: An age of ambiguity.* Boston: Educational Associates.

Gerson, K. (1993). *No man's land: Men's changing commitments to family and work*. New York: Basic Books.

Gilbert, L. A. (1985). *Men in dual-career families: Current realities and future prospects*. Hillsdale, NJ: Lawrence Erlbaum.

Gilbert, L. A. (1988). *Sharing it all: The rewards and struggles of two-career families*. New York: Plenum.

Gilbert, L. A. (1993). *Two careers/one family: The promise of gender equality*. Newbury Park, CA: Sage.

Gilbert, L. A. (1994). Current perspectives on dual-career families. *Current Directions in Psychological Science, 3*, 101–104.

Gilbert, L. A., & Dancer, L. S. (1992). Dual-earner families in the United States and adolescent development. In S. Lewis, H. Hootsmans, & D. Izraeli (Eds.), *Crossnational perspectives on dual-earner families* (pp. 151–171). Beverly Hills, CA: Sage.

Gilbert, L. A., Rossman, K. S., Hallett, M. B., & Habib, K. (1994). *Contextual family variables associated with young adults' work-family intentions*. Paper presented at the annual meeting of the American Psychological Association, Los Angeles.

Gilder, G. (1973). *Sexual suicide*. New York: Bantam.

Goldberg, H. (1976). *The hazards of being male*. New York: New American Library.

Goldner, V. (1985). Feminism and family therapy. *Family Process, 24*, 31–47.

Goldner, V. (1988). Generation and gender: Normative and covert hierarchies. *Family Process, 27*, 17–31.

Gould, R. (1974). Measuring masculinity by the size of a paycheck. In J. Pleck & J. Sawyer (Eds.), *Men and masculinity* (pp. 96–100). Englewood Cliffs, NJ: Prentice-Hall.

Gove, W. R. (1972). The relationship between sex roles, marital status, and mental illness. *Social Forces, 51*, 34–44.

Gove, W. R., & Hughes, M. (1979). Possible cause of the apparent sex difference in physical health: An empirical investigation. *American Sociological Review, 44*, 126–146.

Gove, W. R., & Tudor, J. (1972). Adult sex roles and mental illness. *American Journal of Sociology, 73*, 812–835.

Griswold, R. L. (1993). *Fatherhood in America: A history*. New York: Basic Books.

Gross, A. (1978). The male role and heterosexual behavior. *Journal of Social Issues, 34*, 87–107.

Guinsburg, P. F. (1973). *An investigation of the components of romantic and platonic heterosexual relationships*. Doctoral dissertation, University of North Dakota. (University Microfilms No. 73–39, 623)

Hare-Mustin, R. T. (1989). The problem of gender in family therapy theory. In M. McGoldrick, C. M. Anderson, & F. Walsh, (Eds.), *Women in families: A framework for family therapy* (pp. 61–77). New York: Norton.

Harrison, J., Chin, J., & Ficcarrotto, T. (1989). Warning: Masculinity may be hazardous to your health. In M. S. Kimmel & M. A. Messner (Eds.), *Men's lives* (pp. 296–309). New York: Macmillan.

Hartley, R. L. (1959). Sex-role pressures in the socialization of the male child. *Psychological Reports, 5*, 459–468.

Hewlett, B. S. (1991). *Intimate fathers*. Ann Arbor: University of Michigan Press.

Hochschild, A. (1989). *The second shift*. New York: Viking.

Hoffman, L. W. (1989). Effects of maternal employment in the two-parent family. *American Psychologist, 44*, 283–292.

Jaffe, D. T., & Kanter, R. M. (1976). Couple strains in communal households: A four-factor model of the separation process. *Journal of Social Issues, 32*, 169–191.

Kanin, E. (1967). Reference groups and sex conduct norm violations. *Sociological Quarterly, 8*, 495–504.

Komarovsky, M. (1976). *Dilemma of masculinity*. New York: Norton.

Lamb, M. (1987). The emergent father. In M. Lamb (Ed.), *The father's role: Cross-cultural perspectives* (pp. 3–25). Hillsdale, NJ: Lawrence Erlbaum.

Levant, R. (1990). Coping with the new father role. In D. Moore & F. Leafgren (Eds.), *Problem-solving strategies for men in conflict* (pp. 81–94). Alexandria, VA: AACD.

Levant. R., & Kelley, J. (1989). *Between father and child*. New York: Viking.

Levinson, D., Darrow, C., Klein, E., Levinson, M., & McKee, B. (1978). *The seasons of a man's life*. New York: Knopf.

Lewis, C., & O'Brien, M. (Eds.) (1987). *Reassessing fatherhood*. London: Sage.

Luepnitz, D. A. (1988). *The family interpreted: Feminist theory in clinical practice*. New York: Basic Books.

Lynn, D. B. (1966). The process of learning parental and sex-role identification. *Journal of Marriage and the Family, 28*, 466–470.

Maccoby, E. E. (1990). Gender and relationships: A developmental account. *American Psychologist, 45*, 513–520.

Majors, R., & Billson, J. M. (1992). *Cool pose: The dilemmas of black manhood in America*. New York: Lexington Books.

Miedzian, M. (1991). *Boys will be boys: Breaking the link between masculinity and violence*. New York: Doubleday.

Mirande, A. (1985). *The Chicano experience*. Notre Dame, IN: University of Notre Dame Press.

Nock, S. L., & Kingston, P. W. (1991). Time with children: The impact of couples' work-time commitments, *Social Forces, 67*, 59–85.

Nordstrom, B. (1986). Why men get married: More and less traditional men compared. In R. A. Lewis & R. E. Salt (Eds.), *Men in families* (pp. 31–53). Newbury Park, CA: Sage.

O'Donovan, D. (1988). Femiphobia: Unseen enemy of intellectual freedom. *Men's Studies Review, 5*, 14–16.

O'Leary, V. E., & Donahue, J. M. (1978). Latitudes of masculinity: Reactions to sex-role deviance in men. *Journal of Social Issues, 34*, 17–28.

O'Neil, J. M. (1982). Gender-role conflict and strain in men's lives. In K. Solomon & N. Levy (Eds.), *Men in transition: Theory and therapy* (pp. 5–44). New York: Plenum.

Osherson, S. (1986). *Finding our fathers: The unfinished business of manhood*. New York: Free Press.

Osherson, S., & Krugman, S. (1990). Men, shame, and psychotherapy. *Psychotherapy, 27*, 327–339.

Parsons, T., & Bales, R. F. (1955). *Family socialization and interaction process*. Riverside, NJ: Free Press.

Peplau, L. A., Rubin, Z., & Hill, C. T. (1977). Sexual intimacy in dating relationships. *Journal of Social Issues, 33,* 86–109.

Pettit, E. J., & Bloom, B. L. (1984). Whose decision was it? The effects of initiator status on adjustment to marital disruption. *Journal of Marriage and the Family, 32,* 54–67.

Pleck, J. H. (1980). Men's power with women, other men, and society: A men's movement analysis. In E. Pleck & J. H. Pleck (Eds.), *The American man* (pp. 417–433). Englewood Cliffs, NJ: Prentice-Hall.

Pleck, J. H. (1981). *The myth of masculinity.* Cambridge, MA: MIT Press.

Pleck, J. H. (1987). American fathering in historical perspective. In M. S. Kimmel (Ed.), *Changing men: New directions in research on men and masculinity* (pp. 83–97). Beverly Hills, CA: Sage.

Pleck, J. H. (1993). Are "family-supportive" employer policies relevant to men? In J. C. Hood (Ed.), *Men, work, the family* (pp. 217–237). Beverly Hills, CA: Sage.

Pollack, W. S. (1990). Men's development and psychotherapy: A psychoanalytic perspective. *Psychotherapy, 27,* 316–321.

Pruett, K. D. (1988). *The nurturant father.* New York: Warner Books.

Pruett, K. D, & Litzenberger, B. (1992). Latency development in children of primary nurturing fathers: Eight-year follow-up. *Psychoanalytic Study of the Child, 47,* 85–101.

Robertson, J. M., & Verschelden, C. (1993). Voluntary male homemakers and female providers: Reported experiences and perceived social reactions. *Journal of Men's Studies, 1,* 383–402.

Rotundo, E. A. (1987). Patriarchs and participants: A historical perspective on fatherhood in the United States. In M. Kaufman (Ed.), *Beyond patriarchy: Essays by men on pleasure, power, and change* (pp. 64–80). Toronto: Oxford University Press.

Rotundo, E. A. (1993). *American manhood: Transformations in masculinity from the revolution to the modern era.* New York: Basic Books.

Rubin, L. B. (1976). *Worlds of pain: Life in the working-class family.* New York: Basic Books.

Ruether, R. (1974). Misogynism and virginal feminism in the fathers of the church. In R. Ruether (Ed.), *Religion and sexism* (pp. 150–183). New York: Simon & Schuster.

Rytting, M. B. (1976). *Self-disclosure in the development of a heterosexual relationship.* Unpublished doctoral dissertation, Purdue University.

Scarr, S., Phillips, D., & McCartney, K. (1990). Facts, fantasies, and the future of child care in the United States. *Psychological Science, 1,* 26–35.

Shiffman, M. (1987). The men's movement: An empirical investigation. In M. S. Kimmel (Ed.), *Changing men: New directions in research on men and masculinity* (pp. 295–314). Beverly Hills, CA: Sage.

Shweder, R. A. (1994, January 9). What do men want? A reading list for the male identity crisis. *New York Times Book Review,* pp. 3, 24.

Siegel, M. (1987). Are sons and daughters treated more differently by fathers than mothers? *Developmental Review, 7,* 183–209.

Solomon, K. (1982). The masculine gender role: Description. In K. Solomon & N. Levy (Eds.), *Men in transition: Theory and therapy* (pp. 45–76). New York: Plenum.

Spain, D. (1988, November). *Women's demographic past, present, and future.* Paper presented at the Radcliffe Conference on Women in the 21st Century, Cambridge, MA.

Stacey, J. (1990). *Brave new families: Stories of domestic upheaval in late 20th-century America.* New York: Basic Books.

Staples, R. (1982). *Black masculinity: The black male's role in American society.* San Francisco: Black Scholar Press.

Strong, B., Wilson, S., Robbins, M., & Johns, T. (1981). *Human sexuality* (2nd ed.) St. Paul, MN: West.

Thompson, E., Jr., Grisanti, C., & Pleck, J. (1985). Attitudes toward the male role and their correlates. *Sex Roles, 13,* 413–427.

Thompson, L., & Walker, A. J. (1989). Women and men in marriage, work, and parenthood. *Journal of Marriage and the Family, 51,* 845–872.

Thorne, L., & Yalom, M. (1982). *Rethinking the family: Some feminist questions.* White Plains, NY: Longman.

Tschann, J. (1988). Self-disclosure in adult friendship: Gender and marital status differences. *Journal of Social and Personal Relationships, 5,* 65–81.

Unger, R. K. (1990). Imperfect reflections of reality. In R. T. Hare-Mustin & J. Marecek (Eds.), *Making a difference: Psychology and the construction of gender* (pp. 102–149). New Haven, CT: Yale University Press.

U.S. Bureau of Labor Statistics. (1991). *Labor force statistics derived from the current population survey: A databook.* Washington, DC: U.S. Government Printing Office.

U.S. Bureau of Labor Statistics. (1992). *Labor force statistics derived from the current population survey: A databook.* Washington, DC: U.S. Government Printing Office.

U.S. Department of Labor, Women's Bureau. (1991). *Facts on working women.* Washington, DC: U.S. Government Printing Office.

West, C., & Zimmerman, D. H. (1987). Doing gender. *Gender and Society, 1,* 125–151.

Wheeler, L., Reis, H., & Nezlek, J. (1983). Loneliness, social interaction, and sex roles. *Journal of Personality and Social Psychology, 45,* 943–953.

Whitehurst, C. (1977). *Women in America: The oppressed majority.* Santa Monica, CA: Goodyear.

Wilkinson, R. (1984). *American tough: The tough-guy tradition and American character.* Westport, CT: Greenwood Press.

Williams, J. (1977). *The psychology of women: Behavior in a biosocial context.* New York: Norton.

Wright, P. H., & Keple, T. W. (1981). Friends and parents of a sample of high school juniors: An exploratory study of relationship intensity and interpersonal rewards. *Journal of Marriage and the Family, 43,* 559–570.

Zedleck, S., & Mosier, K. L. (1990). Work in the family and employing organization. *American Psychologist, 45,* 240–251.

Zilbergeld, B. (1978). *Male sexuality.* Boston: Little, Brown.

Zilbergeld, B. (1992). *The new male sexuality: The truth about men, sex, and pleasure.* New York: Bantam.

CHAPTER 10

Understanding the Dark Side of Masculinity: An Interactive Systems Model

GARY R. BROOKS AND LOUISE B. SILVERSTEIN

I T IS EASIER, and riskier, than ever to write about the dark side of male behavior. After centuries of celebrating patriarchal manhood, a new gender consciousness has arisen. Feminist scholarship has written women back into history, highlighting the former marginality of women and challenging the misogyny that is deeply embedded in Western culture. This feminist challenge to "hegemonic masculinity" (Carrigan, Connell, & Lee, 1987, p. 64) and to the view of women as the "subordinate sex" (Bullough, 1974, p. 1) has made it possible to perceive more clearly the multiple problems with traditional masculine role ideals. In contrast to the point of view that celebrated traditional masculinity with concepts such as the "epic" or "chivalric" male (Doyle, 1989, p. 27), the deconstruction of masculinity proposes that men are constrained by the rigid role prescriptions implicit in the traditional male role and by patriarchal expectations for male-female relationships (Levant, 1992). From this perspective, the dark side of masculinity not only harms women but damages men's lives as well.

This critique of traditional masculinity has become so well established that some writers argue it has reached "male-bashing" proportions (Baumli, 1986; Farrell, 1987). Illustrative of this complaint were the reactions to Shere Hite's book *Women and Love* (1987) and to the film *Thelma and Louise* (1991). Although many men found these works to be simple statements of the obvious—that many women are deeply dissatisfied with men and with contemporary female-male relations—others saw them as part of a growing trend of unfairly criticizing men. Faludi (1991) asserts that sensitivity to the criticism of men has increased to the point that it now represents a "backlash" phenomenon. This reactionary men's movement, represented by the writings of

Baumli (1986), Hayward (1988), and Farrell (1987), zealously refutes most charges leveled against men. Similarly, the mythopoetic men's movement is viewed by many as encouraging misogyny (Hagan, 1992) through a call for rediscovery of the "wild man" and celebration of the "deeply masculine" (Clatterbaugh, 1990, p. 90).

Unfortunately, criticism of aspects of the traditional male role has been perceived by some as synonymous with criticism of men. Although we agree that a great deal is wrong with traditional male roles—that there is indeed a "dark side" to masculinity—this chapter is intended neither to inflame sensitivities nor to "bash" men. Instead, its purpose is to catalog and analyze the multiple shortcomings of traditional masculinity as it has been historically defined. Some manifestations of this dark side can be categorized as acts of commission—for example, violence, sexual abuse and sexual harassment, substance abuse, and self-destructive behavior. Other aspects of the dark side represent acts of omission—for example, relationship inadequacies, absent fathering, and social-emotional withdrawal.

Dark side behavior has usually been understood as the problem of a few deviant men. We call this "aberrant male" theory because it holds that there is nothing wrong with traditional masculine role socialization. Rather, dark side behavior is understood to emanate from the personality deficits of undersocialized men. We reject this theory as limited because it blames individual men rather than identifying the problems inherent in the gender socialization process itself. Although we agree that individual men must be held accountable for their behavior, we believe that the solution to dark side behavior must be found at a societal level as well as an individual one.

We will argue, in contrast, that the origins of dark side behavior are not limited to the *under*socialization of some men but rather exist to a lesser degree in the *normative* masculine role socialization of all men. By "normative masculinity" we mean the values, attitudes, and behaviors that are learned by most men during the course of their socialization within contemporary U.S. culture. The definition of normative masculinity we use is based on David and Brannon's (1976) typology: an emphasis on physical toughness and emotional stoicism, aggression, competition, achievement, and success; and an avoidance of anything feminine. Following Levant (1992; Chapter 8), this gender-informed analysis of the dark side of masculine role socialization makes a compelling case for the reconstruction of normative masculinity. This point of view has significant implications both for intervening with troubled men and for raising the next generation of boys.

This chapter begins with a discussion of the wide range of behaviors we view as dark side behavior, including various forms of violence, sexual dysfunctions, socially irresponsible behaviors, and relationship inadequacies. We then turn to the question of the etiology of these behaviors in men. We review and critique all of the theories that have been proposed to explain the dark side of masculinity. These include the "aberrant male" hypothesis, the biological hypothesis, the gender identity paradigm, the gender role strain model, and the social constructionist hypothesis. In the following section, we then examine the prospects for transforming masculinity and offer a new theoretical framework for understanding dark side behavior: the "interactive systems model" of gender role strain. This model attempts to address the cultural, social, psychological, and political variables that operate to create and maintain dark side behavior in men. The chapter concludes with specific recommendations for cultural change and for mental health practitioners in general.

Scope of the Problem

VIOLENCE

Male violence represents the darkest feature of masculinity. No other issue, however, better illustrates the culture's ambivalence about what a "real man" should be. Fasteau (1975) points out that violence can be thought of as the "crucible of masculinity"—that is, the acid test of masculinity—since moral violence in the form of war and recreational violence in the form of professional sports have long been celebrated as examples of noble manhood. Rotundo (1993) points out that, since the 19th century, American culture has considered interpersonal violence in the form of boys fighting with their peers a positive way of building youthful character.

Given that violence has been prescribed by traditional masculine norms, the extraordinary prevalence of male-on-male violence and male violence against women should not be surprising. Yet the statistics continue to be startling. A recent analysis of prevalence studies suggests that between 21% and 34% of women in this country will be physically assaulted by an intimate adult partner, while between 14% and 25% of adult women have been raped (Goodman, Koss, Fitzgerald, Russo, & Keita, 1993, p. 1055).

Male Violence Against Women in the Family

Abuse in couple relationships is not limited to physical aggression and sexual assault but includes a wide range of acts of psychological violence by husbands toward their wives, such as verbal harassment, sexual coercion, restraint of normal activities, and denial of access to resources (Browne, 1993). This discussion, however, focuses primarily on physical violence by men toward their intimate partners.

C. Everett Koop, the former surgeon general, identifies domestic violence as "the number one health problem for women in the United States, causing more injuries to women than automobile accidents, muggings, and rapes combined" (quoted in Hart, 1993, p. 18). In their summary of the prevalence of domestic violence, Harway and Hansen (1993b) report that a number of studies have indicated that one of every six wives has been hit by her husband at some point during her marriage. Relationship violence is not limited to the context of the nuclear family. In two national surveys, Straus and Gelles (1990) found that violence also occurred in 22% to 67% of dating couples.

Using probability sampling techniques, Straus and Gelles (1990) have estimated that a minimum of 2 to 3 million women are assaulted by their male partners each year in the United States. Most of the assaults involve "minor" violence (e.g., pushing, slapping, shoving, or throwing things). However, assaults take the form of severe beating in 3 out of every 100 cases (Straus & Gelles, 1990). Violence is most likely to escalate when a woman attempts to report the abuse or leave the battering relationship (Browne & Dutton, 1990).

Browne (1993) points out that figures based on these types of national surveys represent marked underestimates of the problem. Such surveys typically do not include groups of women who are especially at-risk, such as very poor women, those who do not speak English well, military families, and individuals who are hospitalized, homeless, or incarcerated. Thus, the actual figures may be two to five times higher than current estimates.

Between 50% and 70% of men who batter their wives also abuse their children and/or abduct them as a way of terrorizing their wives (Finkelhor, Hotaling, & Yllo, 1988). Batterers also destroy family belongings and property. Although accurate data are not available, battered women seeking shelter in programs report that property destruction averages $10,000 per perpetrator (Hart, 1993).

Rape and Sexual Assault

Kaplan, O'Neil, and Owen (1993) characterize sexual assault of women as a critical problem in contemporary U.S. society. They report that research studies vary widely in their estimates of the prevalence of rape, but that somewhere between 5% and 44% of women are raped at some point in their lives. A similar range is found in estimates of the prevalence of assault on college campuses, from a low of 15% to a high of 78% (Kaplan, O'Neil, & Owen, 1993).

Koss (1993) reports that the Uniform Crime Reports, a compilation of crimes reported to local authorities, found that 102,555 crimes qualified as rapes in 1990. However, she notes that national samples of adolescents, college women, and adult women suggest that rape incidence is 6 to 15 times higher than reported.

Most sexual assault of women is committed by their intimate male partners. Using a random sample of 930 women, Russell (1982) found that 14% of ever-married women report being raped by a husband or ex-husband. This figure is more than twice that for assaults by strangers. Rape and sexual assault are more common in relationships in which other forms of physical aggression are ongoing (Browne, 1993). Violent episodes seem to include sexual as well as nonsexual physical attacks.

In a recent study of the sexual behavior of 518 college men, 34% reported that they had engaged women in unwanted sexual contact (kissing and fondling), 20% reported that they had attempted unwanted intercourse, and 10% reported that they had completed unwanted intercourse (Ward, Chapman, Cohn, & Williams, 1991). Similar findings were reflected in a study of 196 college men (Kaplan et al., 1993). Of the sample of primarily white, Catholic, suburban men, 49% reported that, since the age of 14, they had engaged in some form of sexual aggression toward women. Despite the fact that 54% of the men had attended a rape awareness workshop, 30% reported sexually aggressive behavior in the past year, while 16% reported at least one incident of the more serious forms of sexual assault (attempted rape, coercive intercourse, or rape) in the past year. Although only 2.5% of the young men viewed themselves as "very likely to rape," 46% reported that they were somewhat likely to force sex if they did not get caught or punished. These data on the likelihood of forcing sex are comparable to data reported in earlier studies (Briere & Malamuth, 1983; Malamuth, 1981).

Sexual Harassment: Male Violence Against Women in the Workplace

The definition of sexual harassment as violent behavior is not generally accepted within popular culture. Cultural beliefs about sexual harassment parallel earlier beliefs about rape and domestic violence. Within popular culture, women have traditionally been seen as overstating the problem and provoking the behaviors. Fitzgerald (1993), in contrast, argues that sexual harassment should be considered a form of violence against women because, like rape and domestic violence, it functions as a form of social control. Just as women who go to bars are viewed as "asking for" rape, and women who argue with their partners or refuse to perform certain household duties are thought to be "asking for" physical violence at home, so women who choose to enter formally male-dominated professions are thought to be "asking for" harassment (p. 1072).

Although the majority of incidents of harassment involve intrusive, unwanted, and coercive sexual attention, harassing behavior often is expressed as rape or sexual assault. Fitzgerald cites government reports estimating that approximately 12,000 female federal workers were victims of rape or attempted rape by supervisors or coworkers in a two-year period alone (p. 1071). These experiences often continue for an extended period of time, that is, for six months or longer. Large-scale surveys of working women suggest that one of every two women will be harassed at some point during her academic or working life. Studies suggest that rates are highest in workplace environments where women have traditionally been underrepresented.

SEXUAL EXCESS

Amid the many criticisms of male behavior are growing questions about the most fundamental aspects of male sexuality. At one time, sex manuals commonly portrayed male-female sexual problems as the outgrowth of women's "frigidity" or the resulted of Victorian sexual repression. More recently, attention has been given to problems in male sexual socialization. Zilbergeld (1983) attacked the "myth" that "female sexuality is complex, mysterious, and full of problems, while male sexuality is simple, straightforward, and problem-free" (p. 1). For Solomon (1982), sexual dysfunction is one of the six defining features of masculinity.

In the public sphere, men's sexual behavior has become notorious over the past decade. The behavior of leading public figures, such as Gary Hart, Wilbur Mills, Jimmy Swaggert, Paul Rubens (Pee Wee Herman), Robert Packwood, Mike Tyson, Clarence Thomas, Woody Allen, and Bill Clinton, has provoked questions about their sexual (mis)conduct. The public exposure of the sexual behavior of these men has frequently inspired other men to distance themselves as far as possible from association with the miscreants. The distancers have more or less claimed that the men under fire are qualitatively different and deviant. Illustration of this righteous distancing was provided by Sen. Orin Hatch during the Senate hearings investigating Anita Hill's allegations of sexual harassment by Clarence Thomas. Hatch argued that Clarence Thomas was not capable of engaging in the acts attributed to him because such acts were performed only by a small number of deviant men. Subsequently, however, serious questions about the claim that male sexual harassment is a rare exception to a more honorable code were raised by the U.S. Navy's Tailhook scandal. This incident involved complaints by 80 women of sexual assault by their fellow officers. Thus, the country was presented with a picture of male sexual misconduct as a group norm, rather than as isolated behaviors confined to a few aberrant men.

Promiscuity

The cultural ideology of manhood has assumed that men's sexuality has a significant dark side in that men have been viewed by moral and biological conservatives as ruled by sexual urges. Although for a while women were considered more sexually motivated than men (see Doyle, 1989, p. 31, on the "spiritual male"), a preoccupation with sexual impulses has generally been seen as men's "nature" and sometimes as their "downfall." The moral conservative position is that sexual promiscuity is an inherent feature of male functioning. Gilder (1973) stated that "the crucial process of civilization is the subordination of male sexual impulses and psychology to long term horizons of female biology.... It is male behavior that must be changed to create a civilized order" (p. 24). A similar theme has been expressed by some sociobiologists who claim that male primates are biologically programmed to seek many sexual partners as an evolutionary strategy for ensuring their success in projecting their genes into succeeding generations (Trivers, 1972).

Social constructionists have raised persuasive arguments against the neoconservative and sociobiological position (see, for example, Silverstein's [1993] critique). However, popular culture still accepts the myth of a biological basis for male promiscuity. Social constructionists, in contrast, have argued that it is male sexual *socialization* that sets the stage for men's casual, or "nonrelational," view of sexuality (Goldberg, 1983; Gross, 1978; Levant, 1992; Zilbergeld, 1992). According to this conceptualization, young males are given the message that sexual activity is a way to validate one's masculinity. An integral feature of this masculinity validation is the presentation of sexual behavior as a contest with women in which men use a variety of means to obtain intercourse while women are expected to resist. Sexual activity thereby becomes a form of "conquest" and evidence of masculine prowess. Greater masculinity is bestowed upon young males who have frequent sex with multiple partners and with minimal regard for intimacy, tenderness, or compassion. This socialization norm is illustrated by the commonly heard adolescent male dictate—"Find 'em, feel 'em, fuck 'em, forget 'em."

Whether promiscuity is viewed as an inevitable aspect of male behavior or as a product of traditional male role socialization, the picture is relatively clear—within patriarchal cultures, men are far more likely than women to engage in casual or nonrelational sex. In reporting on gender differences in sexuality, Shibley Hyde (1993) identifies attitudes toward casual sexual activity as a principle difference between men and women. The data on the sexual activity of heterosexual men and women outside of marriage also support this contention. Men and women are both sexually active outside of marriage, but men are far more likely to report their sexual activities as "solely physical" in nature. Men have many more outside partners, but "what they do not have are many emotional attachments" (Blumstein & Schwartz, 1983, p. 279).

For gay men, the integration of sexuality and intimacy is particularly challenging because of the societal stigmatization of homosexuality. Hetrick & Martin (1984) pointed out that, unlike other minority groups, homosexual youth cannot rely on their families to prepare them to assume a social identity. Jewish families can warn their children about the prevalence of anti-Semitism and suggest strategies for dealing with it. Similarly, black families can prepare their children for dealing with racism and provide corrective experiences for building a positive identity as a person of color.

Gay adolescents, in contrast, usually have no family support for dealing with the homophobia that is endemic in patriarchal society. In fact, their families often share that homophobia. Thus, gay adolescents do not have the family and social support framework for building either a personal or social identity. In terms of sexual behaviors, they have few opportunities to learn the management of sexuality in a positive manner. Nongay adolescents have role models and direct instruction in courtship procedures and the social responsibilities associated with sexuality. In addition, nongay youth have many different community-based contexts for making nonsexual social contacts and forming relationships with members of both sexes. In contrast, gay adolescents are forced to rely almost exclusively on the sexualized context of gay bars. Because of the absence of social and sexual support systems, sexual activity is often the only means available for making social contact.

This problem is further intensified for gay male adolescents by the heterosexism of patriarchal culture, which socializes them as heterosexual men. They have often internalized the male gender norms of avoiding intimacy and proving their "masculinity" through many sexual conquests. Thus, gay men have historically exhibited the same sexually promiscuous and nonrelational sexuality of heterosexual men.

Pornography

Use of pornography is a "male" activity that has been described as "the largest entertainment industry in America" (Gaylor, 1985). The pornography industry grosses more than $10 billion per year; 6 of the 10 best-selling magazines are "male entertainment" publications; there are four times as many "sex emporiums" as McDonald's franchises (Gaylor, 1985). Feminist critics have recently taken on the pornography industry, arguing that it teaches males to denigrate and debase women and sets the stage for interpersonal sexual violence (Dworkin, 1985; MacKinnon, 1985). Particularly impressive in this regard has been the research of Donnerstein and Linz (1987), which demonstrated that regular viewing of violent pornography desensitizes men to violence against women and decreases compassion for rape victims. Although Donnerstein and Linz were most critical of "aggressive" pornography (porn-ography that includes images of violence against women), others have criticized *all* pornography. Many attack the way pornography objectifies women (Russell & Lederer, 1980) and perpetuates misogyny (LaBelle, 1980). More recently, attention has been given to the highly adverse effects on men of this major source of sexual misinformation and distorted interpersonal values (Fracher & Kimmel, 1987; Moye, 1985; Segal, 1990; Zilbergeld, 1992).

Sexual Addiction

Carnes (1983) described what he viewed as an extreme variant of male preoccupation with sexual experiences—sexual addiction. The core of Carnes's work is an effort to apply an addiction model to the topic of sexuality, suggesting that a sexual addict is someone who has a pathological relationship with sexuality that is both unduly central to well-being and mood-altering. Carnes posits a four-stage addiction cycle that includes "preoccupation, ritualization, compulsive sexual behavior, and despair" (p. 9).

Carnes's ideas about sexual addiction are not presented here as scientifically validated concepts free of significant conceptual flaws. They are noted because they seem to represent one of the few attempts to acknowledge the pathological aspects of extreme sexual preoccupation. That is, Carnes raises important questions about the common sexual socialization message given to men that there are no limits to the benefits of sexuality. In this vein, Carnes extends the notion of male sexual preoccupation carried to extremes, as in the "Don Juan Complex" (Wagenvoord & Bailey, 1978), and may offer a new perspective on the penalties of the "Playboy Philosophy," which has been commonly offered to males as a model of healthy sexuality (Lederer, 1980).

SOCIALLY IRRESPONSIBLE BEHAVIORS

Alcoholism

Alcoholism has long been one of the most problematic issues of public health policy. Alcohol abusers occupy up to one-half of all hospital beds in America at any given time (Robertson, 1988) and attempt suicide at rates 75 to 300 times those of nonabusers (Berglund, 1984). Alcoholism has been linked to higher rates of automobile accidents, a range of physical diseases, violent crime, absenteeism in the workplace, and shortened life span (Calahan, 1978). A national study on mental health concluded that 19.2% of Americans will suffer from alcohol or drug abuse during their lifetimes (*Time*, 1984). Nationwide, drunk driving accounts for approximately 25,000 deaths per year; an additional 500,000 suffer from alcohol-related accidents, costing in excess of $10 billion (*New York Times*, 1989). Of late, there has been increased concern about the role of alcohol use in boating and airplane fatalities—between 5% and 10% of airplane pilots have alcohol in their blood while flying (Stephenson, 1991).

Alcoholism and masculinity seem to go hand in hand. Although exact figures vary, all studies indicate that men are far more likely than women to abuse alcohol. Conservative estimates suggest that men are twice as likely to experience alcohol problems (Calahan, 1978), while other authors cite a rate of four or five alcoholic men for each woman who abuses alcohol (Grant, Harford, Hasin, Chou, & Pickering, 1992; Cooper, Russell, Skinner,

Frone, & Mudar, 1992). Other prevalence data indicate that while only 1 in 50 women becomes an alcoholic, 1 in 10 men does (Heilman, 1973). Despite efforts to implicate biological factors in etiology, most researchers see alcohol abuse as a product of differential gender socialization—that is, drinking is more compatible with the male gender role (Grant et al., 1992; Cooper et al., 1992).

Drug Abuse

Drug addiction, in the form of using illicit drugs, is commonly viewed as one of the most pressing contemporary social problems. It is estimated that over 6 million Americans are either selling or using drugs and that one in every five inner-city babies is born addicted to drugs (Stephenson, 1991). The "War on Drugs" has attracted an increasing percentage of law enforcement resources, while the courts have become backlogged with drug-related cases (one-fourth to one-half of all cases). The health care system is braced for dramatic increases in the number of AIDS patients, increasingly afflicted as the result of drug-related behaviors.

Like alcohol abuse, illicit drug addiction is largely a "male" problem. "Although addiction does not discriminate against women, it does seem to be a disease that is closely associated with men" (Diamond, 1987, p. 333). According to Department of Justice figures, over 85% of drug offenders are male (Stephenson, 1991).

HIGH-RISK BEHAVIORS: ADOLESCENT MALE ACTING-OUT AND RISK-TAKING

While adolescent girls are likely to internalize distress and experience higher rates of depression, adolescent males externalize distress through a wide range of acting-out behaviors (Nolen-Hoeksema, 1990; Peterson, Compas, Brooks-Gunn, Stemmler, Ey, & Grant, 1993). In a large-scale study of Minnesota adolescents, Harris, Blum, and Resnick (1991) found that a higher percentage of teenage boys reported frequent antisocial acts (e.g., vandalism, assaultive behavior, shoplifting) than did teenage girls. More than 10% of junior high school boys, but only 6% of same-age girls, reported committing at least one antisocial act in the past year.

Harris et al. (1991) indicated that the gender-related trends they found in antisocial acting-out were also reflected in the data on substance abuse and risk-taking behavior. Nearly twice as many high school boys (29%) as girls (13%) reported heavy drinking on a relatively frequent basis. Similarly, adolescent males were at greater risk for injury or death from automobile or motorcycle accidents. They were also far more likely to sustain head injuries from engaging in high-risk behaviors, such as diving into shallow bodies of water. Although teenage girls attempt suicide at least three times as often as boys do, boys use more lethal methods and die approximately four times more frequently (Garland & Zigler, 1993).

Data on gay male and lesbian adolescents has not yet been well integrated into mainstream psychological research. Thus, the actual prevalence of depression, risk-taking behaviors, and suicide among this population is difficult to determine. Hetrick and Martin (1988) pointed out that the social stigma society places on homosexuality has a particularly devastating effect on the intrapsychic development of personal identity in gay adolescents. These authors argue that the homophobia explicit in patriarchal societies is internalized by gay adolescents and contributes to self-loathing, dissociation, and a negative self-concept. Depressive symptomatology and high rates of suicide and high-risk behaviors, particularly the practice of unsafe sex with multiple partners, are the consequences of this internalization of society's stigmatization of homosexuality (Dworkin & Gutierrez, 1992). Hetrick and Martin (1988) report that 25% to 30% of gay adolescents have attempted suicide at least once.

Antisocial and risk-taking behavior also varies by race, class, and ethnic group. Black males have higher rates than white males of mental disorders, injuries, accidents, mortality, morbidity, AIDS, homicide and suicide, drug and alcohol abuse, criminal behavior, and imprisonment (Majors & Billson, 1992). Assaultive violence—that is, nonfatal and fatal interpersonal violence—occurs more frequently to young Latino and African-American men than to young white men (Hammond & Yung, 1993). The incidence of fatal violence for young Latino men has been reported to be approximately three to four times greater than that for white men. Similarly, the 1988 mortality rates for men between the ages of 15 and 24 show that African-American men are homicide victims at an annual rate of 101.8 per 100,000, compared with 11.5 for white men of the same age (Hammond & Yung, 1993, p. 143). Majors and Billson (1992) report that although the highest suicide rate (20 per 100,000) is reported for white males, suicide for black males has increased in recent years (11.6 per 100,000) and is now the third leading cause of death among 18- to 29-year-olds.

Adult Male Physical Self-abuse

Men die 7 to 10 years sooner than women (Hazzard, 1989; Verbrugge, 1985; Waldron, 1983). Although numerous explanations have been given for this, including biological inferiority (Madigan, 1957; Montagu, 1974) and greater environmental risk (Retherford, 1975), the most compelling case has been made for psychosocial factors. Waldron (1976) estimated that three-fourths of the difference in life expectancy between women and men can be accounted for by gender-related behaviors. Of particular interest here is the fact that men generally take very poor care of themselves. Not only are they more likely to abuse alcohol, to smoke, and to expose themselves to far higher rates of accidental injury (Harrison, Chin, & Ficcarrotto, 1989), but they also are less likely to perform routine preventative health behaviors (Nathanson, 1977). Perhaps because of men's discomfort with the passive and dependent aspects of the patient role, they ignore warning signs of illness and avoid needed bed rest when sick (Skord & Schumacher, 1982). Many men's studies writers seem to agree with the statement of Harrison et al. (1989) that "the male sex-role may be hazardous to your health" (p. 296).

Heart disease, cancer, and cerebrovascular disease are among the most deadly afflictions for black men. Black men die at a higher rate than white men from such causes as hypertension, cirrhosis of the liver, and lung disease. These health problems are exacerbated by the fact that African-American men, like most men, rarely visit doctors or follow treatment recommendations. Majors and Billson (1992) assert that young black men's seemingly indifferent management of health issues is further complicated by high-stress jobs, poor nutrition, lack of education, and substance abuse.

Absent Fathering

Emotionally uninvolved and physically absent fathers are now seen as representative of another aspect of the dark side of masculinity. Before industrialization, when work was intertwined with family life, fathers interacted closely with their children, training boys, and sometimes girls, in work skills (Pleck, 1987; Stearns, 1991). Fathers were usually responsible for discipline and for imparting religious and moral traditions. Since the late 19th century, in contrast, mothers have come to be regarded as the primary parent.

The transformation of parenthood into motherhood occurred at the moment when industrialization separated the location of paid work from the household. Thus, fathering, a role for men within the family, became defined as something that occurred outside the family. This limitation of fathering to the provision of material resources has had dramatically negative consequences for men's relationships with their children.

For poor, ethnic minority men, racial discrimination in the arena of paid work leads to high rates of unemployment or underemployment. These men are thus unable to fulfill the traditional role of provider. For them, the definition of fathering often does not extend beyond procreation. Thus, they have little or no contact with their children. Working- and middle-class fathers who define their fathering role in terms of providing financial security to the family often become preoccupied with work. As a consequence, these men often have little intimate contact with their children.

One study reported that, on average, men living with their families spend 12 minutes a day with their children (Lamb, 1987). Gottfried and Gottfried (1988) found that fathers spent, on average, 26 minutes per day in direct interaction with children below the age of six. As children got older, that time period decreased to 16 minutes per day. U.S. data suggest that fathers tend to spend more time with younger children and more time with sons.

Although the publicity given to minority fathers creates an image of ethnic differences in fathering behavior, data suggest that nonpayment of child support by white, middle-class fathers parallels the lack of paternal investment of poor, minority fathers. In 1985, although close to 90% of custodial mothers were awarded child support, only 54% received any money at all. The exception to this trend is among fathers earning more than $50,000 annually. Among these fathers who excel at the provider role, 90% do comply with child support orders (Okin, 1989).

Homelessness, Vagrancy, and Dropping Out

Not all men participate in the dominant cultural institutions of work and family life. Those who remain outside these social structures pose a challenge to mainstream culture. Many of these nonparticipants are dismissed as asocial or antisocial, and many of their problems are relegated to the criminal justice system. (Department of Justice figures indicate that seven of eight "vagrants" are male.) Recently, there seems to be a somewhat more compassionate tone to the discussions of this issue. For example, the term "homeless" has become more popular than earlier pejorative terms such as "bums" or "vagrants." Although this trend may reflect more positive attitudes toward "dropout" men, it may be no more than a response to the recent increase of women and children in the homeless population.

Marin (1991), for example, argues that sympathy for the homeless is generally reserved for the "innocent victims"—women and children. Although more than 70% of the homeless population is male (Wright, 1989), a recent issue of *American Psychologist* (American Psychological Association, 1991) devoted several chapters to the special problems of homeless women and children. In contrast, none of the special problems of homeless men were discussed. Perhaps this perspective is informed by the long-standing tradition of viewing the unattached male as a romantic figure—the hobo or the dropout. Nevertheless, it may also arise from a general lack of compassion for a population of men who are poorly understood.

To date, the psychological community has not examined how male socialization may contribute to the problem of men's social alienation and familial estrangement or abandonment. Clearly, alcohol plays a role; a large percentage of this population abuses alcohol. However, other aspects of the male role—poor control of violent impulses, emotional inexpressiveness, difficulties seeking help, and preoccupation with work rather than family roles—may have some etiologic culpability. A man may be more likely to leave his family if he cannot fulfill the provider role.

RELATIONSHIP DYSFUNCTIONS

Thus far, we have enumerated dark side behaviors that are negative by-products of the traditional male role. However, more recent critiques of masculinity have gone beyond complaints about the fact that men have not changed to focus on that that they have not changed *enough.*

Inadequate Emotional Partners

Criticism of the dark side of masculinity has moved beyond outcries against some men's extreme acts of violence to encompass a broader range of shortcomings that seem to be present in most men. The most common complaint reflects dissatisfaction with how men behave in intimate relationships. As women have become more empowered in instrumental roles (formerly the domain of men), they have expected men to make complementary advances in relationship-maintenance roles (traditionally the domain of women). Men's shortcomings as nurturers and emotional communicators are increasingly identified as sources of distress. The newest dark side of masculinity may be "inadequate partnering."

A prime example of relationship inadequacy has been men's continued attachment to male-dominant relationship models and their resistance to more egalitarian models. Women have increasingly taken on breadwinner roles and have grown impatient with men who continue to expect to exercise power and privilege within a relationship context. Blumstein and Schwartz (1983) noted that couples are more satisfied when at least one partner is "relationship-centered." Women, who are typically expected to perform that role, have needed men to function more in that capacity, but men have not responded well. The controversial research of Hite (1987) illustrated the depth of women's dissatisfaction. She reported that her survey of women found 98% of respondents wanting more verbal closeness from their male partners, and 95% reporting emotional and psychological harassment from their partners. Although many have criticized Hite's research methodology, most have acknowledged that her work "struck a nerve . . . reflecting some important changes in women's attitudes toward heterosexual relationships" (*Family Therapy Networker,* 1988, pp. 14–15).

Non-nurturing Fathers

In the last two decades, new cultural expectations have created the "modern father" role, which includes caretaking and nurturing as well as providing resources. This new definition of fathering places far greater emphasis on how well a man attends to the emotional needs of his children. Men's capacity for nurturing has been well documented (Hewlett, 1987; Lamb,

1987; Pollack, 1990; Silverstein, 1993) Articles in the popular press have suggested that a dramatic change has occurred in fathering behavior. Supposedly, the "new father," or the "nurturant father," has become the mainstay of the nontraditional, or role-sharing family in Western industrialized countries. Unfortunately, the available data suggest that the changes are not yet of dramatic proportions. LaRossa (1989) distinguished between the "culture" (changing norms) and the "conduct" (what is actually done) of fatherhood, noting that the latter has been far slower to change than the former.

Fathers are now routinely present during childbirth, whereas they were excluded from the delivery room just 30 years ago (Hewlett, 1992). This is not an insignificant change. Many fathers report that the emotional bonding achieved in the first hours with their infants substantially affects their self-evaluations as fathers and as men (Cowan, 1988; Osherson, 1986). However, there is considerable scholarly debate about how much this subjective experience has been translated into specific behavioral changes after the mother returns home from the hospital.

Conclusions vary depending on the research methods used to collect the data. If a study relies on self-report data from the fathers, his participation in child care tends to be overstated. If mothers' reports are used, role-sharing behavior is only slightly overstated. If observational data measures are used by independent raters, the data suggest that the proportional relation between the work done by mothers and fathers has changed very little over the past 20 years. Although fathers do more in the 1990s than they did in the 1970s, mothers have also increased their workload. Thus, mothers generally do two thirds of the total amount of housework and child care, while fathers shoulder only one-third of the burden (Googins, personal communication, May 14, 1993; Hochschild, 1989).

Many explanations have been offered to account for the disparity between the culture and the conduct of fatherhood. Bronstein and Cowan (1988) suggested that many mothers are ambivalent about sharing parenting roles and subtly make paternal involvement more difficult. Levant and Kelley (1989) saw the problem as men's lack of preparation for the fathering role and called for training to remediate fathering skills deficits. Scanzoni (1982) and Bernard (1981) suggested that men have been reluctant to give up the privilege of being cared for and to assume the responsibility of giving care. Kiselica, Stroud, Stroud, and Rotzien (1992) and Silverstein (1993) implicate legal, social, and institutional resistance and call for public policy supports for men to encourage their greater involvement with their children.

Nonparticipative Household Partners

In addition to the unequal responsibility that mothers and fathers assume for child care, numerous studies have documented the continuing lack of equity between husbands and wives when it comes to household chores. Although husbands' contributions to household maintenance have increased over the 20 twenty years, wives continue to work between 13 hours (Douthitt, 1989) and 17 hours (Googins, 1993) more per week at home chores and child care than do their husbands. In a study of 50 couples, Hochschild (1989) reported that unequal responsibility for household tasks was the most frequent source of marital conflict. The question of unequal responsibility for household management is a complex and controversial area of research that is addressed more fully in Chapter 9 of this volume.

The Etiology of Dark Side Behaviors

We turn now to an examination of the possible causes of dark side behavior in men. Several hypotheses as to the etiology of these behaviors have been presented in the literature. We review five explanations for dark side behavior: the "aberrant male" hypothesis, the biological hypothesis, the psycho-social-developmental hypothesis (or gender role identity paradigm), the men's studies perspective (or gender role strain/conflict paradigm), and the social construction hypothesis. Each of these hypotheses will be reviewed and critiqued. Because of the continuing dialogue within the field of men's studies between the proponents of the identity and strain paradigms, we devote most of our discussion to these two contrasting explanations for dark side behavior. An integration of several of these perspectives into a new explanatory paradigm will then be presented.

THE "ABERRANT MALE" HYPOTHESIS

There seems to be no shortage of "ugly" men—violent men, sexually abusive men, male chauvinist pigs, substance-abusing men, socially irresponsible men, and interpersonally dysfunctional men. Many recent authors have focused on what they view as the forlorn state of contemporary manhood. Ehrenreich (1983) cataloged the negative aspects of the male gender and argued that, rather than changing for the better, modern men are changing only superficially or in negative ways. This negative opinion of men is well represented in popular books such as *The Peter Pan Syndrome* (Kiley, 1983), *Women Who Love Too Much* (Norwood, 1985), and *Men Are Just Desserts* (Friedman, 1983). These books are representative of a genre popular in the past decade—books that appeal to women who are unhappy about men. This pessimistic view may be best illustrated by *Men Are Not Cost-effective* (Stephenson, 1991) and *Refusing to Be a Man* (Stoltenberg, 1989). The former, an exhaustive cataloging of the damage done to society by men, recommends "nothing short of men repaying for their own criminal gender. Men must pay for being men" (p. 451). The latter takes one of the most radical stances, arguing that the entire construction of masculinity is unethical and that equality will only be possible when men refuse to identify with traditional masculine values.

Men seem to have had a range of reactions to the past decade's wave of criticism of them and their behavior. Denial and backlash have been common. Some men have adopted the position that critics' charges are grossly exaggerated and that men are being victimized by an organized cadre of male-hating feminist sympathizers (Doyle, 1976; Farrell, 1993; Haddad, 1985; Limbaugh, 1992). Although these arguments strike many as outrageous and absurd, at least they are straightforward and open to direct refutation. More subtle is another argument that disguises the problems and deflects responsibility—the "few bad apples" or "aberrant male" postulate. Those arguing from this point of view acknowledge the offensive acts of men and often urge punishment for the offenders. To paraphrase their position—"Yes, there are some sick and evil men, who abuse women (power, drugs, alcohol, pornography, etc.), but these men are a distinct minority. Most men are fundamentally decent."

An excellent illustration of this point of view is found in the literature on men's violence and on the sexual exploitation of female patients by male psychotherapists. In both areas, the primary emphasis is placed on identifying, punishing, and quarantining the offending males, with considerably less emphasis placed on rehabilitation. Far too absent in this literature is discussion of how violence and sexual exploitation are, to some extent, normative for all men. For example, Wright (1985) argued that sexual intimacy between male therapists and female clients is a relatively insignificant issue for most men and is primarily a problem of "life context of the therapist" and "the character structure of the therapist" (p. 115). This point of view does not acknowledge that all men who are socialized within a patriarchal cultural milieu are given mixed messages on these matters. There may be important differences between men who violate an ethical boundary and those who do not. However, no assumption should be made that men who do not commit the overt offenses are untouched by the issues.

Brooks (1990, 1992) argues that the study of violence and sexual exploitation must include an examination of the conflicting cultural messages routinely given to men about these issues. The principle thesis is that men who are violent or sexually exploitative are not necessarily *under*socialized but perhaps are *over*socialized. Men who are not violent, or who do not sexually exploit, may refrain from these behaviors *in spite of* normative male socialization. Brooks proposes that, rather than focusing exclusively on a few men labeled "aberrant," mental health experts should look at the ways in which *all* men are socialized toward this offensive behavior.

THE BIOLOGICAL HYPOTHESIS

If we reject the idea that most male dark side behavior is attributable to a few deviant, aberrant, or morally inferior men, then we are left with the task of explaining how men come to act in such offensive ways. The biological perspective has argued that testosterone generates a tendency in males of all species to exhibit dark side behavior. A typical example of this point of view is a discussion of nonhuman primate behavior that was recently published in a prominent family therapy journal (Kraemer, 1991). We believe that this theoretical perspective is based on an outdated (mis)understanding of non-human primate behavior.

Over the past two decades, primate research, like almost all areas of academic research, has undergone a feminist revision. Haraway (1989) has pointed out that the first 20 years of primate field research (from 1955 to 1975) reflected a white, male, capitalist bias. The theoretical perspective that emerged from this context suggested several generalizations about primate behavior: Primate males are more aggressive than females; males dominate females; males have short-term bonds with sexually receptive females; and males are uninvolved with infants. With the entrance of large numbers of women into primatology in the 1980s, several new observations about primate behavior have emerged. These include: Female influence is at least as important as male dominance; long-term affiliative, as well as short-term sexual, relationships exist between males and females; and the amount of male involvement with infants varies (Haraway, 1989).

The feminist revision of primate theory has now become generally accepted as mainstream research within the discipline of primatology. However, it has not yet been integrated into social science thinking about nonhuman and human primate behavior (Silverstein, 1993). This new theoretical consensus proposes that behavioral differences between male and female primates previously thought to be based primarily on genetic variables are now thought to vary depending on a complex interaction between genetic, demographic, ecological, and social variables. When comparisons are made across many primate species, the male and female potential for sex, aggression, and parental involvement has been shown to overlap considerably (Smuts, Cheney, Seyfarth, Wrangham, & Struhsaker, 1987). Thus, the biological hypothesis that differing levels of testosterone in males generate high levels of aggression and sexual promiscuity has not been supported by more recent interpretations of nonhuman primate behavior.

THE PSYCHOSOCIAL-DEVELOPMENTAL HYPOTHESIS: THE GENDER ROLE IDENTITY PARADIGM

This theoretical model posits the existence of an intrapsychic structure called a "gender role identity." The development of a coherent and consistent gender role identity is seen as necessary for healthy psychological integration. The fact that boys are raised primarily by their mothers (i.e., by an opposite-sex parent) with little emotional connection to their fathers (i.e., to the same-sex parent) is thought to generate a conflictual gender role identity in men. Within this theoretical framework, male dark side behavior, particularly negative attitudes and behaviors toward women, originates because of the inherently problematic nature of male gender role identity.

We present the theories of Chodorow (1978, 1987, 1989), Fast (1984), and Pollack (1992a, 1992b) in order to provide a detailed description of the assumptions embedded within the identity paradigm. We then discuss the aspects of the paradigm that we find most problematic.

Chodorow's Theory of Gender Identity Development

Chodorow based her theory of gender identity development on psychoanalytic object relations theory (Mahler, Pine, & Bergman, 1978). This theory proposed that all infants form a primary attachment to their mother. This attachment involved a prolonged psychic merging with her that is then followed by a progression toward psychological separation from her.

Chodorow (1978) speculated that, because boys are male, mothers experience them as different and tend to "push them out of the pre-oedipal relationship" (p. 166). Similarly, she proposed that, when a boy realizes he is a different biological sex than his mother, he is forced to give up his attachment to her in an effort to establish a gender identity that is consistent with his biological sex. As a boy proceeds through the separation process, his sense of himself as masculine is threatened by his original identification with his mother.

Chodorow (1978) hypothesized that because fathers are usually emotionally and/or physically absent from the emotional life of the family, most boys do not have an actual *person* with whom to identify but rather must develop a *"positional* identification with aspects of the masculine role" (p. 175). Because only women mother, boys are deprived of a personal identification process that integrates "positive affective processes and role learning" (p. 175).

We see Chodorow's theory as a clear statement of the identity paradigm, since it proposes that a boy's intrinsic sense of maleness is threatened by the organization of the traditional nuclear family: he must identify with a female attachment figure and is deprived of a male with whom to identify. Pleck (1981; Chapter 1) has proposed that this is the core argument of the identity model.

Interestingly, Chodorow's theory has not been consistently interpreted as reflecting the identity model. It is true that her critique (1978, pp. 165–166) rejected Freud's (1905) teleological assumption that women's biology creates primary parenting as their destiny. However, as we read Chodorow, she did not reject the identity model altogether. Rather, she replaced the Oedipal model (which focuses on the conflictual nature of *women's* development) with a pre-Oedipal, object relations model of gender identity development (which emphasizes the problematic nature of *men's* development).

Instead, Chodorow's theory has been associated with the social constructionist hypothesis. These differences of opinion about Chodorow's thinking may arise because her theory actually includes two contrasting components: one addressing the social construction of gender *roles*, and another discussing the process of gender *identity* formation.

In our view, Chodorow's major contribution has been to deepen our understanding of the social construction of gender *roles*. Chodorow integrated Parsons's analysis of the public-private split in postindustrialized society into a theory about gender role socialization. Parsons (1964) pointed out that the sexual division of labor within the postindustrial nuclear family relegates women to the private realm of the family, while limiting men to the public world of work. Chodorow expanded Parsons's observation by underlining the fact that this sexual division of labor in parenting is based on the needs of production in a capitalist economy, not on biological differences between the sexes. Chodorow's unique contribution has been to identify how this public-private split generates differences in gender *role* expectations and, by extension, psychological and behavioral differences in men and women. However, Chodorow herself explicitly rejected role training as a hypothesis for understanding gender differences (1978, pp. 30–35).

Fast's Concept of Gender Identity

Fast (1984, pp. 12–16), like Chodorow, was interested in revising Freudian theory about women's psychological development. Freud's (1905) view was that, originally, all children assume that all people are male. Therefore when children become aware of sex differences, girls experience themselves as incomplete, whereas boys simply confirm a sense of their maleness. Fast proposed that, prior to age three, both boys and girls assume that all people are the same and that all sexual possibilities are open to them. Somewhere between ages three and four, children discover sex differences and realize that their own experience is limited. Boys realize that they will not be able to have a baby, and girls realize that they will not be able to have a penis. This recognition of limits then triggers a sense of loss and deprivation in both boys and girls.

Fast thus described a child's gender identity development as proceeding from an overinclusive self-representation, wherein all sexual and gender possibilities are open to them, to a more differentiated sense of self, wherein sex and gender are experienced as limited. She defined gender identity as a matrix within which the developing child renunciates "early gender-indiscriminate self representations and identifications now found to be physically impossible or gender-inappropriate (to grow a baby in one's body, to have a penis, to be physically active, to be tender)" (p. 12). Fast proposed the establishment of a coherent and consistent core gender identity as a necessary component of psychological health. Within the identity paradigm, "when sex differences become salient, the girl and the boy become aware that attributes [previously] included in their developing self structures cannot or *must* not in fact be theirs" (p. 13; our emphasis). The problematic nature of failing to distinguish between *socialized characteristics,* such as activity level and tenderness, and *biological attributes,* such as the ability to have a baby or a penis, is discussed below in our critique of the identity paradigm.

Pollack's Theory of Developmental Trauma for Boys

Pollack (1990, 1992a, 1992b) has expanded Chodorow's theory about gender identity development in boys. In agreement with Chodorow, Pollack proposes that the realization that he is a different sex from his mother catapults a little boy into a sense of psychological separateness from her. Building on Fast's proposal that this understanding is achieved at about age three, Pollack (1992a) examines the consequences of that realization for the small boy.

Pollack (1992a) points out that a three-year-old is not developmentally mature enough to give up the intense attachment he has for his mother, especially because she has probably been his primary, perhaps even his only, attachment figure, given the structure of family life in patriarchal culture. Pollack (1992b) suggests that the need to separate from mother at such an early age may result in "a 'traumatic disruption' of the boy's early holding environment" (p. 13). He further proposes that this premature separation from mother is the cause of a "normative (gender-linked) developmental trauma" (1992b, p. 13) within the normal course of gender identity formation for boys.

To summarize, Chodorow and Pollack base their theoretical formulations about gender role identity in boys on the formation of a core gender identity. They see this core gender identity as inherently conflictual because of the little boy's primary intrapsychic identification with a female attachment figure. For example, Chodorow (1987) concluded that the sense of maleness in men is conflictual and problematic because "underlying, or built into male gender identity is an early, nonverbal, unconscious, almost somatic sense of primary oneness with the mother" (p. 259). Similarly, Pollack (1992b) argues that because boys experience a traumatic disruption of their attachment to mother, "they have a more problematic course toward identity" and "are left at risk for disruptions in their affiliative connections" (p. 14).

Both theorists then explain dark side behavior as a consequence of the early disruption of the young boy's attachment to his mother. According to this formulation, the premature nature of this disruption requires the development of a wide array of defensive psychological maneuvers. The little boy must guard against his longings to maintain his attachment to his mother by rejecting his dependency feelings, assuming a "tough guy" stance, and devaluing anything associated with his earlier closeness to mother (Chodorow, 1978). Similarly, Pollack (1992a) argues that men tend to overvalue independence, to undervalue connection, and to feel anger toward women.

A Critique of the Identity Paradigm

From our point of view, the identity paradigm is problematic for two reasons. First, the establishment of a consistent and coherent gender role identity is seen as necessary for psychological well-being. This theoretical position accepts the cultural mythology that gender, like sex, is a binary concept. Since gender is culturally, rather than biologically, constructed, it is not limited to only two possibilities. We would argue that the cultural prescription to achieve a coherent and consistent gender role identity is, by definition, psychologically dysfunctional. We believe that the attempt to achieve a consistent gender role identity pressures an individual to conform to a gender role that is restricted to one of only two possibilities.

Finally, certain important assumptions that are integral to the identity paradigm have not been confirmed by empirical research. The notion that gender identity formation is a universal process that can be observed cross-culturally has not been documented. Similarly, the assumption that boys require a male identification figure in order to achieve a sense of themselves as male has not been supported by research on children being reared in non-nuclear family structures.

Gender Constancy Versus Gender Role Identity

Within the identity paradigm, a consistent gender identity is defined as a prerequisite for the development of a coherent gender *role* identity. Both are seen as necessary components for psychological well-being. Yet the definition of gender identity actually includes within it two contrasting theoretical concepts: gender constancy and gender role identity. *Gender constancy* refers to a cognitive understanding of the biologically based limitations of behavior, namely that one is, and will always be, only one sex. *Gender role identity*, in contrast, refers to the internalization of cultural expectations about what is appropriate or inappropriate behavior for members of each sex. Yet the construct of gender identity does not distinguish between these two concepts.

This theoretical inconsistency began with Fast's (1984, p. 12) definition of gender identity (see above) in which she made no distinction between (a) the *biological* attributes of the ability or inability to give birth or to have a penis, and (b) the *socialized* characteristics of physical activity and tenderness. Her definition of gender identity thus included both the acquisition of gender constancy and the internalization of gender role norms. Within the identity paradigm, therefore, *gender identity* has been used to refer to gender constancy while at other times it has been used to define a sense of what it means to be male or female *within a given cultural context*, that is, to refer to gender role identity.

The linkage of gender role identity and gender constancy within the identity paradigm causes the concept of gender, like the attribute of sex, to be treated as if it were a binary concept. Thus, feminine gender role identity and masculine gender role identity are seen as independent and internally consistent constructs. This explication generates an essentialist stance that posits an intrinsic "male" nature standing in contrast to an intrinsic "female" nature. From our point of view, gender differences, unlike biological sex differences, cannot be viewed within a binary framework.

An extreme example of the difficulties that arise when gender is defined as binary is the presence in Samoa and Tahiti of something like a "third gender." In Samoa, some male individuals are raised to fulfill feminine gender roles (Haworth, 1993). These men are called *fa'afafine* and dress as women, work in traditionally "feminine" occupations such as nursing and teaching, and have sex with heterosexual men. Based on cultural expectations, these little boys develop a gender role identity that is neither masculine nor feminine, but fa'afafine.

Another example of a variation in gender categories is the *mahu* of Tahiti (Gilmore, 1990, p. 207). These men dress as women, dance and sing as women do, participate in women's crafts, and have sex with heterosexual men. Like the Samoan fa'afafine, they are respected members of their community. These cross-cultural examples dramatically illustrate the theoretical pitfalls of defining gender characteristics as inextricably linked to the biological attribute of sex.

Empirical Research

A final objection that we have to the identity paradigm is the absence of research to support its assumptions. For example, Chodorow described a process of gender role identity formation within the context of the Western, industrialized, patriarchal, nuclear family. She then assumed that this process, which prescribes only two complementary masculine and feminine gender roles, is universal across cultures. However, the cross-cultural data from Tahiti and Samoa cited above indicate that some societies endorse the formation of two contrasting gender role identities for men. Gilmore (1990) pointed out that some cultures (e.g., Tahiti and Semai) define masculine and feminine roles as virtually identical rather than as complementary.

Similarly, Chodorow assumed that a male identification figure is necessary for boys to achieve an appropriate masculine gender role identity. Yet research on children raised by lesbian mothers (Golombok, Spencer, & Rutter, 1983; Patterson, 1992) has failed to support this contention. The research has suggested that neither a female parent nor a male parent is necessary for gender identity formation, sex role socialization, or the development of a heterosexual orientation in children of either sex. If Chodorow's position about the necessity of a male identification figure is taken to its logical conclusion, normal gender role identity formation for boys cannot occur within father-absent families. This decidedly antifeminist position is another aspect of the identity paradigm that we find problematic.

THE MEN'S STUDIES PERSPECTIVE: THE GENDER ROLE STRAIN/CONFLICT PARADIGM

The "gender role strain/conflict" paradigm (O'Neil, Helms, Gable, David, & Wrightman, 1986; Chapter 6; Pleck, 1981; Chapter 1) sees gender differences as a result of cultural pressures on individuals to conform to gender role norms. Gender roles are seen as operationally defined, internally inconsistent, constantly changing, and inevitably producing a degree of psychological dysfunction in all people. From this theoretical perspective, many dark side behaviors can be characterized as a by-product of the psychological strain men experience as they struggle to conform to a psychologically dysfunctional gender role.

The gender role socialization of boys, especially prior to age 12, has been considered by some theorists to be more restrictive than that of girls (O'Leary & Donahue, 1978). An early study found that experimentation with "cross-gender" behavior was more strongly discouraged in boys, usually more so by their fathers than by their mothers (Lamb, Owen, & Chase-Lansdale, 1978). This finding of early restrictiveness in role options, however, should not be interpreted as evidence that women have greater role flexibility across the life cycle. Nolen-Hoeksema (1990) has shown that, as girls enter adolescence, they also begin to take on the emotional baggage that results from pressure to conform to rigid gender role mandates. Similarly, other feminist theorists have argued that male violence against women is utilized as a form of social punishment toward women who refuse to conform to a traditional gender role (Fitzgerald, 1993). To avoid a hierarchy of suffering, we assume that both boys and girls, men and women, are equally pressured, although in different ways, to conform to restrictive gender roles.

Defining the Male Role

Although the prescribed male role may emphasize different features depending on race, ethnic group, age, and social class, there is a great deal of consensus as to what constitutes the traditional male role in patriarchal cultures. The typography cited most often has been that of David and Brannon (1976), who identified four primary elements of the male role: (a) No Sissy Stuff (avoidance of anything feminine), (b) the Sturdy Oak (emphasis on physical toughness and emotional stoicism), (c) Give 'em Hell (emphasis on being aggressive and forceful), and (d) the Big Wheel (preoccupation with competition, achievement, and success).

Similarly, the "masculine mystique" and gender role conflict described by O'Neil (1982, p. 15; Chapter 6) emphasizes restrictive emotionality, health care problems, obsession with achievement and success, restricted sexual and affectionate behavior, and concerns with power, control, competition, and homophobia. The "elements of the male role" noted by Doyle (1989) were the "anti-feminine element," the "success element," the "aggressive element," the "self-reliant element" and the "sexual element" (p. 146).

Gilmore (1990) is another theorist who attempted to define masculinity. He hoped to discover a universal psychic structure of manhood. Thus, he approached his task from the perspective of the identity paradigm. However, we believe that his analysis actually supports the gender role strain paradigm. In brief, Gilmore found that *most* societies have a manhood cult based on the ideals of competition, risk-taking, stoic resolve in the face of danger, and the rejection of feminine aspects of self. However, this finding was not universally true for all societies.

Gilmore carefully examined the two exceptions to this traditional definition of masculinity: the people of the Polynesian island of Tahiti, and the Semai people who live in the mountains of the Malay peninsula. In Tahiti, women are permitted to do virtually everything that men do, even holding political office, and men are not afraid of appearing effeminate. Gilmore pointed out that within this cultural context, the male role is defined as almost the opposite of macho: Passivity, timidity, and no taste for competitive striving are valued traits. Semai culture, similarly, appears to have little gender role differentiation. Neither men nor women are aggressive, and passivity and compliance are the most valued traits for both sexes. In a similar vein, Lepowsky (1994) has recently described the culture of Vanatinai, an island in the Louisiade Archipelago of Papua New Guinea, as a culture in which very few gender differences in behavior exist. In these societies that are exceptions to the general rule of patriarchal domination of women by men, men are allowed to be passive and dependent and a manhood cult is unnecessary.

Despite his discovery of these societies that do not have a manhood cult,

Gilmore (1990, p. 222) never relinquished his attachment to the identity paradigm. However, if masculinity is not uniform across all cultures, then one cannot propose a universal psychic structure to manhood. Therefore, we interpret Gilmore's cross-cultural data as a refutation of the identity paradigm.

Instead, Gilmore's analysis lends support to the hypothesis that dark side behaviors are directly related to the degree of difficulty involved in performing the male role in a given society. Gilmore noted that in most societies, men are assigned the roles of providing women and children with food and other resources and with protecting them from the threat of warfare. His cross-cultural comparisons indicated that the male role in every culture is defined by the ideal personality traits that are necessary for performing the provider and protector functions.

For example, when the provider role requires men to brave dangerous situations to provision their families with food (e.g., diving for fish in shark-infested waters, as the Truk Islanders must do), masculine gender role socialization generates personality characteristics such as risk-taking and remaining calm in the face of danger. Similarly, when provisioning the family requires hard, unrelenting physical labor (e.g., the lifestyle of farmers in southern Spain), the male role prescribes hard work and self-sacrifice in order to convince men to accept the obligation of continually doing work that provides very little personal satisfaction. If a society is threatened by warfare, as most of the countries in the world have been, then masculine socialization will emphasize aggression and emotional dissociation, qualities that are necessary to perform well as a soldier. Within these harsh economic and political contexts, dark side behaviors become inextricably linked to a normative definition of the male gender role.

Majors and Billson (1992) have used the role strain paradigm to explain the etiology of dark side behavior in young African-American men. These authors argue that the excessive violence and criminal behaviors typical of some inner-city minority youth are stress reactions to the history of oppression blacks have experienced in U.S. society. Majors and Billson propose that young African-American men, in response to these stresses, often adopt the "cool pose" (p. 1) of pride, strength, and control.

Majors and Billson propose that African-American men historically have defined manhood in terms of the traditional gender roles of "provider, protector, and procreator" (1992, p. 1). However, institutionalized racial discrimination has blocked consistent access to the means to fulfill these roles. Faced with blocked opportunities and cultural invisibility, young black males often assume a cool pose to deal with their anxiety about their second-class status. Cool pose is thus a survival strategy for dealing with anxiety and recovering self-respect.

Majors and Billson point out that cool pose can be both an adaptive coping mechanism for dealing with oppression and a self-destructive stance toward the world. Because cool pose does not allow for any expression of weakness or uncertainty, rather than helping black men cope with violence and oppression it can often lead to violence and risk-taking behavior. Because it denies the existence of a wide range of human emotions, such as fear, vulnerability, and indecisiveness, it represents a false self that ultimately is destructive to mental health. Thus, in agreement with Gilmore, Majors and Billson conclude that it is the harsh environment of institutionalized racism that generates the dark side of masculinity in young African-American men. We would argue that it is the existence of institutionalized racism that makes the fulfillment of the traditional male role of family provider exceedingly difficult, if not impossible. From our point of view, it is the inability to fulfill the provider role that generates cool pose in young minority men.

The men's studies perspective explains dark side behavior as largely the result of oversocialization to normative masculinity. Thus, men are violent because the traditional masculine role prescribes aggressive behavior. Men are sexually permissive because traditional masculinity defines "real men" as those who can demonstrate their power and potency by creating many offspring. Men are misogynist because traditional male socialization forbids men from expressing characteristics that are associated with feminine gender roles and encourages negative views of women.

From our point of view, the men's studies or gender role strain paradigm is the best description to date of the dark side of masculinity. However, we believe that this paradigm needs to be expanded to provide a more comprehensive explanatory framework. We try to provide this framework later in the chapter.

FEMINIST THEORY: THE SOCIAL CONSTRUCTIONIST HYPOTHESIS

Feminist theory has explained male dark side behavior as a natural outgrowth of male power within patriarchal society. Miller (1986) analyzed gender differences in the behavior of men and women from the perspective of gender-linked inequalities in power. Her point was that membership in a group that has power over others generates personality characteristics that are associated with the use and abuse of power. Similarly, membership in a group that has no power, and therefore is dependent for its survival on the dominant group, generates a contrasting set of personality characteristics.

She argued that women, like members of other subordinate groups, have developed interpersonal empathy and emotional sensitivity because their survival has required that they be sensitive to men's needs and emotions. Men, like members of other dominant groups, have developed a sense of entitlement and a tendency to oppress others because they have had the power to do so. Theoretically, if the power relations between the sexes were reversed, women would become more violent and oppressive simply by virtue of becoming members of the dominant group. Similarly, men would become more empathic and sensitive because their newly subordinate status would require them to do so.

Male dark side behaviors have thus been understood as strategies for maintaining male entitlement and privilege. Men's sexual violence has been characterized as an outgrowth of both men's normative socialization and their desire to maintain control over women (Brownmiller, 1975; Miller, 1986). Similarly, Bullough (1974) argued that widespread misogyny validates the oppression of women, although it is often disguised as a veneration of women and a noble desire to protect them. O'Neil and Egan (1992a) have analyzed the ways in which men's power and privilege hurt women in intimate relationships. Sattel (1976) described men's emotional inexpressiveness less as a product of flawed male socialization than as a sociopolitical strategy to maintain control of social situations. Alcohol and substance abuse have been viewed, to some extent, as outgrowths of male entitlement. Male abandonment of familial responsibility has been characterized as a "revolt against the breadwinner ethic" (Ehrenreich, 1983). From this theoretical perspective, dark side behaviors are the result of the unequal power relations between men and women within patriarchal culture.

Prospects for Change

In this section, we attempt to develop a systemic framework for deepening our understanding of the dark side of masculinity. We call this framework the "interactive systems model of gender role strain" because it addresses the cultural, social, psychological, and political contexts within which individual behavior occurs. The model reflects a synthesis of several theoretical approaches: the gender role strain paradigm; an ecological perspective on the origins of gender roles; the Bowen family systems theory view of the impact of chronic anxiety on behavior; and the social constructionist analysis of gender-linked power differentials within patriarchal society.

Our model follows directly from the work of several theorists discussed in the previous section who have made important contributions to understanding the etiology of dark side behavior. Pleck's (1981; Chapter 1) development of the gender role strain model represents a profound paradigm shift that set the stage for interpreting dark side behaviors as by-products of role stress rather than as problems in identity formation. O'Neil and his colleagues (see especially Chapter 6) have spent the last 15 years establishing an empirical research base that allows gender role conflict/strain to be operationally defined. This research provides scientific evidence linking role conflict and strain to dark side behavior. Similarly, Levant's (1992) synthesis of the overall field of men's studies points to the ways in which the reconstruction of traditional masculinity would "lighten" the dark side of masculinity.

Although we disagree with Chodorow's and Pollack's conclusion that dark side behavior emanates from problems of gender identity formation, we value their attempts to describe the defensive processes that lead to such behavior. We would agree that, given the way masculinity is currently constructed, mothers and sons tend to disrupt their early attachment, and fathers and sons tend to remain emotionally distant from each other. However, we believe that these relationship problems originate from the cultural prescription to produce boys who can conform to the current restrictive male role.

From our point of view, it is not the attachment to a primary identification figure who happens to be female that causes a little boy's sense of masculinity to be conflictual. Rather, it is the restrictive definition of the male role itself. Therefore, we would not agree that the premature disruption of the little boy's attachment to his mother is an inevitable by-product of masculine gender role socialization. We believe, in contrast, that a boy could develop a coherent sense of himself as masculine, *and at the same time remain intimately attached to his mother,* if the masculine gender role were redefined to be less restricted and less psychologically dysfunctional.

In our view, the gender role strain/conflict paradigm provides the best *description* of the mechanism (i.e,. socialization to a restrictive gender role), through which psychological conflict and strain become linked to normative masculinity. However, this paradigm does not explain why so many cultures have embedded violence, risk-taking, emotional dissociation, and misogyny within a normative definition of masculinity. Why have dark side behaviors not been associated with normative definitions of femininity? Why, across so many other variations in cultural organization (e.g., industrialized and nonindustrialized, Western and non-Western, collective and individualistic), does the dark side of masculinity occur with such consistency?

The strain/conflict paradigm also does not explain the psychological processes activated in some men that cause them to overconform to normative masculine traits. Why does strain, in general, lead to overconformity rather than to rejection of the cultural norms prescribed by normative masculinity? These are some of the questions we address in this section as we develop our interactive systems model.

AN ECOLOGICAL PERSPECTIVE

Our first step in expanding the role strain paradigm is to include an ecological perspective. If we return to Gilmore's (1990) analysis of masculinity, his cross-cultural data suggested that certain ecological variables are critical in constructing the male role within a given society. He examined the similarities in the environmental contexts of Tahiti and Semai, the two societies that do not have a manhood cult (pp. 217–219). He noted a variety of environmental conditions these cultures share in common: Natural resources are plentiful; there are no serious hazards involved in the production of food or other economic necessities; and neither society feels threatened by invaders or warfare. These ecological factors would also be true for the Vanatinai culture that Lepowsky (1994) observed.

Within the ecological context of plentiful resources, relative ease in the production of food, and the absence of external threat, men do not have to prove themselves by taking risks, and there is no pressure to sacrifice self for the good of society. There is also no emphasis on separate public/masculine and private/feminine spheres, and a high degree of power-sharing between the sexes exists.

In contrast to the ecological contexts that do *not* generate manhood cults, Gilmore pointed out that most societies must contend with scarce resources and continual external threat of invasion. Gilmore argued that since most societies assign the most dangerous tasks to men, a young boy must be pressured to develop a personality structure that compels him to put aside his personal goals and accept responsibility for society's goals. Gilmore concluded that it is a manhood cult that exhorts men to work for socially approved goals, even to the point of self-sacrifice.

Gilmore's observation that most societies assign the most dangerous tasks to men is crucial to understanding why dark side behaviors have been inextricably linked to normative masculinity rather than to normative femininity. We propose that, to ensure that men conform to dangerous roles, societies pressure men to give up a personal definition of self and create a pseudo-self. Only by denying many authentic features of self (e.g., the need for emotional connection, dependency longings, fear of physical injury and death, etc.) can men adequately perform the roles of provider and soldier.

A BOWEN FAMILY SYSTEMS PERSPECTIVE

We understand the consequences of the need to deny self from a Bowen family systems perspective (Kerr & Bowen, 1988). Bowen theory proposed that the need to give up self generates an increased level of chronic anxiety. As anxiety increases, individuals tend to regress to stereotyped forms of behavior. We believe that it is the overwhelming anxiety associated with the need to "give up self" that produces a tendency to overconform to masculine role ideals.

The anxiety associated with male gender role strain is debilitating for two reasons. First, the degree to which men must give up self often is extreme in terms of human psychological functioning. In contrast to the role of nurturer, which has been assigned to women, the role of provider requires men to leave the private world of the family, that is, to separate from attachment figures and familiar surroundings. Because most cultures exist in an economic context that requires hard work, the amount of time a man must spend away from his family is considerable. When the provision of resources requires dangerous activity, such as hunting or deep-sea diving, men must willingly put themselves at physical risk. Similarly, fulfilling the role of soldier necessitates risking physical injury and death.

Conforming to these role demands requires denial of, or dissociation from, a wide range of emotions. Dependency longings, separation anxiety, fear of the unknown and of strangers, body anxiety, annihilation anxiety, and so forth, are all profound emotions that men must deny or compartmentalize in order to conform to the masculine role. It is important to note that women are also pressured to give up self to fulfill societal goals. The process of socialization which prepares women to fulfill the role of nurturing parent leads them to deny their autonomy needs, their drive toward mastery and competence, and their competitive impulses.

However, in our view, cultural expectations for women are not as psychologically toxic as those for men. Although women's psychological development has been damaged by socialization within patriarchal culture, women are allowed to acknowledge their dependency longings, their need for intimate relationships, and their sense of vulnerability. We hypothesize that it is the denial of these basic human needs in the socialization of men that generates a debilitating level of personal fragility and sets the stage for the expression of the dark side of masculinity.

A second aspect of male gender role socialization that generates anxiety is the coercive effect of the manhood cult itself. Because men are asked to give up self to such an extent, many men might refuse to do so if the consequences of refusal were not profound. Gilmore (1990) found that most societies consistently threaten men with public humiliation or hazing, physical punishment, and threats of social ostracism. The anxiety that is generated by the fear of the consequences of *not* conforming to cultural expectations generates the tendency in many men to overconform to the normative definition of masculinity.

Since the standards of normative masculinity for most cultures prescribe competitive behavior, aggression, risk-taking, emotional detachment, and the rejection of feminine aspects of self, overconformity to these ideals leads to an exaggerated expression of these personality characteristics. This exaggeration of traditional masculine gender role traits becomes translated into the dark side of masculinity. For example, the ability to take risks, the denial of body anxiety, and the emphasis on aggressive behavior are necessary characteristics for the successful performance of the role of soldier. When these behaviors are transferred to an inappropriate context—for example, from the battlefield into the family living room—then these traits become translated into the dark side behavior of male violence against women and children and against other men in society. Similarly, emotional detachment and denial of the need for intimacy are personal characteristics required for men to perform well as competitive workers in the public world. When these personality features are overdeveloped (and other personality traits such as empathy and capacity for intimacy are underdeveloped) and transferred to the private world of the family, they can become the dark side behaviors of absent fathering and dysfunctional relational partners.

Men's studies proponents have pointed out that men are constrained by extremely harsh mandates about acceptable "male" behavior, as well as by their meager training in emotional skills (David & Brannon, 1976; O'Neil, 1982; Chapter 6). Balswick (1988) has written extensively about how the male gender role deprives men of opportunities for emotionally rich interpersonal relationships. The need to repress (or suppress) important and wide-ranging aspects of self thus becomes a primary source of chronic anxiety in the psychological makeup of men.

THE SOCIAL CONSTRUCTIONIST HYPOTHESIS

In addition to the pressure to give up self and the anxiety that results from that pressure, male power within patriarchy is another variable that contributes to the expression of many dark side behaviors in men.

In our view, the social constructionist analysis of dominant and subordinate groups explains this gender difference. As the dominant group in patriarchal culture, men have the privilege (and one might even say the duty or obligation) to act out aggressively against others. Their membership in the dominant group provides them with the opportunity to abuse power. The dark side behaviors of violence and sexual assault are closely related to the fact that men are socialized to dominance (although in their minds their motives are better understood as protecting the "weak").

Just as the manhood cult coerces men to conform to masculine gender role norms, women are similarly threatened with dire consequences if they fail to conform to feminine gender role norms. Women are subjected to the same forms of social control as men: public humiliation, physical punishment, and social ostracism. In addition, women are far more likely to be sexually assaulted and harassed. Yet women do not exhibit dark side behaviors. Women, in contrast, are socialized to be subordinate to others. Thus, the anxiety engendered in women by the societal pressure to give up self generates *self*-directed, rather than *other*-directed, dark side behaviors—for example, eating disorders, underachievement, depression, and suicide attempts.

We believe that any theoretical framework that aspires to explain the etiology of dark side behavior must include the acknowledgment that the power inequality between men and women contributes to the dark side of masculinity. In this regard, Gilmore's observation about the assignment of the most dangerous societal tasks to men is again a relevant point. Our point of view is that one aspect of male privilege and power in patriarchal society derives from the difficult and dangerous nature of the male role.

We believe that because men are required to risk their lives as soldiers, patriarchy rewards them with male privilege and power. Cross-cultural research has confirmed that an emphasis on warfare correlates positively with the subordination of women in many societies. Ross (1985) studied data on 90 preindustrial societies. He found that frequent warfare, which requires that most men spend some part of their lives as soldiers, is positively associated with a higher level of internal oppression of women than is a more peaceful cultural context. In the more warlike societies, the separation between the public and private realms is extreme, sex roles are rigidly defined, and the domination of women by men is substantial. Similarly, Whitten-Stovall and Whitten-Stovall (1989) found that variables such as marriage by purchase, postmarital restrictions on women, and male property rights correlate with an emphasis on war in preindustrial societies. Thus, power and privilege over women seem to be the consolation prizes that patriarchy offers men in return for asking them to sacrifice their lives for their country.

THE INTERACTIVE SYSTEMS MODEL OF GENDER ROLE STRAIN

Our interactive systems model attempts to address a wide range of variables that sustain dark side behavior within the cultural, social, psychological, and political systems of any given society. As we ponder the prospects for change, we believe that changes must occur at each of these systemic levels. At the cultural level, masculine and feminine gender roles must be redefined. The male gender role must be redefined to deemphasize the provider and protector functions, and highlight the nurturing function. Correspondingly, within the feminine gender role definition, the providing and protective functions must become more prominent.

This cultural transformation would lead to changes in the process of gender role socialization. If men were expected to nurture, then attachment, intimacy, and emotional connection would be placed at the center of masculine as well as feminine gender role socialization. Similarly, if cultural norms for women included their acceptance of responsibility for providing economic resources for themselves and their families and for protecting themselves, little girls would be encouraged to develop personality characteristics that emphasize autonomy, achievement, and mastery.

Thus, cultural change in the definition of gender roles would lead to a restructuring of family relationships at the social level. Changing the traditional sexual division of labor in families would be a necessary precondition for transforming masculine and feminine roles. This has begun to happen in the recent societal trends of working mothers (i.e., coprovisioning by women) and nurturing fathers (i.e., conurturing by men).

Within this role-sharing context, mothers would be committed to raising boys who could become intimate fathers; therefore, close attachments between little boys and their mothers would not need to be disrupted. Similarly, because the provider function would no longer be considered primarily a male responsibility, cultural norms would no longer expect adult men to be as preoccupied with the public world. This would free time and energy for men to be involved in intimate relationships with their children. Since masculine and feminine role definitions would be far more similar, boys would not need to achieve a sense of separation from their mothers as opposite-sex parents. This socialization process would be possible in the context of any family structure (i.e., in families headed by mother only, father only, or a lesbian or gay male couple, as well as in a heterosexual nuclear family). Both men and women would be socializing both boys and girls to develop a wide range of personality characteristics related to expanded rather than restricted gender roles.

These changes in the socialization process and in family relationships would dramatically decrease the psychological stress associated with conforming to gender role norms. Within a cultural context that prescribes very few differences between feminine and masculine gender role norms (like Tahiti and Vanatinai), many more options for self-definition would then become available for individuals of both sexes. Thus, the pressure to give up self to fulfill restricted gender roles would lessen.

Individuals of both sexes could choose from a wider array of culturally sanctioned behaviors (like the fa'afafine in Samoa). Without the psychological stress associated with giving up self to conform to psychologically restrictive gender roles, levels of chronic anxiety would be reduced. This would dramatically reduce the need for the psychological defenses individuals invoke to deal with role strain and conflict. From this perspective, male dark side behaviors (as well as women's more internalized dark behaviors) should decrease.

In addition to changes at the cultural and social levels, changes in the political system of patriarchy would also have to be achieved to address the dark side of masculinity most effectively. We believe that redefining the feminine gender role to include providing and protecting would impart to women some of the power and privilege associated with those roles. This would decrease the economic and political dependence of women on men and thus help to equalize the power relations between them.

However, our goal is not to change women into men, or men into women. Rather, it is to transform patriarchy into a new social order that is less oppressive for men as well as for women. From a cross-cultural perspective, this type of transformation has only been achieved in an ecological context characterized by abundant resources and low external threat of invasion. The challenge for our generation is to establish an egalitarian social order *despite* the context of scarce economic resources and a continual threat of war. In contrast to the domination of the weak by the strong, we must create collaborative relationships among equals. Until this goal is attained, at the international, societal, and personal levels, the dark side of masculinity will continue to plague both men and women.

Implications for Mental Health Professionals

There can be no arguing with the fact that only a small percentage of men actually commit offensive acts such as rape, but this observation misses the point. The fundamental problem with the "aberrant male" point of view is its stance that only a few men are sick while all other men are untouched by the dark side issue. This position pathologizes some men and misses the opportunity for more creative interventions. When we reject the aberrant male perspective and embrace a position that examines normative masculinity, we encounter several major advantages in our therapy approaches to men who engage in dark side behaviors.

First, by implicating the larger culture as well as offender males, we broaden our intervention repertoires. Instead of focusing exclusively on the individual "deviancy" of these men, and looking at how they are, in a distorted and exaggerated fashion, acting out role messages presented to all men, we can approach them with more understanding. Though their acts continue to be censured, and they continue to be held fully accountable for their behavior, they can nevertheless be seen in cultural context and approached with no less (and no more) compassion than they deserve.

Second, this approach allows us to discover new explanations for offenders' reluctance to give up certain behavior patterns. When we examine the larger cultural and political context, we see that these behaviors are not as simple as sometimes thought; men often receive mixed messages and substantial benefits from their offensive actions. An obvious example is the complex subject of violence. Though some violent men are castigated, many are celebrated, and violence frequently seems to yield interpersonal benefits. A more subtle example is the commonly reported male malady—emotional inexpressiveness. An approach that considers emotional inexpressiveness purely as a skill deficit ignores an important contextual issue—emotional inexpressiveness sometimes benefits men. As was noted earlier, Sattel (1976) suggested that male inexpressiveness needs to be understood from a sexual politics perspective in that it "facilitates the instrumental requisites of the male power role" (p. 474).

A third advantage of this approach is that it provides a necessary tool for men to translate the resocialization messages of therapy into their lives in the outside world. It is a major mistake to assume that male role programming ends as men become adults. Traditional male value messages are prominent in the culture and in familial systems. Potential for change is greater when men are provided with cultural consciousness-raising and tools to negotiate value clashes.

Finally, this approach offers a welcome change from exclusive emphasis on problem resolution and rehabilitation. An approach that considers gender-based value conflicts in *all* men has the potential to intervene in a proactive or preventative fashion. All men can be taught about the likelihood of certain interpersonal problems that are the product of overly rigid gender role definitions.

REMEDYING BLINDNESS TO MEN'S VIOLENCE

Taken as a whole, the data that we have presented on the dark side of masculinity paint a picture of men out of control. However, as Browne (1993) points out, the psychological community has been slow to become involved in proactive interventions with couples. Standard procedures of psychological history-taking have not routinely included questions about a history of family violence. Even when partner violence has been known, the reality of risk to a woman victim has frequently not been understood, and a willingness to intervene with the male perpetrator has been absent.

Harway and Hansen (1993a) also report surveying 405 members of the American Association of Marriage and Family Therapists participated in a study of therapists' sensitivity to family violence. Therapists were mailed a questionnaire presenting one of two actual cases in which family violence was implicated. (In one case, unbeknownest to the study participants, the woman was later killed.) Respondents were 53% women, 47% men; 54% had a master's degree, and 32% a doctorate. When asked to provide a conceptualization of the case, 40% of the practitioners failed to address the issue of male violence. Even those who addressed the violence underplayed its seriousness. More than half of the respondents said they did not believe the level of violence required immediate action (p. 44). The responses did not vary based on the sex of the respondent.

In a second study, 405 members of the American Psychological Association (Practice Divisions 12, 29, 42) responded to mailed questionnaires. Respondents were 71% male and 29% female, with 99% possessing doctorates. The questionnaire presented another case of rather extreme domestic violence. Respondents were asked for a DSMIII-R diagnosis and were subsequently informed that the husband murdered his wife. The most frequent diagnosis was one focusing on the couple's marital problems; the next most frequent indicated pathology in both husband and wife. Only 16% of respondents diagnosed the husband alone. After the respondents were informed about the lethal outcome of the case, only 50% indicated that the correct intervention would have been to seek protection for the wife. Another 27% said they would want to assess the couple further to ascertain the seriousness of the violence (Harway & Hansen, 1993a, p. 47).

Our hope in taking a clear and direct look at the dark side of masculinity is to move the professional psychological community toward more active intervention. The feminist movement injected the concept of "the personal is political" into therapy with women to make the point that many problematic behaviors are not the personal problems of individual women but rather the result of the socialization process for all women. Similarly, the new psychology of men is now redefining dark side behaviors not as the personality problems of a few aberrant men but rather as the product of normative masculine socialization in patriarchal culture.

Within this new conceptual framework, men must be held fully accountable for their behavior, and the victims of their violence must be protected. However, expanded interventions for boys and men must also be developed if the dark side of masculinity is to be transformed. Mental health practitioners must develop therapeutic approaches that address men's psychic pain by acknowledging the gender role strain all men experience. Only then will we achieve a situation that currently seems unimaginable—men in pain actively seeking therapy rather than avidly avoiding it.

GENDER-SENSITIVE PSYCHOTHERAPY AND ASSESSMENT

A vital component of gender-aware psychological practice is the recognition of the crucial role of power in relationships. Psychologists practice in a cultural context in which men have generally had political and economic leverage over women and have often used that leverage to maintain power or to sabotage women's growth. Therapists must pay close attention to the complex ways power differentials impact on the potential of both partners to change. For example, treatment of women victimized by violence must be informed by a full understanding of many women's limited resources and behavioral options. Feminist therapists, in reaction to the ways in which power differences were invisible within family therapy practice, have developed a wide range of "women-friendly" assessments and interventions (Avis, 1988; Braverman, 1988). However, Bograd (1991) points out that, "to be truly systemic, family therapists must also critically examine men's subjective experiences and their interrelationships with larger social structures and processes" (p. xiii).

Psychological practice with male clients is not likely to be fully successful, or culturally ethical, if male socialization is not understood. Participation in the masculine gender world affects how a male client perceives problems, attributes causality, reacts emotionally, seeks symptomatic relief, evaluates the potential benefits of seeking professional help, and behaves in psychotherapy. Psychotherapy with men takes off when we infuse it with attention to the core issues of traditional male identity—work, violence, emotional dissociation, sexuality, patriarchal fathering, and risk-taking.

The men's studies perspective provides several advantages for working within a gender-sensitive framework with men. It allows therapists more easily to differentiate between normative role behavior and psychopathology. It also provides for the possibility of being empathic with men's inner experience as they struggle to conform to contradictory gender role norms. This point of view is especially helpful for managing the countertransferential problems inherent in work with dark side behaviors. In terms of psychological assessment, Brown (1986) argued that "gender role analysis" enhances assessment and guards against the risk of overpathologizing clients or "punishing via diagnosis" (p. 245).

A principal objective of gender-sensitive interventions is the promotion of increased flexibility in male role behavior. Solomon (1982) proposed the adoption of "gender role psychotherapy," in which male gender roles are a major focus of intervention. Similarly, Brooks (1990) noted several potential areas in which therapists could encourage role flexibility: (a) lessening the traditional emphasis on work and career issues; (b) reinforcing male interpersonal behaviors besides those of taking charge and seeking to dominate; (c) balancing emphasis on emotional stoicism with the need to acknowledge vulnerabilities and become more emotionally expressive; (d) promoting new models of fathering; and (e) promoting emotional intimacy among men.

PROFESSIONAL EDUCATION AND TRAINING

As the mental health field has begun to grasp the many ways in which gender socialization affects therapy clients, it has been painfully slow in acknowledging another critical population affected by gender socialization—mental health professionals ourselves. Psychotherapists are "gendered" beings in that we, like our clients, are strongly influenced by our socialization as men or women.

Despite the increased recognition of gender as a "fundamental category" (Goldner, 1988), graduate programs continue to provide clinical training that is primarily "generic"—a "one size fits all" approach. Many observers have commented upon the resistance of training programs to offering coursework in gender issues (Bloom, 1991; Coleman, Avis, & Turin, 1990; Edwall, 1991) and have suggested possible explanations. Some of the reasons they note are the customary ones, such as limited resources, finite amounts of training time, and the expected resistance to anything unfamiliar (Philpot, 1992). However, more troubling explanations have also been put forth. For example, some authors (Gilbert, 1987; Pope, Keith-Spiegel, & Tabachnick, 1986) suggest that many training programs assume that gender socialization affects clients but should not affect therapists. Pope et al. (1986), in their description of the "sometimes inhuman training system" (p. 147), observed that therapists are often reluctant to admit a common gender-based reaction to clients (sexual attraction) for fear that they will be considered personally immature or unable to manage countertransference feelings.

Another possible reason for inattention to gender issues is the rudimentary state of knowledge about gender effects in therapist-client interactions. Mintz and O'Neil (1990) reported that, "while theory suggests important process differences between the possible pairs [i.e., therapist-client gender pairings] and critical process issues within each of these pairs, empirical investigation is greatly lagging behind theory development" (p. 385). In other words, as yet, we have little research data to support our hunches about how women and men interact as therapists and clients. However, though much remains invalidated about the exact effects of gender in psychotherapy, we do have enough information to argue that gender issues are too important to continue to be ignored. Gilbert (1987) suggested that before mental health professionals can train nonsexist therapists, they must examine their own sexism.

MEN'S CONSCIOUSNESS-RAISING GROUPS

Stein (1982) described men's consciousness-raising (CR) groups as "social phenomena" that may add appreciably to the benefits of more traditional psychotherapy groups and may, for some men, "supplement or replace traditional masculine activities such as athletic events and club or lodge meetings" (p. 306).

The feminist movement was the first grass-roots movement to rely heavily on CR groups. Women, uncomfortable with the traditional biases of mental health theory and practice, preferred CR groups because of the absence of the power hierarchies inherent in the therapist-patient format (Kirsh, 1974). Additionally, CR groups placed less emphasis on intrapsychic and individual change and more emphasis on societal change, consistent with the feminist critique of traditional psychotherapy (Brodsky & Hare-Mustin, 1980).

The situation for men is different because men have not been subject to the same maltreatment from the traditional mental health community. In fact, men may actually benefit from the "acceptance of lesser power and the accompanying position of dependency on the therapist" (Stein, 1982). Nevertheless, there may be ways in which CR activities have important advantages for men.

First, CR groups adopt a nontherapy focus and do not think of participants as "patients." This nonpathological orientation makes CR groups abundantly more appealing to traditional men, who are most typically reluctant to consider psychotherapy (Levant, 1990; Scher, 1990). Therapy requires men to violate certain prescriptions of the male role by admitting vulnerability and asking for help, whereas CR groups provides a face-saving way of talking about the problem areas faced by all men.

Another major advantage of CR groups is that they provide the opportunity to interact in an all-male group environment. Individual therapy may provide considerable gains to many men, yet it cannot provide the benefits of a group setting. In groups, men have a unique opportunity to relate differently with other men. Common problematic male-male behavior patterns—for example, excessive competition, faulty communication styles, failures of empathy—can be addressed in a group setting. Likewise, men's traditional reliance on women to perform expressive and socioemotional tasks (Aries, 1976) can be overcome when women are not available.

Finally, CR groups may provoke a change in men's "relationships with social institutions" (Stein, 1982, p. 295). Unlike therapy groups, in which more emphasis is placed on individual accommodation to social institutions, CR groups are more likely to inspire men to challenge the social institutions themselves.

Reshaping Culture

We have argued that the etiology of dark side behavior is rooted in the way patriarchal culture defines masculinity rather than in the intrapsychic world of individual men. Thus, transforming the dark side of masculinity requires more than change on the part of individual men. Rather, major aspects of patriarchal culture will have to be altered.

Redefining Fathering

We agree with Chodorow's (1978) point that men should be involved in the nurturing of young children. However, as we understand Chodorow, she objected to the fact that only women mother because she believed that a boy requires a masculine identification figure to develop not only his masculine gender role identity but also an integrated sense of self. Thus, Chodorow's interest in men becoming primary caretakers was not based on transforming the masculine *role* but rather on providing boys with a personal identification figure.

Our point of view, in contrast, is that active nurturing by fathers is important in order to redefine normative masculinity. Since the large-scale entrance of women into the workforce, women have assumed a breadwinning role in families. Thus, many of the personality characteristics formerly associated exclusively with men—for example, ambition, assertiveness, and competence in the public world—are in the process of becoming accepted as part of the feminine gender role. If emotional attachment and nurturing were placed at the center of a cultural (re)definition of masculinity, then gender role prescriptions would overlap for both sexes. Gender role socialization would be transformed from a restrictive, strain-inducing process to one that generates flexibility and growth for both men and women.

However, given the general lack of governmental supports, the negative attitudes of the workplace, the continuing pay differential between women and men, and direct resistance from many men and women, what are the prospects that American fathers will significantly increase their involvement with their children? Anthropologists (e.g., Draper, 1975; Hewlett, 1991) have noted that in hunter-gatherer cultures in which women's contribution to subsistence is equal to, or greater than, men's contribution, men tend to participate more in child care. Scanzoni (1982) has expanded this observation to suggest that men participate in child care and housework only if women have the economic power to demand that they do so. He describes marriage as an "institution consisting of a struggle between conflicting interest groups" (p. 32). Scanzoni proposed that when husbands are the only providers of economic resources, wives accept the sole obligation for housework and child care. Similarly, Bernard (1981) stated that the father's role as sole provider gives him the privilege "to be taken care of, rather than to give care" (p. 81).

Based on this economic analysis of the politics of relationships, Scanzoni (1982) proposed that the single most important factor in equalizing the power balance between marital partners is the amount of money the wife earns on her own. Scanzoni reasoned that as women become coproviders, they will be more likely to demand that their husbands share responsibility for household management and child care.

Scanzoni (1982) warned, however, that men probably will not see women's demands as legitimate, and evidence of male resistance is plentiful. (See Ehrenreich, 1983; Faludi, 1991; and Solomon, 1982, for a thorough analysis of men's negative reactions to women's increased empowerment.) Not all male resistance should be attributed to political reactivity, however. Many other factors inhibit men's potential for change: institutional resistance, public attitudes and perceptions of "new" male models, and men's unrealistic fears of the implications of new masculine identities.[1]

Pleck (1993) argues strongly that the push for "family-supportive" workplace policies, although not always perceived as such, can be a critical vehicle for men to develop new family roles. He notes, for example, that although

[1]It should be noted that there is controversy about the long-term trend in the rate of men's participation in domestic labor and child care. Though some argue that there has been no change, Pleck (1993) argues that there is a slow but steady trend toward greater male participation.

men have been reluctant to use formal paternity leave benefits, they have been more likely to use "informal" leave and otherwise "negotiate the demands of their jobs to meet family needs" (p. 14). Pleck notes that official policy is only part of the story; corporate culture maintains an unspoken belief that men who take family leave are "unmanly." One researcher noted that "we haven't escaped the notion that house- husbands are, to a certain degree, wimpier than persons who are not" (quoted in Alexander, 1990, p. B1).

Corporate culture is not the only repository of fears of creeping wimpishness. Men themselves are insecure about the implications of making adjustments to new male roles. Although there is clear evidence that new family roles and new relationship models offer significant benefits for men (Cowan, 1988; Gilbert, 1985; O'Neil & Egan, 1992b; Osherson, 1986; Robertson & Verschelden, 1993), no significant change will take place unless men continue to be willing to experiment with new behaviors. An important question then is, How do we encourage more men to venture into new ways of being and relating? In this regard, the testimony of other men may be pivotal. At an early age, men learn that if they do not diligently follow masculine role mandates, they will be subject to the harsh rebuke of other men. Traditional male role behavior is so well conditioned that even the most trivial "nonmasculine" act invokes substantial anxiety about how other men might react. Change, therefore, requires that men confront other men about this issue. This interaction can be accomplished best in a compassionate and supportive environment where men share the experiences, fears, and successes of what O'Neil and Eagan (1992b) call the "gender role journey."

TRANSFORMING BOY CULTURE

If society is going to change role norms for adult men, then the socialization of young boys must also change. According to Rotundo (1993), boy culture emerged in the early 19th century when boys were largely freed from the necessity of work in the family. The new freedom from responsibility allowed them to roam the streets of the cities and the fields of rural America, beyond the range of adult supervision. Through these activities, boys developed separate, cohesive, and independent peer groups. Within these groups, certain values, such as mastery, loyalty, and self-control, were revered, while others, such as domesticity and restraint, were despised. Boy culture emphasized physical prowess and daring, emotional and physical stoicism, and loyalty to allies. Embedded within these activities was a high level of aggression toward each other. Older boys routinely bullied younger ones, territorial battles were fought along racial or ethnic lines, and animals were sadistically killed and tortured. Fierce independence from authority was valued, frequently to the point of vandalism and antisocial activities.

Pittman (1990) described a similar phenomenon in his concept of the "male chorus"—a voice in the head of a man that will "hiss or cheer as he attempts to approximate the masculine ideal" (p. 42). According to Pittman, the purpose of the male chorus is the psychic incorporation of male role ideals. The male chorus is composed of "all the guys' comrades and rivals, all his buddies and bosses, his male ancestors, and his male cultural heroes, his male models of masculinity, and above all, his father" (p. 42). Pittman saw the male chorus as invisible, omnipresent, and inescapable as a constant critic of the manliness of a man's actions.

Although both Pittman and Rotundo describe positive aspects of boy culture, they also see it as the social institution that transmits many problematic values, such as the suppression of emotion, the repression of empathy, and a concern with competition and dominance.

Another critic of contemporary boy culture is Miedzian (1991), who has argued that boys in contemporary culture are encouraged to be "obsessionally competitive" rather than simply assertive and competent. In particular, she castigates organized sports as one of the aspects of boy culture that acculturates boys to a fixation with dominance and an insensitivity to violence.

Miedzian (1991) challenges the assertion that participation in organized sports teaches children the importance of teamwork and fair play. She argues, in contrast, that the emphasis on winning actually deprives children of the pleasure of playing the game. Miedzian also objects to the point of view that sports provide an outlet for releasing aggression in a socially sanctioned manner. Miedzian and others (Meissner, 1992; Smith, 1983) have presented persuasive arguments that many sports, particularly football and boxing, sanction violent assault, encouraging small boys to deny their own fear of injury and to repress empathy for their opponents. A particularly compelling piece of evidence is Miedzian's citation of the work of Koss and Dinero (1988), who found that college athletes are responsible for approximately one-third of reported campus sexual assaults.

Organized sports for males, rather than being a harmless outlet for aggression, may actually encourage violence and link masculinity to many dark side behaviors, such as the repression of empathy, violent assault of the other, and denial of fear and physical vulnerability.

Thus, cultural changes in the ways men father need to be accompanied by similar changes in the process through which little boys learn how to act like adult men. For example, as an antidote to the violent aspects of boy culture, Miedzian (1991) recommends that schools begin routinely to include childcare programs in the regular curriculum from kindergarten through sixth grade. The goal of these programs would be to improve the nurturing and caretaking skills of all children. However, for boys, this type of program would specifically provide a corrective socialization experience. Active participation in child care would suggest that accepting responsibility for the care of young children is part of being a "real man." Particularly vital in this kind of activity would be women and men with a clear appreciation of new models of masculinity. These adult role models would provide behavioral alternatives for developing males.

MEN'S SOCIAL ACTIVISM

A major contribution of the feminist movement has been its opposition to the sexist social system that pressures women into limited, traditional gender roles and its emphasis on social activism to reshape that system. In a similar fashion, social activism may also have an important place in countering men's dark side behaviors, both by promoting men's growth as individuals and by posing challenges to the social institutions that perpetuate traditional behavior.

O'Neil and Eagan (1992b) present a model of gender role growth they call the "gender role journey." This model conceptualizes gender role growth as taking place in stages, beginning with the first awareness of gender role pressures, progressing through the emotional disequilibrium of new role possibilities, and eventually producing integration and gender role transcendence. These authors see social activism as both an inherent feature and a natural outgrowth of the gender role journey.

Besides the personal benefits of social activism are the benefits that can be produced only when sexist social institutions are altered. In this vein, it should be noted that the growing "men's movement," a social movement many see as a natural extension of the women's movement, can serve as yet another catalyst for liberating men from traditional role restrictions (Brod, 1987). Other observers acknowledge that, while many men are talking about their role restrictions and participating in weekend retreats, few are activists in social causes. Many critics are particularly unhappy with the followers of Robert Bly and the mythopoetic men's movement, which has been seen as likely to produce only short-term relief for a few men, making no significant impact on the institutions that oppress all men and all women (Hagan, 1992; Kaufman, 1987; Kimmel, 1989). Some men's groups, however, are committed to social change. The National Organization of Men Against Sexism (NOMAS) describes itself as a "pro-feminist, gay affirmative, male positive, anti-racist organization, that sponsors anti-rape, anti-violence, and anti-pornography programs." (See Shiffman, 1987, or Clatterbaugh, 1990, for a description of the profeminist men's movement.)

Conclusion

Most people would agree with the adage, "If it isn't broken, don't fix it." Many people might similarly agree with the point of view that the traditional code of masculinity has functioned very well and should not be subject to tampering. This point of view is manifest in the mythopoetic men's movement's call primarily for rediscovery of the essential masculinity of the "wild man" and reconnection with the "deep masculine archetype" (Bly, 1987, p. 17).

We ardently disagree with this perspective. Instead, we align ourselves with the men's studies and feminist views that call for a fundamental restructuring of masculinity, and in that vein, we have suggested ways to alter mental health practices and transform culture.

Although it is simple to call for the transformation of social institutions, it is difficult to imagine how patriarchal culture would have to change if masculinity (and femininity) were to be truly transformed. Such a transformation would require a reordering of the priorities of work and family life, as well as a new world order that valued the global community above the interests of ethnic groups or nation-states. If masculinity is to be reconstructed, then providing and soldiering would have to be supplemented with nurturing and peacekeeping as cornerstones of the traditional masculine role. We would argue, however, that societies in which relationships between men and women are egalitarian now exist only in the realm of feminist science fiction, for example, in the work of Octavia Butler (1987, 1988, 1989) and Marge Piercy (1991). Even science fiction does not yet imagine a world organized by egalitarian relationships between nation-states and collaborative decision-making rather than the dominance of the weak by the strong.

We realize that advocating for societal change generates profound anxiety, particularly when significant loss is anticipated. However, we believe that the reconstruction of masculinity, while it would involve loss of patriarchal privilege for men, would produce many benefits for men as well as for women. This chapter, which reflects a collaboration between a radical feminist and a profeminist men's studies proponent, has been both painful and joyful to write. Both of us have had to change, and both of us have been challenged to develop more flexibility. We believe that by enthusiastically embracing a new and broader conceptualization of masculinity, men will experience far greater role flexibility, improved self-care, wider definitions of personal worth, and richer, more caring relationships with women, their children, and other men. We view the transformation of masculinity as an important step in moving society to an "elsewhere" (Haraway, 1989, p. 380): a new social order in which differences are respected and relationships are based on by equality and cooperation.

References

Alexander, S. (1990, August 24). Fears for careers curb paternity leave. *Wall Street Journal*, pp. B1, B4.

American Psychological Association (1991). Special issue: Homelessness. *American Psychologist, 46.*

Aries, E. (1976). Interaction patterns and themes of male, female, and mixed groups. *Small Group Behavior, 7,* 7–18.

Avis, J. M. (1988). Deepening awareness: A private study guide to feminism and family therapy. In L. Braverman (Ed.), *A guide to feminist family therapy* (pp. 15–46). New York: Harrington Park Press.

Balswick, J. O. (1988). *The inexpressive male.* Lexington, MA: Lexington Books.

Baumli, F. (Ed.). (1986). *Men freeing men: Exploding the myth of the traditional male.* Jersey City, NJ: Atlantis Press.

Berglund, M. (1984). Suicide in alcoholism. *Archives of General Psychiatry, 41,* 888–891.

Bernard, J. (1981). Societal values and parenting. *Counseling Psychologist, 9,* 5–11.

Bloom, J. B. (1991, January). The challenge of curriculum transformation. In *Proceedings of the National Council of Schools of Professional Psychology Midwinter Conference on Women's Issues in Professional Psychology Preconference Papers.* Tucson, AZ. (Quoted in Philpot, 1992, p. 64.)

Blumstein, P. & Schwartz, P. (1983). *American couples: Money, work, sex.* New York: Morrow.

Bly, R. (1987). The pillow and the key: Commentary on the fairy tale of Iron John, part 1. St. Paul, MN: Ally Press.

Bograd, M. (Ed.). (1991). *Feminist approaches for men in family therapy.* New York: Harrington Park Press.

Braverman, L. (1988). *A guide to feminist family therapy.* New York: Harrington Park Press.

Briere, J., & Malamuth, N. M. (1983). Self-reported likelihood of sexually aggressive behavior: Attitudinal versus sexual explanations. *Journal of Research in Personality, 17,* 315–323.

Brod, H. (1987). Introduction: Themes and theses of men's studies. In H. Brod (Ed.), *The making of masculinities: The new men's studies* (pp. 1–17). Winchester, MA: Allen & Unwin.

Brodsky, A. M., & Hare-Mustin, R. (1980). *Women and psychotherapy.* New York: Guilford Press.

Bronstein, P., & Cowan, C. P. (Eds.). (1988). *Fatherhood today: Men's changing role in the family.* New York: Wiley Interscience.

Brooks, G. R. (1990). The inexpressive male and vulnerability to to therapist-patient sexual exploitation. *Psychotherapy: Theory, Research, Training, 27,* 344–349.

Brooks, G. R. (1992). Gender-sensitive family therapy in a violent culture. *Topics in Family Psychology and Counseling, 1,* 24–36.

Brown, L. S. (1986). Gender-role analysis: A neglected component of psychological assessment. *Psychotherapy, 23,* 243–248.

Browne, A. (1993). Violence against women by male partners: Prevalence, outcomes, and policy implications. *American Psychologist, 48,* 1077–1087.

Browne, A., & Dutton, D. G. (1990). Escape from violence: Risks and alternatives for abused women. In R. Roesch, D. G. Dutton, & V. F. Sacco (Eds.), *Family violence: Perspectives in research and practice* (pp. 75–94). Burnaby, BC: Simon Fraser University Press.

Brownmiller, S. (1975). *Against our will: Men, women and rape.* New York: Simon & Schuster.

Bullough, V. (1974). *The subordinate sex: A history of attitudes toward women.* Athens: University of Georgia Press.

Butler, O. (1987). *Dawn: The xenogenesis trilogy* (vol. 1). New York: Warner Books.

Butler, O. (1988). *Adulthood rites: The xenogenesis trilogy* (vol. 2). New York: Warner Books.

Butler, O. (1989). *Imago: The xenogenesis trilogy* (vol. 3). New York: Warner Books.

Calahan, D. (1978). Implications of American drinking practices and attitudes for prevention and treatment of alcoholism. In G. A. Marlatt & P. A. Nathan (Eds.), *Behavioral approaches to alcoholism* (pp. 6–26). New Brunswick, NJ: Rutgers.

Carnes, p. (1983). *Out of the shadows: Understanding sexual addiction.* Minneapolis: CompCare.

Carrigan, T., Connell, B., & Lee, J. (1987). Toward a new sociology of masculinity. In H. Brod (Ed.), *The making of masculinities: The new men's studies* (pp. 63–100). Boston: Allen & Unwin.

Chodorow, N. (1978). *The reproduction of mothering.* Berkeley: University of California Press.

Chodorow, N. (1987). Feminism and difference: Gender, relation, and difference in psychoanalytic perspective. In M. R. Walsh (Ed.), *The psychology of women: Ongoing debates* (pp. 249–264). New Haven, CT: Yale University Press.

Chodorow, N. (1989). *Feminism and psychoanalytic theory.* New Haven, CT: Yale University Press.

Clatterbaugh, K. (1990). *Contemporary perspectives on masculinity: Men, women, and politics in modern society.* Boulder, CO: Westview Press.

Coleman, S., Avis, J. M., & Turin, M. (1990). A study of the role of gender in family therapy training. *Family Process, 29*, 365–374.

Cooper, M. L., Russell, M., Skinner, J. B., Frone, M. R., & Mudar, P. (1992). Stress and alcohol use: Moderating effects of gender, coping and alcohol expectancies. *Journal of Abnormal Psychology, 101*, 139–152.

Cowan, C. (1988). Becoming a father: A time of change, an opportunity for development. In P. Bronstein & C. Cowan (Eds.), *Fatherhood today: Men's changing role in the family* (pp. 13–35). New York: Wiley.

David, D. S., & Brannon, R. (1976). *The forty-nine percent majority: The male sex role.* Reading, MA: Addison-Wesley.

Diamond, J. (1987). Counseling male substance abusers. In M. Scher, M. Stevens, G. Good, & G. Eichenfield (Eds.), *Handbook of counseling and psychotherapy with men* (pp. 332–342). Newbury Park, CA: Sage.

Donnerstein, E., & Linz, D. (1987). Mass-media sexual violence and male viewers: Current theory and research. In M. S. Kimmel (Ed.), *Changing men: New directions in research on men and masculinity* (pp. 198–215). Newbury Park, CA: Sage.

Douthitt, R. A. (1989). The division of labor within homes: Have gender roles changed? *Sex Roles, 20*, 693–704.

Draper, p. (1975). !Kung women: Contrasts in sexual egalitarianism in foraging and sedentary contexts. In R. R. Reiter (Ed.), *Toward an anthropology of women* (pp. 77–109). New York: Monthly Review Press.

Doyle, J. A. (1989). *The male experience* (2nd ed.) Dubuque, IA: William. C. Brown.

Doyle, R. (1976). *The rape of the male.* St Paul, MN: Poor Richard's Press.

Dworkin, A. (1985). Against the male flood: Censorship, pornography, and equality. *Harvard Women's Law Journal, 8,* 4–12.

Dworkin, S. H., & Gutierrez, F. J. (Eds.). (1992). *Counseling gay men and lesbians: Journey to the end of the rainbow.* Alexandria, VA: American Association for Counseling and Development.

Edwall, G. (1991, January). Above the glass ceiling: Raising the roof. In *Proceedings of the National Council of Schools of Professional Psychology Midwinter Conference on Women's Issues in Professional Psychology Preconference Papers.* Tucson, AZ. (Quoted in Philpot, 1992, p. 65.)

Ehrenreich, B. (1983). *The hearts of men: American dreams and the flight from commitment.* Garden City, NY: Anchor.

Faludi, S. (1991). *Backlash: The undeclared war against American women.* New York: Crown.

Family Therapy Networker. (1988). Shere bashing, *12,* 14–15.

Farrell, W. T. (1987). *Why men are the way they are.* New York: McGraw-Hill.

Farrell, W. T. (1993). *The myth of male power: Why men are the disposable sex.* New York: Simon & Schuster.

Fast, I. (1984). *Gender identity: A different model.* Hillsdale, NJ: Analytic Press.

Fasteau, M. F. (1975). *The male machine.* New York: Dell.

Finkelhor, D., Hotaling, G. T., & Yllo, K. (1988). *Stopping family violence: Research priorities for the coming decade.* Newbury Park, CA: Sage.

Fitzgerald, L. (1993). Sexual harassment: Violence against women in the workplace. *American Psychologist, 48,* 1070–1076.

Fracher, J., & Kimmel, M. (1987). Hard issues and soft spots: Counseling men about sexuality. In M. Scher, M. Stevens, G. Good, & G. Eichenfield, (Eds.), *Handbook of counseling and psychotherapy with men* (pp. 83–96). Newbury Park, CA: Sage.

Freud, S. (1905). Three essays on the theory of sexuality. In J. Strachey (Ed. & Trans.), *The standard edition of the complete psychological works of Sigmund Freud* (vol. 5). London: Hogarth Press.

Friedman, S. (1983). *Men are just desserts.* New York: Warner Books.

Garland, A. F., & Zigler, E. (1993). Adolescent suicide prevention: Current research and social policy implications. *American Psychologist, 48,* 169–182.

Gaylor, L. (1985, July/August). Pornography: A humanist issue. *The Humanist, 15,* 34–40.

Gilbert, L. A. (1985). *Men in dual-career families: Current realities and future prospects.* Hillsdale, NJ: Lawrence Erlbaum.

Gilbert, L. A. (1987). Female and male emotional dependency and its implications for the therapist-client relationship. *Professional Psychology: Research and Practice 18,* 555–561.

Gilder, G. (1973). *Sexual suicide.* New York: Bantam.

Gilmore, D. (1990). *Manhood in the making: Cultural concepts of masculinity.* New Haven, CT: Yale University Press.

Goldberg, H. (1983). *The new male-female relationship.* New York: Morrow.

Goldner, V. (1988). Generation and gender: Normative and covert hierarchies. *Family Process 27*, 17–31.

Golombok, S., Spencer, A., & Rutter, M. (1983). Children in lesbian and single-parent households: Psychosexual and psychiatric appraisal. *Journal of Child Psychology and Psychiatry and Allied Disciplines, 24*, 551–572.

Goodman, L. A., Koss, M. P. , Fitzgerald, L. F., Russo, N. F., & Keita, G. P. (1993). Male violence against women: Current research and future directions. *American Psychologist, 48*, 1054–1058.

Gottfried, A. E., & Gottfried, A. W. (1988). *Maternal employment and children's development.* New York: Plenum.

Grant, B. F., Harford, T. C., Hasin, D. S., Chou, P., & Pickering, R. (1992). DSM-III-R and the proposed DSM-IV alcohol use disorders, United States 1988: A nosological comparison. *Alcoholism: Clinical and Experimental Research, 16*, 215–221.

Gross, A. (1978). The male role and heterosexual behavior. *Journal of Social Issues 34*, 87–107.

Haddad, R. (1985). Concepts and overview of the men's liberation movement. In F. Baumli (Ed.), *Men freeing men* (pp. 281–289). Jersey City, NJ: New Atlantis.

Hagan, K. L. (1992). Introduction. In K. L. Hagan (Ed.), *Women respond to the men's movement* (pp. xi–xiv). San Francisco: Pandora.

Hammond, W. R., & Yung, B. (1993). Psychology's role in the public health response to assaultive violence among young African-American men. *American Psychologist, 48*, 142–154.

Haraway, D. (1989). *Primate visions.* New York: Routledge.

Harris, L., Blum, R. W., & Resnick, M. (1991). Teen females in Minnesota: A portrait of quiet disturbance. In C. Gilligan, A. G. Rogers, & D. L. Tolman (Eds.), *Women, girls, and psychotherapy* (pp. 119–135). New York: Harrington Park Press.

Harrison, J., Chin, J., & Ficcarrotto, T. (1989). Warning: Masculinity may be hazardous to your health. In M. S. Kimmel & M. A. Messner (Eds.), *Men's lives* (pp. 296–309). New York: Macmillan.

Hart, B. (1993). The legal road to freedom. In M. Hansen & M. Harway (Eds.), *Battering and family therapy: A feminist perspective* (pp. 13–28). Newbury Park, CA: Sage.

Harway, M., & Hansen, M. (1993a). Therapist perceptions of family violence. In M. Hansen & M. Harway (Eds.), *Battering and family therapy: A feminist perspective* (pp. 42–53). Newbury Park, CA: Sage.

Harway, M., & Hansen, M. (1993b). An overview of domestic violence. In M. Hansen & M. Harway (Eds.), *Battering and family therapy: A feminist perspective* (pp. 1–12). Newbury Park, CA: Sage.

Haworth, A. (1993, May). Samoa: Where men think they are women. *Marie-Claire* (U.K. edi.), 50–54.

Hayward, R. (1988, April). Play mr. for me. *Spectator, 12*, 22–28.

Hazzard, W. (1989). Why do women live longer than men? Biological differences. *Postgraduate Medicine, 85*, 271–278, 281–283.

Heilman, R. (1973). *Early recognition of alcoholism and other drug dependence.* Center City, MN: Hazelden.

Hetrick, E. S., & Martin, A. D. (1984). Ego-dystonic homosexuality: A developmental view. In E. M. Hetrick & T. Stein (Eds.), *Psychotherapy with homosexuals* (pp. 1–21). Washington, DC: American Psychiatric Press.

Hetrick, E. S., & Martin, A. D. (1988). The stigmatization of the gay and lesbian adolescent. *Journal of Homosexuality, 51,* 163–183.

Hewlett, B. S. (1987). Intimate fathers. In M. Lamb (Ed.), *The father's role: Cross-cultural perspectives* (pp. 292–330). Hillsdale, NJ: Lawrence Erlbaum.

Hewlett, B. S. (1991). *Intimate fathers.* Ann Arbor: University of Michigan Press.

Hewlett, B. S. (1992). *Father-child relations: Cultural and biosocial contexts.* New York: Aldine de Gruyter.

Hite, S. (1987). *Women and love: A cultural revolution in progress.* New York: Knopf.

Hochschild, A. (1989). *The second shift.* New York: Viking.

Kaplan, R. S., O'Neil, J. S., & Owen, S. V. (1993, August). *Misogynous, normative, progressive masculinity and sexual assault: Gender role conflict, hostility toward women and hypermasculinity.* Paper presented at the annual convention of the American Psychological Association, Toronto.

Kaufman, M. (1987). *Beyond patriarchy: Essays by men on pleasure, power, and change.* Toronto: Oxford University Press.

Kerr, M. E., & Bowen, M. (1988). *Family evaluation.* New York: Norton.

Kiley, D. (1983). *The Peter Pan syndrome: Men who have never grown up.* New York: Dodd-Mead.

Kimmel. M. (1989). From pedestals to partners: Men's responses to feminism. In J. Freeman (Ed.), *Women: A feminist perspective* (pp. 581–594). Mountain View, CA: Mayfield.

Kirsh, B. (1974). Consciousness-raising groups as therapy for women. In F. V. Burtle (Ed.), *Women in therapy* (pp. 326–354). New York: Bruner/Mazel.

Kiselica, M. S., Stroud, J., Stroud, J., & Rotzien, A. (1992). Counseling the forgetten client: The teen father. *Journal of Mental Health Counseling, 14,* 338–350.

Koss, M. P. (1993). Rape: Scope, impact, interventions, and public policy responses. *American Psychologist, 48,* 1062–1069.

Koss, M., & Dinero, T. E. (1988). Predictors of sexual aggression among a national sample of male college students. In R. A. Prentky & V. L. Quinsey (Eds.), Human sexual aggression: Current perspectives (special issue). *Annals of the New York Academy of Sciences, 528,* 133–146.

Koss, M. P., Gidycz, C. A., & Wisniewski, N. (1987). The scope of rape: Incidence and prevalence of sexual aggression and victimization in a national sample of higher education students. *Journal of Consulting and Clinical Psychology, 55,* 162–17.

Kraemer, S. (1991). The origins of fatherhood: An ancient family process. *Family Process, 30,* 377–392.

LaBelle, B. (1980). The propaganda of misogyny. In L. Lederer (Ed.), *Take back the night: Women on pornography* (pp. 23–29). New York: Morrow.

Lamb, M. (1987). The emergent American father. In M. Lamb (Ed.), *The father's role: Cross-cultural perspectives* (pp. 3–25). Hillsdale, NJ: Lawrence Erlbaum.

Lamb, M. E., Owen, M. J., & Chase-Lansdale, L. (1978). The father-daughter relationship: Past, present, future. In C. B. Knopp & M. Kirkpatrick (Eds.), *Becoming female* (pp. 73–84). New York: Plenum.

LaRossa, R. (1989). Fatherhood and social change. *Men's Studies Review, 6,* 1–9.

Lederer, L. (Ed.). (1980). *Take back the night: Women on pornography.* New York: Morrow.

Lepowsky, L. (1994, March 29). Sexes are equal on one South Sea isle. *New York Times,* pp. C1, C11.

Levant, R. (1990). Psychological services designed for men: A psychoeducational approach. *Psychotherapy, 27,* 309–315.

Levant, R. (1992). Toward the reconstruction of masculinity. *Journal of Family psychology, 5,* 379–402.

Levant. R., & Kelley, J. (1989). *Between father and child.* New York: Viking.

Limbaugh, R. (1992). *The way things ought to be.* New York: Pocket Books.

MacKinnon, C. A. (1985). Pornography, civil rights, and speech. *Harvard Civil Rights-Civil Liberties Law Review 20*(1), 1–20.

Madigan, F. (1957). Are sex mortality differentials biologically caused? *Millbank Memorial Fund Quarterly, 35,* 202–213.

Mahler, M. S., Pine, F., & Bergman, A. (1978). *The psychological birth of the human infant.* New York: Basic Books.

Majors, R., & Billson, J. M. (1992). *Cool pose: The dilemmas of black manhood in America.* New York: Lexington Books.

Malamuth, N. M. (1981). Rape proclivity among males. *Journal of Social Issues, 37,* 138–157.

Marin, p. (1991, July 8). Born to lose: The prejudice against men. *Nation,* 46–51.

Meissner, M. (1992). *Power at play. Sports and the problem of masculinity.* Boston: Beacon Press.

Miedzian, M. (1991). *Boys will be boys; Breaking the link between masculinity and violence.* New York: Doubleday.

Miller, J. B. (1986). *Toward a new psychology of women* (2nd ed.). Boston: Beacon Press.

Mintz, L. B., & O'Neil, J. M. (1990). Gender roles, sex, and the process of psychotherapy: Many questions and few answers. *Journal of Counseling and Development, 68,* 381–387.

Montagu, A. (1974). *The natural superiority of women.* New York: Collier.

Moye, A. (1985). Pornograpy. In A. Metcalfe & M. Humphries (Eds.), *The sexuality of men* (pp. 185–197). London: Pluto Press.

Nathanson, C. A. (1977). Sex roles as variables in preventive health behavior. *Journal of Community Health, 3,* 142–155.

New York Times (1989, June 17). The costs of alcohol and tragedy (p. 22).

Nolen-Hoeksema (1990). *Sex differences in depression.* Stanford, CA: Stanford University Press.

Norwood, R. (1985). *Women who love too much: When you keep wishing and hoping he'll change.* Los Angeles: J. P. Tarcher.

Okin, S. M. (1989). *Justice, gender and the family.* New York: Basic Books.

O'Leary, V. E., & Donahue, J. M. (1978). Latitudes of masculinity: Reactions to sex-role deviance in men. *Journal of Social Issues, 34,* 17–28.

O'Neil, J. M. (1982). Gender-role conflict and strain in men's lives. In K. Solomon & N. Levy (Eds.), *Men in transition: Theory and therapy* (pp. 5–44). New York: Plenum.

O'Neil, J. M., & Egan, J. (1992a). Men's gender role transitions over the life span: Transformation and fears of femininity. *Journal of Mental Health Counseling, 14,* 305–324.

O'Neil, J. M., & Egan, J. (1992b). Men's and women's gender role journeys: Metaphor for healing, transition, and transformation. In B. Wainrib (Ed.), *Gender issues across the life cycle* (pp. 107–123). New York: Springer.

O'Neil, J. M., Helms, B. J., Gable, R., David, L., & Wrightman, L. (1986). Gender-role conflict scale: College men's fear of femininity. *Sex Roles, 14,* 335–350.

Osherson, S. (1986). *Finding our fathers: The unfinished business of manhood.* New York: Free Press.

Parsons, T. (1964). *Social structure and personality.* New York: Free Press.

Patterson, C. (1992). Children of lesbian and gay parents. *Child Development, 63,* 1025–1042.

Petersen, A. C., Compas, B. E., Brooks-Gunn, J., Stemmler, M., Ey, S., & Grant, K. E. (1993). Depression in adolescence. *American Psychologist, 48,* 155–168.

Philpot, C. L. (1992). Introducing gender-sensitivity training into family psychology programs. *Topics in Family Psychology and Counseling, 1,* 64–80.

Piercy, M. (1991). *He, she, it.* New York: Fawcett Press.

Pittman, F. (1990). The masculine mystique. *Family Therapy Networker, 14*(3), 40–52.

Pleck, J. H. (1981). *The myth of masculinity.* Cambridge, MA: MIT Press.

Pleck, J. H. (1987). American fathering in historical perspective. In M. S. Kimmel (Ed.), *Changing men: New directions in research on men and masculinity* (pp. 83–97). Newbury Park, CA: Sage.

Pleck, J. H. (1993). Are "family-supportive" employer policies relevant to men? In J. C. Hood (Ed.), *Work, family, and masculinities* (pp. 217–237). Newbury Park, CA: Sage.

Pollack, W. S. (1990). Men's development and psychotherapy: A psychoanalytic perspective. *Psychotherapy, 27,* 316–321.

Pollack, W. S. (1992a). Should men treat women? Dilemmas for the male psychotherapist: Psychoanalytic and developmental perspectives. *Ethics and Behavior, 2,* 39–49.

Pollack, W. S. (1992b). *No man is an island: Reframing the psychology of men.* Invited address to the Division of General Psychology of the American Psychological Association. Presented at the Centennial Meeting of the American Psychological Association, Washington, DC, August 1992.

Pope, K. S., Keith-Spiegel, P. , & Tabachnick, B. G. (1986). Sexual attraction to clients: The human therapist and the (sometimes) inhuman training system. *American Psychologist, 41,* 147–158.

Retherford, R. (1975). *The changing sex differential in mortality.* Westport, CT: Greenwood Press.

Robertson, J. M., & Verschelden, C. (1993). Voluntary male homemakers and female providers: Reported experiences and perceived social reactions. *Journal of Men's Studies, 1,* 383–402.

Robertson, N. (1988). *Getting better: Inside Alcoholics Anonymous.* New York: Morrow.

Ross, M. H. (1985). Internal and external conflict and violence: Cross-cultural evidence and a new analysis. *Journal of Conflict Resolution, 29,* 547–579.

Rotundo, E. A. (1993). *American manhood: Transformations in masculinity from the revolution to the modern era.* New York: Basic Books.

Russell, D. E. H. (1982). The prevalence and incidence of forcible rape and attempted rape of females. *Victimology: An International Journal, 7,* 81–93.

Russell, D. E. H., & Lederer, L. (1980). Questions we get asked most often. In L. Lederer (Ed.), *Take back the night: Women on pornography* (pp. 23–29). New York: Morrow.

Sattel, J. W. (1976). The inexpressive male: Tragedy or sexual politics? *Social Problems, 23,* 469–477.

Scanzoni, E. (1982). *Sexual bargaining: Power politics in the American marriage* (2nd ed.). Chicago: University of Chicago Press.

Scher, M. (1990). Effect of gender role incongruities on men's experience as clients in psychotherapy. *Psychotherapy, 27,* 322–326.

Segal, L. (1990). *Slow motion: Changing masculinities, changing men.* New Brunswick, NJ: Rutgers University Press.

Shibley Hyde, J. (1993). Cited by J. Bales, Gender differences largest in views on sex, Hyde finds. *APA Monitor, 24*(11), 7.

Shiffman, M. (1987). The men's movement: An exploratory empirical investigation. In M. S. Kimmel (Ed.), *Changing men: New directions in research on men and masculinity* (pp. 295–314). Newbury Park, CA: Sage.

Silverstein, L. (1993). Primate research, family politics, and social policy: Transforming "cads" into "dads." *Journal of Family Psychology, 7,* 267–282.

Skord, K. G., & Schumacher, B. (1982). Masculinity as a handicapping condition. *Rehabilitation Literature, 43*(9–10), 284–289.

Smith, M. (1983). *Violence and sport.* Toronto: Butterworth.

Smuts, B., Cheney, D. L., Seyfarth, R. M., Wrangham, R. W., & Struhsaker, T. T. (Eds.). (1987). *Primate societies.* Chicago: University of Chicago Press.

Solomon, K. (1982). The masculine gender role: Description. In K. Solomon & N. Levy (Eds.), *Men in transition: Theory and therapy* (pp. 45–76). New York: Plenum.

Stearns, p. (1991). Fatherhood in historical context: The role of social change. In F. W. Bozett & S. M. H. Hanson (Eds.), *Fatherhood and families in cultural context vol. 6, Focus on men* (Springer Series) (pp. 28–52). New York: Springer.

Stein, T. S. (1982). Men's groups. In K. Solomon & N. Levy (Eds.), *Men in transition: Theory and therapy* (pp. 275–307). New York: Plenum.

Stephenson, J. (1991). *Men are not cost-effective.* Napa, CA: Deimer, Smith Publishing.

Stoltenberg, J. (1989). *Refusing to be a man: Essays on sex and justice.* Portland, OR: Breitenbush Books.

Straus, M. A., & Gelles, R. J. (1990). How violent are American families? Estimates from the National Family Violence Resurvey and other studies. In M. A. Strauss & R. J. Gelles (Eds.), *Physical violence in American families* (pp. 95–132). New Brunswick, NJ: Transaction.

Time (1984, October 15). Report on national study (p. 80).

Trivers, R. (1972). Parental investment and sexual selection. In B. Campbell (Ed.), *Sexual selection and the descent of man, 1871–1971* (pp. 136–179). Chicago: Aldine.

Verbrugge, L. M. (1985). Gender and health: An update on hypothesis and evidence. *Journal of Health and Social Behavior, 26,* 156–182.

Wagenvoord, J., & Bailey, J. (1978). *Men: A book for women.* New York: Avon.

Waldron, I. (1976). Why do women live longer than men? *Journal of Human Stress, 2,* 1–13.

Waldron, I. (1983). Sex differences in human mortality: The role of genetic factors. *Social Science and Medicine, 17,* 321–332.

Ward, S. K., Chapman, K., Cohn, E., & Williams, K. (1991). Acquaintance rape and the college social scene. *Family Relations, 40,* 65–71.

Whitten-Stovall, B., & Whitten-Stovall, R. (1989, October). *The psychosexual component of nuclear family violence.* Paper presented at the meeting of the American Public Health Association, Chicago.

Wright, J. D. (1989). *Address unknown: The homeless in America.* New York: Aldine de Gruyter.

Wright, R. H. (1985). Who needs enemies? *Psychotherapy in Private Practice, 3,* 111–118.

Zilbergeld, B. (1983). *Male sexuality.* Toronto: Bantam.

Zilbergeld, B. (1992). *The new male sexuality: The truth about men, sex, and pleasure.* New York: Bantam.

PART IV

THE VARIETIES OF
MASCULINITY

CHAPTER 11

Men of Color: Ethnocultural Variations of Male Gender Role Strain

RICHARD F. LAZUR AND RICHARD MAJORS

Introduction

Male gender roles vary from race to race and from culture to culture (Kimmel & Messner, 1992). They vary as a man develops, matures, and acquires his place in the world. Yet despite this social constructionist understanding, men of color have often been overlooked in the study of male gender roles and their effects upon the quality of life. This chapter examines how men of four cultures of color in the United States—African-American, Latino, American-Indian,[1] and Asian-American—express gender role strain. From the social constructionist perspective, it addresses how these men remain true to their cultural values while adapting to the demands of the dominant society.

Constrained by economic roadblocks and societal discrimination, men of color are frequently considered foreigners by the dominant culture. Often limited by educational opportunities, they are subtly but effectively kept in a subservient status. To be a man of color means confrontation between ethnic identity and demands from the popular culture. Power, success, and even providing for his family are defined within the context of the dominant racial and cultural belief systems. Reconciling cultural and male identities with economic and social obstacles is critical for men of color.

Among ethnic groups, certain attitudes and behaviors are valued and expected among the members. To belong, an individual adopts these perspectives and behaviors. While individual men integrate the male gender role in their own unique ways, the culture of the ethnic group offers survival tech-

---

[1]While many readers may prefer the term "Native American," the authors wish to honor the tradition of the "American-Indian," a term that has returned to popular usage.

niques to guard against inferior status and feelings of oppression. African-American males have adopted distinctive actions and attitudes known as "cool pose" (Majors, 1983, 1986, 1988, 1990, 1991, 1994; Majors & Mancini Billson, 1992). Emphasizing honor, virility, and physical strength, the Latino male adheres to a code of machismo (Ruiz, 1981; Stevens, 1973; Valdés, Barón, & Ponce, 1987). The American-Indian male struggles to maintain contact with a way of life and the traditions of elders while faced with economic castration and political trauma (Braveheart-Jordan, 1993; Schacht, 1993; Schroeder, 1991). Asian-American men resolve their uncertainty privately, in order to save face, and surrender personal autonomy to family obligations and needs (Huang & Ying, 1989; Sue & Sue, 1993). While individual differences and wide variations exist within social classes, these characteristics reflect male gender role strain and socialization across these four cultures of color in the United States.

In his seminal work, *The Myth of Masculinity* (1981), Pleck examined traditionally held beliefs about male gender roles and offers an alternative paradigm from which to view them. From a social constructionist perspective, Pleck suggested that gender roles are operationally defined by widely shared beliefs about what these roles should be. Both men and women maintain notions of what the expected behaviors are for their own and the opposite sex. However, work and family demands make it difficult, if not impossible, to strictly adhere to these prescriptive behaviors. Gender roles are contradictory and inconsistent. Pleck observed that violations frequently occur, and that when they do, they incur social condemnation. This consequence causes people to overconform. He also noted that certain prescribed characteristics, like male aggression and emotional inhibition, are dysfunctional and provoke negative psychological consequences.

Being a man reflects an individual psychology that has integrated attitudes and behaviors from a lifetime of interaction with the world. If a man's personal world encompasses a dominant culture different from his own, he must acknowledge the similarities and differences between his own culture and the dominant one and come to terms with a suitable personal fit (Atkinson, Morton, & Sue, 1993). In such a way, a man of color comes to experience his own unique male gender role.

The Role of Culture

Men are not born, growing from infants through boyhood to manhood, to follow a predetermined biological imperative, encoded in their physical organization. To be a man is to participate in social life as a man, as a gendered being. . . . Our sex may be male, but our identity as men is developed through a complex process of interac-

tion with the culture in which we both learn the gender scripts
appropriate to our culture and attempt to modify those scripts to
make them more palatable. (Kimmel & Messner, 1992, pp. 8, 9)

The social constructionist view asserts that "the meaning of masculinity
varies from culture to culture" (Kimmel & Messner, 1992, p. 9) and, within a
given culture, is modified over time. Men of the same age but different cultures and ethnicity experience their masculinity differently. As a man
matures, his concept of masculinity is modified and redefined according to
his life experiences and his interchanges with the environment. The male
gender role varies according to location, time, and popular beliefs.

Family, friends, and societal expectations play an integral role in the
development of gender roles. Cultural norms affect how the individual male
comes to know his role in society. He learns the expectations and adopts and
modifies them to his unique person. He carries them out in his everyday
behaviors. He interacts with those around him. Through this interaction
with his environment, a man projects an image of self to the world, which
responds to that image and offers feedback. The environment lets him know
whether his behaviors are acceptable or not. Lazur (1983, 1992) calls this
interaction a "conversation." It involves a give-and-take between the individual and the world. Each person projects a particular self-image through
self-presentation (Goffman, 1959). These presentations are influenced by
societal norms that govern what is acceptable and what is not (Goffman,
1955). The norms become incorporated into the individual and dictate
behaviors, thus influencing one's culture.

It is the norms of the culture that define gender roles. "*Sex role norms* are
widely shared prescriptive beliefs about what the sexes ideally *should be*"
(Pleck, 1981, p. 11). Each culture has its own set of beliefs. While similarities
may exist, "ethnic groups within races differ in cultural content. . . . People
of the same racial origin and of the same ethnic groups differ in their cultural
matrices. All browns, or blacks, or whites, or yellows, or reds, are not alike in
the culture in which they live and have their being" (Moore, 1974, p. 41).

Through interaction with the culture, a man masters the male gender role.
The conversation he engages in with the culture helps him to define his
unique fit between personal needs and societal expectations. In the process
of the conversation, he comes to know what it means to be a man within his
cultural context. It is this mercurial variation for the individual that powers
gender role strain. Work and family demands require responses from the
individual man on their own merits, not only because of gender role expectations. Life experiences, level of maturity, and comfort with self also influence how the individual adheres to gender role expectations. Although a
member of the culture, each man expresses his own unique masculinity. In
his conversation with the world, he assesses gender role expectations, com-

pares them with his needs, and responds in a way that balances both his needs and societal prescriptions. His response, in turn, is evaluated by the social environment as to how it meets that environment's needs. Feedback is offered in terms of either acceptance or disapproval.

Through his conversation with the culture, a man operationalizes gender role norms. He sees their inconsistencies and conflicting demands. At times, a response is required that opposes his natural inclination. This is especially true in work or family settings where the prescribed behaviors are dysfunctional. Not wishing to perpetuate the dysfunction, he violates the gender role. He does so at the risk of provoking social condemnation and/or negative psychological consequences. He engages in conversation with the world and offers alternative behaviors that can either be integrated into the social norms or put him at risk of being perceived as nonconforming and suffering the social consequences. It is through this process that a man defines his meaning-making system. He interconnects with the culture but defines his own individual male gender role.

For a man of color, defining his own gender role involves integration of the dominant society's restrictions. Measuring himself against the standard that dictates the male gender role for the dominant culture yet denies equal access to the opportunities that sustain that standard evokes in the man of color frustrations, unexpressed emotions, and a drive for survival. Whether African-American, Latino, American-Indian, or Asian-American, he feels oppressed and at a disadvantage because his skin color, physical characteristics, and family heritage are not of the dominant culture. Despite federal legislation and politically correct lip service from those around him, he is understood from his meaning-making system only insofar as it reflects the norms of the dominant culture. If he displays attitudes or conduct discordant with the dominant culture—even though they may be vital to his family's culture—he is proscribed. That is, if he acts according to *his* culture, those in the dominant culture view him as "different," bar his access to resources, and may even engage in acts of violence against him. If he acts according to the prescriptions of the dominant culture, he ascribes to a system that, in effect, negates him, and he is considered by his own people to have "sold out." Whatever his choice, a man of color is constantly faced with the challenge of dealing with the consequences of how he acts. This pressure creates in him additional stress and conflict in fulfilling the male gender role.

Notwithstanding this treacherous reality of life in the United States, a man of color has to find a way to not only survive but to flourish. He has to identify and acknowledge the similarities and differences between his own and the dominant culture. He has to take into account the obstacles that interfere with his acceptance. The conflict and stress arise from the task of finding the suitable personal fit: deciding how he is going to integrate, if at all, his two different cultures. He must identify for himself and those around him what is important to him as a male, and he must express it in his every-day actions. He must develop his own meaning-making system with regard to the male gender role.

The African-American Male

Generations of discrimination, oppression, and racism have left their mark on African-American men. With the highest rates of mortality, substance abuse, unemployment, and imprisonment among all groups, they have been labeled an "endangered species" (Gibbs, 1984, 1989). One belief of the male gender role identity paradigm is that "Black males are particularly vulnerable to gender role identity problems" (Pleck, 1981, p. 25). Believed to have been emasculated by slavery, to be an irresponsible breadwinner and parent, and relegated to menial jobs, the African-American male is perceived as having to prove his manhood. Building his hypothesis on this belief, Moynihan (1965) attributed the social problems found in African-American families to the absence of men and the dependence on women as heads of household, ignoring political and economic realities. By focusing on gender roles, Moynihan sidestepped the societal issues of racism, oppression, and injustice.

However, those realities exist. It was not apathy or gender role confusion that caused African-American men to fail to provide for their families; they failed because financially they could not do so (Frazier, 1939). Economically and politically impotent, African-American males lack adequate access to the educational, commercial, and social resources historically mastered by European-American men. Yet despite these obstacles, African-American men continue to define the male gender role for themselves in the terms of the dominant culture. This inability to acquire what is valued and possessed by the other culture results in feelings of frustration, alienation, bitterness, and rage. No longer willing to accept what is doled out, African-American men attempt to achieve the goals of the male gender role by defending against exploitation and expressing their distrust toward the dominant society.

By adopting "a ritualized form of masculinity that entails behaviors, scripts, physical posturing, impression management, and carefully crafted performances that deliver a single, critical message: pride, strength, and control" (Majors & Mancini Billson, 1992, p. 4), the African-American male embraces a coping strategy of cool pose (Majors, 1983, 1986, 1988, 1990, 1991, 1994; Majors & Mancini Billson, 1992). He proclaims to the world that he is an African-American male.

The goals of cool pose are social competence, protection, and conveying a sense of pride. Creating, acting, and redefining himself through handshakes, walking, eye work, body stance, and facial expressions, the African-American male proclaims to the world that he is proud, in control, powerful, and strong. It is his way of counteracting stress and adapting to environmental circumstances. Cool pose also expresses bitterness, anger, and distrust toward the dominant culture and preserves an African-American man's sense of dignity, pride, and respect.

Kochman (1981) observed a difference between the styles of the dominant and African-American cultures. European-American behavior is low-stimulus, impersonal, nonchallenging, and dispassionate, while the African-American mode is high-stimulus, emotional, rhythmic, animated, and assertive. "While blacks are more interested in expressing than controlling their impulses, whites value self-restraint, understatement, and diffusion of intense situations" (Majors & Mancini Billson, 1992, p. 53). This difference in styles creates judgments, anxieties, and misgivings between the races, especially in urban areas at night. The resultant disquietude perpetuates a cycle of power/control. While cool pose signifies distrust of the dominant culture, it also engenders pride, self-respect, and social competence. It encapsulates masculinity for some African-American males but is not the sole means of expressing the male gender role.

The African-American male's attempt to maintain his identity comes at a cost. By protecting himself against the dominant society, his behaviors often interfere with authentic heterosexual relationships. Cool pose behaviors impede his attempts to develop an open, expressive emotional relationship with a woman. While some African-American women may find his display of power and virility exciting, it can hinder emotional intimacy. Not able to turn the cool pose behaviors off and on at will, the African-American male has difficulty disclosing himself or expressing feelings in a meaningful way to those with whom he wishes to be close. He proves himself at the cost of intimacy.

Another cost is mistreatment of self and other African-Americans. Not able to express his feelings, fears, or worries, yet constantly under pressure to prove his manhood, his emotions burst forth in expressions of assault, accident, or homicide or are buried in alcoholism or substance abuse. "For many Black men, heavy drinking is the norm and is perceived as an attribute of manhood and camaraderie" (Parham & McDavis, 1987, p. 25). Longtime racism, discrimination, and oppression have resulted in homicide, drug abuse, suicide, and accidents being the leading causes of death among African-American men. Alcoholism, diabetes, hypertension, neglect of other treatable diseases, and inadequate health care (Gibbs, 1984, 1989; Parham & McDavis, 1987) have shortened the African-American male's average life span. Pent-up frustrations and unexpressed emotions have the potential to explode against others, especially other African-Americans. Parham and McDavis (1987) observed that the majority of perpetrators of crimes against African-American males are also African-American. If cool pose behavior guards against oppression and second-class treatment from European-American males, it takes its toll on African-Americans.

The toll is most evident on African-American adolescent males. Adopting cool pose tenets, the African-American adolescent male distances himself from uncool activities like achieving success in school. In the midst of developing an identity yet full of self-doubt, confused about how to express himself, and confronted by the contrast between self and the dominant culture, the adolescent male often seeks identity refuge in a gang. Promoting a masculine culture, the gang embraces initiation rites, displays of strength and daring, camaraderie, and even fashion.

> The gang can become a family that offers belonging, pride, respect, and empowerment that may be absent in the home or denied by society.... African-American gang members have their own rules and culture. They are consumed with symbols that identify and promote a masculine cultural display: distinctive handshakes, hairstyles, stance, walks, battle scars, turf wars, hand signals, language, and nicknames. (Majors & Mancini Billson, 1992, pp. 50, 51)

The costs are often immense. Gang warfare, crime, possession and use of weapons, substance abuse, dropping out of school, and risk-taking behaviors are destructive and endanger the next generation of African-Americans, both male and female. Continuing to overcome centuries of oppression, African-American adolescent males fight to find a way to leave their mark on the world, often at the price of their lives.

The African-American man redefines and operationalizes his male gender role in the struggle to better his life and the lives of those he loves. He attempts to gain status and economic parity. He wards off the power differential with the dominant culture by adopting a certain physical style of interacting with the world. He proclaims his competence, projects his pride, and protects himself. It is one of the few ways he can assert his manhood in the dominant culture.

The Latino Male

Lending the English language a word to describe the essence of virility, *machismo* involves "physical strength, sexual attractiveness, virtue, and potency" (Ruiz, 1981, p. 191). With this clear definition of what it means to be masculine, men of various Hispanic countries attempt to integrate the cultural demands of their heritage into the male gender role. Mexican-Americans, Puerto Ricans, Cubans, and the men of South American nations all have masculine identifications and behaviors prescribed by their societies.[2]

When the term is applied by non-Latinos, however, "'macho' often is defined in terms of physical aggression, sexual promiscuity, dominance of women, and excessive use of alcohol" (Ruiz, 1981, p. 192).

> What has happened over the years is that English has usurped the word and reworked the definition, turning it into the functional equivalent of male chauvinism. The sociological and psychological impact of this has been to stereotype unfairly Hispanic men as being exaggeratedly masculine in their behavior. While there is no doubt that chauvinism and sexism occur among Hispanic men, we doubt that they exist to a greater degree than in other groups. (Valdés, Barón, & Ponce, 1987, p. 210)

Latinos are the fastest-growing group in the United States, owing in part to immigration and high fertility rates (Gibbs, 1989). In addition to their cultural diversity, they exhibit

> variation in racial characteristics. Hispanics represent a mixture of several racial groupings. Some families trace their bloodlines directly back to Spain and consequently retain Caucasian features. Other families share multiple bloodlines comprising [the] Native-American, African, and Caucasian races. (Valdés, Barón, & Ponce, 1987, p. 209)

Naturally then, Latino men express male gender roles in various ways. Shifts occur across generations as Puerto Rican families acculturate (Inclan & Herron, 1989). Moving from an agrarian to an industrial economy changes the Puerto Rican family: Where once children would have stayed within the family, they now live in a culture that encourages individual autonomy. This change creates stress and conflict within the family. "The first generation tends to uphold its culture of origin and values in the new host culture" (Inclan & Herron, 1989, p. 256), while second and third generations have a foot in both the culture of origin and the new environment.

> Prior to the development of capitalism, the home was the center and focus of all human activity—work, recreation, family life, etc., and all members of the family—men, women, children—participated alike. Capitalism brought with it a split . . . [and] wage-labor . . . now began to be performed at the work center and was primarily the responsibility of men. . . . Characteristics such as unemotionality, toughness, and performance-minded[ness] became institutionalized and reinforced as male characteristics while the realm of the emotional, personal life was valued in women. (Inclan, 1983, p. 6)

---

[2]While more than 20 nationalities can be categorized as Latino, only those in a majority in the United States—Mexican-Americans, Puerto Ricans, and Cubans—will be considered here. Stevens (1973) observed a difference between those cultures affected by "outside" conquering cultures and those where indigenous autonomy prevails. Machismo prevails in the former, whereas the latter honor the matrilineal family structure.

While traditionally Latino males were expected to be strong and forceful, to withhold affectionate emotions, and to be the provider and protector of the family (Ramirez, 1989), male dominance among Mexican-Americans is part of

> the status structure within which their interactions occur. This emphasis is crucial because it alerts us to the importance of structural variables in understanding sex stratification. Furthermore, it casts doubt on interpretations which treat culture (the systems of shared beliefs and orientations unique to a group) as the cause of male dominance. If male dominance is universal, then it cannot be reduced to the culture of a particular category of people. (Baca Zinn, 1982, p. 30)

Although machismo influences the patriarchal structure, gender roles may still vary, as Ramirez and Arce (1981) observed. They espoused traditional values, but when observed during real life, Mexican-American men tend to share the day-to-day decision-making with women, and there is greater equality and opportunity for women in this culture than its traditional values would lead one to expect. True, some families remain patriarchal with domineering husbands, while others are matriarchally dominated with docile males (Falicov, 1982), but there appears to be movement toward an egalitarian system.

Confronted with the male gender role demands of the dominant culture yet denied economic and political access to its resources, Latino men have undergone increasing stress. Alcohol has been viewed as providing relief from the sense of powerlessness, inferiority, and subordination. "Hispanic men have markedly higher rates of alcoholism, arrest for drunken behavior, deaths due to cirrhosis of the liver, and deaths due to alcohol-related traffic accidents than do non-Latino American males" (Panitz, McConchie, Sauber, & Fonseca, 1983, p. 31). The high incidence of poverty, cultural pride in the manufacture of alcohol in the homeland, absence of religious strictures, responsibility for extended family members, and the machismo ethos are cited as major influences.

In an attempt to tease out the significance of machismo, Neff, Prihoda, and Hoppe (1991) found that while Mexican-American and African-American males are more likely to be highly macho, Mexican-Americans are more likely to be heavy drinkers (5–6 drinks at a sitting) than either European-American or African-American males. For these groups, high machismo was generally associated with a low probability of heavy drinking. The authors cite a model of powerlessness wherein the individual compensates for what he does not yet have. "Machismo is no more strongly related to alcohol use among Mexican-Americans than among Anglos or blacks" (Neff, Prihoda, & Hoppe, 1991, p. 461).

The study also found that high macho males are more likely to have low self-esteem than are low macho males. Neff et al. argue that, "although 'machismo,' per se, is typically not discussed as a core element of Anglo culture, machismo effects are significant in all Anglo subgroups" (p. 461).

Using dominoes as a metaphor of how Puerto Rican males interact, Inclan (1983, 1991) has observed a cultural shift with the advent of industrialization as means to economic development. With the change in the social structure, dominoes came to represent a way for men to connect outside the worksite and to express a full spectrum of "interpersonal possibilities—from aggressivity [*sic*] and competition to support and collaboration—all framed in the 'pretend' language of playing a game" (1983, p. 7). At times serving as respite from conflict at home, dominoes represent loyalty and partnership among Puerto Rican men. During play, a "no talking" rule exists. "It's a structure where communication and affect can be exchanged in safe and metaphorical ways. It is one of a variety of responses that a people has developed to deal with male-male relationships in their special set of historical circumstances" (1983, p. 14).

Within the various cultures of the Latino community, the male gender role also varies according to the nationality, ethnic identity, acculturation into the dominant culture, responsibilities to the extended family, poverty, and machismo of the individual man. The progressive aspects of machismo can be celebrated. However, as Pleck (1981) noted, violation of gender roles leads to social condemnation and negative psychological consequences. Baca Zinn (1982) observed: "Perhaps manhood takes on greater importance for those who do not have access to socially valued roles. Being male is one sure way to acquire status when other roles are systematically denied by the workings of society" (p. 39).

The Latino man draws upon his culture of machismo to define his male gender role in the face of the demands of the dominant culture. Confronted with economic and social obstacles that impede his access to power and success, he attempts to reconcile the differences and integrate the standards of his own culture with those of the dominant one. However, he pays the price in stress, which takes its toll not only on him but on those he loves and on the community in which he lives.

The American-Indian Male

An ethnic group indigenous to the North American continent and the only one legally defined by Congress (Trimble & Fleming, 1989), "American-Indians" are a highly heterogeneous people "comprised of approximately 530 distinct tribes of which 478 are recognized by the U.S. government" (Sue & Sue, 1990, p. 176). Even though differences in family structure, language, and customs exist between tribes, an individual with 25% Indian blood is considered American-Indian (Trimble, 1988; Sue &

Sue, 1990).[3] Culture plays an important role in the definition of gender roles for the American-Indian, but little has been written about those roles and how the changes within the culture affect American-Indian men. Once the providers of food and game for the community, American-Indian males have been run over by the dominant culture (Braveheart-Jordan, 1993; Schroeder, 1991), leading to the unavailability of male role models and the conflict of living in a dominant culture that is frequently incompatible with the core identity.

Cooperative by nature, the American-Indian tribe plays an important role in individual identity. Seeing themselves individually as extensions of the tribe, "this identity provides them with a sense of belonging and security, with which they form an interdependent system" (Sue & Sue, 1990, p. 177). Everyone is essential to the tribe's functioning (Schacht, 1993). Individual behaviors are judged according to how they benefit the tribe. If others benefit from the behavior, then it is good. In Eskimo villages above the Arctic Circle, whale hunters are revered for bringing food to the entire community.

Establishing a sense of affinity, the tribe encourages interdependence. Grandparents, aunts, uncles, and cousins play instrumental roles in teaching the child how to function. Skills are taught and customs passed through the generations by oral tradition. Maternal uncles are frequently responsible for instructing boys in the skills, traditions, and cultural values necessary for survival and spiritual harmony. The life force of nature is honored and esteemed within others and within the self. The duality of forces, the masculine and feminine, which beget energy and channel life, is venerated. Even in hunting, the animal's life is honored for the good it offers to others.

However, as government regulations have restricted the use of land, American-Indians have been confined and the traditions of the past changed. The traditional male roles of hunter, warrior, teacher, and leader have been nullified. The dominant culture holds power, prestige, and influence, which it exerts in ways that are antithetical to American-Indian tradition. "As members of a conquered nation, they have replaced ancient behaviors in service of survival, often at the cost of health" (Schroeder, 1991).

Examining the cumulative trauma for multiple generations when a way of life that had existed for thousands of years was wiped out in a single generation, Perez (1993) attributes current problems of American-Indian life to the stress incurred by dependence on a dominant foreign force. Heart disease, accidents, cancer, chronic liver disease and cirrhosis, and suicide are the leading causes of death among American-Indian males (U.S. Department of Health and Human Services, 1992). One-third of American-Indian males

[3]The authors recognize the uniqueness of the individual American-Indian cultures. Unfortunately, space does not allow for a more detailed description of the individual peoples; only salient shared characteristics are considered here. Clearly, more work in this area needs to be done.

in the state of New Mexico die before reaching age 35 (DeBruyn, 1993). The rate of suicide among Alaska Native American males is 10 times the national average. Within a 16-month period, one village of 550 people experienced "eight suicides [one of whom was female], dozens of attempts, two murders, and four drownings" (Weaver, 1988, p. A2). Alcohol, the destruction of the subsistence lifestyle, poor educational opportunities, and few jobs have made an impact. American-Indian males have lost the core activities that were integral to their identity.

A Tsimshian Indian, Doug Modig, declared, "Our culture has been destroyed" (Weaver, 1988, p. A3). Another, Thelkla Hootch, said, "The men are not what they were. Men had dog teams, they'd go out in the morning. Everybody helped each other. My grandfather would go hunt ducks and seals. They don't do that anymore. They're on welfare, food stamps. . . . It's not like it used to be" (Weaver, 1988, p. A3). The effects of the dominant culture have been profound.

Rectifying the distortions of history—distortions often internalized by American-Indians themselves—DeBruyn (1993) clarifies the role of the Lakota warrior. Warriors were the protectors willing to bravely sacrifice themselves to defend their people. War was the last resort, not a thing of glory, as depicted by European-American culture. Schacht (1993) suggests that when the American-Indian male was unable to fill the protector role, he lost an important identity. Losing relatives and friends to the invasion by the dominant culture was extremely painful. Unable to do his job of protecting the community led to self-hatred and a learned helplessness in the realization that there was no escape from the pain.

Unable to counteract the intrusions of the dominant culture, American-Indian males have found that their attempts to integrate into it have been equally destructive. "Frequent relocation, substandard living conditions, and chronic unemployment in both urban and reservation areas have taken their toll on Indian people" (La Fromboise & Graff Low, 1989, p. 116). Denied access to the resources necessary for a subsistence lifestyle and to educational and economic opportunities, the American-Indian male is often compelled to work in the city, leaving behind his culture and ancient ways of life. Faced with racism, stereotypic images (Trimble, 1988), and the great number in people in a city, many feel overwhelmed and unable to cope. Despite these hardships, the economic future appears to be better for American-Indians in urban areas, and the majority of American-Indians live outside of trust lands, villages, pueblos, and reservations (La Fromboise & Graff Low, 1989).

However, in leaving, they become unavailable for tribal ceremonies. Traditional practice holds that everyone is essential to the tribe's function. If they leave, they will not be present during crucial times in ceremonial events. The community feels abandoned, creating a conflict that makes it difficult to function (Schacht, 1993) and presents a difficult choice: loyalty to the tribe, or economic survival.

Drawing a parallel to domestic violence in a family, Schroeder (1991) likens the dominant culture to the powerful father who beats a boy's mother, the American-Indian culture. Witnessing this abuse and uncertain about their cultural identity, American-Indian males lack adequate male gender role models. Wanting to protect his mother but fearing retaliation, the boy regards the father with disgust and hatred; however, as a male, he looks to the father as his primary source of socialization as a man. Wanting to connect with his mother but also believing that she should be able to protect him, the boy feels contempt for her. "As a culture, as Native-American males have witnessed this desecration of the traditional values, they have very much wanted to defend that, yet have been unable, to with the understandable results of powerlessness, hopelessness, and depression—self-defeating behaviors that would happen in an individual transferred to a cultural level" (Schroeder, 1991).

The effects have been profound. Calling it the "great invisible wound of this country," Schacht (1993) acknowledges the American-Indians' cumulative unresolved grief, which has been ignored by society. "It's never talked about. Nobody is even standing over the graves saying, 'This is a terrible tragedy and something ought to be done about it.'" A way of life, a culture, was destroyed. Children were shipped to boarding schools, provider and protector roles were stripped from the men, and language and customs were extinguished. Adrift, individuals were caught between two worlds. Pent-up feelings could not be expressed. The American-Indians suffer unresolved cultural grief and anger as a people.

A case can be made for calling what is happening to the American-Indians genocide. DeBruyn (1993) applies to the history of American-Indians the definition spelled out by the United Nations 1948 General Assembly's Convention on Genocide.

> Genocide means any of the following acts committed with intent to destroy in whole or in part a national, ethnical, racial, or religious group and includes five types of criminal actions:
> - killing members of the group,
> - causing serious bodily or mental harm to members of the group,
> - deliberately inflicting on the group conditions of life calculated to bring about its physical destruction in whole or in part,
> - imposing measures intended to prevent births within the group, and
> - forcibly transferring children of the group to another group.

These acts have been committed against American-Indians. The effects have been felt by generations of American-Indians seeking their identity as a people. For healing to occur, the anger, grief, and other unexpressed emotions need to be acknowledged and proclaimed.

Drawing upon the grief work done with survivors of the Holocaust, Braveheart-Jordan (1993) proposes that the American-Indian male confront the past, learn the history of his people, and acknowledge his anger and other feelings as he begins the grief process. She and her colleagues lead workshops in which men come to understand and internalize the concept of the "survivor syndrome." Collective responses reduce the sense of isolation and victim-blaming, normalize the experience, and put the blame where it belongs. By sharing a cathartic group experience with other members of the tribal community, survivors are able to share their feelings and mobilize and channel them in individual constructive actions. In such a way, community/cultural values are restored.

Perhaps as American-Indian men grieve the losses of their culture, they will draw upon the amazing strength and resources of previous generations. Then they will be able to use that strength to define the male gender role in such a way as to continue to contribute to the welfare of their people. In so doing, they will reclaim their place in American life.

The Asian-American Male

Observing that members of the dominant culture are unable to distinguish among Asian subgroups and treat all Asian-Americans the same, with no regard for individual and ethnic differences, Chan (1992) distinguishes "thirty separate and distinct ethnic groups, each with their own values, customs, languages, behavior and tradition" (p. 8). Though they all have cultural roots in Confucian and Buddhist traditions, Chinese, Korean, Japanese, and Taiwanese customs differ from each other and from Cambodian, Laotian, and Vietnamese customs. Degree of acculturation also leads to differences: The obligations of a fourth-generation Chinese-American differ from those of an immigrant. To address all Asian-American male gender roles the same would be simplistic; however, little research has been published on any Asian-American male's experience of gender roles. Consequently, this section attempts to integrate the information—much of it found in counseling literature—that is available.

Although customs and religions vary, Sue and Sue (1993) found several similarities between the various Asian-American cultures. Parents instill a sense of obligation to family that is maintained throughout life. Family needs supersede personal autonomy. Even if married, sons maintain a strong allegiance to parents. Emotions are restrained, especially in public. Authority is rooted in a patriarchal system; males are highly valued. "The father's behavior in relationship to other family members is generally dignified, authoritative, remote, and aloof" (Sue and Sue, 1993, p. 200).

Influenced by the teachings of Confucius, Chinese home life is governed by a strict sense of order, with prescribed roles. In return for ensuring the family's economic well-being and social status, the father has unchallenged authority and the loyalty and respect of all family members. Emotional well-being is the responsibility of the mother. Firstborn sons are the "the most valued child, [and] received preferential treatment as well as more familial responsibilities. . . . [They are] expected to provide emotional support to the mother, assume responsibility for the educational and character development of younger siblings, and bring honor and financial support to the family" (Huang & Ying, 1989, pp. 36, 42). These expectations place extreme pressure on firstborn Asian-American males (Hirasma, 1980; Lee, 1982).

A hierarchical family structure characterized by male authority, restrictive emotional displays, and family obligation is also evident in Japanese-American families (Nagata, 1989). For instance:

> It was not uncommon for third generation (Sansei) children to have acquired only the most basic and straightforward facts about their elders' internment experience [during World War II]. . . . They gained little understanding of the personal and group impact of being abruptly removed from homes and incarcerated in desolate locales;. . . or of the extent of racial hatred and wartime hysteria that prevailed. (Nakanishi, 1988, p. 167)

The effects upon Japanese-American families, especially males, of such stoicism has been profound (Sue & Sue, 1990).

Both Chinese- and Japanese-Americans tend to be well educated and to exceed the national median income and have low rates of delinquency, divorce, and psychiatric contact (Sue & Sue, 1990). While they reflect an image of success, closer analysis indicates that poverty is equally prevalent among these groups, more than one wage earner often contributes to the family income, and wages are often not commensurate with education and training. Because disgrace and shame are often associated with public acknowledgment of problems, they are more often resolved within the context of the family rather than through outside resources.

Based on Confucian traditions but influenced by Roman Catholic missionaries, Vietnamese culture values the family as the basic social unit. Extended family interdependence is important. Roles and responsibilities within the family hierarchy are clearly delineated. Elders are respected, and children are seen as the future. "Both children and adults feel a sense of inferiority if children do not achieve goals set by the family" (Huang, 1989, p. 295).

Less socially prescribed, Cambodian culture is influenced by Buddhist teachings. In this patriarchal society, the extended family is acknowledged but the family structure is formed by the couple. Buddhist tradition upholds respect for life in all its forms, the presence of suffering, and the importance of honesty and gentleness. This morality, codified by Cambodian civil law, counterbalances the father's sovereignty as head of the family. Even though he is highly regarded, the husband shares authority with his wife (Huang, 1989).

Noting the plight of Cambodian, Laotian, and Vietnamese immigrants following the Vietnam War, Huang (1989) determined that although loss and culture shock are integral components of the refugee experience, children rate their fathers "as slightly more willing to 'Americanize'" (Huang, 1989, p. 290) than mothers, who are the least happy family members. Physical and sexual assault by sea pirates had a profound impact upon the children, and "adolescent males [were] overwhelmed by fear, shame, rage" (Huang, 1989, p. 292). Many teenage boys, "detached from the native culture and unable to secure a niche in American society, [would] group together [into a gang] for reasons of identity, protection, and economics" (Huang, 1989, p. 292).

Whether he is recently emigrated or several generations acculturated makes a difference in the Asian-American man's attitude and response to the male gender role. It is the balance between the family and the dominant culture that influences how individual Asian-American males prescribe the role for themselves. As Chan (1992) differentiates:

> The distinction between the public and private self is really the very important concept in Asian cultures. The public self is that which conforms to gendered and familial role expectations. The public self behaves in a manner which follows social norms, which seeks to avoid actions which would bring shame upon one's family and one's community. . . . The private self is never seen by anyone other than one's most intimate relationships. (Chan, 1992, p. 9)

Integrating the public and private selves, an Asian-American man's attitude and response to the male gender role differs depending on the amount of time he has spent in this culture. Family values and loyalties, religious philosophy, and economic pursuits are integral parts of male gender role strain. The individual man attempts to make sense of his gender role for himself within the context of his culture and the demands of the world at large.

Discussion

Men of color must overcome societal prejudices, economic obstacles, educational constraints, and, at times, acts of violence to assert their place in the dominant culture. Motivated by the same goals that impel men of the dominant culture, men of color forge the male gender role by balancing personal needs with cultural demands and the expectations of the world at large. However, to date that effort has been ignored by the men's studies literature.

As Kimmel and Messner (1992) have articulated, male gender roles vary from culture to culture and are modified over time within a culture. Even more evident, within a culture, there are variations as well as individual differences. Gender roles are operationally defined by widely shared beliefs (Pleck, 1981). These widely shared beliefs are part of the cultural attitudes. As such, they are important ingredients in the individual man's definition of his gender role.

Through an interaction with the environment, a man comes to know what others expect of him. Family, peers, and societal demands prescribe attitudes and behaviors that comprise his gender role. There is a give-and-take, a conversation, in which the individual projects his particular self-image into the environment. The congruence of this image with societal expectations regulates the environment's response to him. If he is congruent, the feedback is positive and he is accepted. While some differences are tolerated, if he is widely divergent from societal expectations of the male gender role, he is more likely to be ostracized.

This is what constitutes gender role strain. Widely shared beliefs create a norm against which the man and the environment are likely to compare and contrast his attitudes and behaviors. In addition to these norms, stereotypic perceptions of the way each gender acts operationally define gender roles. However, life-cycle inconsistencies, historical changes, and other contradictions make it difficult if not impossible to conform to gender roles (Pleck, 1981). Violations occur. The degree of the violation dictates environmental sanctions. While some behaviors can be tolerated by the environment, if they are too divergent, negative consequences are imposed. If a man fails to live up to critical aspects of the male gender role, or is imagined to have so failed, the environment dictates that he compensate. Often he does so by overconforming (Pleck, 1981).

Through his conversation with the environment, a man evaluates the expectations, compares them with his own needs, determines the risks of noncompliance, and acts accordingly, attempting to balance gender role prescriptions with his own needs. A conversation between the individual and the environment (including cultural attitudes and expectations) assists the man in defining how he wants to live the male gender role possibilities. While men have been criticized for adhering to rigid gender role definitions, it is the rigidity of the expectations and restrictions placed on women that has brought attention to how men fulfill gender roles. Many qualities of male gender roles are highly adaptive for society; however, the constrictions needlessly block the fulfillment of human potential.

As men in the dominant culture examine the usefulness of these constrictions, it is assumed that men of color should do the same. Applying the same paradigm, no matter how useful to one culture, to different cultures is to implicitly deny the importance of the differences and the value of alternative ways of viewing the same kind of life event. Different cultures have different expectations. Not to honor these differences is tantamount to oppression.

For a man of color, a paradigm for understanding gender roles must emerge from his culture and be relevant to it. More research, along with increased dialogue between the culture and dominant expectations, are needed. Without both these contributions to understanding, the differences will be exaggerated and misunderstanding will predominate.

Racism in its various forms needs to be confronted. In his essay "why [sic] is this men's movement so white?" Gordon (1993) raises the issue of European-Americans' fear of African-American men. "But with your fear around confronting male power, I also feel you are afraid of me. *Are you afraid of me?* Are you afraid of who and what I represent? Are you afraid of my blackness?" (p. 15). "For black Americans, racism has been a fact of life for over three centuries" (Jones, 1988, p. 126). Suggesting that racism needs to be addressed on both the individual and institutional levels, Jones asserts that "the dual power to define difference as deficient and to reinforce conformity to prevailing standards is the essential character of cultural racism" (p. 131). He adds, "Two basic beliefs are necessary to convert the problem of racism to our collective advantage: there is strength in diversity, and . . . we are no stronger as a nation than the weakest among us" (p. 133).

For men of color to confront the male gender role, European-American men must also be aware of how facets of their role in the dominant culture suppress and restrain men who are not part of the dominant culture. For too long, the dominant culture has preserved economic, educational, and societal obstacles that have restricted and effectively maintained men of color in a subservient position. Just as European-American males are becoming increasingly aware of the repression of women, so too is it necessary to examine the power differential and their resulting economic supremacy over other males.

The end result is going to be disruptive. Whenever there is a shift in power, those who perceive they are losing it become entrenched and seek to restabilize the equilibrium in their favor. While the dominant culture may give lip service to parity, little has been done to accept, much less integrate, cultures of color in the power structure of the United States.

To do so would create conflict and pain. It would mean changing how things are done and examining traditional and current models, finding the similarities and differences with those of other cultures. In effect, it would mean that the European-American male would have to do what a man of color has always had to do: examine himself to determine how he fits in, if at all.

Economic factors will have to be examined. Traditionally valued as the breadwinner, men have long felt that making money is an essential component of the traditional male gender role. However, men of color have long been discriminated against in this arena. Denied access to the economic opportunities of the dominant culture, men of color have had to work harder, longer, and against greater odds to accomplish less than their European-

American counterparts. And when men of color do succeed, the perception that their color gave them an unfair advantage diminishes their sense of accomplishment and self-worth.

By the year 2000, two-thirds of the American workforce will be people of color and women (Johnston, 1987). The effects on business will be profound. European-American men will be faced with one of the most demanding challenges to their identity: The source of power and control will be threatened by the very people needed to sustain it!

While elaboration of these issues is outside the purview of this chapter, the issues themselves need to be raised. In addressing the context, perhaps some understanding of the impact of male gender role strain on men of color can be attained. However, more research needs to be done.

Data needs to be collected on the expression of male gender roles across cultures in the United States. While African-American, Latino, American-Indian, and Asian-American are four common cultures of color in the United States, they certainly are not the only ones. In reviewing the literature for this chapter, the authors were unable to find information on several cultures, and what was available was limited. Many cultural attributes are generalizations, and each culture is characterized by wide variation within social class and among individual males in their understanding of the male gender role. More participants representing these cultures would add a dialogue of exploration and discovery to the men's studies literature.

Paradigms of other worldviews need to be integrated into the definition of male gender roles; what works in one culture may not apply in another. Other perspectives need to be offered. Changes in definitions as individual men mature and redefine their male gender roles also needs to be respected. Longevity studies within a culture need to be done. Most important, men of the dominant culture need to listen to their brothers of color and learn from their experiences. Regardless of culture, a man participates in an interactive process of defining and redefining his awareness, behaviors, and beliefs about his male gender role. There is much work left to be done. This is just a beginning.

References

Atkinson, D. R., Morton, G., & Sue, D. W. (1993). *Counseling American minorities: A cross-cultural perspective* (4th ed.). Dubuque, IA: William C. Brown.

Baca Zinn, M. (1982). Chicano men and masculinity. *Journal of Ethnic Studies, 10*(2), 29–44.

Braveheart-Jordan, M. (1993, August). Healing historical trauma in Native-American men. In J. Perez (Chair), *Impact of historical trauma on Native-American men.* Symposium presented at the annual meeting of the American Psychological Association, Toronto.

Chan, C. (1992). What's love got to do with it? Sexual/gender identities. *American Psychological Association Division 44 Newsletter, 8*(3), 8–11, 18.

DeBruyn, L. (1993, August). Historical factors impacting the mental health of Native-American men. In J. Perez (Chair), *Impact of historical trauma on Native-American men.* Symposium presented at the annual meeting of the American Psychological Association, Toronto (cassette recording no. 93-083).

Falicov, C. J. (1982). Mexican families. In M. McGoldrick, J. K. Pearce, & J. Giordano (Eds.), *Ethnicity and family therapy* (pp. 164–186). New York: Guilford Press.

Frazier, E. (1939). *The Negro family in the United States.* Chicago: University of Chicago Press.

Gibbs, J. T. (1984). Black adolescents and youth: An endangered species. *American Journal of Orthopsychiatry, 54,* 6–21.

Gibbs, J. T. (Ed.). (1989). *Children of color: Psychological interventions with minority youth.* San Francisco: Jossey-Bass.

Goffman, E. (1955). On face—work. *Psychiatry, 18,* 213–231.

Goffman, E. (1959). *The presentation of self in everyday life.* New York: Doubleday/Anchor.

Gordon, M. D. (1993, Summer/Fall). why [*sic*] is this men's movement so white? *Changing Men, 26,* 15–17.

Hirasma, T. (1980). Minority group children and behavior disorders: The case of Asian-American children. *Behavior Disorders, 5*(3), 186–196.

Huang, L. N. (1989). Southeast Asian refugee children and adolescents. In J. T. Gibbs (Ed.), *Children of color: Psychological interventions with minority youth* (pp. 278–321). San Francisco: Jossey-Bass.

Huang, L. N., & Ying, Y. W. (1989). Chinese-American children and adolescent. In J. T. Gibbs (Ed.), *Children of color: Psychological interventions with minority youth* (pp. 30–66). San Francisco: Jossey-Bass.

Inclan, J. E. (1983, February). *Interpersonal relations among Puerto Rican men; or, why so much dominoes?* Paper presented at the meeting of the Association of Anthropological Study of Play, Baton Rouge, LA.

Inclan, J. E. (1991, March). *Playing dominoes: Relationships among Latino men.* Paper presented at the midwinter meeting of the American Psychological Association, divisions of psychotherapy, independent practice, and family psychology, San Antonio, TX.

Inclan, J. E., & Herron, D. G. (1989). Puerto Rican adolescents. In J. T. Gibbs (Ed.), *Children of color: Psychological interventions with minority youth* (pp. 251–277). San Francisco: Jossey-Bass.

Johnston, W. B. (1987). *Workforce 2000: Work and workers for the 21st century.* Indianapolis: Hudson Institute.

Jones, J. M. (1988). Racism in black and white: A bicultural model of reaction and evolution. In p. A. Katz & D. A. Taylor (Eds.), *Eliminating racism: Profiles in controversy* (pp. 117–135). New York: Plenum.

Kimmel, M., & Messner, M. (1992). *Men's lives* (2nd ed.). New York: Macmillan.

Kochman, T. (1981). *Black and white styles in conflict.* Chicago: University of Chicago Press.

La Framboise, T. D., & Graff Low, K. (1989). American-Indian children and adolescents. In J. T. Gibbs (Ed.), *Children of color: Psychological interventions with minority youth* (pp. 114–147). San Francisco: Jossey-Bass.

Lazur, R. F. (1983). *What it means to be a man: A phenomenological study of masculinity.* Unpublished doctoral dissertation, Massachusetts School of Professional Psychology, Newton.

Lazur, R. F. (1992, August). Warrior child: Narcissistic injuries of the male sex role. In M. R. Wong (Chair), *Snips and snails and puppy dog tails: Men and shame.* Symposium presented at the centennial meeting of the American Psychological Association, Washington, DC.

Lee, L. (1982). Social systems approach to assessment and treatment for Chinese-American families. In M. McGoldrick, J. K. Pearce, & J. Giordano (Eds.), *Ethnicity and family therapy* (pp. 164–186). New York: Guilford Press.

Majors, R. (1983). *Cool pose: A new hypothesis in understanding antisocial behavior in lower socioeconomic status males.* Unpublished manuscript, University of Illinois, Urbana.

Majors, R. (1986). Cool pose: The proud signature of black survival. *Changing Men: Issues in Gender, Sex, and Politics, 17,* 5–6.

Majors, R. (1988). Cool pose: A new approach toward systemic understanding and studying of black male behavior. *Dissertation Abstracts International, 49–01,* 259B.

Majors, R. (1990). Cool pose: Black masculinity and sport. In M. Messner & D. Sabo (Eds.), *Sport, men, and the gender role: Critical feminist perspectives* (pp. 109–114). Champaign, IL: Human Kinetics.

Majors, R. (1991). Nonverbal behavior and communications styles among African Americans. In R. Jones (Ed.), *Black psychology* (3rd ed.) (pp. 269—294). Berkeley, CA: Cobb & Henry.

Majors, R. (1994). *The American black male: His present status and future.* Chicago: Nelson & Hall.

Majors, R., & Mancini Billson, J. (1992). *Cool pose: The dilemmas of black manhood in America.* New York: Lexington Books.

Moore, B. M. (1974). Cultural differences and counseling perspectives. *Texas Personnel and Guidance Association Journal, 3,* 39–44.

Moynihan, D. (1965). *The Negro family: The case for national action.* Washington, DC: U.S. Government Printing Office.

Nagata, D. K. (1989). Japanese American children and adolescents. In J. T. Gibbs (Ed.), *Children of color: Psychological interventions with minority youth* (pp. 67–113). San Francisco: Jossey-Bass.

Nakanishi, D. T. (1988). Convergence in race relations research: Japanese-Americans and the resurrection of the internment. In P. A. Katz & D. A. Taylor (Eds.), *Eliminating racism: Profiles in controversy* (pp. 159–180). New York: Plenum.

Neff, J. A., Prihoda, T. S., & Hoppe, S. K. (1991). "Machismo," self-esteem, education and high maximum drinking among Anglo, black, and Mexican-American male drinkers. *Journal of Social Studies, 52*(5), 458–463.

Panitz, D. R., McConchie, R. D., Sauber, S. R., & Fonseca, J. A. (1983). The role of machismo and the Hispanic family in the etiology and treatment of alcoholism in Hispanic American males. *American Journal of Family Therapy, 11*(1), 31–44.

Parham, T. A., & McDavis, R. J. (1987). Black men, an endangered species: Who's really pulling the trigger? *Journal of Counseling and Development, 66,* 24–27.

Perez, J. (Chair). (1993, August). *Impact of historical trauma on Native-American men.* Symposium presented at the annual meeting of the American Psychological Association, Toronto.

Pleck, J. (1981). *The myth of masculinity.* Cambridge, MA: MIT Press.

Ramirez, O. (1989). Mexican-American Children and Adolescents. In J. T. Gibbs (Ed.), *Children of color: Psychological interventions with minority youth* (pp. 224–250). San Francisco: Jossey-Bass.

Ramirez, O., & Arce, C. H. (1981). The contemporary Chicano family: An empirically based review. In A. Barón, Jr. (Ed.), *Explorations in Chicano psychology* (pp. 3–35). New York: Praeger.

Ruiz, R. A. (1981). Cultural and historical perspective in counseling Hispanics. In D. W. Sue (Ed.), *Counseling the culturally different: Theory and practice* (pp. 186–215). New York: Wiley.

Schacht, A. (1993, August). Psychological and behavioral consequences of historical trauma in Native-American men. In J. Perez (Chair), *Impact of historical trauma on Native-American men.* Symposium presented at the annual meeting of the American Psychological Association, Toronto.

Schroeder, J. (1991, August). Gone are the buffalo: Gender role stress in Native American men. In R. F. Lazur (Chair), *Buffalo, dominoes, and machismo: Exploring racial and cultural male sex roles.* Symposium presented at the annual meeting of the American Psychological Association, San Francisco.

Stevens, E. (1973). Machismo and marianismo. *Society, 10,* 57–63.

Sue, D. W., & Sue, D. (1990). Counseling the culturally different: Theory and practice (2nd ed.). New York: Wiley.

Sue, D., & Sue, D. W. (1993). Ethnic identity: Cultural factors in the psychological development of Asians in America. In D. W. Atkinson, G. Morten, & D. W. Sue (Eds.), *Counseling American minorities: A cross-cultural perspective* (4th ed.). Dubuque, IA: William. C. Brown.

Trimble, J. E. (1988). Stereotypic images, American Indians, and prejudice. In P. A. Katz & D. A. Taylor (Eds.), *Eliminating racism: Profiles in controversy* (pp. 181–202). New York: Plenum.

Trimble, J. E., & Fleming, C. M. (1989). Providing counseling services for Native-American Indians: Client, counselor, and community characteristics. In P. B. Pedersen, J. G. Draguns, W. J. Lonner, & J. E. Trimble (Eds.), *Counseling across cultures* (3rd ed.) (pp. 177–204). Honolulu: University of Hawaii Press.

Valdés, L. F., Barón, A. Jr., & Ponce, F. Q. (1987). Counseling Hispanic men. In M. Scher, M. Stevens, G. Good, & G. A. Eichenfield (Eds.), *Handbook of counseling and psychotherapy with men* (pp. 203–217). Newbury Park, CA: Sage.

U.S. Department of Health and Human Services (1992). *Health United States 1991* (DHHS Publication No. PHS 92-1232). Washington, DC: U.S. Government Printing Office.

Weaver, H. (1988, January 10). A people in peril: A generation of despair. *Anchorage Daily News,* pp. A2, 3.

CHAPTER 12

Roles, Identities, and Sexual Orientation: Homosexuality, Heterosexuality, and Bisexuality

JAMES HARRISON

I would call the "net product" of "identity" theory that part of its gross product that could not without noticeable loss of convenience be reformulated in available language *minus* "identity."
I believe that to be zero.   LEITES, 1971

And I saw no male role I could play that was acceptable to me.
                                                        BRODKEY, 1994

Introduction

This chapter discusses the relevance of the male gender role strain paradigm (Pleck, 1981) for understanding the experience of homosexual and bisexual men. Since by definition bisexuality involves homosexual expression, all general observations about homosexuality are equally applicable to bisexuality. Later I have some things to say specifically about bisexuality, as well as about heterosexual men's attitudes toward same-sex intimacy.

This is not an easy topic to take on. Its boundaries are amorphous. On the one hand, the topic could almost be dismissed as insignificant. Since homosexual men are also men, it could be argued that male role strain would likely affect the class of homosexual men in the same way it affects the class of heterosexual men, while recognizing that it will affect individuals differently. The difference lies in the culture's prejudice against, and fear and stigmatization of, same-sex love, intimacy, and eroticism. By cultural accident, homosexual men have sometimes been considered not to be "real" men—that is, to have failed to fulfill the male role and achieve a complete male identity. This common assumption is wrong, complicates the picture, and obfuscates the issues. On the contrary, homosexual men are fully and completely, biologically and culturally, men—whose sexual attraction is directed toward persons of the same sex. The erroneous assumption requires stepping back to explore how the issues came to be posed this way. Without doing so, we can get mired in the polarized academic tar pits of "role" versus "identity," or "essentialism" versus "constructivism," or "them" versus "us," without achieving any better understanding.

Before going further into the issue, be forewarned that the terms "role" and "identity," and all their derivatives, have no consistent, agreed-upon, operational definitions in the academic, scientific, or popular literature. The meaning of the words must be discerned from the context, and one struggles to find consistency even within some authors.

BASIC QUESTIONS

Of the many basic questions about male homosexual orientation, at least four are important to consider here. The first two are ethical; the third is psychological, and the fourth is cultural.

1. Is homosexual status intrinsically good or bad?
2. Is homosexual activity intrinsically right or wrong?
3. Is homosexuality a preference or a way of being?
4. Is homosexuality unique to contemporary Western culture, or is it a human universal?

This observer has a point of view concerning each of these questions that is derived from a career-long inquiry into biological, social, psychological, anthropological, historical, and ethical issues, as well as clinical work in psychology with clients of both sexes and a variety of sexual orientations. That view can be summarized briefly: First, homosexual status is a "good," though a minority variant within the range of normal human possibilities, similar in this respect to such traits as left-handedness. Second, its expression in behavior can be evaluated by the same criteria by which we would evaluate the rightness or wrongness of any other activity—by the context and consequences. Third, sexual orientation is not "chosen" in any meaningful sense of the idea of adult choice but is recognized during maturation and usually experienced as unchangeable. Fourth, same-sex erotic interaction is found in all known human cultures. However, the word *homosexuality* was not invented until the late 19th century, in conjunction with the emerging distinction between status and behavior; the word is distinctly as product of Euro-American culture. Non-European cultures do not use this word unless they are utilizing a European language, nor do such cultures understand same-sex eroticism in the same way European-derived cultures do.

To argue my case, it is necessary for me to take a long step backward and ask how we got to this point.

Historical and Cultural Context

My point of view is similar to the consensus view that is emerging among contemporary, empirically oriented psychologists, biosocial scientists, historians, and other thoughtful scholars (Friedman & Lerner, 1986). Needless to say, it is not yet understood by the proverbial man in the street, nor by many who shape attitudes and set policy in our society. Rather, the more common view remains that homosexuality is sin, sickness, and/or crime. Even some scholars who have tried to study homosexuality objectively have called it "deviance," implying different from the standard, wayward. Why is there so much divergence between my point of view and the more common one?

There is no one answer to this question, but there are at least four components to it: (1) taking the received culture for granted; (2) the general negativity toward sex (embarrassment, titillation, and shame) in our culture; (3) the social location of the observer; and (4) a tendency to project unwanted traits onto the "other" to enhance the value of the self or the group.

This chapter is not about universal human experience but rather about the beliefs, attitudes, and values that have evolved in our own culture, broadly conceived, and within its subvariations: Western, Euro-American, or Judeo-Christian culture, as you prefer. For that reason, it is necessary to ask how the commonly received point of view came to be.

Culture here is understood as the shared assumptions about value, meaning, communication, and "fund of knowledge" of any subset of persons and about the way they organize their lives: families, communities, organizations, occupational groups, ethnic groups, minority groups (e.g., left-handed persons, Harvard graduates, queers, Vietnam vets, etc.). Religious groups, regions, nations, linguistic groups, corporations, and even families all have cultures. Individuals participate in several of these larger groups, and the culture of an individual can be understood as an idiosyncratic, not necessarily integrated, composite of parts of all these potentially overlapping cultures. This fact makes generalization difficult, because no individual integrates the dimensions of the larger common culture he or she experiences in the same way. For the purpose of this article, two components of culture are especially relevant: language and religion.

LANGUAGE

Language is evolutionary and symbolic. Words do not have meaning apart from contexts. When are specific words coined and why? When do meanings of words change? What are the cultural contexts in which words are used? Without understanding the historical context, it is virtually impossible to read even a text that is only 100 years old, though basic vocabulary and grammar have not changed significantly. Quite apart from written, literary language, all reflective people can cite examples of private language that is not understandable to persons who are not a member of the subculture from which these culturally specific code languages emerge. "To boot" and "bug" have very specific meanings to people who use computers. Ask any computer-illiterate New Yorker what these words mean and the answer may be, "A shoe store on Columbus Avenue at 72nd Street," and, "A hidden microphone placed by organizations like the CIA or the KGB."

Have I made the point that all language that is not operationally defined is metaphorical? Now consider the private languages of subpopulations that have had lower social status, such as women, Jews, blacks, homosexuals, automobile salesmen, or lawyers (Rossi, 1974). Members of these groups have, at will, the ability to speak jargon, in standard English format, that is incomprehensible to persons who do not participate in their cultures. "The butch AC/DC solicitor dropped a hairpin, but the fagela didn't take the bait." No end of harm is done by people who do not recognize the historical quality of language. For example, Christian fundamentalists who tend to absolutize the King James version of the English Bible are rarely aware that the word *homosexual* does not appear in it.

RELIGION

A second component of culture is religion. If there is any everyday dimension of culture about which people are more ill informed than language, it is religion. Religion has to do with explanations about the unknown, ideas about meaning, and guidelines for right actions—in Tennyson's words, "Believing where we cannot prove" (1942). Religion is universal: Everybody has one, private or public, primitive or developed, idiosyncratic or traditional. For some it is ecology, for others, secular humanism. For still others, various versions and interpretations of the traditional religions constitute this component of culture.

Premodern cultures did not distinguish between language, religion, law, and the culinary arts. Differentiation of the various components of culture emerges only when cultures collide. "We would like to know their smelting techniques, but who would want their recipes?" or, "Can we buy their airplanes without being contaminated by their rock music?" So let's take a quick running review of the "Source" (Michener, 1965), "Quelle," origins, or assumptions we still make about religion in postmodern Western culture.

Ancient Semitic Sources

Hebraic, nomadic shepherds evolved a belief that their God was the best God into a belief that their God was the one and only. This belief is commonly translated into the notion of "the chosen people," which has sometimes been interpreted as "God likes us better than them," or, in a more enlightened phrasing, "We have more responsibility than those who are not aware of our standards." The latter statement reflects the assumption that is the origin of authentic universalism or catholicity. Expressed in the concrete style of ancient Hebraic culture: The measure you use for yourself is the measure you use for your customer, and the rules of hospitality within your family also apply to the stranger within your gate. This is a generally appealing ideal: You should not only be fair with your family and friends but with strangers as well. In scientific terms, it implies a "bureau of standards." In pragmatic American terms, it makes society work.

The ancient Hebraic tribes were small in comparison with the surrounding peoples. Their leaders dreamed that they would become stronger. Any act of adult physical intimacy had to be in the service of population increase. Or, in modern language, they were the first pronatalists.

Nomadic Hebraic culture came in contact with town-dwelling, agrarian, Palestinian cultures with a more highly developed technology and division of labor. They attributed the management of the unknown to multiple sources of power, or Gods, all of whom had to be appeased to ensure the success of various enterprises. Urban cultures with higher population density are in greater danger of exhausting their stores and experiencing famine in lean years than rural populations. Literal child sacrifice had not yet been repudiated as a way of giving back something to the source of life. Since there is an analogical relationship between sexual intercourse and the fertilization of the ova in both animal and plant crops, it is not surprising that Palestinian rituals included ceremonial, polymorphous sexual expression. These people became known as Philistines, and ever since, that term has come to connote bacchanalian forms of sexual expression.

These Middle Eastern cultures, Hebraic and Palestinian, in their multiple variations, however much in competition with one another, spoke related languages and were modest in dress—perhaps a consequence of the semi-desert, semitropical climate, which made exposure to the sun dangerous. This modesty in the Hebraic culture was specifically connected to cultic practice: Nakedness or an uncovered head before God produced shame in this culture. Doubtless, a trace of this standard can be found in the dress codes of modern Islam and in the prevalence of shame about nakedness and sexuality in traditional European cultures. Shame is a universal emotion, but it is not intrinsically connected to nakedness or sexual expression in all cultures.

Hellenic Sources

About 500 years B.C.E., all of the Middle East came under the domination of the Greek empire, which celebrated the beauty of the human body and whose school was called a "gymnasium." Nakedness caused no shame.

Families were for procreation and few women attained literacy, so we know very little about the lives of women, since public life was for men. Physical intimacy between mentor and student was integrated into the educational process. These "Greek"-speaking peoples were technologically superior to "Semitic"-speaking peoples, who in turn considered the culture of the former an abomination.

Furthermore, instead of formulating concrete rules of good conduct that were understood as revealed by God, these Greeks invented philosophy—they themselves weighed abstract principles and their consequences, one against the other. They made a distinction between the ideal and the real, the spiritual and the physical, a formulation that could be considered dualistic in comparison with concrete Hebraic monism. They developed basic mathematics and observational science, which were essential for technical development. They also had principles of right sexual conduct; these principles varied from region to region but did *not* exclude sexual expression between persons of the same sex.

This collision of cultures is the source out of which Western, Euro-American, or Judeo-Christian culture evolved. Rabbinic Judaism, Christianity, and Islam may be understood as Hebraic sects that emerged from differing syntheses of Semitic and Hellenic cultures. But all affirmed monotheism, justice tempered by mercy as the ethical ideal, and a universal standard requiring fair treatment of outsiders—in principle if not in practice.

Christian Synthesis

Early Christianity as a Hebraic sect repudiated Greek culture. Paradoxically, the Greek language was the international language of the day and became the base language of Christianity. Like a Trojan horse, Greek culture survived as the conceptual framework of Christianity; theology replaced philosophy, and much of the content of classical Greek culture was rejected. Observation and measurement of the real world became irrelevant because the Christians thought they knew all that was necessary for their cosmic well-being. The Hebraic ethic, universalized without ethnic barriers, was the ideal of the Christians message of love and forgiveness and had great appeal.

The emergence of a medieval synthesis produced a more or less stable, if static, society. Not everyone was included in the synthesis—not the pagans or the heathens (words that literally mean "country folk" and "people who live on the heather," respectively). But much of European society found a place in a hierarchy organized under God, represented by the chief bishop (*episcope*, Gk., "supervisor," Lt., "overseer"), administered by priests or preachers (same etymological root, *presbyter*, Gk., "elder"), and paralleled in secular society by the "holy emperor," the regional nobles, and the local chief man. Greek dualism had become institutionally expressed in the ideal spiritual church and the real secular government.

Christianity was no longer a religion of appeal and persuasion, but the official religion of empire. Religious dissent was the equivalent of treason. The modern European languages as we know them today had not yet taken shape. The independent nation-state had not yet emerged.

However, as Christianity expanded across different linguistic and cultural groups, it became impossible to resolve differences of meaning and interpretation into one universally agreed-upon formulation. The breakup of the medieval synthesis resulted in civil wars, neighbor against neighbor, parish against parish, village against village. After all, isn't truth worth dying for? But what is truth?

Islam: A New Synthesis

Meanwhile, Arabic peoples who had lived among both Hebraic and Greek Christian communities, and who had assimilated bits and pieces of both Judaism and Christianity, found a leader in the sixth century who taught a new synthetic religion, Islam, which repudiated neither Judaism and Christianity nor ancient Greek knowledge. Islam, being also a religion of the book, promoted literacy. The followers of Islam used Greek technical knowledge for exploration, manufacturing, architecture, navigation, and trade. It seemed that Islamic culture would dominate the world. Islam did not consider pleasure intrinsically bad as long as it did not undermine social responsibility. Physical intimacy between persons of the same sex was publicly celebrated as long as it did not threaten the procreative institution of family.

Renaissance to Enlightenment: Another Synthesis

Fearing encroaching Islam and reversing traditional Christian practice, Europeans began to reclaim the ancient Greek knowledge in a series of movements resulting in the Renaissance, the invention of movable type, the Reformation (in which it was realized that you don't have to pay a franchise fee if you have the recipe book), and the Enlightenment, during which the *imago dei* in mankind was defined as "reason."

Modern Culture

The 18th-century philosophers set about to answer a practical question: What is the minimum necessary agreement that reasonable people can come to if society is to exist? That reason rather than external authority would supply the criteria for answering this question was revolutionary and ultimately called into question all received wisdom, including the presupposition that reason itself was sufficient. The various modern answers were all concerned with the emerging idea of individual persons—their worth, freedom, and rights (Bentham, 1984).

What Does Love Have to Do with It?

Up until this time, there had been no concept of sexual orientation. Social organization was by role: ruler/ruled, parent/child, husband/wife. Medieval Christianity had gradually formed the position that sexual expression was acceptable solely within marriage, solely for reproductive purposes. Pleasure was suspect as a motive. Celibacy had become the ideal. Other sexual acts were condemned. The most common term for condemned sexual behavior came to be "sodomy," derived from a clearly mistaken reading of a Hebraic biblical story.

SEXUAL ORIENTATION AS STATUS OR CONDITION

However important the achievements of the Enlightenment (which made modern democracies possible by affirming the individual's right to life and liberty), not all human experience could be reduced to the perfect symmetry of an 18th-century garden, a neoclassical building, or a Haydn concerto. Scientific investigation could discover order, but apart from order there was also the unexpected, the accidental, the irregular, chaos. Just as the Enlightenment enabled individuals to question tradition, the reactive Romantic movement affirmed the storm, the exotic, and the exception. Together, both validated individual persons in asserting their individuality over social expectation. Mary Wollstonecraft and George Eliot come to mind as examples.

No culture has ever been univocal, even the culture of a single family or a small tribe. Without innovators and deviants, our species would surely have remained preliterate hunter-gatherers, if we had survived at all. Variations and adaptability are the qualities that have enabled our species to become the dangerously dominant one.

Along with the emergence of the idea of individual actualization, some persons began to conceive of themselves as constitutionally different in their erotic predisposition and asserted their right to expression of same-sex intimacy. They rejected the appellation "sodomite," but no other word was readily available. (Though available words did exist in Greek and Latin, and in the European dialects before Roman domination, when the classical texts were translated into modern languages they were "Bowdlerized" to conform to sexually repressed Christian sensibilities.) The perfectly honest dialect words, like *fuck*, were considered vulgar in the Latinized culture. It was necessary to invent new words.

In 1836 Heinrich Hoessli coined the term *mannmaennliche liebe*, literally, "man-man love." Karl Ulrichs (1865) used the term "Uranian," and later "urning"—as if such persons were from a different planet—and also the term "the third sex." In 1861 John Addington Symonds (1975) used the term "inversion." The more common modern word, *homosexual*, was not invented until 1869 by a Hungarian physician named Karoly Maria Benkert. *Heterosexual* was not coined until sometime later (Katz, 1983). Edward Carpenter suggested "the intermediate sex" in 1908. These pioneers who asserted that patterns of sexual desire were statuses, apart from acts, and who sought acceptance for individual differences among persons were the exception rather than the rule. The continued existence of negative sanctions suppressed complete freedom of expression, as illustrated by Walt Whitman's ambivalence between the self-affirmation in his poetry and his unwillingness to make common cause with early homosexual rights advocates (Rowse, 1983).

Premodern views had been incorporated into most codes of law, including English common law, on which most American law is based. Blackstone (1811) called homosexuality a "crime against nature," a term still used in North Carolina law. The Napoleonic code, which was formulated during the Enlightenment, is the exception that proves the rule.

Benkert's new word *homosexual* was intended as a scientifically neutral, nonjudgmental, descriptive term for same-sex intimacy. The word *bisexual* was originally a biological term that referred to the presence of male and female organs in one individual, synonymous with *hermaphrodite,* a condition common in plants, shellfish, and some species of lizards but never a complete actuality in mammals. Hence the terms "pseudo-hermaphrodite" and "intersexed person" came into use (Money & Ehrhardt, 1972).

Usage of the term "bisexual," metaphorically extended in meaning to refer to persons who enjoy sexual intimacy with persons of their own and the other gender, is a product of modern psychiatry (Freud, 1925, 1933).

However inevitably it changes, culture evolves slowly—not on all fronts at the same rate, and not with inner consistency. Once the idea occurred that homosexuality was a condition rather than an act, then the possibility emerged that homosexuality was not morally wrong. Yet that notion was contrary to prescribed social roles in the common culture. The traditional treatment for sin was punishment. Traditional legal codes have tended to define anything the church labels "sin" as "crime" in the eyes of the state.

The Medical Model

Still maintaining the assumption that persons should adhere to traditional social roles, the medical model provided the alternative of cure instead of punishment. If sickness, there must be a cause. So most investigation about homosexuality in the first half of this century focused on cause and "cure." However, in this case the cure has been the cause of the disease.

Freud (1933b) was equivocal about homosexuality, viewing it not as an illness but as a developmental arrest—at least an arrest in the process of fulfilling expected social roles. Yet he also recognized the possibility that some homosexual people are exceptional in their achievements. Lacking the genius of his innovative thought, followers who sought to turn Freud's thought into orthodoxy were among the most adamant in declaring homosexuality a disease.

Identification, Imitation, Introjection, and Identity

Freud (1993b) struggled to articulate a theory of male development. "Heterosexuality" and "masculinity," discovered in the 19th century, came to be seen as achievements rather than just the way boys grow up. Freud lived during the first century of social mobility facilitated by the railway, the first reliable and affordable mode of mass transportation. Adult children did not inevitably live in the compound or village with their parents. The new technology led to the emergence of the nuclear family, which in Freud's terms was called the Oedipal triangle. Previously, boys had just grown up to be men. In this strange new world where men worked away from home and women stayed home, how could a boy learn to be a man if raised by women?

In retrospect, we know that Freud knew better but also tended to equate masculinity, activity, and heterosexuality, and that he made a parallel equation of femininity, passivity, and homosexuality (Freud, 1933). In spite of its value in probing the complexity of human motivation, self-understanding, and the dynamics of anxiety management and maintenance of self-esteem, the psychoanalytic tradition wrestled for half a century with a problem of its own making.

In traditional psychoanalytic thinking, the term "identity problem" became a code word for homosexuality. Eric Erikson (1959) coined the phrase "identity crisis," and in his writing it is clear that he intended a comprehensive definition of sense of self by the term "identity." "Thus, strange as it may seem, it takes a well established identity to tolerate radical change" (Erikson, 1964, p. 96). Yet it is a commentary on the fear of difference in our culture that the term "identity crisis" also came to be understood in sexual terms by more pedestrian thinkers (Karlen, 1971).

Identity was a concept that psychology borrowed from her mother philosophy but used without as much thoughtfulness as Mom put into it. On reflection, we might recognize that identity has no meaning apart from change, development, or maturation.

By separating the concept of identity out of its original dialectical matrix and turning it into an entity, psychoanalytic theory has created an absurdity.

Identity is nothing more nor less than our experience of continuity within change.

Identity has become such a shibboleth, the sociologist Mary McIntosh (1968) could even argue in favor of the idea of "the homosexual role," in opposition to the concept of diagnosis or condition. She defined "role" as a social "construction":

> For [it is] not until he [*sic*] sees homosexuals as a social category, rather than a medical or psychiatric one, that the sociologist can begin to ask the right questions about the specific content of the homosexual role and about the organization and functions of homosexual groups. (Quoted in Plummer, 1991, p. 43.)

Not until modern psychological research demonstrated that homosexuality fits no criterion by which we ordinarily define sickness was there a strong basis for understanding sexual orientation simply in terms of human difference—for which a cure was neither desirable nor necessary (Gonsiorek & Rudolph, 1991; Hooker, 1957). And not until homosexuality could be removed from the category of pathology was it conceptually possible to grasp that categorizing a person as a member of a sex and categorizing a person in terms of which sex they are erotically attracted to are two separate issues.

What About the Words Gay and Lesbian?

Whatever word is used to refer to a stigmatized population eventually deteriorates. Observe how rapidly we have transitioned from *colored* to *Negro* to *black* to *African-American*. The word *homosexual* is of mixed parentage: It combines a Greek root for "same" with the Latin root for "sex," (i.e., half of a whole). However, more problematic is that its half-century association with clinical diagnosis has made the original neutral word suspect. Some homosexual people asserted their right to a label of their own choosing, and the word *gay* has come into standard usage—despite its origin as a French term for female prostitutes who lived the *gai* life during the end of the last century. Many women who wish to differentiate their experience from that of homosexual men prefer the word lesbian, for the home island of the poet Sappho. Many contemporary gay people have reclaimed the terms "queer," "faggot," and "fairy" and, with increasing historical awareness, realize that these words neither stigmatize nor hurt but rather affirm the desirability of not being ordinary.

Back to the Present

At the beginning of this essay, I indicated that it would be important to explore four basic questions and briefly indicated my point of view on each of them. Now I wish to elaborate my perspective in the context of my galloping summary of the history of Western civilization.

First, is homosexuality good sexuality? Yes, if it enables a person to be self-affirming, fully integrated, with high self-esteem. Yes, if it enables a person to play a constructive social role in creativity and nurturance. Yes, if it enables a person to give love, affirmation, and healing to another.

Second, is homosexual behavior "right"? Yes, if it is fully and mutually consensual and does no harm to self or others (Tietje & Harrison, 1994). Yes, if it brings pleasure and release from tension and bridges even temporarily the existential isolation of one human being from another. In other words, the value and ethical status of homosexuality depend on the context, consequence, and meaning of actions, as they do in heterosexual expression. The idea that physical intimacy should be expressed only by heterosexual couples within marriage has led to loneliness, mismatches, ruined lives, and mistreated children, who have been sacrificed on the altar built of unnatural celibate ideals. Sexual orientation is discovered developmentally, for some early in life, and for others not until later years. However, a social atmosphere that encourages repression is likely to distort or delay that discovery.

Third, is homosexuality a choice, a lifestyle, or a pattern of behavior that can be changed by will, through the intervention of psychologists, endocrinologists, or religions conversion? No, people do not choose their sexual orientation, though it is conceivable that some children reject unsavory forms of relationship that they experience as typical family life and, on some very basic level, choose to be different.

Sexual orientation of any sort, including homosexuality, is not unidimensional. Rather, it evolves during early childhood through the interaction of multiple factors, including genes, hormones, social learning, children's symbolic interpretation of events in their individual families, and communal and social settings during the period in which linguistic and cognitive development takes place. There may be some genetic predisposition in some families, but the disposition alone is not considered a necessary or sufficient condition for the development of homosexual orientation. The directionality is formed early in life, along with an emergence of a sense of self and the ability to use gender-specific personal pronouns. The fine-tuning takes place during puberty and late adolescence coincidental with the completion of cognitive development; at this stage, individuals are capable of understanding the subjunctive mood in grammar and the conditions under which the violation of ordinary rules is not only justifiable but may be necessary for the preservation of good.

Variation in sexual orientation is better understood not just by the valuable two-dimensional Kinsey scale (Kinsey, Pomeroy, & Martin, 1948) but also in the multidimensional matrix, suggested by Money (1986), in the ideas of "sexual signatures," or "love maps." Every person's self-understanding of their identity, including their sexual orientation, is unique.

Fourth, is homosexuality an essential and universal aspect of human existence, or is it a social construction of a specific time in human cultural evolution or within specific cultures? This is perhaps the most frequently discussed topic among all serious scholars and within the gay community in this decade, and it is likely to so continue until a broader synthesis or an encompassing new paradigm emerges (De Cecco & Shively, 1972–94). Here the issues become politicized, and there is a danger that empirical science will be ignored. It is perhaps the only area in which the gay community and the religious right have some agreement!

If homosexuality is an essential dimension of variability in human nature, like left-handedness, then homosexual persons should have all the rights and respect accorded to any other human being, and social accommodations should be made equivalent to left-handed desks in school. Yet others say if this essential variant is a function of a recessive gene or an intrauterine hormonal variation, then some means may be found to prevent the occurrence of homosexuality—gene-splicing, hormonal intervention, or abortion.

On the other hand, if homosexuality is a social construction, it must serve a functional purpose and contribute to the survival of individuals and extended families and to the well-being of society itself. For example, homosexuality may serve to limit population growth beyond the possibility of species survival and may provide an advantage to extended families in the next generation by providing additional nurturance by aunts and uncles, relieving the burden on parents. But, say others, if homosexuality is a social construction, then what has gone wrong with society that it has created conditions under which persons of the same sex may establish intimate relationships? Perhaps marriage should be required, divorce outlawed, fluorine and chlorine taken out of the water supply, and religious observation enforced by the government in order to restore "family" values.

This either-or question, in my view, has all the profundity of the question "Does an elephant have a trunk or a tail?" It is an open question, subject in part to an empirical or observational answer—if we are tall enough, far enough away, open-minded enough, and patient enough to see the whole beast. In my own view, the answer is not essentialism or constructionism, but "both-and." The determinants for any individual are likely to be an idiosyncratic mixture of various biological, cultural, and learning components. Every aspect of human existence is biologically grounded and mediated; however, the specific way an individual develops is a function of accidental circumstance within the range of life sustaining possibility and social learning, at home, in school, through interpersonal experience, and so on. I count myself among the social constructionists, but I do not believe our constructions are floating in insubstantial ether but rest on essential biological foundations. Our selfhood is a product of interpersonal relationships, which are symbolic interactions across time and among persons that are firmly grounded in biological possibility. Who doubts that biology demonstrably manifests diversity? I think the either-or debate takes energy away from more fruitful exploration of the complexity of human existence and of how we may more healthily relate to one another. Many who distinguish themselves from essentialists by calling themselves social constructionists seem to be unaware that this is only a new name for an old argument, which historically has been called nominalism versus realism (Boswell, 1982–83).

The ethical questions of right and wrong are not dependent on the argument between essentialists and social constructionists, as some gay people believe. Rather, the ethical questions depend on one's ethical theory and how ethical issues are analyzed. Are rules absolute and universal and found in one source? If so, which source? Or are ethical issues decided on the basis of how persons are treated and the consequences thereof? Clearly, this author affirms the latter position: Individual persons should be treated as ends in themselves, and each actor is responsible for not doing harm to self and others.

BOTH-AND

Perhaps by now I have made my point that I do not believe either-or thinking gets us very far. Toward the conclusion of my plane geometry class in high school, my teacher, Alma Kiser, made a few points about solid geometry, which could be easily visualized, and suggested there were multidimensional geometries. I could imagine a fourth dimension existing in time but could not grasp what other referent multidimensional geometry could possible have. Many years later in graduate school, I encountered multiple regression analysis in statistics: the process of finding the line one can draw in a scatter plot that best describes the interrelationship between multiple independent variables and a dependent variable. How do you visualize the line that best fits all the data points in hyperspace? Just like human life, it cannot be reduced to two dimensions. Before, I had always worried about the relevance of a psychological experiment that could account for only 3% of the variance in the issue under investigation. Then I realized that if anyone can account for 3% of the reason for something being the way it is, that is important.

THERE REALLY IS A GAY IDENTITY

An immense amount of valuable research has been conducted on homosexuality and bisexuality. To my knowledge, however, none of the research is relevant to the issue this paper addresses: whether role strain or role identity is the more powerful heuristic model for understanding the problems inherent in being homosexual. In part, the research is irrelevant because there is no terminological clarity, as I have argued above. More important, however, the word *identity* has been aggressively claimed by gay people because it had been used so consistently to describe their imputed lack thereof. And surely believing so made it so, for how could gay people have a sexual identity when their lives were denied them?

The notion of "gay" identity or "positive gay identity" (Berzon & Leighton, 1979) is surely a social construction of a specific period of history in which the idea of individual rights, freedom of speech and press, failed censorship, population mobility, and empirical scientific research all converged. Gay identity means no more and no less than the emergence of a self-identified subset of persons who repudiate inferiority by virtue of their minority status as persons who are erotically attracted to persons of their own sex. We have discussed the roots of this convergence above. If a symbolic moment must be set for the crystallization of gay identity, it is recognized as the Stonewall Revolution of the spring of 1969, an event at which more people claim to have been present than could possibly have fit on the streets of the area known as Greenwich Village in New York City. A few men refused to be arrested by New York City police at a bar, some because they insisted on their right to peaceable assembly and others because they feared public disclosure were they known to have been there. Truly their resistance was a shock that is still ringing around the world. That it happened in the United States, a heterogeneous, prosperous country without deep roots, after a time of high mobility during and after World War II, is no accident. Nor is it an accident that it occurred in the decade after Evelyn Hooker (1957) had demonstrated scientifically that psychologists and psychiatrists could not reliably determine who was and who was not homosexual unless individuals so identified themselves. Nor is it an accident that it happened in the context of a struggle by African-Americans to be full citizens of a country for which they had fought, and at the time of the resurgence of the movement for women's equality. Not a few but many gay people were thinking, "Me too."

There is strength in numbers. The broader intellectual framework on which social construction rests is sometimes called the "sociology of knowledge" (Plummer, 1981), which in my view might better have been called the sociology of opinion. During the late 19th century, a few people dared to assert openly that they had erotic feelings toward members of their own sex. The idea of orientation did not exist, and punishment was prescribed only for "behavior." Now the recognition of orientation exists whether or not it is expressed in behavior.

How did this shift in perspective take place? Some have suggested that it took place by labeling, that is, by being *"imposed* by formal control agents— police, psychiatrists—on unsuspecting victims.... But this view is now recognized as wholly inadequate; *self-constructed, symbolic, self-labeling* is a much more fundamental theoretical and empirical problem" (Plummer, 1981, p. 67).

Some have hoped that the achievement of gay identity would result in a higher sense of human solidarity whereby those who had been discriminated against would not discriminate against others and those who had been mistreated would not mistreat others (Altman, 1973). Alas, this hope has proven elusive.

There is a homosexual community of sorts, and there are gay subcultures (Altman, 1982), but not all homosexual people participate in them. Indeed, one of the most negative comments that one homosexual person who openly works for gay rights and gives to charities can say about another who takes advantage of gay culture but does not participate in building it is, "He may be homosexual, but he certainly isn't gay."

Thus, it is clear that homosexual identity consists solely in the definition of sexual orientation; it is not likely to carry any essential, necessary, or intrinsic correlates, such as being more sensitive, having better taste, or being better educated. Nevertheless, there are probably some culturally defined differences in the homosexual subculture that are a function of historic discrimination and oppression: migration to larger cities, higher representation in careers that permit personal freedom and require travel. Gays may be overrepresented in the health and religion fields because these professions have sometimes promised deliverance from an attributed fault, and it may not be coincidental that shamans in many other cultures have homosexual relationships. There is perhaps more social interaction in the homosexual community across ethnic, cultural, and class boundaries because gay people have a characteristic in common that transcends all other categories of difference. These are empirical questions. Unfortunately, it is never possible to get a truly accurate sample representing any stigmatized group, and especially one that is not visible.

And finally, it is important to say that sexual orientation and status as a member of a sex are two different categories, best represented as a 2×2 Latin square diagram:

	Male	Female
Homosexual		
Heterosexual		

In other words, the term "gay identity" has meaning vis-à-vis the term "male identity" only insofar as the stereotype of male identity excludes emotional attachment and physical intimacy with other men.

Nevertheless, according to W. I. Thomas's famous dictum, "If men define situations as real, they are real in their consequences" (Thomas, 1928; Harrison, 1978). It is no surprise that in our culture virtually all of the negative epithets directed toward gay men are terms suggestive of women: "nelly," "sissy"—your imagination can take over from there. Some homosexual men act in an effeminate way, the behavior of others is indistinguishable from that of presumed heterosexual men, and still others express an exaggerated hypermasculinity. One explanation for such a range of expression would be that homosexuality is not a unified phenomena, and different people have brain or cognitive structures that can either intensify or moderate behavioral traits. Insofar as we have a common idea of effeminacy, it is clear that some heterosexual men could be so described. Another possibility is that in cultures that severely punish homosexual acts, homosexual persons have developed the ability to play roles, which can hide their orientation or selectively reveal it (Bullough & Bullough, 1993). A third is that youth who are labeled homosexual early in life and are never allowed self-identification may accept the reality of the cultural stereotype. A fourth may be that some gay men have been injured by the stereotype, are angry, and flaunt a caricature of it—this behavior is sometimes called "camp." In addition, there is some evidence suggesting that children who grow up to identify themselves as homosexual men preferred activities more similar to those enjoyed by girls and avoided rough-and-tumble play when they were boys (Bell, Weinberg, & Hammersmith, 1981; Green, 1987).

And there are many men who have no gay or homosexual identity at all but enjoy "getting it off" with another man so long as they are the inserter in any sexual interaction—leaving aside assessment of who might be "active" or "passive" under such circumstances. Even with the current awareness of the danger involved in sexual activity with unknown partners, there is much casual sex at truck stops or "tearooms" (Humphries, 1979). Some speculate that the largest single category of homosexual men are heterosexually married. And finally, apart from self-identification, some cultures do not identify a man as homosexual if he is the "dominant" person in the interaction, regardless of the sex of his partner.

IDENTITY AND BISEXUAL MEN

The issue of identity presents a more difficult set of problems for bisexual men. Some, both in the professional psychiatric community (Rado, 1965) and within the self-identified political gay community, have denied that there is such a thing as bisexuality. The term "bisexuality" is suspect in the gay community because it has been used by so many men a more socially tolerable category that permits public identifications as heterosexual while avoiding the stigma of the homosexual label.

However, the empirical evidence stands with Kinsey (Kinsey, Pomeroy, & Martin, 1948) and Money (1986). Clearly, sexual orientation is not distributed in the population on a Gaussian curve, with the mode, median, and mean being bisexual. Rather, sexual orientation is positively skewed in its distribution, more like left-handedness. The analytical problem is lack of a clear definition. Some people are more person- than gender-focused in their capacity for arousal and under different circumstances may find sexual interaction satisfying with specific members of either sex. Is such a person bisexual, sequentially heterosexual, or homosexual?

Certainly, there are many young men who find the power of their emergent sexuality so powerful that, in the vernacular, "they could have intercourse with a telephone pole." It is the experience of these young men from which the notion emerged that homosexuality is a developmental phase that normal boys go through, but a developmental "arrest" that homosexual men never come out of.

Those who hold this view overlook the opposite phenomenon. There are some men who discover a gay cohort in adolescence and like them better than ostentatiously self-assertive heterosexual boys. Such persons may enjoy sex with other boys, establish relationships, participate actively in the gay community, and become gay-identified. Later such a man may, for a variety of reasons, experience heterosexual arousal, meet an appropriate woman, discover that heterosexual men are not all culturally and artistically illiterate, and realize that, while still able to respond erotically to men, he has fallen in love with a woman.

In addition, there are unequivocally gay men who are deeply identified as "family men." These men would prefer to suppress their strongest sexual desire in order to fulfill their wish to be married to a woman and to parent children. Some will say, "I love my wife and enjoy sex with her; I can repudiate homosexual gratification except in fantasy and dreams." Others say, "I love my wife but don't want to have sex." Others admit, "I hate my wife but cannot risk separation, divorce, or an extramarital affair." Others believe, "I can maintain my marriage and a male lover as well." And beyond these variations is every conceivable combination of shift in self-identity and consequent action.

In sum, bisexuality is a reality, but it does not lend itself to a clear identity in the same way that can be claimed by those who fall toward the two ends of the Kinsey scale—if sexuality must be reduced to a one-dimensional phenomenon. A bisexual man does not alternate equally between partners of each sex unless he is incapable of establishing a relationship.

Fewer men identify themselves as bisexual today. Most who are aware of their inner complexity would say that they are predominantly of one sexual orientation or the other but recognize their capacity for arousal in the other direction—with the right person under the right circumstances.

THERE IS NO GAY ROLE BUT THERE ARE GAY ROLES

The concept of identity is useful in discussing the experience of homosexual and bisexual men, but the concept does not have much content. Similarly, the concept of role is useful, but its meaning is purely contextual, like the meaning of a role in a play.

I have insisted categorically that homosexual men are men who vary from other men only in their erotic orientation. The question of role strain for homosexual men, then, is the question of how they may experience role strain as a stigmatized minority.

Here it may be helpful to cite several of the ten propositions that Pleck (1981) used to operationalize his role strain theory; these three are particularly applicable to the experience of gay youth and homosexual men.

1. Roles are operationally defined by stereotypes and norms. Insofar as the stereotyped male role includes expressing heterosexual desire, young men who do not so express themselves experience self-doubt, inadequacy, and, if their secret is discovered, stigmatization and shame. Most boys learn to hide their real feelings and to act like they expect other boys to act. It is not unusual for two adult men who have known each other from childhood to say, "But I thought you were straight."
2. Roles are contradictory and inconsistent. Boys like to have fun. Sexual play is common and is often included in the form of roughhousing and wrestling, and sometimes explicitly as sexual interaction. Heterosexual boys lose interest. Homosexual boys respond in a variety of ways. Neither labeled, self-identified, aware, nor playing a role, the homosexual boys cannot understand why they are responding differently from their peers. One person of my acquaintance, who grew up in rural Michigan in a homogeneous, traditional Protestant community, observed that he never connected what he did with what was condemned in church. "We thought there were no homosexuals in our town. What was condemned was not what *we* did or experienced." Gradually the circle of boys who engaged in sexual play narrowed. But my friend continued sexual activity within the narrower circle without shame or guilt—knowing only that it was boy stuff you didn't tell parents about, like a lot of other adventure-seeking activity.
3. The proportion of individuals who violate gender role norms is high. This is certainly the case for most gay men, and prior to self-affirmation as a man who is different, attempts to avoid such violations may result

in severe role strain. However, the opposite may be the case for the many homosexual men who try not to publicly or visibly violate role norms to avoid stigmatization and harassment.

Violating gender role norms leads to social condemnation. Not until adolescence—when the pressure is on to date or go to the prom, expectations that seem like girl stuff—is there experience of strain. For my friend, strain emerged only in late adolescence. Rehearing biblical readings (St. Paul or Leviticus) and his research at the county library after becoming aware of his difference, set things off: "I discovered that what I had thought was good was thought to be sinful, sick, or something I expected to grow out of. Only through labeling with words like *gay* or *faggot* did my experience become a problem, because what was expected was not who I was."

Some boys catch on that they had better keep their thoughts, feelings, and experiences a secret. Some succeed in leading an active sexual life, at the price of a bad conscience. Some develop a negative identity, which results in the justification: "If I'm a delinquent in this area of my life, I may as well break all the other rules." Some suppress their sexuality out of fear and temporarily sublimate it into artistic activities, which give some permission for role-playing and role disconformity. Others are so terrified that they avoid any involvement in music, dance, or art (in which "girls" are supposed to excel) and thus develop a pseudomale role.

Other young gay men experience serious negative consequences because they do not hide their feelings and experience from trusted but ill-informed parents, teachers, physicians, and ministers. For today's youth, the elders are likely to be better informed, as are most physicians and educated clergy. However, some parents are stunned, hurt, and disappointed and want their child fixed at any cost. Competent physicians and psychologists assist parents in working through their own conflicts while enabling their young adult children to clarify the meaning of their experience and fantasies without condemnation. Nevertheless, there are still some doctors and counselors who are ready to exploit the fears of a homosexual man or his parents by offering cures, and who "blame the victim" for not fulfilling the required condition when the cure does not work. Even more tragic than the condemnation by trusted parents and older role models is the young person who is victimized by a misinformed minister, who can add guilt to shame and intensify both into a sense of failure and fear.

As discussed, hiding their difference may lead some boys to overconformity. Seymour Kleinberg (1978) has described subsets of self-identified gay men who exaggerate traditional signs of masculinity—often even engaging in potentially dangerous tests of strength and endurance. The current vogue among gay men of working out at a gym and showing muscle is one example.

However, many heterosexual men are so terrified of being thought gay that they avoid expressing qualities that are generally thought to be essential to humanity, like loving, caring, gentleness, nurturance, and enjoyment of beauty (Harrison, 1987). At the extreme, some have reverted to a retributional form of religious justification in so-called fag-bashing, or "killing queers for Christ."

A colleague working as an openly gay person in a job as chief social worker in a public institution in a midwestern city recently told me about an experience with one of his staff, whom we will call Bill. Bill is a very intelligent young man in his twenties with a bachelor's degree; he is making the transition from paraprofessional status to the beginnings of graduate study. At first, he seemed distant and avoidant. My colleague speculated about whether Bill was awed by his experience and authority or feared closeness or guilt by association. Months passed, and Bill became more relaxed. Traveling together to a conference gave them the opportunity for long talks. Finally, my friend asked, "Do you know I am gay?" Bill responded, "Yes, it caused a bit of conversation in the department before you came."

> FRIEND: "At first I noticed you were distant from me. Were you afraid of me because of my status or . . . ?"
>
> BILL (laughing): "I was afraid that you would hit on me."
>
> FRIEND (also laughing): "Doesn't that suggest an unusually high opinion of yourself?"

As the conversation continued, Bill told my friend about his lack of respect for and distance from his father, whom he believed had destroyed his own life, and made his wife and sons miserable, by suppressing his homosexuality, sublimating it into a distorted, rigid, and ethically vacuous form of ritualized religion.

In spite of Bill's wish to be open and accepting, he was still fearful about something he did not understand. Yet he was crystal clear about the costs of his father's repression of selfhood and the misery it had brought to him and his family.

Conclusion

The term "identity" is useful as a way to reference that idiosyncratic constellation of qualities in each of us that persists over time and makes us the person we are: character, if you will. However, when we single out sexuality as a preeminent dimension of self, we are enacting the return of the repressed. Because our Judeo-Christian culture has so poorly dealt with sexuality, we find we are obsessed with it. Christian fundamentalists' preoccupation with homosexuality gives them opportunities to engage in the prurient and salacious spreading of misinformation.

As I grew up, my identity was that of a child surrounded by loving grandparents, parents, aunts, uncles, and cousins by the dozens, of all ages. My family was poor but literate. I was smart and assumed everyone was as smart as I was. Capable of being the best in class, I was surprised that most boys tried to best me on the playground.

My identity resided in being a boy, American, southern, North Carolinian, Presbyterian. We were chosen, had good taste, standard American grammar, once born. Educated white southerners are defiantly assertive about their freedom, privacy, and right to be idiosyncratic. Many with less opportunity become the victims of fear-mongers like Jesse Helms and poorly educated preachers who imagine family life in the past to have been like the storybook lives of wealthy Victorians. My identity was that of one who believed in the work ethic and in fairness. Like my friend from the Midwest, sexuality had little or nothing to do with it. Not until I could read did I discover there was a problem. And being basically trusting, I thought that it was one that I would "grow out of." But I was smart enough to keep my own confidence, because I knew the consequence of openness. For me, there was neither role nor identity. Nor was there guilt, only potential shame in being found out to be different. Even now as a mature adult, sexual orientation plays little part in my identity.

However, it plays an immense and important part in the communities of persons who are achieving their adult sense of self. It is worth noting that a valuable book about gay experience (Mass, 1990) has the *I* word in the title but no chapter heading or index entry on the subject. Similarly, a recent edition of the newsletter of the Society for the Psychological Study of Ethnic Minority Issues (1994) is entitled "Identity Development." For stigmatized or marginalized persons, the term "identity" has come to mean self-assertion against prejudice. This is a derivative meaning claimed in defense against those who have innocently or maliciously presumed that gay and lesbian persons, or persons with other minority status, have defective identity.

The existence of the stigma deserves as much explanation as the existence of the phenomenon of same-sex love and attraction. Perhaps this obvious point cannot be perceived in Western scientific inquiry until impartial scientific methods of observation have been utilized to understand cultures other than our own and to discover that same-sex expression not only is not stigmatized in many cultures but in some is formally prescribed. Only if one makes the unscientific assumption that Western culture is superior to, and the norm for, all other cultures, in all aspects, can one conclude that heterosexuality is superior to homosexuality in every way.

Like other men in our society, gay men seek an identity: to be a specific, individuated personhood. But that identity is not focused on sexual orientation unless coping with stigma, prejudice, guilt, and shame has been a serious problem. Otherwise identities are idiosyncratic and multifaceted. Insofar as gay men confront restrictive role definitions, they experience strain. Most specifically, gay men must transcend the role definition that prohibits feeling affection and love for another man. The gay man has the biological assistance of sexual desire, however, to assist him in overcoming that prohibition.

In this regard, it is perhaps the healthy heterosexual man who experiences the greater strain and who may pay the higher cost. How many men mistrust their honest emotions and restrict expressions of feelings toward parent, friend, and children? Would it not be a strange world indeed, if men could not care about each other? What is the price that we pay as a society, and the psychological loss for women, children, and many heterosexual men themselves when men cannot be free in expressing warmth and pleasure in another man's company?

References

Altman, D. (1973). *Homosexual: Oppression and liberation.* New York: Avon.

Altman, D. (1982). *The homosexualization of America: The Americanization of the homosexual.* New York: St. Martin's.

Bell, A. P., Weinberg, M. S., & Hammersmith, S. K. (1981). *Sexual preference: Its development in men and women.* Bloomington: Indiana University Press.

Bentham, J. (1984). An essay on paederasty. In R. Baker & F. Elliston (Eds.), *Philosophy and sex* (rev. ed.) (pp. 353–369). Buffalo: Prometheus.

Berzon, B., & Leighton, R. (1979). *Positively gay.* Millbrae, CA: Celestial Arts.

Blackstone, W. (1811). *Commentaries on the laws of England.* Oxford: Clarendon.

Boswell, J. (1982–83). Revolutions, universals, and sexual categories. *Salmagundi, 58–59,* 89–113.

Brodkey, H. (1994, February 7). Dying: An update. *New Yorker,* p. 71.

Bullough, V. L., & Bullough, B. (1993). *Cross dressing, sex and gender.* Philadelphia: University of Pennsylvania Press.

Carpenter, E. (1908). *The intermediate sex: A study in some transitional types of men.* London: Mitchell Kinnerly.

De Cecco, J. P., & Shively, M. G. (Eds.). (1972–94). *Journal of Homosexuality.* New York: Haworth Press.

Erikson, E. H. (1959). Identity and the life cycle. *Psychological Issues, 1* (1), 1–164.

Erikson, E. H. *Insight and responsibility.* New York: Norton.

Freud, S. (1925). Some psychical consequences of the anatomical differences between men and women. In J. Strachey (Ed. and Trans.), *The standard edition of the complete psychological works of Freud* (vol. 19). London: Hogarth Press.

Freud, S. (1933). New introductory lectures on psychoanalysis. In J. Strachey (Ed. and Trans.), *The standard edition of the complete psychological works of Freud* (vol. 22). London: Hogarth Press.

Friedman, R., & Lerner L. (1986). *Toward a new psychology of men.* New York: Guilford Press.

Gonsiorek, J. C., and Weinrich, J. D. (1991). The definition and scope of sexual orientation. In Gonsiorek, J. C., and Weinrich, J. D. (Ed.), *Homosexuality: Research implications for public policy* (pp. 1–12). Newbury Park, CA: Sage.

Green, R. (1987). *The "sissy boy" syndrome and the development of homosexuality*. New York: Basic Books.

Harrison, J. B. (1978). Warning: The male sex role may be dangerous to your health. *Journal of Social Issues 34*(1), 65–86.

Harrison, J. B. (1987). Counseling gay men. In M. Scher, M. Stevens, G. Good, & G. A. Eichenfield (Eds.) *The handbook of counseling and psychotherapy with men* (pp. 220–231). Newbury Park, CA: Sage.

Hooker, E. (1957). The adjustment of the overt male homosexual. *Journal of Protective Techniques, 21*, 18–31.

Humphries, L. (1979). Exodus and identity: The emerging gay culture. In M. Levine (Ed.), *Gay men: The sociology of male homosexuality*. New York: Harper & Row.

Karlen, A. (1971). *Sexuality and homosexuality*. New York: Norton.

Katz, J. (1983). *Gay/lesbian almanac: A new documentary*. New York: Harper & Row.

Kinsey, A. C., Pomeroy, W. B., & Martin, C. E. (1948). *Sexual behavior in the human male*. Philadelphia: W. B. Saunders.

Kleinberg, S. (1980). *Alienated affections: Being gay in America*. New York: St. Martin's.

Leites, N. (1971). *The new ego*. New York: Science House.

Mass, L. D. (1990). *Homosexuality as behavior and identity*. Binghamton, NY: Harrington Park Press.

McIntosh, M. (1968). The homosexual role. *Social Problems, 16*(2), 182–192.

Michener, J. A. (1965). *The source*. New York: Random House.

Money, J., & Ehrhardt, A. A. (1972). *Man and woman, boy and girl: The differentiation and dimorphism of gender identity from conception to maturity*. Baltimore: Johns Hopkins University Press.

Money, J. (1986). *Love maps*. New York: Irvington.

Pleck, J. (1981). *The myth of masculinity*. Cambridge, MA: M.I.T. Press.

Plummer, K. (1981). *The making of the modern homosexual*. Towata, NJ: Barnes and Noble.

Rado, S. (1965). A critical examination of the concept of bisexuality. In J. Marmor (Ed.), *Sexual inversion* (pp. 170–189). New York: Basic Books.

Rossi, A. (1974). *Research and politics on sex and gender*. Unpublished paper presented at Vassar College, Poughkeepsie, NY.

Rowse, A. L. (1983). *Homosexuals in history*. New York: Dorset Press.

Society for the Psychological Study of Ethnic Minority Issues. (1994). Melinda Garcia (Ed.), Identity development. *Focus, 8*(1). Washington, DC: Division 45, American Psychological Association.

Symonds, J. A. (1975). *A problem in Greek ethics* New York: Arno. (Originally published in 1861)

Tennyson, A. (1942). The Presbyterian hymnal (No. 175). Philadelphia: Presbyterian Board of Christian Education. (Originally published in 1850)

Thomas, W. I. (1928). *The child in America*. New York: Knopf.

Tietje, L., and Harrison, J. (1994). Homosexuality II / Ethical Aspects. In W. T. Reich (Ed.), *Encyclopedia of bioethics*. New York: Macmillan.

Ulrichs, K. H. (1865). Vindex. *Social-juristiche studien uber mannmannerliche geschlectliebe* (Social-legal studies on male-male love). Leipzig: Matthes.

Coda: A New Psychology of Men: Where Have We Been? Where Are We Going?

WILLIAM S. POLLACK AND RONALD F. LEVANT

Where Are We Now?

The O. J. Simpson murder trial, the Anita Hill–Clarence Thomas hearings, Sen. Bob Packwood's diary scandal, the rape trial of William Kennedy Smith, and the Tailhook incident have bombarded us. Americans seem transfixed by questions of gender role and painfully divided along gender lines. Feminist scholars have rightfully taken to task our traditional, phallocentric, gender-biased psychology of human development, reengineering it to fit girls' healthy growth and adult women's relational lives. But where does that leave men? Men have either been left trying to atavistically piece together the shards of "leftover" patriarchical theories and life experiences—creating a dangerous, angry backlash against women's strides for recognition and power—or become mired in a hopeless muddle of painful loss and confusion.

A solution, we believe, can be created, one that is *empathic* to male development and experience while gender-sensitive and aware and respectful of women's needs and rights as well. Such a solution requires that we create a new psychology of men, and this volume is an important, groundbreaking move in that direction. *A New Psychology of Men* brings together cutting-edge, state-of-the-art research, theory, and application aimed at diminishing gender-role strain and enhancing male-female communication.

Pleck updates his now classic paradigm of gender role strain and raises serious concerns about the forces of backlash, which could insidiously move us again toward patriarchical control. Pollack reconstructs psychoanalytic theory, putting to rest the normative societal drive for premature separation-individuation in boys—an unnecessary traumatic abandonment—and he recasts unconscious dynamics in an experience-near and empathic structure for boys and men. Bergman expands the relational school of women's growth and development to encompass men's issues, especially their struggle with relational dread. Krugman unearths the deep-seated forces of unconscious shame within men—forces that often pressure them into schizoid isolation or toward aggressive and hurtful interactions.

To place this theoretical reframing of masculinity on a firm empirical basis, Thompson and Pleck review the significant research gender role strain within the last 20 years, moving toward a broader vision of our concept of masculinity/ties. O'Neil, Good, and Holmes report on the significant results of their own measure of gender role strain, the Gender Role Conflict Scale, and find important evidence for how gender-based role conflict may be hazardous to men's emotional security, self-esteem, and well-being. Eisler—himself the originator of a prominent gender role scale, the Masculine Gender Role Stress Scale—reviews an impressive set of studies on men's physiological/biological health (especially their cardiovascular reactivity); these studies link traditional masculine roles with physical health and indicators of physical illness. Type A may well turn out to be what one of us has previously referred to as "Type M" (see Chapter 2).

Levant begins the process of applying this new vision of men's psychology by arguing for a reconstruction of masculinity. This process involves the creation of a new masculinity, or masculinities, based on recognizing the contemporary crisis of masculinity, analyzing its roots, and then separating out those aspects of traditional male activity that remain valuable to men and women alike and those that are dysfunctional and must be transformed. Brooks and Gilbert take a penetrating look at two of men's most significant roles in society and show how the male gender socialization process has inhibited their full capacity to function as fathers and husbands in a balanced family life. They make some very cogent suggestions for change. Brooks and Silverstein probe the "dark side" of masculinity, most especially men's proclivities toward impulsivity, aggression, and violence. They highlight a central fault underlying traditional masculine behavior and make important suggestions on how to remediate this pressing dilemma.

Lazur and Majors expand our knowledge of masculinity beyond the borders of white, middle-class America, across the frontiers of ethnicity and class, looking particularly at four subcultures in the United States: African-American, Latino, American-Indian, and Asian-American. Harrison also takes up the theme of the varieties of masculinity by enhancing our understanding of homosexual and bisexual men and by posing several provocative questions about how the gay experience elucidates and/or confounds our understanding of so-called heterosexual men's lives.

Where Do We Go from Here?—Quo Vadis?

"Tempora mutantur, et nos mutamur in illis"
(Times change, and we change with them).

As we attempt to create the foundation for a new psychology of men in the last half of the last decade of the 20th century—at fin de siècle—we feel an understandable inclination to predict those changes we expect to see in men's roles, relationships, and, indeed, our concepts of masculinity as we edge toward the 21st century. Unlike the ancient seer Teiresias, we profess no special power to foretell the future, but we can speak of both trends observable and goals necessary to forge a new psychology of men.

First, we must stress that we are at the very early, beginning stages—both academically and societally—of the dawn of men's consciousness of an engendered sense of self. The growing women's movement, along with the economic changes wrought by the dual-earner family, will make a new psychology of men, we believe, a pressing necessity rather than merely an intellectual interest. Owing to the burgeoning of new biological knowledge (most especially discoveries about the human genome and the findings of evolutionary biology), some of it relating to sex differences, the challenge will be to integrate this new information into a more complex model of the social construction of gender. Otherwise, we may not be able to avoid the inevitable backlash and the reemergence of an essentialist model of gender and a patriarchal power structure. If the 1990s are indeed the decade of the brain, we must see how we can harness our hearts and minds to integrate the new biological insights about sex into our psychosocial knowledge of the social construction of gendered human experience.

As the recognition of diversity has been an important move forward in the psychology of women, we believe that the same insight must, and will, occur in the psychology of men. All men may be created equal, but not all men enjoy equal advantages. We need—more and more—to develop understandings of the varieties of masculinity and, in particular, the difficulties for men in oppressed classes or stigmatized minorities. The best opportunities for all men to effect change will occur when we make genuine possibilities for transformation available to gay men, men of color, and men mired in the underclass of poverty. Increasingly, society and men themselves must recognize that Jim Harrison (1978) is right: The traditional male role is truly "hazardous to your health." Resocialization, reconstruction, and reframing may well become the order of the day. Men must stop killing themselves in droves. To achieve such transformation, the impetus must emerge not just from an ideology of change but also from pragmatic and mundane concerns for health and longevity.

Although *A New Psychology of Men* is not primarily about applied intervention or psychotherapy, most of the chapters reviewed above beg for implementation. In the arena of research, apart from some preliminary use of phys-iological measures (see Chapter 7), most of the research conducted to date has employed self-report measures. To solidify our scientific foundation and develop our understanding of the problem, we need to work toward greater utilization of a multitrait-multimethod (Campbell & Fiske, 1959) paradigm of psychological measurement. In addition, we must move toward integrating issues of men's health and illness with research on men's social roles. On the theory end, there is a need for better integration—within the framework of a social constructionist perspective—between modern psychoanalytic and developmental psychology, cognitive and behavioral psychology, and the new findings from biology. We need, if you will, a bio-psycho-social model of the construction of gender that is also informed by a depth psychology of unconscious processes, in individuals and groups.

To make such applications meaningful, we need practical psychoedu-cational interventions to help men examine themselves and rethink the accepted wisdom about what their roles should be, as well as more targeted, prescribed/engendered psychotherapy models that are empathic to men's needs. All change involves loss, and the integration of loss requires mourn-ing. It behooves us to create therapeutic interventions that can help men to bear and put into perspective their sense of loss about traditional masculin-ity—no matter how politically unacceptable or personally dysfunctional those roles may have been. This is the only way genuine change can emerge.

Central to the changes that a new psychology of men should generate are a new set of relations between men and women. There is a great need to resolve the "crisis of connection" (Levant, 1994) between the genders and to promote empathic intergender dialogue. Men and women must move toward a more empathic understanding of the other's experience, rather than assuming that the other gender can or should be measured by the yard-stick of their own personal frame of reference. Neither "half" can be the "bet-ter half." For this to happen, we hope that men will take it upon themselves to address the terrible problem of male violence against women and against men themselves. If a new psychology of men fails to stem the tide of vio-lence and to remediate power imbalances, we believe it will have failed to achieve its essential purpose.

Also, we see the need for men to become more involved as fathers. As this occurs, we think men will come to experience fathering as their second-greatest chance for connection and intimacy. Many of our so-called deadbeat dads may well turn out to be "deadpan" dads: men who are depressed and confused, who lack the social support necessary to take on a nurturant role, and who were not taught the skills of parenting in their own childhood. So what we refer to today as the *new* father, through the right type of interven-tions, may become the typical father—involved and emotionally expressive and connected to children, family, and significant others.

To liberate men and their families from the drudgery of endless duty, changes in the workplace must occur to accommodate men's increasing interest and involvement in their family lives. It is hard to overstate the significance of the changes required in our attitudes toward the work-family balance for men (as well as women) if we are ever to see a world with greater gender balance and committed fathers.

In this more courageous world of the new masculinities, we can expect men to become more openly connected and emotionally expressive. Consequently, men may become less anxious that exhibiting such traditional "female" traits as caring and closeness will make them "less" of a man. With that change, we hope that much of the scourge of homophobia will wither away. We can look forward to a time when men may be close to one another as well to women, when male-male friendship will not be a dangerous break with rigid gender expectations but rather an experience that supports and enhances men's self-esteem.

As we raise the next generation, the boys who will become men in the 21st century, we look forward to a time when these boys will be able to safely stay in the "doll corner" as long as they wish, without being taunted or called "sissy" or "faggot." Then parents will be able to raise their sons as well as their daughters to be human partners, sharing the varied and diverse capacities for instrumental or expressive ways of being—no longer bifurcated along the rigid lines of gender.

As such a *new psychology of men* takes hold in the close-touch world of work and family, one can only imagine the larger, global implications for a world where men need not fight to show their strength and are no longer stridently and endlessly searching to prove their masculinity. The implications for achieving gender harmony and peace go well beyond the scope of this volume, but in the words of Shakespeare, "Tis a consummation devoutly to be wished."

References

Campbell, D. T., & Fiske, D. W. (1959). Convergent and discriminant validation of the multitrait-multimethod matrix. *Psychological Bulletin, 56*(2), 81–108.

Harrison, J. (1978). Warning: The male sex role may be dangerous to your health. *Journal of Social Issues, 34*, 65–86.

Levant, R. F. (1994, August). *Changing gender role relationships and the family.* Paper presented at the Presidential Mini-convention "Psychology Looks at the Family" at the annual convention of the American Psychological Association, Los Angeles.

Index

Abandonment, in developmental trauma, 41
Aberrant male hypothesis, 281, 295–96
Acting-out, adolescent, 289–92
Action empathy, 237, 238
Action solutions, and male subculture, 111–12
Activism, social, 323
Adaptation, and shame, 12–15
Addiction, see Alcoholism; Drug abuse; Substance abuse
Adolescence: African-American males and, 343; dark side of masculinity seen in high-risk behavior in, 289–92; gay adolescents and, 287, 376; sexual behavior in, 255–58, 286
Affiliation, self psychology on development of, 49–50
African-American men, 341–43; adolescents among, 343; antisocial and risk-taking behavior among, 290; "cool" pose among, 17, 341–43; gender role conflict and, 178, 181, 197; gender role strain and, 305; health issues for, 291; male role as protector and, 267; violence in retaliation for shaming among,

117–18; see also Men of color
Age, and gender role conflict, 180
Aggression and aggressiveness: competition learned in male development and, 75; gender role discrepancy and, 14–15; gender role stress and, 209; gender role trauma and, 16; male development and, 70; male identity-ism and, 26; male relational dread and, 82; male role as protector and, 267; shame and, 94, 107, 109, 110, 114–15; socialization and later expression of, 240–41
Alcoholism, 84, 208; dark side of masculinity and, 288–89, 307; homelessness and social alienation and, 292; men of color and, 342, 345; shame and handling of, 94, 108, 117, 120–21; see also Substance abuse
Alexander, S., 321
Alexithymia, 44, 238–40
Allen, D., 135
Altman, D., 374
Alvarez, M., 46, 237
American Association of Marriage and Family Therapists, 314
American-Indian men, 338,

346–50; see also Men of color
American Psychological Association (APA), 117, 292, 315–16
Anderson, R. D., 149
Anderson, S. M., 136
Androgyny, and gender role conflict, 168
Anger: emotional socialization and, 237; gender role discrepancy and, 15; gender role stress and, 215; socialization and later expression of, 46, 47, 240–41
Anti-femininity in Men Scale, 135
Antisocial behavior, 289
Antisocial personality disorders, 118–19, 208
Anxiety, 208; domestic violence and, 94; gender role conflict and, 188; gender role discrepancy and, 15; gender role stress and, 215; manhood cult and, 310; masculine personality characteristics and, 17; shame and, 117
Arce, C. H., 345
Archer, J., 131, 149, 154, 155, 177, 182
Aristophanes, 36–37, 41
Arnold, W. J., 176, 178, 179, 182, 186, 188
Arrindell, W. A., 215
Ashmore, R. D., 155, 156